HITLER'S INVASION OF EAST ANGLIA, 1940

AN HISTORICAL COVER UP?

In Memoriam
Herbert Philip Bowman 20 July 1926-16 November 2002

HITLER'S INVASION OF EAST ANGLIA, 1940

AN HISTORICAL COVER UP?

MARTIN W. BOWMAN

Pen & Sword
AVIATION

First published in Great Britain in 2019 by
PEN AND SWORD AVIATION
an imprint of
Pen & Sword Books Limited
Yorkshire – Philadelphia

Copyright © Martin W. Bowman, 2019

ISBN 978 1 52670 548 8

The right of Martin W. Bowman to be identified as the author of this work has been asserted by her in accordance with the Copyright, Designs and Patents Act 1988.

A CIP record for this book is available from the British Library
All rights reserved. No part of this book may be reproduced or transmitted in any form or by any means, electronic or mechanical including photocopying, recording or by any information storage and retrieval system, without permission from the Publisher in writing.

Printed and bound in the UK
by TJ International

Typeset in Times New Roman 11/13.5 by
Aura Technology and Software Services, India

Pen & Sword Books Ltd incorporates the imprints of Pen & Sword Archaeology, Atlas, Aviation, Battleground, Discovery, Family History, History, Maritime, Military, Naval, Politics, Railways, Select, Social History, Transport, True Crime, Claymore Press, Frontline Books, Leo Cooper, Praetorian Press, Remember When, Seaforth Publishing and Wharncliffe.

For a complete list of Pen and Sword titles please contact
PEN & SWORD BOOKS LTD
47 Church Street, Barnsley, South Yorkshire, S70 2AS, England
E-mail: enquiries@pen-and-sword.co.uk
Website: www.pen-and-sword.co.uk

Or

PEN & SWORD BOOKS
1950 Lawrence Rd, Havertown, PA 19083, USA
E-mail: Uspen-and-sword@casematepublishers.com
Website: www.penandswordbooks.com

Contents

Prelude	The Veil of the Unknown	viii
Chapter 1	'Fall Gelb'	1
Chapter 2	The Death Ray	42
Chapter 3	The Last Ditch	74
Chapter 4	If the Invader Comes	88
Chapter 5	The Invasion that never was	113
Chapter 6	'The Germans have Landed'	135
Chapter 7	Caught like Fish in a Frying Pan	148
Chapter 8	'Even a Small Invasion might go a Long Way'	161
Chapter 9	Unternehmen Brandenburg Concerto	176
Chapter 10	Went the day Well?	197
Appendix A	Unternehmen Seelöwe (Operation 'Sealion') Order of Battle August 1940	215
Appendix B	Commando Operations 1940-43	219
Appendix C	Airborne Operations 1941-43	226
Appendix D	Operation 'Biting' February 1942	235
Appendix E	Operation 'Jubilee'; the raid on Dieppe, 19 August 1942	238
Appendix F	Operation 'Deadstick', June 1944	240
Appendix G	'Secrecy over Wartime File Remains Baffling'	244
Index		268

In history you don't ever get positive, conclusive evidence.
Dr. James E. Crisp
North Carolina State University

Author's Note

History is not an exact science; it is an agreed upon lie. Therefore the contents of this book are factual, save for Chapter Nine, in which I make no apology for using the false document technique to create verisimilitude in a work of fiction. By inventing and inserting documents that appear to be factual, an author tries to create a sense of authenticity beyond the normal and expected suspension of disbelief for a work of art. The goal of a false document is to convince an audience that what is being presented is factual. In this case Chapter Nine is speculative but while false documents intentionally blur the boundaries between narrative non-fiction and fact, if the factual clues presented in the preceding chapters are studied and pieced together then some or all of its parts may indeed have happened.

At this juncture I would like to record my appreciation for the valuable contributions made by James Hayward; Jim Drane of the National Trust; David Kibble-White; Peter D. Antill BA (Hons) MSc (Econ) PGCE (PCE) and The Museum of the British Resistance Organisation (B.R.O.) at the Parham Airfield Museum in Suffolk.

At present we lie within a few minutes' striking distance of the French, Dutch and Belgian coasts and within a few hours of the great aerodromes of Central Europe. We are even within cannon-shot of the Continent.

So close as that! Is it prudent, is it possible, however much we might desire it, to turn our backs upon Europe and ignore whatever may happen there? I have come to the conclusion - reluctantly I admit - that we cannot get away. Here we are and we must make the best of it. But do not underrate the risks- the grievous risks - we have to run.

Broadcast by Winston Churchill, 16 November 1934.

Prelude

The Veil of the Unknown

The reader of these pages in future years should realise how dense and baffling is the veil of the Unknown. Now in the full light of the aftertime it is easy to see where we were ignorant or too much alarmed, where we were careless or clumsy. Twice in two months we had been taken completely by surprise. The overrunning of Norway and the breakthrough at Sedan, with all that followed from these, proved the deadly power of the German initiative. What else had they got ready - prepared and organised to the last inch? Would they suddenly pounce out of the blue with new weapons, perfect planning and overwhelming force upon our almost totally unequipped and disarmed Island at any one of a dozen or score of possible landing-places? Or would they go to Ireland? He would have been a very foolish man who allowed his reasoning, however clean-cut and seemingly sure, to blot out any possibility against which provision could be made.
Their Finest Hour by Winston S. Churchill.

On Monday 28th August 1939, having been advised to report to the Recruiting Depot at Bradford, Yorkshire, 19-year-old Jim 'Dinty' Moore caught the train from his home in Hawes at the head of Wensleydale and set off on the first leg of a journey that would last six years and five months. During the summer of 1939 he had been accepted as a wireless operator. AC2 Moore's feelings were a mixture of excitement and apprehension and he certainly had no idea that within twelve months he would be flying over Western Europe as a member of the crew of a Bristol Blenheim. 'During the summer of 1939 the Royal Air Force prepared itself for war as best it could, with the faint hope, as in previous years that war could be averted by the politicians. In so far as the aircrew were concerned, they believed they were ready to fight, not realising that in many cases their aircraft were to prove to be no match against the Luftwaffe. Being young they did not appreciate, nor want to appreciate, the horrors of war, even though most of them knew some of those who had survived the appalling battles of Flanders during the 1914-18 War, a mere twenty years earlier.'

On Sunday morning, 3rd September, 'Dinty' Moore was sitting in a barrack block at Padgate, a training establishment on the outskirts of Warrington, having joined the RAF only four days earlier, when the radio in his hut was switched on and instead of the normal programmes serious music was being played. 'It was then solemnly announced that the nation was to be addressed by the Prime Minister, Neville Chamberlain.'

Arthur Neville Chamberlain, born 18 March 1869 and educated at Rugby School, was a Conservative politician who had served as Prime Minister from May 1937. He remembered the horrific losses of the First World War and was determined to avoid hostilities with Adolf Hitler's Germany, if at all possible. Chamberlain is best known for his appeasement foreign policy and in particular for his signing of the Munich Agreement in September 1938, which conceded the German-speaking Sudetenland region of Czechoslovakia to Germany. On 30 September Chamberlain flew back to London in triumph, stating he had reached agreement with Hitler. Large crowds mobbed Heston aerodrome where he was given a letter from King George VI assuring him of the Empire's lasting gratitude and urging him to come straight to Buckingham Palace to report. The streets were so packed with cheering people that it took Chamberlain an hour and a half to journey the nine miles from Heston to the Palace. After reporting to the King, Chamberlain and his wife appeared on the Palace balcony with the King and Queen Elizabeth. He then went to Downing Street where both the street and the front hall of Number 10 were packed. As he headed upstairs to address the crowd from a first-floor window someone called to him, *Neville, go up to the window and say 'peace for our time'*. Chamberlain turned around and responded, *No, I don't do that sort of thing*. Nevertheless, he recalled the words of his predecessor, Benjamin Disraeli and his return from the Congress of Berlin in his statement to the crowd: *My good friends, this is the second time there has come back from Germany to Downing Street peace with honour. I believe it is peace for our time. We thank you from the bottom of our hearts. Now I recommend you go home and sleep quietly in your beds.* The RAF was stood down. There was no applause, only heartfelt relief but no one felt proud of themselves. They

HITLER'S INVASION OF EAST ANGLIA, 1940

knew that as Britain's first line of defence they would be overwhelmed by the Luftwaffe onslaught had it come. Of the 750 fighters that Fighter Command possessed, only ninety were Hurricanes. The rest were obsolete biplanes.[1]

On 15 March 1939 Germany invaded the Czech provinces of Bohemia and Moravia, including Prague. On 23 August Hitler and Joseph Stalin, the leader of Communist Russia, surprised the world by signing the German-Soviet Non-Aggression Pact, in which the two countries agreed to take no military action against each other for the next ten years, making the invasion of Poland by the German Army a certainty. The British Government then signed a formal treaty with the Polish Government in the faint hope that knowing Britain would stand by Poland, whatever the cost. Hitler would cancel his orders for the invasion of that unfortunate country.[2] Hitler knew his Armed Forces were not prepared for war on two fronts, making several unacceptable proposals to the British Ambassador, in an attempt to prevent the British and French from interfering. Finally, after some hesitation, he gave the order for the invasion of Poland that began on Friday, 1st September 1939, telling his generals, 'Our enemies are small worms. I saw them at Munich.' Despite Chamberlain's plea to Hitler to withdraw his troops from Poland, which the dictator ignored, Britain was left with no option, even though it was ill prepared, other than to declare war on the evil represented by the Nazi Regime in Germany. Consequently, at 11 o'clock on Sunday 3rd September 1939, Chamberlain made his historic broadcast to the nation, announcing that 'Britain was at war with Germany'.

---

1 *Duel of Eagles* by Peter Townsend (Weidenfeld & Nicolson, 1970). Born 1914 in Rangoon, Burma and educated at Haileybury College, Townsend joined the RAF in 1933 and trained at RAF Cranwell. He served in Training Command and as a flying instructor at RAF Montrose. He was stationed at RAF Tangmere in 1937 and was a member of 43 Squadron RAF. The first enemy aircraft to crash on English soil during WWII fell victim to fighters from Acklington on 3 February 1940 when he and two other Hurricane pilots of 'B' flight, 43 Squadron, shot down a Heinkel 111 of 4./KG 26 near Whitby. Townsend was awarded the DFC in April 1940. Two more He 111s were claimed by Townsend, on 22 February and 8 April and a sixth share on 22 April. By May 1940 he was one of the most capable squadron leaders of the Battle of Britain, serving throughout the battle as commanding officer of 85 Squadron, flying Hawker Hurricanes.

2 Britain and France had signed military assistance treaties with Poland and two days after Germany invaded Poland, on 1 September 1939, they declared war on Nazi Germany. Neither country mounted significant offensive operations however and for several months no major engagements occurred in what became known as the 'Phoney War' or 'Twilight War'. Winston Churchill in particular wished to move the war into a more active phase, in contrast to Prime Minister Neville Chamberlain.

THE VEIL OF THE UNKNOWN

His address began: *This morning the British Ambassador to Berlin handed the German Government a final note saying that unless we hear from them by 11 o'clock that they were prepared, at once, to withdraw their troops from Poland, a state of war would exist between us. I have to tell you that no such undertaking had been received and that, consequently, this country is at war with Germany.* 'The remainder of his speech was drowned by cheers and excited conversation for, it must be remembered', wrote Jim Moore 'we were all youngsters who were actually excited at the prospect of being at war with our old enemy. Such is the innocence of youth. Considering that the last war, the war to end all wars, had ended only twenty years earlier with an appalling loss of life, we should have had a clearer idea of the reality of war. I suppose those who were actually involved were reluctant to talk of their experiences and our attitude had been influenced by books recording the heroics. On the same day, speaking in the Reichstag, Adolph Hitler declared: *I will not wage war against women and children. I have ordered my Air Force to restrict itself to attacks on military objectives*. Despite this lofty pronouncement it did not prevent the aerial bombardment of the city of Warsaw and the killing of thousands of men, women and children a few days later.

Britain's declaration of war was followed by months of comparatively little military activity, a period referred to in history books as the 'Phoney War'. Hitler was prepared to offer Britain fairly generous peace terms but when the possibility arose, that Britain would not sue for peace, he had been ready since May 1939 to wage long-term economic warfare against Britain, using the Luftwaffe and the navy to cut her supply lines. Better still, instead of spending months and years in squeezing Britain slowly into submission by economic warfare, Hitler reasoned that by invading he could finish her off in a matter of weeks and turn his attention to invading the Soviet Union. The Kriegsmarine concluded that if the conditions they thought necessary for the invasion were fulfilled, such as the elimination of the RAF and Royal Navy, these would in themselves induce the British to surrender: further resistance would be pointless. An invasion, as such, would surely be unnecessary?

In the small hours of 11 March 1938 when German panzers had moved up to the Austrian border to annex the German-speaking nation for the Third Reich, the possibility of British intervention had been considered and on 18 February 1938 the Luftwaffe Chief of Air Staff, General Hans-Jürgen Stumpf, asked General Hellmuth Felmy, commanding Luftflotte 2, to prepare an operational plan for air attack on Britain. On 12 March Hitler accompanied German troops into Austria, where enthusiastic crowds met them. Hitler appointed a new Nazi government and on 13 March the Anschluss (Union) was proclaimed. By 22 September General Felmy indicated that a strategic Luftwaffe assault on Britain could not be decisive. In 1939 Stumpf sent Felmy another request - urgent this time - with the Sudetenland crisis blowing up, to prepare plans for an air campaign against England.[3] But a May 1939 planning exercise by Luftflotte 3 found they were not ready to do much damage to Britain's war economy, beyond laying naval mines. Once Britain and France declared war, Hitler was concerned that resources would be overstretched: his 'Directive No. 6' proposed a swift attack, but his generals needed more time to prepare their forces. On 22 November 1939 Joseph 'Beppo' Schmid the Head of Luftwaffe intelligence presented a report entitled 'Proposal for the Conduct of Air Warfare' stating that 'Of all Germany's possible enemies, Britain is the most dangerous.' The report argued for a counter to the British blockade and said 'Key is to paralyse the British trade'. Instead of the Wehrmacht attacking the French, the Luftwaffe with naval assistance was to block imports to Britain and attack seaports. 'Should the enemy resort to terror measures, for example, to attack our towns in western Germany' they could retaliate by bombing industrial centres and London.[4]

On 15 November 1939 under orders from Grossadmiral (Grand Admiral) Erich Johann Albert Raeder, Commander in Chief of the German

---

[3] Felmy was convicted as a war criminal in 1948 during the Hostages Trial in Nuremberg when he was accused of war crimes in Greece and was given a sentence of fifteen years. On 15 January 1951 he was released early. On 14 December 1965 Felmy died in Darmstadt in what was then West Germany.

[4] Parts of this appeared on 29 November in 'Directive No. 9' as future actions once the coast had been conquered. On 24 May 1940 'Directive No.13' authorised attacks on the blockade targets, as well as retaliation for RAF bombing of the Ruhr. After the defeat of France the High Command (OKW) felt they had won the war and some more pressure would persuade Britain. On 30 June the OKW Chief of Staff Alfred Jodl issued his paper setting out options: the first was to increase attacks on shipping, economic targets and the RAF: air attacks and food shortages were expected to break morale and lead to capitulation. Terror bombing of civilians could be considered and invasion would be a last resort. Destruction of the RAF was the first priority. Hermann Göring's operational directive issued the same day authorised redeployment of the Luftwaffe and intensified attacks with the main emphasis on destruction of the RAF. They were to block seaborne supplies to Britain. There was no mention of invasion.

THE VEIL OF THE UNKNOWN

Kriegsmarine,[5] a small team headed by Vice Admiral Otto Schniewind of the Naval War Staff carried out a feasibility study to examine the military, naval and transportation implications of a possible invasion of Britain.[6] Known as 'Study Red', the study proposed a landing on the south coast of England with disembarkation from German home ports, concluding that: 'if a victory in the West or a stabilization of the front permits forces to become available, a landing operation across the North Sea to the south coast on a large scale would appear to us to be a possible means of forcing the enemy to sue for peace.' The plan was based on the assumption that Dutch and Belgian ports had first been captured and were available and the bulk of the British Army would be in France and could be prevented from returning across the Channel. Before a landing could take place all the artillery, anti-aircraft and British troops manning the coastal defences had to be eliminated, the RAF had to be destroyed and the Royal Navy had to be prevented from approaching the landing area. Equally, a choice would have to be made between a short sea crossing from the French Channel ports, which were open to RAF air attacks or a long sea crossing from ports beyond British bombing range, in the Low Countries, North Germany, or the Baltic. Finally, if German troops were to be landed in sufficient numbers, a beach landing would be too slow: a major British port on the

---

5 Raeder (24 April 1876-6 November 1960) had, in 1939, became the first person to hold that rank since Alfred von Tirpitz. Raeder argued strongly against Operation 'Sealion' as Weserübung had almost destroyed the German surface fleet. He felt that the war at sea could be conducted far more successfully via an indirect strategic approach, by increasing the numbers of U-boats and small surface vessels in service to wage a Handelskrieg as guerre-de'-course is known in Germany against British shipping, which would had the additional benefit from Raeder's viewpoint of bolstering his case for making the Kriegsmarine into the first service at the expense of the Army and Luftwaffe. By mid-1940 Raeder had come to appreciate that submarines were both cheaper and faster to build than warships. He also had doubts about Germany's ability to gain air superiority over the English Channel and the lack of regional German naval superiority. Air supremacy was a prerequisite to successfully preventing destruction of the German invasion fleet by the Royal Navy. Raeder led the Kriegsmarine for the first half of the war; he resigned in 1943 and was replaced by Karl Dönitz. He was sentenced to life in prison at the Nuremberg Trials, but was released early due to failing health.

6 During a visit by Raeder to the Chief of Naval Command nine days earlier, on 6 November, talk turned to the continuation of the war with a possible victory over France. Would the Führer decide to starve Great Britain out by means of a blockade or intend to land on the islands with masses of troops? Hitler had just designated 12 November 1939 as the date for the attack on the west. *Hitler on the Doorstep: Operation 'Sea Lion'* by Egbert Kieser (1987).

east coast would have to be captured by paratroops first. The Luftwaffe said that 'total air superiority' and 'total surprise' was needed and an invasion could only be 'the final act in an already victorious war.' Raeder dispatched copies of 'Study Red' to the OKL and the Oberkommando des Heeres (OKH) headed by General Walther von Brauchitsch[7] who gave orders for Major I. G. Stieff to prepare a counter-report, 'Study Northwest' in which the army experts expressed concern at the numbers of troops available because of their involvement in campaigns in Europe. And, taking into consideration that the Kriegsmarine had been confronted with 'Study Red' in assuming a landing on the English southern coast, Stieff and his team moved the landing north between the Thames Estuary and the Wash. Air Division 7, reinforced by the 16th Infantry Regiment, were to take the ports of Yarmouth and Lowestoft in an airborne operation, while the infantry division and a brigade of cyclists landed in the ports from the sea. South of the ports, a further infantry division was to land on the open coast near Dunwich and on Hollesley Bay in front of Ipswich, in order to prevent enemy counter-operations from there. A second landing wave consisting of two panzer divisions, a motorised infantry division and a reinforced infantry division, was to follow.[8]

In December the Wehrmacht (German army) carried out its study of a landing in England and created a more detailed plan codenamed

---

[7] Heinrich Alfred Hermann Walther von Brauchitsch (4 October 1881-18 October 1948) was born into an aristocratic military family. He joined the 3rd Guards Grenadier Regiment 1901. He served on the staff of several formations that fought over a dozen major battles of World War I, serving with the XVI Corps, 34th Infantry Division and Guards Reserve Corps as a staff officer before taking part in no fewer than twenty-eight notable clashes on the Western Front. He was awarded the Iron Cross and the House Order of Hohenzollern. After Hitler's rise to power in 1933, von Brauchitsch was put in charge of the East Prussian Military District and became a popular officer because of his kindness to the civilian Prussian population in times of local fires. Although he personally disliked Nazism, he borrowed immense sums of money from Hitler and eventually became dependent on his financial help. Brauchitsch primarily served as Commander-in-Chief of the German Army from 1938 and during the two first years of war until 1941. He played a key role in the Battle of France and oversaw the German military campaigns in Yugoslavia and Greece. For his part in Battle of France, Brauchitsch became one of twelve generals promoted to field marshal on 19 July 1940. After a first heart attack in November 1941 and the failed Moscow offensive in December 1941, Hitler dismissed him as Commander-in-Chief of the Army; he spent the rest of the war in enforced retirement and never saw Hitler again. Brauchitsch was arrested on charges of war crimes, but died of a heart attack in 1948 before he could be prosecuted.

[8] Kieser.

THE VEIL OF THE UNKNOWN

'Northwest'. This envisaged a surprise attack across the North Sea to the East Anglian coast from the Thames estuary to the Wash by sixteen or seventeen divisions, backed up by all the paratroops available. The major objective was the capture of London. The first phase of the invasion involved capturing the ports of Lowestoft and Great Yarmouth by a massive airborne assault. Simultaneously, troops would be landed near Hollesley Bay and Dunwich, one of the old Cinque Ports, on the Minsmere Cliffs, nine miles south of Southwold and seven miles north of Leiston, in order to prevent British reinforcements being brought up from Ipswich. In 1086, just twelve years after the Norman Conquest, Dunwich was a thriving port. Just under a hundred years later, in 1173, Robert, Earl of Leicester, tried to land 3,000 Flemish troops here in an attempt to overthrow and depose Henry II and replace him with his son. His plot was delayed by the loyal residents of the village who turned the boats away when they tried to disembark. Because of this, the Earl of Leicester was forced to set sail again, finally landing at Orwell, east of Harwich. In appreciation of their actions, Dunwich was granted a royal charter in 1199, becoming a borough and gaining a council, magistrates and officers. The village may have still been a much larger town, possibly even a city, if it hadn't been for several severe floods in the 13th and 14th centuries, which destroyed several of the churches and reclaimed portions of the land. Its proximity to the coast worked against it as well and the sea ate away at it, leading to its almost complete abandonment by the 19th century. Out in the sea in front of the beach are said to be 27 buried churches, absorbed by the sea,

As in the German Navy plan for the invasion of Britain, the same pre-conditions applied to the Wehrmacht plan, Operation 'Northwest', which depended upon the Kriegsmarine protecting the invasion convoys, neutralising British coastal defences and preventing the BEF returning from France. The Kriegsmarine objected to this plan on the grounds that they could not simultaneously provide cover for the invasion and keep the Royal Navy occupied elsewhere. They also pointed out the need for continuous good weather, without which the Luftwaffe would be unable to operate and the invasion force might well be cut off without supplies. At the end of December in a memorandum, commander-in-chief of the Luftwaffe, Reichsmarschall Hermann Göring, a veteran World War I fighter pilot ace and a recipient of the coveted Pour le Mérite or the 'Blue Max', insisted that the East Anglian landing would 'run into the strongest point of the enemy air defence' and that an invasion 'could only be the last act of a war against England which had already taken a victorious course'. It could not

HITLER'S INVASION OF EAST ANGLIA, 1940

itself bring about victory. Both the German Navy and Army schemes were carried no further than the initial planning stages and then shelved - or so it is claimed.

On 4 April in a speech to the Conservative Party at Central Hall, Westminster Neville Chamberlain stated that he was confident of victory and claimed that the Government had now made good its initial weaknesses and unpreparedness compared with the German aggressor: The result was that when war did break out German preparations were far ahead of our own and it was natural then to expect that the enemy would take advantage of his initial superiority to make an endeavour to overwhelm us and France before we had time to make good our deficiencies. Is it not a very extraordinary thing that no such attempt was made? Whatever may be the reason - whether it was that Hitler thought he might get away with what he had got without fighting for it, or whether it was that after all the preparations were not sufficiently complete - however, one thing is certain: he missed the bus.

The 'Phoney War' ended abruptly on 9 April 1940 with the German invasion of Norway. So fast had been the speed of the German advance, that the British Expeditionary Force had found itself trapped in northern France. At first the situation seemed hopeless, but eventually the British army was saved from complete destruction by the miraculous success of the Dunkirk Evacuation. The bulk of the BEF had escaped to fight another day, but thousands of British soldiers had been killed, wounded or taken prisoner. And to add to the disaster, nearly 500 tanks, 40,000 other vehicles, 400 anti tank guns and 1,000 heavy guns, together with vast amounts of ammunition and lighter weapons had been destroyed or left behind. It would take time to replace such huge losses of equipment and time to rebuild the army's fighting strength - but time was not on Britain's side.

In October 1939 the chief of the German Kriegsmarine, Grossadmiral Erich Raeder had discussed with Adolf Hitler the danger posed by the risk of having potential British bases in Norway and the possibility of Germany seizing these bases before the United Kingdom could. The navy argued that possession of Norway would allow control of the nearby seas and serve as a staging base for future submarine operations against the United Kingdom. But at this time, the other branches of the Wehrmacht were not interested and Hitler had just issued a directive stating that the main effort would be a land offensive through the Low Countries.

At the beginning of April 1940 intelligence reports were received of German shipping massing in ports in Northern Germany. This activity

THE VEIL OF THE UNKNOWN

was part of Unternehmen (Operation) 'Weserübung' the code name for Germany's assault on Denmark and Norway and the opening operation of the Norwegian Campaign. The name comes from the German for Operation 'Weser-Exercise'; the Weser being a German river. After the invasions in the early morning of 9th April (Wesertag; 'Weser Day') envoys of the Germans informed the governments of Denmark and Norway that the Wehrmacht had come to protect the countries' neutrality against Franco-British aggression.

Unternehmen 'Weserübung' saw the first major use of Germany's airborne forces and the first paratrooper attacks in military history.[9] According to the fanatical German parachutist's creed the Luftwaffe Fallschirmjäger paratrooper was the 'chosen one' of the German Army. Each man was to 'seek combat and train to endure any manner of test'. To him the battle would be the 'fulfilment'. 'Cultivate true comradeship, for by the aid of your comrades you will conquer or die' he was told. 'Beware of talking. Be not corruptible. Men act while women chatter. Chatter may bring you to the grave. Be calm and prudent, strong and resolute. Valour and the enthusiasm of an offensive spirit will cause you to prevail in the attack. The most precious thing in the presence of the foe is ammunition. He who shoots uselessly, merely to comfort himself, is a man of straw. He is a weakling who merits not the title of parachutist.' Above all the paratrooper learned never to surrender. 'To you death of victory must be a point of honour. You can triumph only if our weapons are good. See to it that you submit yourself to this law - first my weapons and then myself.' He must grasp the full purpose of every enterprise, so that if his leader was killed he could fulfil it. Against an open foe he was instructed to 'fight with chivalry, but to a guerrilla extend no quarter'. 'Keep your eyes wide open' he was reminded. 'Tune yourself to the topmost pitch. Be as nimble as a greyhound, as tough as leather, as hard as Krupp steel and so you shall be the German Warrior incarnate.'

Fifty-two Ju 52s from 1. and 8. Staffel in Kampfgeschwader 1 transported a kompanie of Fallschirmjäger and a battalion of infantry to the northern part of Jutland. The 1st Fallschirmjäger Division had been formed in 1938 and was the original 'elite' Fallschirmjäger unit. It was this unit that was

---

9 In 1938 both KGrzbV 1 and 2 were deployed against Austria at the time of the Anschluss, each gruppe numbering more than 50 aircraft, the former at Fürstenwalde and the latter at Brandenburg-Briest. Within 18 months the Luftwaffe's strength of Ju 52/3ms had grown to 547 in ten gruppen and a large proportion of this fleet was available for action against Poland in September 1939. In the event, the Polish Campaign did not feature any significant use of air-lifted troops and the Ju 52s were used mainly to airlift fuel and other supplies forward as the Wehrmacht continued its lightning advance.

HITLER'S INVASION OF EAST ANGLIA, 1940

responsible for all of the early German airborne triumphs and many of the later defensive struggles that solidified the Fallschirmjäger reputation in battle. One of the Fallschirmjäger 'Ten Commandments' was 'Never surrender; to you death or victory must be a point of honour.' On the first day of the invasion, the paratroopers seized the Vordingborg Bridge to Zealand linking Copenhagen with its ferry terminal and two airfields at Aalborg in Denmark. The Ju-52/3ms also dropped paratroopers at three key airfields in southern Norway at the cities of Oslo, Stavanger and Kristiansand. The Vordingborg bridge was captured by troops carried in a dozen aircraft of 8/KGzbV 1, while Aalborg airfield, vital to support the operation in southern Norway, was also captured by airborne forces. During the fighting in Norway, wheeled landing gear was replaced with floats to enable the Ju 52/3m's to land in that country's numerous fjords.

The invasion of Denmark lasted less than six hours and was the shortest military campaign conducted by the Germans during the war. The 62 days of fighting made Norway the nation that withstood a German invasion for the second longest period of time, after the Soviet Union. A total force of eleven gruppen with no fewer than 573 Ju 52/3ms commanded by Oberstleutnant Carl-August Baron von Gablenz took part in the invasion of Norway and they flew more than 3,000 operational sorties in eight weeks, lifting 29,000 men, 2,300 tons of stores and over a million litres of fuel. Nothing like this achievement had previously been undertaken. The German navy was supposed to capture Oslo, but Norwegian reservists using old Krupp guns and shore-based torpedoes along the Oslo fiord managed to sink the brand-new heavy cruiser *Blücher* and stop the naval attack in its tracks. Among the key Norwegian positions allotted for capture by airborne forces was Oslo/Fornebu airfield. Bad weather prevented KGzbV 1 from dropping paratroops there, with the result that the Ju 52/3ms of KGrzbV 103 had to land on the airfield while it was still in Norwegian hands. Within six hours the Germans had captured the objective, permitting further airborne forces to be landed by KGrzbV 102 and 107. The Germans moved into the capital in the afternoon, but by that time the government had fled and Norwegian resistance went underground. Paratroops were dropped at Stavanger, where the airport was captured just as speedily. Operation 'Weserübung' however, cost the Luftwaffe more than 150 Ju 52s, most of which were total write-offs.

A number of airfields were captured by paratroops, ably assisted by Bf 110 fighter attacks on ground installations, opening the way for the landing of reinforcements. In response to a request from the Norwegian Government for military assistance, an advanced party of an Allied Expeditionary Force

THE VEIL OF THE UNKNOWN

was landed at Narvik in Northern Norway on 14th April. This was followed the next day by the main force. This futile gesture resulted in the loss of men and equipment which could have been put to better use in the Battle for France. The problems facing the bombers of the RAF in giving much needed support to the Allied Armies were twofold, first appalling weather and second the distances which had to be flown to attack worthwhile targets. For example, the main Luftwaffe base at Stavanger in Southern Norway lay 350 miles across the North Sea from the nearest aerodrome in Scotland and 500 miles from bases in England. Despite intelligence reports of the build-up of German forces along their borders with France, Belgium and Holland, obviously in preparation for the long awaited assault, incredibly no raids were carried out by any aircraft of the Allied Air Forces, due to the anxiety of the French High Command not to provoke the Germans.

The Allies sent troops to Norway met with little success and on 26 April the War Cabinet ordered a withdrawal. Prime Minister Neville Chamberlain's opponents decided to turn the adjournment debate for the Whitsun recess into a challenge to Chamberlain who soon heard about the plan. After initial anger, Chamberlain determined to fight. What became known as the 'Norway debate' opened on 7 May and lasted for two days. The initial speeches, including Chamberlain's, were nondescript, but Admiral of the Fleet Sir Roger Keyes, member for Portsmouth North, in full uniform, delivered a withering attack on the conduct of the Norway campaign, though he excluded Churchill from criticism. Leo Amery then delivered a speech which he concluded by echoing Oliver Cromwell's words on dissolving the Long Parliament: 'You have sat here too long for any good you are doing. Depart, I say and let us have done with you. In the name of God, go!' Chamberlain spent much of 9 May in meetings with his Cabinet colleagues. The following day Germany invaded the Low Countries and Chamberlain went to Buckingham Palace to resign and advise the King to send for Churchill, who later expressed his gratitude to Chamberlain for not advising the King to send for Halifax who would have commanded the support of most government MPs. Chamberlain had led Britain through the first eight months of the war. He died of bowel cancer on 9 November 1940 at the age of 71.

'It may be difficult for the present generation to believe' wrote Jim Moore, 'yet, if our nation had surrendered to the Germans in 1940, as we might well have done, it could well be we who would today be yearning for freedom from a truly evil Nazi regime. On 17 June 1940 the French, having no option, asked for an armistice and surrendered whilst the remnants of

HITLER'S INVASION OF EAST ANGLIA, 1940

the defeated British Army were evacuated from Dunkirk, having lost so many men and almost all their equipment. They were, as a fighting force, almost impotent, being in no condition to successfully withstand a German invasion. On 18 June the RAF was evacuated from Marseilles. At this point there were those [in Britain] who favoured surrender, but fortunately the newly appointed Prime Minister, Winston Spencer Churchill, who truly personified the bulldog spirit, did not agree.

'Let us consider briefly the regime with which we were at war and the plans they had for the British people in the event of a successful invasion of our island. During the 1930s, Adolph Hitler and the Nazi Party had become the ultimate power in Germany, introducing a regime even more ruthless than those in the various Balkan states pre- and post-1939-45. This regime was supported by a regime of terror carried out by three organisations, the SS (Schutzstaffel), Gestapo (Geheime Staatspolizei) and the SD (Sicherheitsdienst) which, between them, stifled any possible resistance to the Nazi Party. Any action carried out by these organisations was deemed to be above the law. The concentration camps, of which much has been written, were introduced, not only to exterminate so-called 'enemies of the regime', but to terrorise the German people.

In so far as the intentions of the Germans, after the invasion of Britain and the defeat of the British Armed Forces, it would have been a vicious affair. In captured German papers, their Army had been directed 'that the able-bodied male population (in Britain) between the ages of seventeen to forty-five will, unless the local situation calls for an exceptional ruling, be interned and dispatched to the Continent.' It was also directed to systematically plunder the wealth of this island and to terrorise its inhabitants. These plans were even more drastic than any introduced by the Germans in Poland. Already Britain's entire stock of gold reserves had been shipped across the Atlantic to Canada for safe keeping. The collections of London's museums and galleries had been removed from the capital, priceless works of art were sent to remote slate mines in deepest Wales. The government also organised a campaign to prepare Britain's civilian population for the certainty of invasion; official posters and leaflets advised the public that when the invaders came they should: 'Stay Put', they were also warned not to believe rumours and not to spread them. New Defence Regulations, introduced under the 'Emergency Powers Act,' made it a punishable offence to spread 'alarm and despondency.' And two of the new regulations: 'Forcing Safeguards' (breaking through roadblocks) and 'Looting' carried the death penalty. The threat of invasion was deemed to be so serious that the arming of the civil population was even suggested in

THE VEIL OF THE UNKNOWN

Parliament. However, this was one measure that the government was reluctant to take any further. Nevertheless, national newspapers carried instructions on how to use Lee Enfield service rifles and make petrol bombs. Several neutral governments were openly sympathetic towards Nazi Germany, many others, including the USA, thought it would only be a matter of time before Britain sued for peace. So serious was the situation that there were those in Britain itself, even within the corridors of power, who were prepared to seek a negotiated peace with the Germans.

'How was it therefore' asked Jim Moore, 'that we inhabitants of this small island, with only the Commonwealth as our Allies, managed to hold out against a rampant and victorious Germany, until 11 December 1941, when Hitler, in the Reichstag, declared war on America, forcing them into the war in Western Europe? Remember, without Britain as a base from which to launch a successful invasion of Europe, no such invasion could ever have taken place. First and foremost, the appointment of Churchill as Prime Minister, who at this critical stage in the history of this country, had the ability to instil in us all the will, not only to resist, but to fight back with every means at our disposal. Second, the courage and determination of the civilian population who, between September 1940 and May 1941 were subjected to a merciless aerial bombardment which claimed the lives of 42,900 men, women and children. Third, the defeat of the Luftwaffe in the Battle of Britain by the courage and determination of the fighter pilots of the Royal Air Force. Fourth, the successful bombing campaign waged by the aircrew of Bomber Command against the ports in which the Germans were assembling their invasion fleet. Last, but certainly by no means least, the men of the Royal and Merchant Navies who kept open the vital supply lines, despite suffering appalling losses at the hands of the German U-boat fleet. Churchill was not content merely to defend, being determined to show the Germans and the rest of the world, we were not defeated and that we had both the will and the ability to carry the war to the enemy. He turned to the crews of the Royal Air Force to carry out aggressive action against the enemy.'

Britain now stood alone against Nazi Germany with no allies and few friends. Following the surrender of France, French generals predicted that within a matter of weeks: 'England will have her neck wrung like a chicken.' These are facts of history that even to this day some would prefer were conveniently forgotten. In the summer of 1940 the outlook for Britain was extremely bleak: either negotiate an armistice on Nazi terms - or face invasion.

Chapter 1

'Fall Gelb'

In November 1939 a former policeman, who had been recruited into the German Abwehr as of 25 August 1939, was despatched to the Netherlands to buy Dutch uniforms. The Abwehr was a German military intelligence organization which had existed since 1920 for the purpose of gathering both domestic and foreign information. Assigned to Abwehrstelle Wehrkreis IV Münster Gruppe II/F, Richard Gerken, born in Bomlitz on 19 March 1900 had very short hair and light blue, watery eyes and was a heavy smoker. He spoke German, Dutch and Danish and had several aliases and was responsible for maintaining contact with agents in the Netherlands and German customs staff who collected data on the situation in the Dutch border areas. His immediate superior was Major von Rosenberg. Gerken's early childhood had been an unhappy one. His mother died when he was two, his father had died in 1912 and his brother was killed in France in 1914. On 21 December 1921 Gerken married 19-year old Thea Koch. The rise of the Nazis transformed Gerken's life. When Hitler replaced the Ministry of War with the OKW and made the organization part of the Führer's personal 'working staff' in June 1938, the Abwehr became its intelligence agency and Vice-Admiral Wilhelm Canaris, a former U-boat commander in World War One, highly intelligent with a gift for languages and having experience of espionage from the earlier conflict, was placed at the head of the organization. Its headquarters was located at 76/78 Tirpitzufer, Berlin, adjacent to the offices of the OKW. When he was instructed to buy Dutch uniforms, Gerken went to the small town of Dennekamp where he knew of an ardent Dutch Nazi who might help him. The Dutchman was more than willing to assist. Gerken, the Dutch Nazi and his 20-year-old son travelled to Amsterdam where they made contact with two other Nazis. Together they went to a clothes store run by a Dutch Jew, Heer Blum and requested that they needed 150 Dutch Army uniforms for an opera performance

HITLER'S INVASION OF EAST ANGLIA, 1940

in Osnabrück of 'The Count of Luxembourg'. Blum was not convinced and so, deeply suspicious, made a note of the car's registration number and phoned the Dutch Police. On 2 November 1939 the police raided the Nazi's home in Dennekamp. Gerkern's two collaborators denied all knowledge of the purchases of uniforms, but the police searching the premises found several trunks filled with uniforms addressed to Richard Gerken. They told the men that they knew that Gerken was an Abwehr agent working in the Netherlands and both father and son broke down and confessed their complicity in the plot. It would seem that the Dutch failed to ascertain the significance of their find. They could not have known that the idea of infiltrating the Dutch defences with German troops wearing Dutch uniforms was none other than Adolf Hitler's and probably only realised their folly when the invasion of Holland began on 10 May 1940.[10]

On Thursday 9 May 1940 a Wellington bomber on 38 Squadron at RAF Marham in Norfolk was brought to readiness for a security patrol to Borkum in the German Friesian Islands. 'The object of the patrol to Borkum' recalled the front-gunner, LAC G. Dick 'was to maintain a standing patrol of three hours over the seaplane base to prevent their flarepath lighting up and thus inhibit their mine-laying sea-planes from taking off. We carried a load of 250lb bombs in case a discernible target presented itself. We took off at 2130 hours. Holland was still at peace and their lights, though restricted, were clearly visible, the Terschelling lightship in particular, obliging by giving a fixed navigational fix. After three hours monotonous circling and seeing next to nothing, I heard Flying Officer Burnell, our Canadian pilot, call for course home. The words always sounded like music to a gunner in an isolated turret with no positive tasks to take up his mind, other than endless turret manipulation and endless peering into blackness. I heard the navigator remark that the lightship had gone out and the pilot's reply, 'Well give us a bloody course anyway. One only had to go west to hit Britain somewhere, or return on the reciprocal of the outward course - drift notwithstanding. After an hour's flying with the magic IFF box switched

---

[10] See *Hitler's Espionage Machine; German Intelligence agencies and operations during World War II* by Christer Jörgensen (Spellmount Ltd, 2004). In 1944 Gerken was given the task of forming 'stay behind' groups of agents for sabotage purposes. When arrested the following year he offered information about arms and explosives dumps hidden in Germany for use after the hostilities had ceased.

'FALL GELB'

on for the past thirty minutes, I gave the welcome call, 'Coast ahead!' Much discussion occurred as to where our landfall really was. I told them I thought north of the Humber, which was 150 miles north of our proper landfall at the Orfordness corridor. I was told to 'Belt up'. As a gunner, what did I know about it? (I had flown pre-war on 214 Squadron for two years up and down the East Coast night and day and was reasonably familiar with it.) Probably pride would not let them admit that they were 150 miles off course, in an hour's flying. Eventually, a 'chance light' showed up and we landed on a strange aerodrome, which turned out to be Leconfield. Overnight billets were arranged at 0400 hours for the visiting crew. However, others were on an early start. They switched on the radio at 0600 hours and gave us the 'gen' that at around midnight Germany had invaded Holland, Belgium and France - hence the extinguished lightship.'

Two days' earlier all telephone and telegraphic communications between Holland and the USA were suspended. On 7 May the Dutch Military Attaché in Berlin had received a warning from well-informed German officers and knew that when dawn broke on Friday 10 May, the Germans would unleash their 'Blitzkrieg' ('Lightning War') against the Low Countries (the Netherlands and Belgium) and France. The German Army would cross the Dutch border as part of 'Fall Gelb' ('Case Yellow') as the German invasion was codenamed.

During the evening before the attack on the Netherlands, German transport aircraft flew over the country heading west toward the North Sea, apparently making for England. The ruse was so carefully planned that when the Ju 52s took off at dawn the next morning for their intended targets in Holland, many German paratroops were unaware of their true destination. Only senior officers had been given any real details and then only on a 'need to know' basis. Operational orders were issued to the troops only after they'd landed and many paratroopers captured in the early fighting believed they had landed in England. Some didn't even know Holland and Germany were at war. While this was happening, over the border in neighbouring Belgium, a group of German troops used light aircraft to land several miles behind the Belgian frontline. The mission for this small detachment from the 34th Infanterie Division was to secure important road junctions and some of them were in civilian disguise or wore Belgian uniform.

Soon after dawn on 10 May the German Ambassador at The Hague, Count Julius von Zech-Burkersroda, called at the Foreign Ministry with a

HITLER'S INVASION OF EAST ANGLIA, 1940

note announcing that German troops were entering the country to protect its neutrality against a threat from the Franco-British army's - despite what Hitler himself had admitted, that the allies would never violate Dutch or Belgian neutrality. Twenty-six years earlier Burkersroda's illustrious father-in-law, Chancellor Bethmann Hollweg, had called the German guarantee of Belgian neutrality 'a mere scrap of paper'. In Brussels, the Belgian Foreign Minister, Paul Henri Spaak, faced the German Ambassador squarely as the latter entered his office bearing a similar note. Spaak cut the German short. 'Forgive me, but I wish to speak first. The German army has just attacked our country. It is the second time in twenty-five years that Germany has committed a criminal aggression against a neutral Belgium... What has just happened is even more odious... than in 1914. No ultimatum, no note, no protest has ever been laid before the Belgian Government. It is through the attack itself that Belgium has learnt that Germany has violated her promises...' As the German Ambassadors were delivering their notes in The Hague and Brussels the Luftwaffe's bombs could be heard crashing down on nearby airfields. Since dawn the German army had been pushing forward on a 175-mile front and Luftwaffe bombers had swept down on seventy allied airfields.[11]

A total of 475 Ju 52/3m transports and forty-five Deutsche Forschungsanstalt für Segelflug (DFS) 230 gliders would be used over Holland to deploy the parachute elements of the airborne troops, as well as transport the elements of the two airborne divisions not landing by parachute or glider; the whole being placed under a special command staff under General Richard Putzier. Developed in 1933, the DFS 230 had a square box-like fuselage structure, shoulder wing and jettisonable wheeled undercarriage. In addition to the pilot, it had room for eight heavily-armed troops who sat close together on a narrow bench located in the middle of the fuselage (half facing forward, half facing back). Entry and exit to the cramped interior was by a single side door. The front passenger could operate its only armament, a machine gun. It was an assault glider, designed to land directly on top of its target, so it was equipped with a parachute brake. This allowed the glider to approach its target in a dive at an angle of eighty degrees and land within 60 feet of its target. It carried a freight cargo of about 1,200kg.

In 1937 in a demonstration arranged before a gathering of senior German officers, 25-year old Hanna Reitsch cast off from a Ju 52/3m at about 1000 metres (3,280 feet) and dived the (DFS) 230 and landed

---

11 *Duel of Eagles* by Peter Townsend.

virtually at the feet of the officers. Within seconds eight soldiers had disembarked and taken up their positions. She was given the honorary title of 'Flugkapitan' by Ernst Udet in 1937, after successfully testing Hans Jacobs' dive brakes for gliders. She flew from Salzburg across the Alps in May 1937 in a DFS Sperber Junior. Udet, the second-highest scoring German flying ace of World War I and a major proponent of the dive bomber was among the assembled officers who witnessed the DFS 230 demonstration.[12] The other assembled senior officers included Generalfeldmarschall Albert Kesselring, Generalmajor Otto Moritz Walter Model and Erhard Milch. It was Milch who oversaw the development of the Luftwaffe as part of the re-armament of Germany following World War I and served as founding Director of Deutsche Lufthansa, formed on 6 January 1926. After just one year its 120 aircraft had flown four million miles to destinations as far-flung as Peking, Moscow and Rio de Janeiro. Milch was a tireless worker who according to his chief of staff Kesselring, managed the Air Ministry practically singlehanded. Hermann Göring said Kesselring only worked when he had to, but then it was with passionate drive. Otherwise he left it to Milch, the organizing brain and Udet, the technical genius.[13]

In September 1938 Hanna Reitsch flew the DFS Habicht ('Hawk') unlimited aerobatic sailplane, with support provided by the Deutsche Forschungsanstalt für Segelflug, in the Cleveland National Air Races. This was followed by another expedition with Professor Walter Georgii, a meteorologist and a pioneer of gliding research, to Libya in North Africa. During the autumn of 1938 a small glider assault command was formed under Leutnant Weiss and it was found that the use of gliderborne troops had many advantages over those dropped by parachute. Their approach was silent, they were not dispersed and they did not have to spend precious time extricating themselves from cumbersome parachutes. Suspended from his parachute by two straps attached to the back of his harness, the German paratrooper had very little control over his movements when in flight. The German soldier could only swivel around on the end of his harness without the means to control

---

12 By 1936, through his political connections, he had been placed in command of the T-Amt (the development wing of the Reichsluftfahrtministerium) (Reich Air Ministry). On 17 November 1941 Udet committed suicide, shooting himself in the head while on the telephone with his girlfriend. Evidence indicates that his unhappy relationship with Göring, Erhard Milch and the Nazi Party in general was the cause of his mental breakdown.

13 *Duel of Eagles* by Peter Townsend.

his descent or his point of contact with the ground. At the DFS Hanna Reitsch test flew transport and troop-carrying gliders, including the DFS 230 which would be used in the 'Blitzkrieg' on 10 May when the world's first operational use of glider-borne troops came with the attack on the Belgian fort of Ében-Émael.

The Belgian defences consisted of one delaying position running along the Albert Canal and then a main defensive line running along the River Dyle, which protected the port of Antwerp and the Belgian capital, Brussels. This delaying position was protected by a number of forward positions manned by troops, except in a single area where the canal ran close to the Dutch border, which was known as the 'Maastricht Appendix' due to the proximity of the city of Maastricht. The Belgian military could not build forward positions due to the proximity of the border and therefore assigned an infantry division to guard the three bridges over the Albert Canal in the area, a brigade being assigned to each bridge. The bridges were defended by blockhouses equipped with machine-guns. Artillery support was provided by Fort Ében-Émael, which occupied a strategic position on the Albert Canal and whose artillery pieces covered two of the bridges.[14] Belgian plans did not call for the garrison of the fort and the attached defending forces to fight a sustained battle against an attacking force; it was assumed that sufficient warning of an attack would be given so that the detachment on the eastern side of the canal could be withdrawn, the bridges destroyed and the garrison ready to fight a delaying action. The defending force would then retire to the main defensive positions along the River Dyle, where they would link up with British and French forces. Having become aware of the Belgian defensive plan, the German High Command made its own plans to disrupt this and seize and secure these three bridges, as well as a number of other bridges in Belgium and the Netherlands, to allow their own forces to breach the defensive positions and advance into the Netherlands.

The force tasked with assaulting Ében-Émael and capturing three bridges across the Albert Canal was primarily composed of Fallschirmjäger from the 1st Parachute Regiment and engineers from the 7th Air Division, as well as a small group of Luftwaffe pilots and men of the 22nd Airlanding

---

14 The fort was equipped with six 120mm artillery pieces with a range of ten miles; sixteen 75mm artillery pieces; twelve 60mm high-velocity anti-tank guns; twenty-five twin-mounted machine-guns; and a number of anti-aircraft guns. One side of the fort faced the Albert Canal, whilst the other three faced land and were defended by minefields; deep ditches; a 20 feet high wall; concrete pillboxes fitted with machine-guns. Fifteen searchlights were emplaced on top of the fort.

'FALL GELB'

Division in November 1939 and was named Sturmabteilung Koch (Assault Detachment Koch) after the force leader, Hauptmann (later Lieutenant Colonel) Walter Koch. One of the pioneers of German military parachuting, he did not survive the war, being killed in 1943 as a result of a car crash while driving at high speed in dense fog. Although composed primarily of parachutists, it was decided that the first landings by the force should be by glider. Adolf Hitler, who had taken a personal interest in the arrangements for the assault force, had ordered that gliders be used after being told by his personal pilot, Hanna Reitsch, that gliders in flight were nearly silent; it was believed that, since Belgian anti-aircraft defences used sound-location arrays and not radar, it would be possible to tow gliders near to the Dutch border and then release them, achieving a surprise attack as the Belgian defenders would not be able to detect them. Fifty DFS 230 transport gliders were supplied for use by the assault force and then a period of intensive training began. A detailed study of the fort, the bridges and the local area was made and a replica of the area was constructed for the airborne troops to train in. Joint exercises between the parachutists and the glider pilots were carried out in the early spring of 1940 and a number of refinements made to the equipment and tactics to be used, such as barbed wire being added to the nose-skids of the gliders to reduce their landing run and the airborne troops trained with flamethrowers and specialized explosives, the latter of which were so secret that they were only used on fortifications in Germany and not on fortifications in Czechoslovakia similar to Fort Ében-Émael.

Hauptmann Koch divided his attack force into four assault groups, each of which was given a specific task. The most important mission was that allocated to 'Group Granite' under Oberleutnant Rudolf Witzig, composed of eighty-five men in eleven gliders whose task would be to assault and capture Fort Ében-Émael. 'Group Steel', commanded by Oberleutnant Gustav Altmann and formed of ninety-two men and nine gliders, would capture the Veldwezelt Bridge; 'Group Concrete', commanded by Leutnant Gerhard Schacht and composed of ninety-six men in eleven gliders, would capture the Vroenhoven bridge; and 'Group Iron', under Leutnant Martin Schächter, composed of ninety men in ten gliders, who would capture the Kanne bridge. The finalized plan for the assault called for between nine and eleven gliders to land on the western bank of the Albert Canal by each of the three bridges just prior to 0530 on 10 May, the time scheduled for 'Fall Gelb' to begin. The groups assigned to assault the three bridges would overwhelm the defending Belgian troops, remove any demolition charges and then prepare to defend the bridges against an expected counter-attack.

HITLER'S INVASION OF EAST ANGLIA, 1940

Forty minutes later, three Ju 52 transport aircraft would fly over each position, dropping a further twenty-four airborne troops as reinforcements as well as machine-guns and significant amounts of ammunition. Simultaneously, the force assigned to assault Fort Ében-Émael was to land on top of the Fort in eleven gliders, eliminate any defenders attempting to repel them, cripple what artillery they could with explosive charges and then prevent the Garrison from dislodging them. Having achieved their initial objectives of seizing the bridges and eliminating the long-range artillery pieces possessed by the Fort, the airborne troops would then defend their positions until the arrival of German ground forces.

By 0435 hours on the morning of 10 May, forty-two Ju 52/3ms carrying the 493 airborne troops that formed the assault force took off from Köln-Ostheim and Köln-Butzweilerhof airfields, each towing a DFS 230 transport glider. The armada of gliders and transport aircraft turned south towards their objectives. The aircraft maintained strict radio silence, forcing the pilots to rely on a chain of signal fires that pointed towards Belgium. The tow-ropes on one of the gliders snapped, forcing the glider to land inside Germany. Another pilot of a second glider released his tow-rope prematurely and was unable to land near its objective. Both gliders were carrying troops assigned to 'Group Granite' and were destined to assault Fort Ében-Émael, thereby leaving the group under strength; it also left it under the command of Oberleutnant Witzig's second-in-command, as Witzig was in one of the gliders forced to land. The remaining gliders were released from their tow-ropes twenty miles away from their objectives at an altitude of 7,000 feet, which was deemed high enough for the gliders to land by the three bridges and on top of the fort and also maintain a steep dive angle to further ensure they landed correctly. After the Ju 52s released the gliders and began turning away, Belgian anti-aircraft artillery positions detected them and opened fire. This alerted the defences in the area to the presence of the gliders.

All nine gliders carrying the troops assigned to 'Group Steel' landed next to the bridge at Veldwezelt at 0520, the barbed-wire wrapped around the landing skids of the gliders succeeding in rapidly bringing them to a halt. Two men were able to reach the canal bank and climb onto the girders of the bridge and disconnect the demolition charges placed there by the Belgian garrison. The defenders held on until a platoon of reinforcements arrived and forced them to retire to a nearby village but the assaulting force could not overcome two field-guns located five hundred metres from the bridge by small-arms fire so several Junkers Ju 87 Stukas were called in and they knocked out the guns. 'Group Steel' lost eight airborne troops dead and thirty wounded.

Ten of the eleven gliders transporting 'Group Concrete' landed next to the Vroenhoven Bridge at 0515, the eleventh glider having been hit by anti-aircraft fire en route to the bridge and being forced to land prematurely inside Dutch territory. The gliders were engaged by heavy anti-aircraft fire as they landed, causing one of the gliders to stall in mid-air. The resulting crash severely wounded three airborne troops. The rest of the gliders landed without damage. One of the gliders landed near to the fortification housing the bridge detonators and allowed the airborne troops to rapidly assault the position. They killed the occupants and tore out the wires connecting the explosives to the detonator set, ensuring the bridge could not be destroyed. The remaining Belgian defenders resisted fiercely by mounting several counter-attacks in an attempt to recapture the bridge. They were repelled with the aid of several machine-guns dropped by parachute to the airborne troops at 0615. Constant Belgian attacks meant that 'Group Concrete' were not withdrawn and relieved by an infantry battalion until 2140. They suffered losses of seven dead and twenty-four wounded.

All but one of the ten gliders carrying the airborne troops assigned to 'Group Iron' was able to land next to their objective, the bridge at Kanne. Due to a navigation error by the pilots of the transport aircraft towing the gliders, one of the gliders was dropped in the wrong area. The other nine gliders were towed through heavy anti-aircraft fire and released at 0535. As the gliders began to descend towards their objective, the bridge was destroyed by several demolition explosions set off by the Belgian garrison. As the gliders came in to land, one was hit by anti-aircraft fire and crashed into the ground killing most of the occupants. The remaining eight landed successfully and the airborne troops stormed the Belgian positions and eliminated the defenders.

Only nine of the eleven gliders from 'Group Granite' actually reached the target, but these landed among the bewildered Belgian troops on the top of the fort's flat grassy expanse. Using explosives and flamethrowers to disable the outer defences of the fortress, the Fallschirmjäger then entered the fortress. Specially created 'hollow cone' demolition charges, which had been thoroughly tested on fortifications in occupied Poland and designed to penetrate up to twelve inches of armoured steel were used with devastating effect. The attackers disabled the fort's guns, killed a number of defenders and trapped the rest of the garrison inside the lower sections of the fortress. As the secondary objectives were attacked, a single glider landed on top of the Fort, from which emerged Oberleutnant Rudolf Witzig. After his glider had unintentionally landed in German territory, he had radioed for another tug and it landed in the field with a replacement glider. Once the airborne troops had broken down fences and hedges obstructing the aircraft, they boarded the new glider and were towed through anti-aircraft fire to the fort. 'Group Granite' held the position until the arrival of German ground forces at 0700 hours on 11 May. The assault cost 'Group Granite' only six killed and nineteen wounded. The supposedly unconquerable fortress had fallen to the glidermen in a matter of hours, opening the way for Colonel-General Fedor von Bock's Army Group 'B' to advance into northern Belgium, which fatally fixed the attention of the French high command there.[15]

The airborne assault on Fort Ében-Émael and the three bridges it helped protect was part of a much larger German airborne operation that involved the 7th Air Division and the 22nd Airlanding Division. The 7th Air Division, comprising three parachute regiments and one infantry regiment, was tasked with capturing a number of river and canal bridges that led to the Dutch defensive positions centered round Rotterdam, as well as the airfield at Waalhaven. The 22nd Airlanding Division, which was composed of two infantry regiments and a reinforced parachute battalion, was tasked with capturing a number of airfields in the vicinity of The Hague at Valkenburg, Ockenburg and Ypenburg. Once these airfields had been secured by the parachute battalion, the rest of the division would land with the aim of occupying the Dutch capital and capturing the entire Dutch government, the Royal Family and high-ranking members of the Dutch military and effect a surrender of the Dutch forces before the fighting even began. The division would also interdict all roads and railway lines in the area to impede the movement of Dutch forces. The intention of the German OKW was to use the two airborne divisions to create a corridor, along which the 18th Army could advance into the Netherlands without being impeded by destroyed bridges. General Kurt Student, who proposed the deployment of the two airborne divisions, argued that their presence would hold open the southern approaches to Rotterdam, prevent the movement of Dutch reserves based in north-west Holland and any French forces sent to aid

---

15   The next major operation in which the DFS 230 took part was the invasion of Crete in May 1941. The attack was led by fifty-three DFS 230 gliders from I. Bataillon/Luftlande-Sturmregiment commanded by Major Walter Koch.

the Dutch defenders and deny the use of airfields to Allied aircraft, all of which would aid a rapid advance by the 18th Army. A total of 400 Ju 52 transport aircraft would be used to deploy the parachute elements of the airborne troops, as well as transport the elements of the two airborne divisions not landing by parachute or glider.

The initial attacks against Holland and Belgium were carried out with complete surprise against the weakest parts of the Dutch or Belgian defences. And, for the first time in modern warfare, the Germans made extensive use of airborne troops to seize and neutralise vitally important strategic positions in advance of their attack. Similar tactics had been used during the opening stages of the Norway invasion on 9 April. German paratroops had captured airfields near Oslo and Stavanger, allowing troop carrying aircraft to fly in large numbers of reinforcements who then went on to take the Norwegian capital. In Holland around 16,000 German troops were planned to be flown in, divided over all targets. Total German strength was around 165,000 men with another 55,000 on the left flank and around 35,000 men as an infantry reserve. These faced 240,000 Dutch army personnel, most of which were concentrated in the Fortress Holland defences. The Luftwaffe opened attacks on Holland by bombing Schiphol, the barracks at Amsterdam and the anti-aircraft defences nearby. This was soon followed by two simultaneous airborne operations, the descent of parachute troops being made on key points in Holland. The individual task forces were instructed to withstand all Dutch counter-attacks for at least three days. At the end of the third day the German ground forces were scheduled to link up with the troops at Moerdijk.

RAF Coastal Command Blenheims on reconnaissance early in the morning of 10 May reported eleven German aircraft crashed on the beach south of the spot where the Amsterdam Canal joins the sea and eleven Junkers on the airfield at The Hague, which was strewn with the abandoned parachutes of German troops. Inside the Ju 52s the German paratroopers each clipped their static line to the anchor line and when his turn to jump came, positioned himself in the open doorway of the transport aircraft, placing his feet wide apart on the edge of the doorway and gripping the handrails on either side of the opening he launched himself out into space by pushing against the hand rails and springing forward in one swift movement. The 'spread-eagled' position reduced the shock imparted by the sudden opening of the parachute canopy and the parachutist fell from the aircraft in an arc, the vertical height of which was about 82 feet, before the parachute canopy unfolded completely. Once oscillation ceased, the parachutist floated steadily down, suspended from his fully opened parachute, the actual rate of fall reaching twelve to nineteen feet per second according to the weight of the soldier. A great deal of attention had been paid during training exercises to mastering the technique of accurate landing - allowing for drift - the object being to place the troops as close as possible to the points to be attacked.

While the paratroopers initially seized the airfield, Dutch troops quickly drove them off before they could be reinforced. The attack, however, resulted in the Dutch high command's focusing on the defence of the capital and rushing its reserves to The Hague. Meanwhile, a far more dangerous German drive, led by paratroopers, was gathering steam on the Netherlands frontier. The Germans dropped small packets of paratroopers to seize the crucial bridges that led directly across Holland and into the heart of the country to open the way for the 10th Panzer Division. Soon after 0300 hours news came in of the first Germans entering the Netherlands: German paratroops had been dropped at four places in the west of the country - north and south of the Moerdijk bridges, near Dordrecht in the western Netherlands, on or near Waalhaven airfield at Rotterdam and around The Hague. At 0400 hours the bridges at Moerdijk were bombed and very soon a battalion of paratroops came down, two companies landing south and two more north of the bridges. After some fierce fighting the Germans managed to capture the bridges intact. At about the same time, a battalion of paratroops was dropped around Dordrecht. Again there was heavy fighting, but the bridge at Dordrecht was in German possession by noon. Probably this bridge could have been withheld longer from the attackers but for some strange decisions taken by the garrison commander, which resulted in chaos and confusion.

While the 'Blitzkrieg' was a highly mechanised style of warfare, its success owed just as much to the elements of surprise, deception and infiltration as it did to armour and aircraft. At Venlo the Dutch destroyed a German armoured train with ten German agents on board, though the railway bridge at Gennep was captured intact. A troop train passed the bridge safely but the Dutch managed to blow up the bridge at Zeeland. At Nijmegen the road and railway bridges were blown up right in front of the infuriated Germans. Nevertheless, on other sectors of the front the Germans broke through and moved deep inside Dutch and Belgian territory with consummate ease. Without doubt, it was the infiltration tactics employed by specialist German units that are the reality behind the stories of parachutists disguised as Dutch policemen and Belgian officers. But who exactly were the men, or perhaps even women, behind the disguises? Many have claimed that German airborne troops did not adopt disguises and many German veterans claimed that they fought in the uniform of the Fallschirmjäger and this uniform alone. But there was another shadowy unit of the German armed forces that definitely did use disguise and deception. Furthermore, they practically turned the use of such ruses into an art form.

During World War I, the legacy of German General Paul Emil von Lettow-Vorbeck's superb guerrilla war in the German East Africa campaign[16] and T. E. Lawrence's use of Arab hit-and-run tactics to fight the Turks in the Middle East had a profound effect on one of Lettow-Vorbeck's junior officers, a young captain named Theodore von Hippel. After the war, Hippel proposed utilizing small, elite units to penetrate enemy defences before hostilities or offensive actions had begun. Many believed that this would be an infringement of the rules of war and furthermore, such saboteurs were not worthy of being called soldiers but Hippel persevered and when he became an officer in the Abwehr, the German high command allowed him to form a battalion and carry out sabotage, capture roads and bridges ahead of the main force and securing strategic targets before they were demolished. Known as the Ebbinghaus battalion, the unit performed magnificently during the Polish campaign. Though it was dissolved shortly afterward, Admiral Wilhelm Canaris gave Hippel the opportunity to form a unit for the Abwehr, on 15 October 1939. Officially founded in Brandenburg and named after the barracks near Berlin's famous Brandenburg Gate where they had first been assembled, they adopted the shorter name of Brandenburg Kompanie. It was commanded by Lieutenant Colonel Friedrich Wilhelm Heinz, commander 1st Battalion Heinz, a man who shared Admiral Wilhelm Canaris' admiration for Paul von Lettow-Vorbeck.

Heinz served in the trenches in the Great War, where he was wounded multiple times and well decorated. Post-war, he was a member of various Nationalist groups including the Stahlhelm and the Freikorps Ehrhardt, where he took part in the Kapp Putsch. He was heavily involved in politics as a right-wing monarchist throughout the inter-war years. He was also a poet and author, developing skills that he later directed to the political arena. He was an early National Socialist party member but he soon baulked at Hitler's dictatorial style. He instead aligned himself closely with the Strasser wing of the party. There is evidence that Heinz was to be murdered in the Night

---

16 von Lettow-Vorbeck, nicknamed affectionately as the 'Lion of Africa' Lettow-Vorbeck was a general in the Prussian Army and the commander of its forces. For four years, with a force that never exceeded about 14,000 (3,000 Germans and 11,000 Africans), he held in check a much larger force of 300,000 British, Belgian and Portuguese troops. Essentially undefeated in the field, Lettow-Vorbeck was the only German commander to successfully invade imperial British soil during the First World War.

of the Long Knives. In the mid-thirties, after he was known to be anti-Hitler, Heinz joined Admiral Wilhelm Canaris' Abwehr intelligence service as a safe haven from the attentions of the Gestapo. He was heavily involved in several of the plots against Hitler. By 1938, Heinz was working actively against Hitler as a member of Hans Oster's group within the Abwehr. During the war, Heinz commanded the first battalion of the Abwehr's Brandenburg commandos and later the fourth regiment of the Brandenburg division. He was wounded many times and was eventually invalided home to take command of a watch battalion in Berlin. On 20 July he was present in the Bendlerstrasse for Stauffenberg's famous coup attempt. He left the Bendlerblock building empty handed as orders to the various police and security units were slow in coming. He survived the coup without more than a single Gestapo interrogation.

After the suicide of Heinz's close friend and Abwehr co-member Werner Schrader on 28 July 1944, the Gestapo found Hans von Dohnanyi's detailed archive of regime crimes, as well as prior coup plans in Schrader's safe. In addition, the Gestapo learned that the archive had for a time been kept in Heinz's brother-in-law's bank vault until Schrader and Heinz had moved it to his office at army high command in Zossen. The archive detailed Heinz's personal involvement in the 1938 Oster plot and an arrest warrant was issued. Heinz went to ground in Berlin and, unlike many of the conspirators who went into hiding, managed to stay hidden until war's end. Friedrich Wilhelm Heinz died in 1968.

As part of 'Fall Gelb', the 100th Special Purpose Battalion commanded by Hauptmann Fleck was ordered to seize the bridges over the Maas and the Maas-Waal Canal at Nijmegen and Westerpoort, east of Arnhem. Late in the afternoon of 9 May the Brandenburgers' 800th Special-Purpose Construction Training Battalion commanded by 30-year old Oberleutnant Wilhelm Walther, had moved up into attack positions. Born on 27 January 1910 in Dresden in an Evangelical Lutheran family, Walther had trained as an architect from 1929 until 1933 at the Technische Hochschule in Dresden until study ended prematurely because the tuition fees could not be paid. On 1st November 1934 his military career began when he joined the Wehrmacht. In March 1940 at a secret training camp at Asperden he was given command of the 4th Kompanie, which consisted of three large platoons who were to take various objectives during the German 'Blitzkrieg'. During Unternehmen 'Weserübung' the speedy capture of four airfields in Denmark and southern Norway was entrusted to Walther's 1st Battalion of 1st Jäger Regiment. Walther and his men arrived over Oslo-Fornebu airfield in conditions of poor visibility. There was to be no paratroop air drop and the Ju 52s would fly straight in to land on the runway but the Norwegian defences opened fire and forced the transports to abort the mission. However, the pilots of the Bf 109 escort, who had been strafing the airfield, landed and opened fire with their machine guns. The Ju 52s put down, the Company deplaned and half an hour later the airfield was in German hands.[17]

The Brandenburg commando detachments, as they were known, were a special purpose unit that was created by and functioned as part of the Abwehr. They would often operate in advance of German troops to seize a vital installation or strategically important position. But, whatever their mission, they would always resort to subterfuge. The Brandenburgers were volunteers recruited from Germans who had lived and worked abroad and were picked for their language skills and knowledge of other countries, particularly those bordering Germany. They were trained to be self reliant, were proficient in a variety of military skills and operated in small teams. To access the bridges easily and then to overtake the guards by surprise and off the platoons were divided into groups of about eight German soldiers, together with some Dutch volunteers mostly living and working in Germany and recruited from the NSB affiliated organization 'Sport and Game'. Walther's assault team and the fourteen other combat teams wore Dutch helmets and army coats, which they put on over their own uniforms. This was referred to as 'halbtarnung' (half camouflage). 'Volltarnung', or 'full camouflage', was the wearing of the complete enemy uniform. Each man carried a submachine-gun concealed beneath the coat. 'Pineapple' and stick type hand grenades were carried in the coat pockets. Pistols were stuck in trouser pockets.

By attacking through the Netherlands, Luxembourg and Belgium, the German Oberkommando der Wehrmacht believed that German forces could outflank the Maginot Line and then advance through southern Belgium and into northern France, cutting off the British Expeditionary Force and a large number of French forces and forcing the French government to surrender. To gain access to northern France, German forces would have to defeat the armed forces of the Low Countries and either bypass or neutralize a number of defensive positions, primarily in Belgium and the Netherlands. Some of these defensive positions were only lightly defended and intended more as delaying positions than true defensive lines designed to stop an enemy attack. However, a number of them were of a more permanent design,

---

17 *Storming Eagles: German Airborne Forces In World War II* by James Lucas (Arms & Armour Press, 1988).

possessing considerable fortifications and garrisoned by significant numbers of troops. The Grebbe-Peel Line in the Netherlands, which stretched from the southern shore of the Zuiderzee to the Belgian border near Weert, had a large number of fortifications combined with natural obstacles, such as marsh-lands and the Geld Valley, which could easily be flooded to impede an attack.

The Germans, executing a plan approved by Hitler, though not contrived by him personally, tried to capture the Ijssel and Maas bridges intact, using commando teams of Brandenburgers that began to infiltrate over the Dutch border ahead of the main advance, with some troops arriving on the evening of 9 May. During the night of 10 May they approached the bridges: several teams had a few men dressed as Dutch military police pretending to bring in a group of German prisoners, to fool the Dutch detonation teams. Some of these 'military policemen' were Dutch members of the Nationaal-Socialistische Beweging, the Dutch Nazi party. The Dutch released reports of German soldiers in disguise to the international news agencies. This caused a fifth column scare, especially in Belgium and France. However, unlike the situation later on in those two countries, in the Netherlands there was no mass exodus of civilian refugees, clogging the roads. Generally German soldiers behaved in a civilised manner towards the Dutch population, forming neat queues at the shops to buy goods rationed in Germany, such as chocolate. After the generally failed assaults on the bridges, the German divisions began crossing attempts over the rivers Ijssel and Maas. The first waves typically were destroyed, due to insufficient preparatory fire on the pillboxes. At most places a secondary bombardment destroyed the pillboxes and the infantry divisions crossed the river after building pontoon bridges; but at some, as Venlo, the attempt was aborted. At Arnhem, Leibstandarte Der Führer led the assault and that day advanced to the Grebbe Line, followed by 207 Infanteriedivision. Despite the destruction of the Wilhelminabrug and the Sint Servaasbrug German troops passed Maastricht, a vital traffic hub, relatively quickly. Even before the armoured train arrived, 3rd Army Corps had already been planned to be withdrawn from behind the Peel-Raam Position, taking with it all the artillery apart from 368 Staal pieces. Each of its six regiments was to leave a battalion behind to serve as a covering force, together with fourteen 'border battalions'. The group was called the 'Peel Division'. This withdrawal was originally planned for the first night after the invasion, under cover of darkness, but due to the rapid German advance an immediate retreat was ordered at 0645, to avoid 3rd Army Corps becoming entangled with enemy troops. The corps joined 'Brigade G', six battalions already occupying the Waal-Linge line and was thus brought up to strength again. It would see no further fighting.

Most of the attempts using commando teams failed and the bridges were blown, on two occasions with Brandenburgers and all. The main exception was the seizure of the Meuse railway bridge in Gennep on 10th May. An eight-man team, led by Leutnant Wilhelm Walther, was given the task of capturing the bridge intact after obtaining information about where demolition charges had been placed. Three Dutch members of the Dutch National Socialist party dressed and armed as gendarmes created the impression that they had intercepted and caught the nine men of the assault team somewhere in the area of the border and were now bringing them in. The group halted 800 metres from the 150 metre long bridge for Walther to go over the attack one more time. At 0200 Walther's team, now disguised as Dutch military police escorting German prisoners, the Brandenburgers took the defenders of the bridge by surprise. Two guard posts were destroyed, but three Brandenburgers were wounded and the team was pinned down as the posts on the far side of the bridge were not yet under German control. Walther advanced across the bridge as the confused defenders hesitated, allowing the rest of the Brandenburgers to destroy the remaining guard posts and seize the detonator minutes before an armoured train carrying the tanks of the largely Austrian 9th Panzer Division commanded by the Hungarian-born Generalleutnant Dr. Alfred Ritter Von Hubicki and shortly followed by a troop train carrying motorized infantry of the SS-Verfügungsdivision rolled over the bridge, both driving right through the Peel-Raam Position at Mill and unloading an infantry battalion behind the defence line.[18]

Many more operations like this took place over the course of the campaign. The bridges over the Maas-Waal Canal were taken by four 'Dutch policemen' with thirty German 'deserters' led by Leutnant Witzel who bluffed their way across and managed to prevent the Dutch defenders from blowing the bridge. A Dutch counter-attack failed under fire from the first German guns to be moved forward. The Malden Bridge, guarded by an NCO and ten enlisted men of the Dutch 26th Infantry Regiment with medium and heavy weapons with which to fight off an attack, was overwhelmed by the small force of Germans who occupied the guard houses and cut the wires

---

18 After the war Walther was arrested by the Dutch military authorities. See *The Brandenburgers - Global Mission* - by Franz Kurowski (J. J. Fedorowicz Publishing, 1997).

to explosive charges that had been laid. With the same surprise and speed, the Germans took the bridge at Hatert. The Dutch were also prevented from blowing the road bridges over the Juliana Canal at Obbicht, Berg, Stein and Urmond in South Limburg which were secured by the platoon led by Leutnant Kürschner and the explosive charges removed from their recesses. Forty men of the Hocke Special Unit, consisting of the 100th and 800th Special Purpose Battalions took the bridge over the Juliana Canal at Oud Roosteren and overran a Dutch infantry squad positioned there. They then tried to cross the bridge over the canal at Roosteren. Having tricked the guard on the east bank when he asked them for the password the group was stopped again at the west end of the bridgier and suspicions were raised, not least their 'steel' helmets, which were made of papier-mâché. After a fire-fight resulting in dead and wounded on both sides, the Brandenburgers succeeded in taking the bridge. The group immediately proceeded to the Maas Bridge near Maaseyk but was spotted and came under heavy fire, which prevented them from reaching the bridge in time and soon after the firing began the bridge was blown up. Under the command of Leutnant Grabert, a fifteen-man V-squad with one man disguised as a Dutch lieutenant marched to Roermond at 0200 but during a brief fire fight, which delayed Grabert and his men from reaching the bridge, with a thunderous roar, it was blown up before their eyes.

The attempted seizure of the bridge north of Roermond near Buggenum by a six-man team commanded by Unteroffizier Hilmer, whose men were disguised as railway workers and carried picks and shovels, also failed. The bridge guard stopped the group and after suspicions were raised, the 'railway workers' suddenly dropped their tools, pulled out their weapons and opened fire. One Dutch sentry was killed and another was wounded, though he was able to warn the west bank and they fired on the Germans from the west bunker. The first two Germans fell to the ground badly wounded. Immediately after the Dutch guards on the east bank had been overrun, Hilmer fired signal flares to summon a German armoured train waiting under steam just beyond the border but when his team reached the middle of the bridge four huge explosions shook the structure and they were hurled into the river along with the rubble. The train arrived twenty minutes later but it could go no further. A Dutch anti-tank gun opened fire, the first rounds struck the locomotive and the crew were forced to abandon it due to the danger of explosion. Despite these setbacks, the spearheads of the 256th Infanterie Division and the Nazi war machine rolled through Holland, Belgium and on into northern France at breathtaking speed. France was an even bigger success for the Fallschirmjäger. In early May 1940 the strength of German airborne forces was nearly that of a light infantry division. But their impact on the opening moves of one of the most important battles of World War II was out of all proportion to their size. In the southern Ardennes, Fieseler Fi-156 Storch ('Stork') light reconnaissance planes famous for their excellent short take-off and landing (STOL) performance dropped members of the Brandenburg Regiment on the bridges immediately to the south of the 10th Panzer Division's route of march.

Waalhaven airfield had already been under attack from the air for several minutes as Sergeant Major Jan Buwalda took off in the 8th Fokker G.1. of 3rd JaVA (No.3 Dutch Fighter Squadron) at 0359 hours.[19] The whole squadron was now airborne and each of the heavy twin-engined fighter aircraft were soon fighting on their own. Buwalda climbed the twin-boom, two-seater up along the wall of fire from the blazing Koolhoven aircraft factory at the edge of the airfield and turned south west in a sky vibrating from the noise of fighting aircraft and explosions. A few minutes earlier, 28 Heinkel He 111 bombers led by Luftwaffe Kommodore Martin Fiebig had crossed the Dutch coast a few miles south of the Hook of Holland. With six other Staffeln (squadrons) of KG 4, they had left their home bases of Delmenhorst, Fassberg and Gütersloh in Germany to attack the Dutch airfields of Schiphol, Ypenburg and Waalhaven. Surprise was to be achieved by making a wide detour over the North Sea and approaching Holland from the West. Seconds after crossing the coast the German pilots reported heavy flak and spotted several Dutch fighters. But Fiebig, leading the Stab (Staff-flight) spearheading the attack, made straight for Waalhaven with the aim of destroying as many Dutch fighters as possible on the ground. Minutes later the first bombs hailed down on the doomed airbase. The Heinkels turned south and Fiebig decided to make another run to blow up the remaining ground installations.

Flying over Zuid-Beyerland, ten miles south of Waalhaven, Jan Buwalda attacked the first enemy bomber he saw; firing his eight nose machine guns

---

19   While the 4th JaVA received a devastating blow, losing all but one of its aircraft, eight 3rd JaVA G.1 fighters were scrambled in time and successfully engaged several German aircraft. The surviving aircraft continued to fly, but with mounting losses, bringing their numbers down to three airworthy aircraft by the end of the first day. Despite the heavy losses of 4th JaVA, some of the planes could be kept in the air, by scavenging parts from various planes. In the 'Five-day War' the available G.1 fighters were mainly deployed in ground attack missions, strafing advancing German infantry units, but also used to attack Junkers Ju 52/3m transports. Although reports are fragmentary and inaccurate as to the results, G.1 fighters were employed over Rotterdam and The Hague, contributing to the loss of 167 Ju 52s, scoring up to 14 confirmed aerial kills.

HITLER'S INVASION OF EAST ANGLIA, 1940

he immediately hit the port engine, which started to trail grey smoke. The bomber slowed and curved away to the northwest, losing height rapidly. Seconds' later three crew members bailed out, barely in time to land safely as their aircraft crashed in the fields near the village of Rockanje and were taken prisoner by a coastal artillery unit. One of them was reported to be furious at ending his war so soon: he was Group-Commander Martin Fiebig of KG 4.

Returning to base, Buwalda spotted another enemy bomber close to the airfield and having sufficient ammunition left started his second duel. After a long, southerly chase towards Dordrecht, he scored several hits and finally shot down his second He 111 at 0425 hours, but within seconds was attacked by a large formation of Bf 109s. Chased by nine enemy fighters, Buwalda tried to escape to the south with his air gunner, Sergeant Wagner, making desperate efforts to keep the attackers at a distance. The starboard engine of the G.1. was hit and badly damaged and the port engine began to lose power. Evasion was impossible; the Fokker was being continually hit and Sergeant Wagner was wounded in one eye. Having no chance, Buwalda made a successful belly landing near Zevenbergen, ten miles south of Dordrecht. He then removed one of the machine guns from his aircraft and fought his way back to Waalhaven with a light AA group through an area where German paratroops had landed in the meantime... another story in itself. This short but remarkable operational life of Fokker G.1., No. 319 is but one example. Similar experiences were recorded by the other seven G-1 crews of Waalhaven and other Dutch Air Force units equipped with Fokker D-XXI single-seaters, T-V 5 five-seat medium bombers, C-5 and C-10 biplanes and Douglas 8A reconnaissance-fighters, an updated version of the Northrop A-17 for the export market, with a more powerful engine and increased bomb load. An order for eighteen Douglas DB8A-3N assault bombers was placed in March 1939.[20] The Fokker D-21 was the first mono-wing fighter design from the Dutch Fokker factory, being designed in 1935 for use by the Dutch Colonial Air Force, which in the end rejected the prototype. In December 1937 the Dutch War Department ordered 36 off D-XXIs for the Dutch Air Force, intended to form two fighter squadrons.[21]

---

20 Lieutenant General G. van der Wolf DFC, writing in the, *RAF Souvenir Book 1972*. Born 1916, he entered military service in 1935, escaped capture in 1940 and came to England with the Dutch military flying school. He flew 85 combat sorties with RAF squadrons in WWII and became C-in-C in 1970.

21 A handful of the Finnish Air Force D-XXIs claimed almost 200 aerial victories over the Russian Air Force during both Finnish-Russo wars.

'FALL GELB'

On 10 May only nine out of sixteen T-5s at Schiphol AFB were ready for action. None of the other seven aircraft could be successfully prepared for action during the May War. By the afternoon four major aerodromes at Waalhaven, Ypenburg, Ockenburg and Valkenburg were in German hands. The Dutch air force had suffered severe losses during this first day of war. At Ypenburg eleven of the assembled dozen DB8A-3Ns took off and formed four patrols. None of the aircraft survived the tragic events of that day. One was shot down by three Bf-110s over the North Sea and the crew perished. Another was shot down by three Bf 109Es and two Bf 110s at Voorschoten. One crew member was killed. Another DB8A shot down a Ju-52 before crashing at Honselersdijk (Delft) with the loss of one crew member killed. A second DB8A also shot down a Ju-52 before making an emergency landing at Schipluiden near Delft. The crew survived. Four DB8As made emergency landings at two airfields and were later destroyed on the ground by German fighters. Two more were shot down with one crew being lost. An eleventh victim was shot down at Nootdorp (Delft) with the crew surviving. Out of 22 crew members eight had died and several had been wounded. In total, 62 of the 125 Dutch aircraft were put out of action. Yet the remaining aircraft still carried out missions during the following days, in the face of German air superiority. For this feat of arms the force was awarded the Militaire Wilier sorde, equivalent to the Victoria Cross.

The Germans at once began to land troops in large numbers from troop-carrying aircraft. The RAF immediately gave all the aid it could to the hard-pressed Dutch. Aircraft of Bomber Command were in action within a few hours, but their efforts proved futile. Rupert 'Tiny' Cooling was second pilot in Sergeant 'Duggie' Douglas' crew, one of two new crews who had arrived on 9 Squadron at Honington in the flat fields of Suffolk three days earlier.

'The mess was quiet at lunchtime. Serious groups gathered round the radiogram, listening silently to the news. A lot was said but little was learned: things did not seem to be going well. It was all far from reassuring. Word went around - briefing at 1500 hours. Tension eased fractionally; at least here was something positive, even if it left two hours to conjure with, to fill with 'ifs' and 'maybes'. Lunch lay in the stomach like a warmed weight of unkneaded dough; there was a slightly greasy feeling in the bowel. Unwilling though they might be, none of the aircrew would have opted out if given any choice. The murmur of voices stilled as the CO walked briskly into the crew room, followed by his flight commanders. The target was the aerodrome at Waalhaven; Rotterdam's airport. It had been seized by German troops. Junkers Ju 52s were flying in men, munitions and supplies.'

HITLER'S INVASION OF EAST ANGLIA, 1940

German bombers started bombing Waalhaven at 0355 hours and an hour later a battalion of paratroops was dropped on and east of the airfield. Though there was some stiff resistance from Dutch troops, Waalhaven fell quickly into German hands. In Rotterdam itself fifty paratroops landed in Feyenoord (South Rotterdam). They moved as fast as they could to the Maas bridges, the last obstacle in the way of the German troops of the XVIII Army, approaching from the south. Twelve Heinkel 59 seaplanes alighted on the river at 0500 hours on both sides of the bridges and landed 150 men who occupied the north and south banks of the Maas at the foot of the bridges. The air force did everything it could. Four times they bombed Waalhaven, causing much damage among the German aircraft, but by the end of the first day of battle the Germans had established themselves firmly on Waalhaven airfield from where they could carry out further operations. South Rotterdam was occupied, the Maas bridges were in their hands and they had a small bridgehead, consisting of only a few houses, on the north bank. It had been observed that during the day about 250 Junkers 52 transport aircraft had landed on Waalhaven and thus it was estimated that there were about 5,000 Germans in South Rotterdam.

Fighting had been going on in and around The Hague, where German paratroops had been dropped on 10th May shortly before 0500 hours. The airborne troops which would land afterwards had received orders to occupy The Hague and capture the Dutch government. To attain this, the airfields of Ockenburg, Ypenburg and Valkenburg had to be taken first. After aircraft bombed and machine-gunned the airfields and barracks, paratroops would be dropped near the airfields to deal with the remaining Dutch forces. After that, German airborne troops would land and then march on The Hague to carry out the rest of the plan. In order to surprise the Dutch completely, the aircraft would fly in a westerly direction over the Netherlands (simulating an attack on England), turn over the North Sea and attack from the west. The Germans were successful, as they managed to get the three airfields in their possession - though with severe losses, partly because the paratroops for Ypenburg and Ockenburg had landed too far south of their targets, so that it was the airborne troops who first had to fight the defenders. Half an hour after the paratroops had come down, Junkers transport aircraft landed on the two airfields. At Ockenburg the attackers were under such heavy fire that even the aircraft crews were forced to take part in the ensuing fight. They suffered heavy losses: few aircraft were able to leave after the airfield had been taken. The rest of the Junkers formed such an obstacle that only a few more could land with reinforcements. The remainder of the troops earmarked for Ockenburg landed on the beach, in the dunes near Kijkduin and at Waalhaven. At Ypenburg of a group of thirteen transport aircraft, were shot down before landing and only a handful of Germans were able to leave the aircraft. Further landings on the airfield were impossible and the remainder of the troops intended for Ypenburg landed on the highway from The Hague to Rotterdam, near Hook of Holland and Waalhaven. Valkenburg was the only place the Germans landed without heavy losses; together with the paratroops, the airborne troops were able to overpower the defenders. Here, however, there was another difficulty for them: the heavy Junkers aircraft had sunk into the soft soil so that the airfield could no longer be used. Besides, the Dutch had been bombarding the airfield with artillery and from the air. More German troops landed on the beach and in the dunes near Katwijk.

Within hours of entering the country, German troops had taken control of the Northern provinces, but the German plan to capture the Dutch Royal Family and Government in The Hague was a complete failure. At 0500 hours on 10 May a dozen rather antiquated open cockpit Heinkel He 59B-1 seaplanes of Staffel 'Schwilben', which were among those used during the initial assault phase of the invasion of Norway to deliver assault parties into the fiords, landed on the River Maas with 120 infantry and combat engineers in a suicidal attempt to capture the Willems twin road and rail bridges in the heart of the city. The elderly biplanes, six on each side of the bridge, taxied on the water so that the assault troops could use inflatable boats to get ashore. Four of the seaplanes were lost before German reinforcements arrived on the scene and the bridge was taken.

The Dutch anti-aircraft gun-fire was particularly effective against the lumbering, low-flying Ju 52/3M tri-motors and many were shot down with the loss of their troop complements. On the first day alone, 157 Ju 52/3ms were destroyed, together with the loss of more than a thousand men. Others stuck in the soft soil and mud when attempting to land on the uncompleted airfield of Valkenburg, while Dutch fighters strafed and destroyed many more transports that had landed on the beach north of The Hague. Although fearfully outnumbered, the Dutch Army Air Service fought valiantly and immediately after the occupation of Waalhaven by the German airborne forces three T.V. 5 medium-bombers of 1st Air Regiment attacked the transport aircraft packed on the airfield. Only one returned to base.

Dutch troops were to counter-attack at last light on 10 May. Thirty-six Wellingtons would crater Waalhaven airfield, destroy the transports and soften up the defences. Each was to carry sixteen 250lb bombs, nose and

HITLER'S INVASION OF EAST ANGLIA, 1940

tail fused for maximum fragmentation. The Wimpys carried twelve 250lb bombs in their bomb bays and all the attacks were to be carried out in dives from 4,000-6,000 feet down to 1,200-1,500 feet. Weather was forecast to be fine; the winds south-westerly. Flak, said the intelligence officer, would be light stuff, mainly 20mm. The Germans had had no time to bring in heavy anti-aircraft weapons. Single-engined fighters were unlikely but there were reports of Bf 110 activity. No mention was made that five out of six Blenheims had been shot down by 110s earlier in the day and over the same target. Take off time was 1730 hours; aircraft would proceed independently.'

Peering through the Perspex dome amidships, 'Tiny' Cooling saw the flickering curtain of flak was hemmed with orange flame and rolling curls of dense black smoke. Jock Gilmour's voice over the intercom caused him guiltily to draw his fascinated gaze from the rising ribbons of glittering sequins to scan the sky for fighters. 'Bomb doors open. Target in sight. Right a little, right.' The last word was drawn out and then chopped as the nose came round to the required heading. Now the lights were directly ahead. The pattern seemed to part; to open up a pathway before closing in behind. Slowly at first the bright stars rose, gathering speed to race towards the aircraft and pass beyond the wing-tips and the tail. 'Left, left. Steady. Bombs gone.' The Wellington jerked perceptively as 4,000lb of metal and high explosive plunged from the gaping belly.

There was a sharp 'twack' like some large and floppy fly swat striking the fabric skin. A triangle of the camouflage covering leapt up to dance upon the upper surface of the starboard wing. Surprised at his own calm and composure, Cooling said, 'Pilot, we've been hit. Starboard mainplane. There's a patch of fabric flapping just outboard of the engine.' The curtain of flak fell away behind. Another aircraft stood out in silhouette against the darkening sky. Cooling's heart thumped almost painfully and then subsided as he recognised another Wellington. A lazy line of grey surf hemmed the dun-coloured sands, suggesting the margin of comparative safety, the Dutch coast. 'U-Uncle' flew on past the Dutch coast. Out over the North Sea Sergeant Douglas handed over control to 'Tiny' Cooling before going aft to see the damage for himself. It was dark when 'U for Uncle' crossed the Suffolk coast.

At the age of 66 Winston Churchill had taken over as Britain's wartime leader and Minister of Defence on 10 May. In his first speech as Prime Minister, Churchill told Parliament that he was putting politics aside and forming a national government which included all parties to wage war against Germany. He said he would tell them what he told his new ministers:

'FALL GELB'

'I have nothing to offer but blood, toil, tears and sweat.' On 10 May the British public had opened their newspapers to read that hundreds of German paratroops had descended from the skies over Dutch cities and tanks had rolled across the Belgian border. The next day the *Daily Express* reported a failed plot to seize the Dutch royal family in which brief mention was made of German troops in disguise. It also assured readers that the 'Blitzkrieg' is being effectively handled' and beneath the subheading 'Shock tactics foiled', it was reported that Dutch forces had taken a heavy toll of the enemy parachutists. During the five days of the campaign against Holland no less than 167 Ju 52/3ms were lost, mostly falling victim to anti-aircraft fire. After the initial assault, operations by the transport units began to tail off, the capture of Belgium and northern France being entrusted to ground-based army units. Having gained a foothold in Rotterdam, seaplanes were then used to ferry in reinforcements.

Next day, Saturday 11 May, six Wellingtons on 149 Squadron bombed Waalhaven again. The German violation of Dutch and Belgian neutrality had opened up a path for British bombers to fly directly from England to the Ruhr where sixty per cent of Germany's industrial strength was concentrated. However, political infighting between the French and British commands delayed matters. The French, with their hands full trying to repel an enemy force from its borders, were alarmed at the repercussions of such an action and Bomber Command, with its sixteen squadrons of Wellingtons, Whitleys and Hampdens, was prevented from carrying out the action. Attempts were made to eliminate the German pockets, but without success. Between The Hague and Katwijk there was exceptionally heavy fighting which resulted in a loss of one Dutch battalion. The motorway from Delft to Rotterdam was still partly in German hands. The Luftwaffe was even able to supply the airborne troops with food and ammunition. Though the Germans were not able to march on Rotterdam, they were successful in that they managed to hold down a contingent of the Dutch army around The Hague, thus keeping them from being used elsewhere. From 11 May onwards the Germans had air superiority, which made operations for the Dutch army more difficult. Furthermore there were many rumours of subversive actions by civilians and disguised Germans in The Hague, which meant that the Dutch troops, continually on the move, got little rest - something which had also happened at Rotterdam. The result of it all was that some of the airborne troops were able to break out a few places and managed to join up. There were three German pockets on Sunday 12 May: Overschie, in the village of Valkenburg and near the Wassenaarse Slag - in all about 1,000 men. On Sunday 19 May a

HITLER'S INVASION OF EAST ANGLIA, 1940

total of 132 serviceable aircraft was available to the Army Air Service but this total included 28 obsolescent Fokker C.V and C.X two-seat reconnaissance aircraft, the latter dating from the mid-thirties; sixteen equally elderly Koolhoven F.K.51 two seat advanced training biplanes and six Lorraine Fokker D.XVII-4 single-seat fighter biplanes of 1933. The 1st and 2nd Fighter Groups were equipped with the lightly armed D.XXI, the AAS's standard single-seat fighter but its bulky Bristol Mercury 8 radial engined and fixed, spatted undercarriage resulted in a maximum speed of only 286 mph.

The battle was joined in Belgium and France where the German 'Blitzkrieg' was equally swift and decisive. On Sunday, 12 May the French government announced that 'all German parachutists landing in French territory wearing any uniform but the German will be immediately shot.' The following day, via the BBC's Foreign Service, the British government broadcast a virtually identical message warning of summary execution for any '[enemy] parachutists descending in Britain in attire other than recognised German uniform.' The *Daily Express,* below the sub-heading, 'Germans disguised as Dutch parsons' reported that 'German troops disguised as peasants and clergymen have been arrested in various towns... those wearing Dutch uniform are being executed.' Another story, obviously connected with the abortive attempt to capture the Dutch royal family, mentions a large plane crashing in a suburb of The Hague with 'nineteen Germans onboard all wearing Dutch uniform - aged 17-19'. The tone of the report suggests that they had all been killed.

An even more sensational story was on page 3. Beneath the heading 'Germans Dropped Women Parachutists as decoys', witnesses onboard an English ship departing Rotterdam told of seeing: 'parachutists descend in women's clothes. They wore blouses and skirts and each carried a sub-machine gun.' The witnesses were unable to confirm if the parachutists really were women or just men in disguise. In the same report it was said that the paratroops had dropped out of the skies 'like vultures,' most of them disguised in Dutch army uniforms, while others were dressed as policemen, priests, peasants and civilians. A senior British commander alleged that German women, who had previously worked in Holland and had local knowledge of The Hague and Rotterdam, were parachuted in alongside the armed troops to act as guides. The *News Chronicle* reported: 'In a number of cases they [the paratroops] have been wearing uniforms calculated to deceive observers into thinking they were friendly.' Another press report revealed that Some German paratroopers captured in Holland had been carrying lists of prominent Dutch citizens who were to be shot. In Britain

'FALL GELB'

Parliament was proposed that all MPs and prominent citizens should be armed with revolvers. Famously, in *The Times* on Tuesday 21st May the Dutch Foreign Minister in exile, Mr. Van der Kleffens, made the astonishing claim that during the invasion of his country the Germans had resorted to: 'such abominable ruses de guerre as the use of disguises of nuns, Red Cross nurses, monks, tram car conductors, policemen, postmen and Dutch troops.' In printing the words of Mr. Van Kleffens, *The Times*, revered as a British institution, gave an air of authenticity to what would become one of the best known pieces of WWII folklore.

There were other stories claiming that German invasion forces had also been assisted by pro-Nazi sympathizers, commonly referred to as 'Fifth Columnists', a phrase that had originated during the Spanish Civil War of 1936-39. It was alleged that they aided the Nazi invaders by providing valuable information about local defences and even carried out acts of sabotage. During the retreat through Belgium it was reported that men dressed as British army officers with a perfect command of English were issuing false orders to British troops. It was also said that the Germans were putting spies among refugees to spread terror. The *Daily Express* cartoon of Saturday 18 May parodied the situation by showing a character labelled 'rumour' tip-toeing ahead of a line of tanks. However, for the men of the British Expeditionary Force serving in northern France the reality of the situation was deadly serious. British soldiers returning from the continent told of suspicious characters mingling with the hordes of fleeing refugees that choked the roads: 'we risked a bullet in the back or a bomb in the truck'. Other stories told of Belgian farmers being shot because they had ploughed what appeared to be arrows in a field pointing to a nearby British Army HQ. One account alleged that soldiers of the Welsh Guards threw a 'suspect' priest into a canal because he was carrying a bible with 'suspicious notations' in it. British officers reported that the Germans had used the elements of 'surprise and confusion' to break through the weaker parts of the Belgian and French defences and that enemy paratroops 'frequently dressed in local disguises'. It was also reported that dummy paratroops were often dropped in amongst the real troops to create the deception of larger numbers. These 'decoy' paratroopers were also reportedly sometimes dressed in British uniforms.

Meanwhile, in Holland the Dutch army took up a defensive position in the hills of Utrecht province near Grebbeberg and at Kornwerderzand at the end of the Afsluitdijk in Friesland. There the fighting was intense. The Grebbeline fell on 13 May. The German plan of attack on the Netherlands aimed at breaking the resistance of the Dutch troops in the shortest possible time, so that German troops would be free for operations in Belgium and France. The capture of Rotterdam was vital to this plan as the city was the gateway to the heart of Holland and its fall would lead to the subsequent capitulation of the army. The Germans therefore planned artillery and air bombardment against Rotterdam but first the garrison commander received an ultimatum to surrender, accompanied by a threat that the city would be destroyed if the German offer was not accepted. One of the Dutch army officers had the impression on 14 May that the German commander in South Rotterdam had done everything in his power to prevent this bombardment but that it had been decided in Germany - by Reichsmarschall Göring - that the attack had to be carried out and the city destroyed. As an excuse for this bombardment the Germans said that British troops were landing on the Dutch coast south of the Maas River, which constituted a danger in the rear of the German troops in the line Moerdijk-Dordrecht-Rotterdam. This meant that a breakthrough to the north had to be forced. However, there were no troops landing on the Dutch coast at that time.

Shortly after the Germans handed over the second ultimatum (the first had been sent back unsigned) at 1330 hours, the bombardment broke loose. The air raid lasted ten minutes. A wide swathe of buildings collapsed and burst into a sea of flames. In the strong wind, the fire storm spread quickly. Flames were visible for kilometres in all directions and it took days for the fire to die down. Apart from hospitals and other essential services, the air raid and the fire also destroyed densely populated residential areas. Almost 900 people died; thousands of Rotterdammers were left without a roof over their head. Within minutes the whole centre of Rotterdam was. Part of the population was leaving the city, adding to the general confusion. Five hours after the attack the first German troops entered the burning city.

The bombardment of Rotterdam and the threat of a similar fate to Utrecht made surrender inevitable and the Commander-in-Chief of the Dutch forces, General Henri Gerard Winkelman decided to lay down arms. At 1650 hours on 14 May, a telex message went out ordering all commanders to stop fighting and to destroy all ammunition, arms and material. After nearly five days of fighting Holland capitulated to the German might on 15 May at 1100. During the five-day war around 2,200 Dutch soldiers lost their lives and 2,700 were wounded. Civilian casualties stood at around 2,000. The Dutch lost virtually all their 125 aircraft in this struggle against overwhelming odds. Most of the gallant efforts by Dutch pilots in May

1940 are not well known, since for Holland the war ended with five years of occupation, when conditions were conducive to wide publicity on such subjects. Little known too are the enemy's aircraft losses in the Netherlands during those five days - no less than 342 aircraft through fighters, anti-aircraft fire and forced landings, among them 34 Bf 109s, thirty He 111s, 21 Ju 88s, eight Bf 110s and 222 Junkers Ju 52 transports out of 400 employed. This tremendous loss of transport aircraft was a heavy blow to the Luftwaffe's Transportgeschwader from which it took more than a year to recover and may well have contributed to Hitler's decision to cancel Unternehmen 'Seelöwe' (Operation 'Sealion'); his plan to invade Britain in summer 1940. Even at the end of June, the Luftwaffe had only 357 Ju 52s, each capable of carrying just twelve parachutists.

Though on the whole it can be said that the Dutch forces put up a good fight and that there were many instances of individual valour, the ultimate result was disappointing. The German airborne troops near Rotterdam and The Hague had managed to hold out against numerically superior forces, which were, however, not well trained and armed and this had a crippling influence on the morale of the Dutch troops. The Dutch command and leadership often left much to be desired. Another important factor in the failure to finish off the remnants of the airborne troops was lack of insight into the real strength of the German troops and their exact positions.[22]

The Dutch capitulation was followed by the Belgians on the 28th. By the early morning of 2 June the remaining troops of the BEF (British Expeditionary Force) had been evacuated from the shores around Dunkirk. Thousands of French troops had still to be evacuated. On the night of 3/4 June, the last night of the evacuation from the beaches of Dunkirk, a force of 142 bombers made widespread attacks on German factories and oil plants from Hamburg to Frankfurt and a few of the Wellingtons made a last attack on German positions near Dunkirk. But bombers built for night attack could do little to check advancing Wehrmacht and by now their attacks on communications could do little to prevent the arrival of supplies on the Western Front. Though there was national euphoria and relief at the unexpected deliverance at Dunkirk, the peril facing Britain was now universally perceived. But on 4 June Churchill told the world that Britain would stand firm: *Even though large tracts of Europe and many old and famous states have fallen or may fall into the grip of the*

---

22 *Airborne Assault Over Holland* by Lieutenant Commander F. C. Van Oosten.

HITLER'S INVASION OF EAST ANGLIA, 1940

Gestapo and all the odious apparatus of Nazi rule, we shall not flag or fail. We shall go on to the end, we shall fight in France, we shall fight on the seas and oceans; we shall fight with growing confidence and growing strength in the air. We shall defend our Island, whatever the cost may be; we shall fight on the beaches, we shall fight on the landing grounds, we shall fight in the fields and in the streets, we shall fight in the hills; we shall never surrender.

On 18 June Churchill had to explain in solemn terms the dire situation while remaining positive and willing to confront the Nazis. (France finally surrendered on 22 June). His oratory in the House of Commons reached its zenith as he declared: *What General Weygand called the Battle of France is over. I expect that the Battle of Britain is about to begin. Upon this battle depends the survival of Christian civilization. Upon it depends our own British life and the long continuity of our institutions and our Empire. The whole fury and might of the enemy must very soon be turned on us. Hitler knows that he will have to break us in this island or lose the war. If we can stand up to him, all Europe may be free and the life of the world may move forward into broad, sunlit uplands. But if we fail, then the whole world, including the United States, including all that we have known and cared for, will sink into the abyss of a new dark age made more sinister and perhaps more protracted, by the lights of perverted science. Let us therefore brace ourselves to our duties and so bear ourselves that, if the British Empire and its Commonwealth last for a thousand years, men will still say, This was their finest hour.*

The Prime Minister's rhetoric with its Shakespearean tones produced loud and prolonged cheers in the chamber and boosted morale but two days later the House of Commons went into secret session to hear from Mr. Churchill a statement on the new situation following the French debacle. Mr. Churchill's inspiring and uplifting words in public masked a stark reality that Britain was open to invasion but Britain's 'Thin Blue Line' - RAF Fighter Command - would have to be overrun first before German troops could land. On 2 July the Oberkommando der Wehrmacht (OKW) issued an instruction stating that the Führer had ordered preparations to be made for the invasion of Britain. On 12 July General der Artillerie Alfred Jodl, Chief of the Wehrmacht Operations staff, indicated that the first wave of the assault would consist of seven divisions with AA protection creating a wide-fronted bridgehead between Weymouth and Margate. The Oberkommando der Marine (OKM) was to assemble rapidly the barges (or 'prahms') and other shipping required to transport the first wave together with their fuel, munitions, weapons and transport. Two further waves were planned with reserves for a fourth wave. Three groups would sail: one from Calais (16th Army), a second from Le Havre (9th Army) and the third (6th Army) from Cherbourg. Accompanying the groups would be Panzer and Gebirgsjüger Divisions (alpine or mountain troops of the German-Austrian Gebirgstruppe) and the Waffen-SS Totenkopf Division. Eight hundred vessels with an average capacity of 500 tonnes were required to transport the invasion force but there were not sufficient barges so Grand Admiral Erich Raeder would have to also use tugs, pontoons and fishing and motor boats.

During the Battle of France, Raeder had met Hitler on 21 May and raised the topic of invasion, stressing the difficulties and his own preference for a blockade. The report issued on 30 June by OKW Chief of Staff Alfred Jodl set out options, with invasion as a last resort once the British economy had been damaged and the Luftwaffe had full air superiority. Raeder emphasised that the Kriegsmarine had been considerably weakened by the Norwegian Campaign. It would be unable to stop the relatively intact Royal Navy from breaking up an invasion fleet, though the Luftwaffe 'might create conditions favourable for an invasion, whether it could was not in the Navy War Staff's province.' On 11 July Raeder got Hitler's agreement that invasion would be a last resort and on the same day the Luftwaffe advised the OKW that getting air superiority would take fourteen to 28 days. On the 13th Hitler met his army chiefs Field Marshal Walther von Brauchitsch and General der Artillerie Franz Halder who presented detailed plans on the assumption that the navy would provide safe transport. Against his previous practice, Hitler showed no interest in the details, but said preparations were to begin. The Kriegsmarine produced a draft plan for achieving a narrow beachhead near Dover. (On 28 July the army responded that they wanted landings all along the south coast of England). Halder noted in his diary: 'The Führer is greatly puzzled by Britain's persisting unwillingness to make peace. He sees the answer (as we do) in Britain's hope on Russia and therefore counts on having to compel her by main force to agree to peace. Actually that is much against his grain. The reason is that a military defeat of Britain will bring about the disintegration of the British Empire. This would not be of any benefit to Germany. German blood would be shed to accomplish something that would benefit only Japan, the United States and others. [Next day] The Führer confirms my impressions of yesterday. He would like an understanding with

Great Britain. He knows that war with the British will be hard and bloody and knows also that people everywhere today are averse to bloodshed.'[23]

On 16 July Adolf Hitler issued 'Führer Directive No.16': 'Since Britain still shows no sign of willingness to come to an agreement in spite of her hopeless military situation, I have decided to prepare and if necessary carry out an amphibious operation against England.' The aim of this operation will be to eliminate the English homeland as a base for the prosecution of the war against Germany and if necessary, to occupy it completely. I therefore order as follows:

1. The landing will be in the form of a surprise crossing on a wide front from about Ramsgate to the area west of the Isle of Wight. Units of the air force will act as artillery and units of the navy as engineers.

    The possible advantages of limited operations before the general crossing e.g. the occupation of the Isle of Wight or of the county of Cornwall are to be considered from the point of view of each Branch of the armed forces and the results reported to me. I reserve the decision to myself. Preparations for the entire operation must be completed by the middle of August.
2. These preparations must also create such conditions as will make a landing in England possible. Viz:
    (a) The English Air Force must be so reduced morally and physically that it is unable to deliver any significant attack against the German crossing.
    (b) Mine-free channels must be cleared.
    (c) The Straits of Dover must be closely sealed off with minefields on both flanks: also the western entrance to the channel approximately on a line Alderney-Portland.
    (d) Strong forces of coastal artillery must command and protect the forward coastal area.

---

23 On 19 July Halder (30 June 1884-2 April 1972) was promoted to Generaloberst. In August he began working on Operation 'Barbarossa', the invasion plan for the Soviet Union. On 23 July 1944, following the failed 20 July assassination attempt on Hitler's life by German Army officers, Halder was arrested by the Gestapo. Although he was not involved in the plot, intense interrogations of the conspirators revealed that Halder had been involved in earlier conspiracies against Hitler. Halder was imprisoned at both the Flossenbürg and Dachau concentration camps. Halder's wife Gertrud chose to and was allowed to, accompany her husband into imprisonment. On 31 January 1945 Halder was officially dismissed from the army.

'FALL GELB'

It is desirable that the English Navy be tied down shortly before the crossing, both in the North Sea and in the Mediterranean (by the Italians). For this purpose we must attempt even now to damage English home-based naval forces by air and torpedo attack as far as possible...'

And so began the German military machine's highly visible preparations for Operation 'Sealion'. Hitler held a meeting of his army and navy chiefs on 31st July in his residence of Berghof. The Luftwaffe was not represented, but Göring was confident that air victory was possible. Like many commanders in other air forces, including the RAF, he was convinced that if attacks on military targets failed, the bombing of civilians could force the British government to surrender. On 1st August the OKW (Oberkommando der Wehrmacht or 'High Command of the Armed Forces') issued its plan, code named Operation 'Sealion', which was scheduled to take place in mid-September 1940. 'Sealion' called for landings on the south coast of Great Britain backed by an airborne assault. Neither Hitler nor OKW believed it would be possible to carry out a successful amphibious assault on Britain until the RAF had been overcome. Raeder believed that air superiority might make a successful landing possible although it would be a risky operation and require 'absolute mastery over the Channel by our air forces'. Many years later Grand Admiral Karl Dönitz admitted that 'we possessed neither control of the air or the sea; nor were we in any position to gain it.'

According to the available evidence, the plan, in its final form, would have been a basic seaborne assault against a stretch of England's south coast from Eastbourne to Folkestone by thousands of enemy troops transported across the English Channel, most of them in converted Rhine barges. Along with the initial seaborne assault, airborne troops would have been used to capture airfields and other strategic points in Sussex and Kent. 'Führer Directive No. 17' dated 1st August 1940, which dealt with a landing operation in the east and south of England, called for the troops of Army Groups A and B to assault the island from the Calais-Le Havre areas in three groups who were supposed to land on the east coast of England between Norwich and Brighton.

A prerequisite to any invasion of England would require the elimination of RAF Fighter Command - at least in the invasion area - and a large invasion fleet of ships and vast numbers of troops and aircraft. After the campaign in the West, the Luftwaffe's air transport units were brought up to their pre-Holland strength and were assembled at airfields in the Lyon, Lille and Arras areas by August 1940. Probably this was achieved using new and repaired aircraft augmented by other, often unsuitable, aircraft, like the two four-engined types; the FW 200 Condor and the Ju 90, which had begun life as the Ju 89 bomber. The use of deception to penetrate or infiltrate defences, particularly points of strategic importance, had been a crucial element of the 'Blitzkrieg'. Without doubt, such tactics would be employed in any invasion of Britain.[24] Following the fall of France, British army intelligence bulletins were prepared for distribution to all major army units. Officers just returned from the continent were sent on tours around Divisional commands to give lectures to their fellow officers. It was impressed upon all officers and men as a matter of urgency that: 'German troops landed by air or sea may be disguised in British uniforms and may be provided with British equipment'. As one particular bulletin put it: 'Enemy airborne troops landing in British uniform or other disguises would (as they had done on the continent) cause confusion and even fighting between our own forces.' Orders were issued to British troops making it clear that 'the rules of war provide for the fact that fighting men who hide under disguise shall be shot immediately'; a sentiment also expressed by sixty-year old General William Edmund Ironside GCB CMG DSO who served as Chief of the Imperial General Staff during the first year of the war before becoming Commander in Chief Home Forces. When referring to enemy paratroops he said: 'shoot them and shoot them without reference to taking any kind of care of their future.'

Any German invasion fleet needed barges and other vessels and many of them, to transport the invasion troops. Along the French coast Wehrmacht troops practiced the use of assault boats and Gebirgsjäger scaled the chalk cliffs similar to those of the Kent and Sussex coast. In Dutch harbours 2,000 hastily converted barges and coupled pontoons, plus 500 other craft, were brought together to carry the men, tanks and artillery of the invasion force. Provision had to be made for the many horses on which the Wehrmacht still

---

24 They were not always successful. In Belgium an advance party of Germans dressed as French and Belgian officers had attempted to stop a British unit about to blow up a bridge across the Yser Canal at Dixmude. Lieutenant Mann of the 12th Lancers threatened the impostors with his revolver and the bridge was successfully demolished, holding up a German motorised column for several hours. In another incident, this time in France, German tanks reportedly flying French colours and crewed by men in French uniform broke into British positions near Merville. Just in time the ruse was discovered and the armour piercing shells of the British 25-pounder field guns smashed into the enemy vehicles at almost point blank range.

relied for moving much of its artillery and supplies.[25] To support the weight of the guns and tanks, concrete was pumped into the bottoms of the barge hulls and sections of the bows were cut away and given ramps and opening doors. To propel the motorless pontoons and slow-moving canal and river barges, aircraft engines were added above their sterns using conversion kits, whilst others were given additional marine engines coupled to complicated drive systems. However, these vessels could not manoeuvre easily if attacked and being slow-moving and shallow-draft vessels they could only operate when the Channel was calm and likely to remain so for a period of time. Heavy-calibre railway guns were moved up to the Pas de Calais to target the English beaches with long-range fire and to close the Straits of Dover to British shipping. German fighter and bomber aircraft moved onto captured French airfields along the Channel coast to menace shipping and attempt to wrest control of the skies from the RAF in preparation for invasion.[26]

'In anticipation of the expected invasion attempt by the Germans' wrote Jim Moore 'the following Battle Order was issued: 'Attacks will be pressed home regardless of cost. Each aircraft should aim to hit one vessel with one bomb and machine gun the enemy whenever possible. Squadrons equipped with gas spray are to be ready to operate with this at the shortest possible notice, but it will only be used as a retaliatory measure'. (Thank goodness this form of warfare was never employed).'

Until the threat of invasion receded, as soon as an aircraft returned from an operation it was immediately re-armed and re-fuelled ready for take-off. Ground crews were always immediately available, some staying with the aircraft 24 hours a day, whilst the aircrew were kept on stand-by. On 21 June, between Maaskuis and Rotterdam, bombers found a hundred or more covered barges, stationary but pointing towards the sea. Each barge was about three hundred feet long and they were tied up in threes. Many similar barges were found on the waterways of Holland. Day by day more

---

25 Horse-drawn transportation was most important for Germany, as it was relatively lacking in natural oil resources. Infantry and horse-drawn artillery formed the bulk of the German Army throughout the war; only one-fifth of the Army belonged to mobile panzer and mechanized divisions. Each German infantry division employed thousands of horses and thousands of men taking care of them. Germany actually used more horses in WWII than it had done in the First. Despite losses of horses to enemy action, exposure and disease, Germany maintained a steady supply of work and saddle horses until 1945. Cavalry in the Army and the SS gradually increased in size, peaking at six cavalry divisions in February 1945.

26 *British Home Defences 1940-45* by Bernard Lowry (Osprey, 2004).

HITLER'S INVASION OF EAST ANGLIA, 1940

reports of barges came in and at the same time the runways on many aerodromes were being extended, bomb craters filled in and - a sinister sign - Junkers 52s were appearing on them.

On Monday 8th July Blenheims made a daylight attack on barges in Dutch canals; some of the bombers attacked from a height of less than 1,000 feet and their crews saw some of the barges alight and the wreckage of others floating on the water. On the same day a canal south of Furnes in Belgium was reported to be packed with barges over a distance of ten miles. On Thursday, 11th July, the day the Battle of Britain began, large concentrations of barges, tightly packed together were seen on the canal between Dunkirk and Furnes while just south of Furnes there was only a small concentration of barges. Blenheims were now out as often as possible attacking barges in the Dutch and Belgium canals. On Friday, 13th July they blew barges to pieces in the Bruges-Ostend Canal and as the main concentration of barges went westwards, or towards the coast, so did the bombing attacks. On Tuesday, 16th July, the day Hitler issued Directive No. 16, authorizing Operation 'Sealion', barges in a canal west of Armentieres were bombed. On Thursday, 18th July Blenheims made a rather heavy attack in daylight on docks and shipping at Boulogne, a port which the Germans might be expected to use for any invasion of Britain.

RAF crews might have slept easier in their beds had it been known that on 23 July Hitler attended a special performance of Gotterdammerung at Bayreuth and left the opera house with the conviction that he must attack Russia. Hitler permitted Admiral Raeder and the other service chiefs to continue with their plans for the invasion of Great Britain until the end of the month. And then at a meeting on 31 July he announced to his stunned service chiefs that the way to defeat Britain in this war would be to attack Russia.

Meanwhile, during September 1940 the Blenheim crews in East Anglia flew more sorties than were flown in any month until 1944 by the crews of 2 Group; for instance, 18 Squadron alone flew 127. Nightly, in company with Hampdens, Wellingtons and Whitleys of Bomber Command, operations were carried out on the concentration of barges being assembled by the Germans in the ports of Boulogne, Calais, Dunkirk, Flushing and so on with considerable success. These raids were a persuasive argument to the German High Command in postponing their plans to invade the British Isles. 'Without wishing to take anything away from the heroic efforts of our fighter pilots during the Battle of Britain' wrote Jim Moore, 'the contribution made by the crews of Bomber Command should also be remembered, as yet another 'Few' who held back the enemy when we were under siege. A few days after the fall of France, the Germans started moving hundreds of barges, each 300 feet long, along the canals of Western Europe towards the North Sea and the Channel ports. These enormous barges were essential to the German invasion force, which they intended to land on the shores of our embattled island. These concentrations of barges were to be the focus of the attention of all the squadrons in Bomber Command during September. We were briefed as to the type of attacks we would be required to make on German naval vessels and troop carrying craft. We were also advised that, should the invasion take place, we would be moving to an aerodrome near Exeter.

'The Germans had either installed or seized from the French some heavy naval guns at Cap Gris Nez on the French coast, which had formed the unpleasant habit of shelling shipping passing through the Straits of Dover and the town of Dover itself. We made three trips in August-September to bomb these guns and followed with attacks on barge concentrations in the ports of Dunkirk, which we visited three times, Flushing, Boulogne, Ostend and Calais. On these trips, which took approximately three hours, the defences were very alert with large concentrations of searchlights and pretty spectacular displays of anti-aircraft fire. We hoped we were doing the maximum amount of damage to these barges, which represented such a threat to our island.'

Sergeant Wireless Operator/Air Gunner Mike Henry, his pilot, Flying Officer 'Sandy' Powell and Sergeant 'Rich' Richmond, observer were flown to RAF Wattisham on 19 August to join 110 'Hyderabad' Squadron.

'The Channel ports in late 1940 were among the most heavily defended targets I can remember. Hitler's intention of preserving his invasion fleet was made clear for his minions ferociously threw up everything but the kitchen-sink. What made matters worse for us was the altitude at which we had been briefed to attack i.e. between 6,000 and 8,000 feet. At that height, light flak was at its deadliest. It came up like an inverted monsoon of vivid colour; from all directions it poured to culminate at the apex of a cone of searchlights. They were at the time, some of the most terrifying experiences of my life. 'How any aircraft can survive in that lot,' I thought as we made our bombing run, 'is a miracle.' But, as we found out, the age of miracles was not past and we came through unscathed. Many, of course, didn't and were seen to plummet, flaming pyres earthwards. Those targets made our first two sorties look like a poor man's Guy Fawkes' night in heavy rain.

'By 21 September the incessant pounding had put twelve transport ships, four tugs and fifty-one barges out of action. A further nine transport vessels, one tug and 163 barges were damaged. One week later, 214 out of the assembled fleet of 1,918 converted Rhine barges had been temporarily or permanently put out of commission, a serious loss of 12 per cent. This undoubtedly contributed to Hitler's decision to break off the invasion preparations on 12 October.[27] When trips to the Channel ports came to an end the Blenheims began to turn their aircrafts' noses towards Germany. So that short interlude of colourful enemy aggression over the French Channel ports came to an end. The threatened invasion was called off and we reverted to other targets. I must add that, while we survived those hectic nights over Dunkirk, Calais and Boulogne, we weren't at all sorry to climb higher into the night sky and just remain prey to the heavier flak.'

After a week of September had gone by, barges on the coast seemed to have become an immediate menace again. The greater part of Bomber Command's effort on the night of 7th/8th September was directed against barges and shipping in Calais harbour, at Dunkirk and at Ostend. In the early hours of the morning and well on into daylight, Whitleys patrolled the coast between Ostend and Boulogne; sometimes coming down to 500 feet in broad daylight, so urgent was the need for immediate information of the German plans. As the day went on, Blenheims reconnoitered the Channel ports and the ports of the Low Countries; they bombed what barges and ships they could find. But this was only the beginning of a sustained attack on all the ports and harbours of northern France, Belgium and Holland. For many nights in succession Bomber Command sent the greater part of its aircraft, though it still maintained its attacks on targets in Germany, to bomb the barges and destroy the docks and jetties from which an invasion would start.

Winston Churchill made the following broadcast to the nation: 'The effort of the Germans to secure daylight mastery of the air over England is of course the crux of the whole war. So far it has failed conspicuously... For him [Hitler] to try and invade this country without having secured mastery in the air would be a very hazardous undertaking. Nevertheless, all his preparations for invasion on a great scale are steadily going forward. Several hundreds of self-propelled barges are moving down the coasts of Europe, from the German and Dutch harbours to the ports of northern France, from Dunkirk to Brest and beyond Brest to the French harbours in the Bay of Biscay.'

---

27 By 21 September the RAF had destroyed or severely damaged 21 transports and 214 barges, only about 12 per cent of the entire invasion fleet, losses that could be made up by reserves. *Operation Sealion: How Britain Crushed the German War Machine's Dreams of Invasion in 1940* by Leo McKinstry (John Murray, 2014).

'FALL GELB'

The attacks went on throughout September, while rumours and threats of the coming invasion went round the world; Sunday 15th September was everywhere reported to be the day when the barges would start, but 15 September came and went. Bomber Command did not relax when the advertised day, or any other advertised day, was passed; on the contrary, some of the heaviest attacks on the ports were made towards the end of the month. The expectation of invasion, the mounting tension, produced its crop of rumour and the production in fantasy of what had long been expected in fact.

On the night of 15/16 September 180 German bombers formed long processions from Le Havre and Dieppe-Cherbourg, all heading for London. Meanwhile, arguments ensued on both sides of the divide. Next day Göring called a conference of his Luftflotten and Fliegerkorps commanders in France and decided to return to a policy of attack on Fighter Command rather than industrial and residential targets by day. Bomber formations would now be reduced in size and Gruppen would bomb targets in the London area with maximum fighter escort to destroy as many RAF fighters as possible. Göring predicted that this would finish off Fighter Command in four to five days. On 10 September the German Naval War Diary had stated: 'The Führer thinks the major attacks on London may be decisive and a systematic and prolonged bombardment of London may result in the enemy's adoption of an attitude which will render 'Sealion' superfluous.' The diarist even went as far as to say that, 'According to the state of preparations today the execution of the operation by 21.9.40 as previously arranged, is thus ensured.'

'In America and on the Continent throughout October and November', continues Mike Henry, 'it was being said that barges had sailed in September but were smashed by our bombers. In particular, this was said to have happened on 15 September, a date for which invasion had been predicted before. This story at least took more account of inherent probability than most other rumours of this war. Steadily, at regular intervals, 'Bomber Command went on with the work of disorganizing the ports which front the English coast. For that matter this work has never stopped. Though the barges may be gone, all these harbours are still of use to the Germans for their shipping which creeps along the coast. Though it may be difficult to disentangle the work of Bomber Command from that of Fighter Command in preventing any attempt at invasion of Britain, there is little doubt that Bomber Command would play a most important part in repelling any future attempt at invasion. Attacks on a far heavier scale than in the past could - and would - be made on the ports from which the Germans proposed to mount an invasion, on any ships crossing the Channel and on any beaches or ports in Britain where Germans succeeded in landing. Attacks as heavy as any on Germany would be made at much closer range and several times in the twenty-four hours. The invasion might well be over before it started.

'Britain's east and south coasts were now the 'frontline' and defences were being constructed as a matter of extreme urgency, on some occasions even civilians were organised into digging trenches. The coast of East Anglia in particular was seen to be especially vulnerable. The low lying coast and open country beyond the beaches would be ideal terrain for the German 'Panzers'. The airfields and top secret Radio Direction Finding (RDF, later radar) stations, vital to Britain's air defence - would also be prime targets in the initial stages of an invasion; *or before.*'

The technology of radio-based detection and tracking evolved independently in a number of nations during the mid 1930s. At the outbreak of war in September 1939 both Great Britain and Germany had functioning systems. In Britain it was called RDF, Range and Direction Finding, while in Germany the name Funkmessgerät (radio measuring device) was used.[28] In February 1940 the invention of the resonant-cavity magnetron by John Randall and Harry Boot of Birmingham University marked a major advance in radar capability. This small device was capable of producing microwave power in the kilowatt range, opening the path to second-generation radar systems. While the benefits of operating in the microwave portion of the radio spectrum were known, transmitters for generating microwave signals of sufficient power were unavailable; thus, all early radar systems operated at lower frequencies (e.g., HF or VHF). After the Fall of France it was realised in Britain that the manufacturing capabilities of the United States were vital to success in the war. Though the United States was not yet a belligerent, Prime Minister Winston Churchill directed that the technology secrets be shared in exchange for the needed capabilities. In the summer of 1940 the Tizard Mission visited the United States and the cavity magnetron was demonstrated at RCA and Bell Labs, etc. The British magnetron was a thousand times more powerful than the best American transmitter

---

28 By mid-1940 the RAF had fully integrated RDF as part of the national air defence. By contrast, The German Funkmessgerät, was neglected, partly due to Adolf Hitler's prejudice against defensive measures and failings by the Luftwaffe in coherently incorporating the new technology.

'FALL GELB'

at the time and produced accurate pulses. The most powerful equivalent microwave producer available in the US (a klystron) had a power of only ten watts. Bell Labs was able to duplicate the performance and the Radiation Laboratory at MIT (Massachusetts Institute of Technology) was established to develop microwave radars. It was later described by noted Historian James Phinney Baxter III as 'The most valuable cargo ever brought to our shores'.

Germany would have stopped at nothing to obtain the cavity magnetron device. Three weeks after Hitler announced his intention to invade England, an apparently ordinary Swedish tramp steamer, with an extraordinary Luftwaffe escort, sailed towards the small island of Heligoland in the North Sea. The 4,150-ton steel-hulled tramp, built by Öresundsvarvet A/B of Landskrona, Sweden and completed in 1926, was owned by Waages Rederi of Oslo, Norway under the name *Saga*. In 1931 when she was engaged in her irregular trade, this itinerant vagrant of the sea had been sold to A. E. Reimann of Stensved, Denmark and renamed *Lundby*. Below decks were one hundred English speaking Germans of number 11 Kompanie, 3rd Battalion Brandenburger commandoes, about to embark upon training for a special mission. As always strict security was maintained, only later would the men be briefed with the barest details of the planned operation. Dressed as British police and Home Guard they would be landed covertly in advance of an invasion force to infiltrate and capture an important radar station - somewhere on the English coast.

Chapter 2

The Death Ray

In view of the many British commando raids on the Continental coast it seems odd that the Germans never tried the equivalent, in Eastern England or anywhere else on the British shores. But whereas the British raided the Continent in the frame of mind that they could not yet invade but hoped eventually to do so, the Germans had let the whole invasion strategy lapse. There have been stories about German raids on the East Coast, such as the recent one about an attempted landing at Shingle Street, beside the RAF's Kings Marshes weapons experimental site near the mouth of the Ore, in Suffolk. (In this case German submarines and burned corpses have featured). But I am pretty confident that all such tales are bogus. There are complete, long-declassified, war diaries for all three services on the wartime Suffolk coast and none give so much as a hint of any German shore raid or landing. Of course they could all be falsified, but I hardly think this likely.'

**The Battle of the East Coast (1939-1945)
by J. P. Foynes published in 1994.**

Albert Percival Rowe of the Directorate of Scientific Research at the Air Ministry has been described as a 'complex character with a strong sense of mission, so, difficult to live with'. In June 1934, aged 36, 'Jimmy' or 'A. P.' Rowe, as he was known, took it upon himself to read every study about the state of air defence in Britain and as a result informed his director, 58-year old Harry Egerton Wimperis that unless science could come effectively to the rescue, any war in the next ten years was bound to be lost. Rowe was born in Launceston, Cornwall. After attending the Portsmouth Naval Dockyard School, he studied physics at the Royal College of Science, University of London, graduating with a first class honours degree in 1921 and postgraduate diploma in air navigation in 1922. Wimperis, an aeronautical engineer, known for the development of the

THE DEATH RAY

Drift Sight and Course Setting Bomb Sight during World War I, devices that revolutionized the art of bombing, took the report seriously and in 1934 he set up the formation of the Committee for the Scientific Survey of Air Defence within the Air Ministry chaired by Sir Henry Tizard to find ways to improve Britain's air defence. At its first meeting on 28 January 1935 one of the first matters to come before the Tizard committee was Radio Direction Finding of aircraft proposed by Robert Alexander Watson-Watt, Superintendent of the Radio Department of the National Physical Laboratory. Born in Brechin, Angus, Scotland, on 13 April 1892 Watson-Watt was a descendant of James Watt, the famous engineer and inventor of the practical steam engine. Nazi Germany was rumoured to have a 'death ray' using radio waves that was capable of destroying towns, cities and people and Wimperis asked Watson-Watt about the possibility of building their version of a death-ray. It was suggested that a high intensity radio beam might be used as a weapon to bring down enemy aircraft. This, it was hoped, would be achieved either by causing their engines to cut-out in mid air, or by disabling the pilot, just like the 'death rays' featured in the *Flash Gordon* comics and films of the time.

Watson-Watt quickly returned a calculation carried out by his colleague, Arnold Wilkins, showing that the device was impossible to construct and fears of a Nazi version soon vanished. However, engineers at the Radio Research Station, Slough, thought it might be possible to use the reflective quality of radio waves to detect the approach of aircraft over long distances. A Post Office Report of June 1932 mentioned that aircraft interfered with radio signals and re-radiated them and Watt considered the possibility of transmitting a radio pulse which would be reflected back by aircraft as a signal to the ground. Further calculations by his scientific assistant, Arnold F. Wilkins enabled Watson-Watt to submit to the Air Ministry on 12 February 1935 a document entitled 'Detection and Location of Aircraft by Radio Methods'.

Using as a basis his experiments in calculating the height of the ionosphere by the reflection of radio pulses, Watson-Watt explained how pulses would be similarly reflected from the metal components of an aircraft and how this reflection could be recorded. Although not as exciting as a death-ray, the concept clearly had potential but at the Air Ministry, Air Vice-Marshal Sir Hugh Caswall Tremenheere Dowding, a 54-year old widower wedded to the service, before giving funding, asked for a demonstration proving that radio waves could be reflected by an aircraft. Dowding was of the opinion that the next war would be won 'by science thoughtfully applied to operational requirements'. In 1931 he had been appointed Air Member for Research and Development and in the mid-1930s he grasped the importance of RDF (later radar) and would integrate it into the defence system. The demonstration Dowding sought was ready by 26 February 1935, the day Hitler received Göring and the War Minister Blomberg at the Chancellery, in order to put his signature to the decree that Göring laid before him, establishing the Reichsluftwaffe as the third armed force. Late that afternoon a Handley Page Heyford aircraft from the Royal Aircraft Establishment at Farnborough flew a straight course up and down a beam transmitted from the nearby BBC short-wave station at Daventry. In a field near Weedon in a caravan towed there by a Morris car, a wireless receiving set to which was attached a cathode-ray oscillograph showed a green spot elongated as the aircraft came nearer, contracting as it went away. The range of this early locating equipment was only eight miles but it had been demonstrated beyond doubt that electro-magnetic energy was reflected from an aircraft and that these reflections could be depicted visually by the cathode-ray apparatus. Such was the secrecy of this test that only four people witnessed it: Watson-Watt, his colleague Arnold Wilkins, A. P. Rowe and their driver, Mr. Dyer. Rowe coined the acronym RDF as a cover for the work, meaning Range and Direction Finding but suggesting the already well-known Radio Directing Finding technology. Rowe's decisions gave priority and most of TRE's resources to the completion of the Chain Home and Chain Home Low systems in 1938-39 and also continuing research in 1940 on developing airborne interception (AI) radar and centimetric radar with the cavity magnetron.[29]

In November 1939 AI.Mk.I-equipped Blenheim IVs of 25 Squadron were detached to Martlesham Heath for night patrols over the North Sea but they made no contact with mine laying seaplanes, which had begun

---

[29] Despite some opposition from Bomber Command who felt that the project would not produce large-scale results, Rowe, assisted by Alec Reeves, also led in the development of the 'Oboe' navigation system and the H_2S radar. Rowe replaced Robert Watson-Watt as Superintendent of the Bawdsey Research Station where the Chain Home RDF system was developed and in 1938-1945 was the Chief Superintendent of the Telecommunications Research Establishment (TRE), which carried out pioneering research on microwave radar. In 1946 Rowe moved to Australia as chief scientific officer for the British rocket programme. The following year he was appointed scientific adviser to the Australian Department of Defence and on 1 May 1948 he became, by invitation, the first full-time vice-chancellor of the University of Adelaide, a position he held until his retirement in 1958.

to operate over the Thames Estuary and East Coast at this time. The AI-equipped Blenheims began operating with 600 (Auxiliary Air Force) Squadron from Manston over the Thames Estuary and the Bawdsey Radar Flight from Martlesham Heath. The AI development team had been evacuated from Bawdsey on the outbreak of war, as the experimental radar station's exposed location rendered it vulnerable to air attack or commando-style raids. Detached to Martlesham Heath for operational patrols it was not until the spring of 1940 that the AI-equipped Blenheims saw combat. On 12th May a Blenheim operating under the control of Bawdsey CH station intercepted a Heinkel He 111 off the Dutch coast and it was claimed by Flight Lieutenant Christopher Dermot Salmond Smith DFC.[30] As the fate of the Heinkel is uncertain, this combat cannot be claimed as the first success by a radar-equipped night-fighter.[31] A Blenheim If fitted with AI.Mk.II from the Fighter Interception Unit (FIU) at RAF Ford achieved the first success on the night of 2nd/3rd July, accounting for a Dornier Do 17 bomber. On the night of the 22nd/23rd July a Blenheim Mk.If flown by Flying Officer Glyn 'Jumbo' Ashfield, with a crew of Pilot Officer G. E. Morris, observer and Sergeant Reginald H. Leyland, AI operator achieved the first airborne radar intercepted kill in history when they were directed to a possible intercept by the controller at Poling Chain Home radar station who reported an incoming raid. The Blenheim crew shot down a Dornier 17Z of 2 Staffel, Kampfgeschwader 3, which crashed into the sea off Bognor Regis, Sussex.

The Prime Minister, Stanley Baldwin, was kept quietly informed of radar's progress. 'Full scale' tests of a fixed radar radio tower system that would soon be known as Chain Home, an early detection system

---

30   Smith of Overy Staithe, Norfolk was born in September 1916 at Bruton, Somerset and educated at Bradfield College. He entered RAF College Cranwell in September 1934 as a Flight Cadet. After graduating in July 1936 he was posted to the School of Air Navigation, Manston for a course. He joined 220 (GR) Squadron at Bircham Newton on 29 November 1936. Smith went to A&AEE Martlesham Heath on 1 June 1938. He was involved with the development of airborne radar and for his service in that field he was awarded the DFC (gazetted 7 May 1940). He joined 25 Squadron at North Weald on 20th September 1940 as a Flight Commander. In November 1941 Smith took command of 79 Squadron at Fairwood Common, Wales. He was killed on 22 December 1941 when his Hurricane IIB Z5255 collided with a He 115 that he intercepted off Southern Ireland. His only brother, Squadron Leader F. M. Smith, was killed aged 25 serving with 94 Squadron on 1 June 1940 when his Gladiator II N2291 crashed at Khormaksar during low level aerobatics. He is buried in Maala Cemetery, Aden (now Yemen).

31   *Night Fighter: A Concise History of Night Fighting Since 1914* by Anthony Robinson (Ian Allan 1988).

that attempted to detect an incoming bomber by radio signals, were conducted during the RAF Air Exercises over London in August 1934. The tests were a complete failure, with the defending fighter only seeing the bomber after it had passed its target even when the 'hostiles' were Vickers Virginia biplane bombers cruising at 75 mph at 7,000 feet. Squadron Leader P. R. Burchall said: 'The recent air exercises, in which something more than 350 aeroplanes were engaged, afford a very illuminating example of the mischief of jumping to faulty conclusions from unsound data. Because the official communiqués have admitted that perhaps 70 per cent of the enemy raiders were able to reach their objectives, a feeling of defencelessness and dismay, or at all events of uneasiness, has seized the public.'

The problem was not the radar, but the flow of information from trackers from the Observer Corps to the fighters, which took many steps and was very slow.[32] Henry Tizard with Patrick Blackett[33] and Air Marshal Sir Hugh Dowding, who on 14 July 1936 had become the first Air Officer Commander in Chief of Fighter Command, set about correcting 'some lamentable deficiencies' at Fighter Command. It was none too soon. Three days after Dowding's appointment, civil war had broken out in Spain and the German 'Legion Kondor' exploited the war for its own ends, sending 370 handpicked pilots and aircrew, devising tactics and honing its skills. In 1935-36, the whole structure of the Royal Air Force was reshaped. What had been a Directorate of Supply and Research was divided into Research and Development and Supply Organisation. In May 1936 a Training Command was established, followed on 14 July by a Bomber Command, Coastal Command and Fighter Command. All these officers were directly responsible to the Air Council through the

---

32 In 1925, following a Defence Committee initiative undertaken the previous year, the formation of an RAF command concerning the Air Defence of Great Britain led to the provision of a Raid Reporting System, itself delegated to a sub-committee consisting of representatives from the Air Ministry, Home Office and the General Post Office. This Raid Reporting System was to provide for the visual detection, identification, tracking and reporting of aircraft over Great Britain and was eventually to become known as the Observer Corps, subsequently awarded the title Royal by HM King George VI in April 1941 in recognition of service carried out by Observer Corps personnel during the Battle of Britain.

33 Patrick Maynard Stuart Blackett, Baron Blackett OM CH PRS was an English experimental physicist known for his work on cloud chambers, cosmic rays and paleomagnetism, winning the Nobel Prize for Physics in 1948. He also made a major contribution in WWII advising on military strategy and developing operational research. His left-wing views saw an outlet in third world development and in influencing policy in the Labour Government of the 1960s.

THE DEATH RAY

CAS. It was a big advance upon the clumsy existing organisation: a Commander-in-Chief of Air Defence with both fighters and bombers under him, standing in an indeterminate relationship to the Chief of the Air Staff.

Dowding designed a 'command and control air defence reporting system' with several layers of reporting that were eventually sent to a single large room for mapping. Observers watching the maps would then tell the fighter groups what to do via direct communications. Between the radar 'plots' of approaching hostile aircraft and the fighters which climbed to intercept them and the guns, searchlights, balloons and air-raid sirens (all of which had their vital functions) there existed a highly intricate system of communications manned by hundreds of men and women. Once the raiders crossed the coast, tracking them was the responsibility of the Observer Corps, which was made up of 32 centres whose 30,000 volunteers manned over 1,000 posts around the clock monitoring the height, speed and strength of the enemy formations overhead. The Observer Corps plotted the 'hostiles' by sight or sound, depending on the visibility and passed their plots by landline to their own Group HQ, which relayed them to the Fighter Command filter room for onward transmission throughout the system. The filter room concept was developed by Squadron Leader Hart at Bawdsey, where the first one was built, but parts were later removed and taken to Bentley Priory in October 1938. The first filter training school opened in March 1940 at Bawdsey. The filter room collated, sorted and filtered all incoming reports before the information was used operationally. This was intended to eliminate duplication and to display identified tracks on the group Operations Room plotting table. The results were broadcast to all operational users within the designated area of responsibility of a fighter group, such as sector Operations Rooms and Observer Corps centres. The filter room was originally part of the group Operations Room but later became a protected building in its own right known as a filter block, built using the cut-and-cover technique in two levels. The roof consisted of a 1 foot thick reinforced concrete sub roof and a thinner upper roof with a 4 feet 6 inch void filled with sand and gravel, the complete area then being covered with earth.

Thought to be one of the most vulnerable installations to air attack, Operations Rooms were protected by 6 feet high earthworks. The standard Operations Room for stations under the ADGB Scheme of 1925 was a brick-built bungalow-like building which accommodated up to three squadrons and which was invariably built immediately behind the station headquarters, connected to it by a corridor. It was often a detached building which required a basement to house a heating chamber. The building was 97 feet 9 inches long and 27 feet 9 inches wide, built with solid walls 13 feet 5 inches wide and faced with red facing bricks. King-post timber trusses with hipped gable ends and large-size purlins supported by vertical struts carried rafters supporting rough boarding and slates. A protected central entrance through the earth bank gave access to a corridor connecting a store and workshop on the far left, while the Operations Room was at the opposite end. The PBX, battery room, wireless and signals office were all in the centre of the building. A protected roof version was very well defended against the effects of incendiaries and bomb blast from near misses. Surrounding the whole building was a nine feet high reinforced-concrete traverse wall with an angled earth bank having a maximum thickness of 17 feet. The building was further protected with a thick-section concrete sub roof slab supported by twenty large section RSJs.

On 2 April 1935 Watson-Watt received a patent on a radio device for detecting and locating an aircraft. In mid-May Wilkins left the Radio Research Station with a small party, including Dr. Edward George 'Taffy' Bowen, to start further research at Orford Ness, an isolated peninsula on the Suffolk coast of the North Sea.[34] By June they were detecting aircraft at a distance of sixteen miles, which was enough for scientists and engineers to stop all work on competing sound-based detection systems. (By the end of the year the range was up to sixty miles). The physics of radio waves had been understood for some time and although it is often stated that radar was a British invention, similar research had been carried out in a number of countries, including France, Russia, Japan, the USA and Germany. The October 1935 issue of the American magazine *Modern Mechanix*, had openly published details of the most recent developments in both German and American short wave radar.

---

34 As early as 1936 it was realized that the Luftwaffe would turn to night bombing if the day campaign did not go well and Watson-Watt had put Bowen in charge of developing radar that could be carried by a fighter. Night time visual detection of a bomber was good to about 300 metres and the existing Chain Home systems simply did not have the accuracy needed to get the fighters that close. Bowen decided that a airborne radar should not exceed 200lb in weight, 8 feet in volume and require no more than 500 watts of power. To reduce the drag of the antennas the operating wavelength could not be much greater than one metre, difficult for the day's electronics. 'AI' - Airborne Interception, was perfected by 1940 and was instrumental in eventually ending the Blitz of 1941. Bowen also fitted airborne radar to maritime patrol aircraft (known in this application as 'ASV' - Air to Surface Vessel) and this eventually reduced the threat from submarines.

THE DEATH RAY

By September 1935 the Air Council was sufficiently impressed with progress to recommend the construction of a chain of ground stations from Southampton to the Tyne. As an intermediate step, in December the Treasury agreed to the erection of five stations between Dover and Bawdsey covering the approaches to London. The building of these five stations was beset with all kinds of difficulty and delay and approval for the main chain of twenty Chain Home (CFI) stations between the Isle of Wight and St. Abbs Head did not follow until August 1937. In an effort to put a radar defence in place as quickly as possible, Watson-Watt and his team created devices using existing available components, rather than creating new components for the project and the team did not take additional time to refine and improve the devices. So long as the prototype radars were in a workable condition they were put into production.

W. J. Clarkson who served at RAF Dunwich during the war was one of a specially picked team of electrical experts assembled in Britain to combat scientifically the menace of the Luftwaffe. 'Radar gets its name from the initial letters of the words, radio, azimuth, direction and range. In general terms radio waves are reflected back by any object in their path, so that if the output from a sufficiently powerful transmitter was concentrated in one beam it is possible to 'sweep' an area and get back an echo from objects such as aircraft or shipping. This echo could be heard on a loud speaker but it was necessary to see it and for this purpose a cathode ray tube was used. The echo could also be seen in an oscilloscope on a very much smaller scale. 'Radio waves travel at 186,000 miles a second' recalled Clarkson 'so that you can see that a target only 93 miles away has to look pretty slippy in reflecting its echo back. Thus, if a pulse has to travel 93 miles out and is reflected 93 miles back, a total of 186 miles it has taken only $1,000^{th}$ of a second, or milliseconds. This is a long time in radar because the echo must be displayed on the tube, plotted and the plot passed on to those concerned. Thus you haven't much time if an enemy plane is coming in at 300 mph. If you mark the tube off in miles, say 200 and the echo appears half way along the line of light shown on it that is obviously 100 miles. The transmitter, like any other transmitter, if it was operated continuously would cause interference and the radar receiver would be useless, particularly as both are close together. Therefore the transmitter sends out a hoop of power for only a couple of microseconds and remains quiet for perhaps the rest of the time up to, say twenty milliseconds. Echoes may be received then from any distance, represented by the time factor. A speed of 186,000 miles a second represented a distance of roughly seven and a half times round the world.

HITLER'S INVASION OF EAST ANGLIA, 1940

'There were many types of radar sets and nearly all employed a rotary device which helped in following a target. Some transmitters only operated for a fraction of a microsecond; that is for a fraction of a millionth of a second. Some sets gave the height, range and direction and speed of an aircraft or a surface vessel. Radar undoubtedly saved the situation in the Battle of Britain. We had pitifully few planes compared with the Luftwaffe but we were able to plot incoming German squadrons long before they arrived and place our own forces in their path. RAF fighters might be having a duel over Essex, Sussex of even Norfolk, but they were there when wanted to meet the raiders over, say Kent. Those Spitfire and Hurricane pilots certainly took some punishment.

'Some of the bigger radar installations used more power than the local plant could supply and at remote places we used big diesels which were another job for the radar mechanic. Detection of hostile aircraft was only part of the work of the radar service and I had to do much travelling between stations as an expert.'

In February 1936 research scientists, including Robert Watson-Watt had moved into Bawdsey Manor to begin research and development into radar for practical military use and it became known as RAF Bawdsey. Built in 1886, it was enlarged in 1895 by Sir William Cuthbert Quilter who was an art collector, one of the founders of the National Telephone Company and the Liberal Unionist Member of Parliament for Sudbury. Requisitioned by the Devonshire Regiment during World War I and having been returned to the Quilter family after the war, the manor, complete with 168 acres of land, out buildings and estate cottages was purchased by the Air Ministry for £24,000 in 1936 to establish a new research station for developing the Chain Home RDF (radar) system. Stables and outbuildings were converted into workshops and 240 feet wooden receiver towers and 360 feet steel transmitter towers were built. The only way to get to Felixstowe, other than by driving forty miles around the Deben estuary via Ipswich was via the motor boat ferry operated by the Brinkley family. In the thirties the ferry was operated by Mr. Charles Brinkley, who had lost his right hand in an accident. Old Felixstowe had a couple of pubs that were popular with the troops called The 'Ferry Boat Inn' (the Feebee) and The 'Victoria'. At 'Grotty Tom's' in Bawdsey village, where the low ceiling with black beams running across it forced tall folk to duck down, 'Tolly' ale could be consumed in large quantities, if you were so inclined (and you usually were inclined when you left!). There was a choice of 'Tolly Mild' and 'Tolly Bitter'. Often one could not tell the difference and it was reckoned that the landlord only had one barrel of beer, connected to the two pumps via a 'T-piece'.

THE DEATH RAY

The experimental radar station was located just northeast of the Manor, about 200 yards distant. The area was wooded and there was a lovely path along the cliff with secluded grottoes where one could get some peace and quiet. The officers mess was housed in the manor house, a magnificent building with fairy tale towers, beautiful wooden wall panels, grand stairways and comfortable rooms set in amongst a peaceful surrounding of trees and shrubs. There was a walled garden and nearby a small pond complete with real live ornamental ducks that tested your brakes when they strayed out in front of your car. By the outbreak of World War II a chain of radar stations was in place around the coast of Britain. All major ports and towns along the east coast were surrounded by manned roadblocks and strong points, most were subject to strict curfew and were virtually 'locked down' after sunset. On the coast itself, beaches were mined and festooned with barbed wire entanglements and civilian access to the shoreline was prohibited.[35]

By 1937 the first three radar stations were ready and the associated system was put to the test. The results were encouraging and an immediate order by the government to commission an additional seventeen stations was given, resulting in a chain of fixed radar towers along the east and south coast of England. The first operational masts (apart from research masts at Orfordness) erected at Bawdsey were followed by masts at Dover in Kent and Canewdon. The latter is a village in the north approximately four miles northeast of Rochford situated on one of the highest hills of the Essex coastline from which St. Nicholas church affords wide views of the Crouch estuary. The name Canewdon derived from the Saxon 'hill of the Cana's people' and not, as is sometimes claimed, from Canute the Great. Canewdon's location was favourable for its vantage point and proximity to the sea for trading and salt production. From Prehistoric and Roman times farmsteads and cemeteries were located on higher ground. In 1915 Agnes Morley was killed by an incendiary bomb which landed on her house when dropped from a Zeppelin. She was the first woman to be killed in mainland Britain and received a 'heroines' funeral. The event was widely reported in the papers of the time. Fearing war with Germany, in 1937 RAF Canewdon was one of four radar sites established to test the use of Chain Home Transmission and Receiver radar sites around the coast to detect

---

35 When war was declared in September 1939, fears of a possible commando raid led to the development activities being relocated, first to Dundee, Scotland and later to Worth Matravers near Swanage in Dorset on the southern coast of England, where they became the Telecommunications Research Establishment (TRE).

enemy aircraft and estimate their range.[36] The Germans were aware of the construction of Chain Home but were not sure of its purpose and concluded that the stations were a new long-range naval communications system.

During the air exercises of 5th-7th August 1937, Britain's embryonic air defence system only just passed its first serious examination but RAF Fighter Command's biplane fighters were often too slow to catch the new Blenheim bombers. On Tuesday, 19th October 1937 there appeared in British newspapers the headline, 'NAZI CHIEF ADMIRES OUR FLYING MEN' and a full report of the official visit to Britain by a delegation from the Third Reich's immense new Air Ministry in Berlin's Leipzigerstrasse led by 35-year old Field Marshal Erhard Milch, who had carefully watched and enjoyed the RAF Hendon pageants where he 'learnt a lot', including the theory of fuel injection for engines from one of the Bristol Company's technical staff. Milch's party included General Hans Jürgen Stumpf, Chief of Air Staff; General Wenniger, German Air Attaché; Major Kriepe; Major Nielsen and Oberstleutnant Polte were met by Air Chief Marshal Sir Edgar R. Ludlow-Hewitt AOC in C Bomber Command, Air Vice-Marshal Patrick H. L. Playfair and Air Commodore D. C. S. Evill. Milch was then invited to inspect the RAF Guard of Honour made up of Handley Page Heyford aircraft of Nos. 99 and 149 Squadrons, each with four aircrew standing to attention in full flying kit beside their aircraft. Photographs and further information of the visit including a close-up of Milch in full Luftwaffe dress uniform and Major General Udet, Director of the Technical Department, inspecting a new Bristol Blenheim fighter bomber appeared the following day. Udet piloted Erhard Milch's personal aircraft, Heinkel He 111 V-16 D-ASAR, conveying Milch, Stumpff and their staffs to Croydon on 17 October. The visitors had been courteously received by King George VI at Buckingham Palace, shown around the factory of the Bristol Airplane Company and given inspection tours of several RAF stations, including Hornchurch, Mildenhall and Odiham. Milch was so impressed with Odiham, a brand new station, that it was decided it would be the location of the Luftwaffe Headquarters following the successful German invasion of Britain.

The officer commanding 11 Group, Air Vice-Marshal Ernest Leslie Gossage, a former artillery officer who became a pilot in the Royal Flying Corps, was at the luncheon given for Milch at Fighter Command. He told John Willoughby de Broke, Commanding Officer of 605 County of

---

36 Nineteen radar stations were ready to play a key part in the Battle of Britain and by the end of the war over fifty had been built.

THE DEATH RAY

Warwick Squadron,[37] who - in his own fashion - told Peter Townsend, 'While the VIPs were warming their back-sides in front of the ante-room fire over drinks General Milch suddenly addressed the assembly in a loud voice, 'Now gentlemen, let us all be frank! How are you getting on with your experiments in the radio detection of aircraft approaching your shores?' Several of the VIPs nearly had a fit and more than one glass was dropped to the floor with a crash. Red in the face with confusion, the host tried to laugh the matter off. 'Come, gentlemen!' said Milch, 'there is no need to be so cagey about it. We've known for some time that you were developing a system of radio location. So are we and we think that we are a jump ahead of you.' Milch was over-optimistic. It was true that the 'Freya' radar set had caused a sensation at the German manoeuvres at Swinemünde in the autumn of 1937, when it plotted an aircraft sixty miles away. Already on order for the Kriegsmarine and the Luftwaffe, delivery was due to begin shortly. But the RAF was just ahead. Milch did not know that during the August air exercises 'hostile' bombers were being 'plotted' by the radar stations at Bawdsey, Canewdon and Dover. The system was far from complete, but it was the basis of what would become the key element in Britain's air defences. The Filter Room, an all-important adjunct which checked and analysed plots before passing them to Fighter Command Operations Room, was installed at Bawdsey. Results were encouraging: formations of six or more aircraft were 'plotted' at ranges of 100 miles at 10,000 feet and more.

'Deeply impressed' by his visit Milch hastened back to Berlin on 25 October to report to his Commander-in-Chief, Reichsmarschall Hermann Göring, who, after helping Adolf Hitler take power in 1933, became the second-most powerful man in Germany. A member of the NSDAP[38] from its earliest days, Göring was wounded in 1923 during the failed coup known as the Beer Hall Putsch. He became addicted to morphine after being treated with the drug for his injuries. In 1927, working in Berlin as the agent for Lufthansa, Göring, whose drug addiction had by now been successfully treated at the Langbro Public Asylum, struck up a close relationship with Milch. Göring founded the Gestapo in 1933 and later gave command of

---

37 He became a Duty Controller in the 11 Group Operations Room at RAF Uxbridge, responsible for the fighter protection of the south-east (when he was mentioned in despatches) and then became Deputy Director of Public Relations at the Air Ministry (1941-44) and Director from 1945 to 1946.

38 The Nationalsozialistische Deutsche Arbeiterpartei (National Socialist German Workers' Party), commonly referred to in English as the Nazi Party, had been a political party in Germany since 1920.

HITLER'S INVASION OF EAST ANGLIA, 1940

it to Heinrich Himmler. Göring was appointed commander-in-chief of the Luftwaffe in 1935. By 1940 he was at the peak of his power and influence; as minister in charge of the Four Year Plan, he was responsible for much of the functioning of the German economy in the build-up to World War II and Hitler promoted him to the rank of Reichsmarschall, a rank senior to all other Wehrmacht commanders.

The Reichsmarschall was not interested in Milch's report of his visit to England. For some time trouble had been brewing between the two top men of the Luftwaffe. It was rooted in Göring's jealousy - 'a bad German characteristic', Milch admitted. Since the Rhineland occupation in 1936 Milch's name became more and more coupled with Göring's as the Luftwaffe's guiding force - much to Göring's displeasure. When Milch told Göring, 'It's time I went. Apparently I have not done my job properly and I should like to go back to Lufthansa, Göring replied. 'On the contrary, you have done your job too well. Everyone thinks you are the head of the Luftwaffe.'

Meanwhile at Bawdsey, the first radar training school was turning out women operators. Watson-Watt had noticed how quickly the girl typists at Bawdsey had adapted themselves in the early days, but when he suggested women operators the Air Ministry objected. Women might be emotionally unstable under fire. Fortunately the Air Ministry relented. Many of these girls later became heroines.[39]

The 'radar' eventually developed at Bawdsey differed from the majority of other existing systems in using a longer wavelength of around twelve metres and it operated on lower frequency ranges. The use of a longer wavelength necessitated the construction of large high pylons to support the aerial arrays. By 1938 the radar chain had been increased from three to five stations. The air exercises of 5-7 August proved promising and provided the reward for Dowding's 'forceful, cogent and entirely outspoken protests' to the Air Ministry. On the assumption that the Luftwaffe would likely mount daily raids of 200 aircraft it was estimated that 10 per cent would be destroyed. (Another basic assumption was that the raids would approach from the east and northeast, from bases inside Germany). Dowding, who had received a letter dated 4 August from the Permanent Under-Secretary of the Air Ministry saying the Air Council would be unable to offer him any further employment in the RAF after the end of June 1939, knew differently. On 23 February the London *Evening Standard* announced that Dowding, now 56, would shortly retire.

---

39 *Duel of Eagles* by Peter Townsend.

THE DEATH RAY

The next day the Chief of Air Staff, Newall telephoned Dowding that 'no change will be made during the present year.' Dowding thought about the situation for a few days and then wrote to the Air Ministry: 'I have received very cavalier treatment at the hands of the Air Ministry during the past two years. I have no grievance over these decisions, except as regards the discourtesy with which they were effected... I can say without fear of contradiction that since I have held my present post I have dealt with and am in the process of dealing with a number of vital matters which generations of Air Staff have neglected for the last fifteen years: putting the Observer Corps on a war footing, manning of Operations Rooms, identification of friendly aircraft, unserviceability of aerodromes and adequate Air-Raid Warning System. This work had to be carried out against the inertia of the Air Staff, a statement which I can abundantly prove if necessary. In spite of my intense interest in the Fighter problems of the immediate future ... there is little in my past or present treatment at the hands of the Air Ministry to encourage me to undertake a further period of service.' Dowding's retirement was deferred, but only until the end of March 1940.

The presence of highly conspicuous pylons dotted around Britain's coast was almost certainly photographed by the airliners of Deutsche Lufthansa as they purposely crossed the Suffolk coast over Bawdsey, en-route from Germany to Croydon. From the 2nd to 4th August 1939 'The Spionage' or 'espionage trip', taking over 48 hours and covering 2,612 miles was made by the re-commissioned German airship LZ130 *Graf Zeppelin*, fully fitted out with a radio-measuring spy basket and technical personnel and which was carrying General Wolfgang Martini, the Luftwaffe's Chief of Signals, on the first of two leisurely reconnaissance flights over the east coast of Britain. Among other tasks, as commander of the LZ130 *Graf Zeppelin* Albert Sammt flew the August 1939 spying flight and its last flight before it was dismantled. Born on 24 April 1889 in Niederstetten, in Württemberg he was the elevator Höhensteuermann (helmsman) of the Zeppelin LZ126 - *USS Los Angeles* on its transatlantic flight in 1924 and an officer on board the LZ129 *Hindenburg* during the catastrophe on 6 May 1937 when it caught fire and was destroyed during its attempt to dock with its mooring mast at Naval Air Station Lakehurst in Manchester Township, New Jersey at the end of its first transatlantic flight.

As well as the 45 crew of LZ130, 28 radio equipment and technicians under the supervision of Dr. Ernst Breuning engaged in the measurements were carried on the radio-listening and radiolocation trip. Although the moon was only two days on the wane there was plenty of cloud when, on

HITLER'S INVASION OF EAST ANGLIA, 1940

the night of 2nd August the great airship lifted off at around 2053. LZ130 overflew Hildesheim at 2338, seen by very few people. The main goal was secretly to investigate the British Chain Home radar system. To do this the airship flew northwards close to the British east coast up to the Shetland Isles and back. Sammt flew the LZ130 up Britain's east coast stopping the engines at Aberdeen pretending they had engine failure in order to investigate strange antenna masts. They drifted freely westwards over land and saw for the first time the new Supermarine Spitfires, which were then photographed as they circled the airship. RDF stations on the east coast picked up a strong radar response from a large slow-moving object over the North Sea. The airship radioed its position off the Yorkshire coast to its home base. The Zeppelin was actually several miles inland over Hull.

The duty signals officer, Flight Lieutenant Walter Pretty said, 'We were sorely tempted to radio a correct message to the airship but this would have revealed we were seeing her on radar, so we kept silent.'[40] The trip continued far enough North for examining any signals that might have come from the Scapa Flow naval base but none of the Thames Estuary. The original route would have covered these stations and the entire southern coast but the weather intervened causing the airship to pause near Bawdsey as it changed course, A. P. Rowe accepted this as proof that Bawdsey was marked for destruction when war began.[41] This initial flight failed in its main objectives, as did a second attempt on the evening of 3 August. Dr. Ernst Breuning explained later that the trip's results were negative and not because the British radar was switched off, as Churchill wrote in his memoirs. General Martini used a strong, impulsive, broadband radio transmission for determining the 'radio-weather', the best wavelengths to use for radio. These impulses severely disturbed the highly sensitive receivers in the 10-12 metre waveband. Breuning repeatedly requested Martini to stop transmitting during the spy trips, to no avail. This made it impossible for the LZ130 to investigate the very wavebands the British were using.

On their return journey, as they neared Frankfurt on the evening of 4 August they were warned by radio that landing was not yet possible. At first they suspected an aeroplane had crashed at the site, but on overflying saw nothing amiss. They turned and flew towards the Rhön Mountains and on asking, were informed 'landing before dusk not possible'.

---

40   *Duel of Eagles* by Peter Townsend.
41   *A Radar History of World War II: Technical and Military Imperatives* by Louis Brown (Institute of Physics Publishing, Bristol and Philadelphia, 1999).

THE DEATH RAY

They decided to return to Frankfurt and speak directly with the landing team (Landemannschaft) using their VHF transmitter, so that they would not be overheard by the French and so that they could speak in Swabian German to Beurle, the landing team leader. Beurle informed them they must not land yet because the British had lodged a diplomatic protest over their actions and a British delegation was at the airfield, with agreement of the German government, to inspect the ship. They were under suspicion. Beurle told them to wait while they thought of something. Shortly, the LZ130 received instructions. They were to hide all the equipment on the ship and not to land at the usual well-lit landing point where a landing team was waiting, but to land at the other end where the 'real' landing team was waiting. Once they had landed there, the technicians were to get off and they would be replaced by a unit of Sturmabteilung. The British delegation waiting at the usual landing place were told that, due to the weather, the airship had to land at another part of the airfield. By the time the British reached the airship, the spy crew was on a bus on their way to their hotel. Although they searched the ship, the British found nothing suspicious on the ship nor in the decoy SA-crew. A few days later, around lunchtime, the watchers at Bawdsey radar station had another surprise. 'The Germans are coming!' they cried as the 'blip' which they estimated at fifty aircraft steadily approached the coast. Seven miles out it turned and headed back towards Germany. For the radar girls it was a taste of things to come, as it was for the Luftwaffe, who this time were only exercising.[42]

With this level of activity the British government was faced with the alarming reality that the Germans knew about Britain's radar defences and it was a foregone conclusion that RDF stations would be targeted by the enemy. It is almost certain that well before war was declared on Sunday morning, 3rd September, German air intelligence experts were studying aerial photographs of Bawdsey Manor and the other RDF stations nearby.

At Darsham (RAF High Street), an early radar station built in 1939 approximately four miles north east of Saxmundham and about five miles from Dunwich had 'Type 1 radar'. Four 240 feet Receive towers were made of wood standing in a close formation and five 360 feet Transmit towers were made of steel. The CH stations were built in three stages. After the initial chain had been completed, various types of emergency standby stations were provided to guard against damage or breakdown of the main station. For High Street an MRU (Mobile Radio Unit) was provided at Hinton about half way between High Street and Dunwich.

---

42 *Duel of Eagles* by Peter Townsend.

HITLER'S INVASION OF EAST ANGLIA, 1940

Peggy Youell and a friend were still schoolgirls just entering their teens and staying with her uncle and aunt in Great Yarmouth when war was declared. That same night the sirens sounded and the girls were bundled under the dining table, scared silly by the elders discussing what to do if gas bombs were dropped. Very soothing! Next morning they were put on the train home to Darsham on the Ipswich-Lowestoft East Suffolk Line. Peggy arrived to find four tents full of soldiers installed in the garden and an anti-aircraft gun in the adjoining field. Rations were meagre and the men had no cooking facilities so her mother, with the help of the so-called cook (an elderly soldier called Joe) cooked meals on her cooking range and oil cooker for about three months. Among these men were several from Ipswich. The Air Force arrived. Their billets were about a quarter of a mile down a lane close by, camouflaged by a wood and their work place was the radar station at Darsham just off the A144 to Bramfield and Halesworth. The local farmer left milk for their 'cuppas' at their house for the RAF personnel to collect on their way to night duty and her mother worked in the NAAFI at the camp. Some would come in and play cards or darts and one or two played the piano for a sing-song. Several had previously been stationed at Bawdsey. The village in the meantime became full of soldiers - the two large residences having been commandeered for the purpose - who were in training. Peggy's mother arranged many concerts, dances, socials and so on for their entertainment in the Village Hall. The Scots Fusiliers taught some of their reels and flings - 'not exactly elegant in Army boots'. Although Peggy feared enemy activity because of the radar station being so near, most noise came from the AA guns when aircraft went overhead on their way to Norwich. The little cottage accommodated several wives, husbands and fiancées of the service people for a night or weekend so they could spend a little time with loved ones.

Dunwich CHL chain just north of Aldeburgh became operational on 1st January 1940. All aircraft and shipping movements detected were plotted and these plots were sent by special telephone lines to the nearby Darsham High Street CH radar station, which added information detected by their equipment and telephoned all plots to the Area Operations Rooms at Bentley Priory. The information could then be relayed to a centralised command that would in turn organise an appropriate response and direct, or vector, fighters to intercept the approaching 'targets.'

The Type 16 broadside array aerials were each mounted on a 25 feet timber gantry 35 feet from the cliff edge about 600 yards north of four terraced Victorian coastguard cottages at Minsmere Cliffs. The transmitter hut was sixty feet above sea level and the receiver, fifty feet, so that with the heights of the gantries the aerials were 85 and 75 feet respectively above sea level. The performance of CHLs placed on relatively low seashore sites like Dunwich fell well below what was possible when a more elevated site such as the cliff tops of Beachy Head was available. The answer to this was to put the aerials on a tower. Experiments putting a CHL on the 200 feet gantries of a transmitter tower at the Douglas Wood CH Station in Scotland proved this to be feasible, so a programme was started to mount on towers those CHLs on low sites to improve detection of low-flying aircraft (100 feet or less).

Following Dunkirk and with Britain facing imminent invasion, the potential vulnerability of all RDF stations like Dunwich was brought even more sharply into focus. The technical site was situated on the cliff top surrounded by a barbed wire fence. Accommodation for WAAFs was at Cliff House, as was the canteen and the recreation room. Other accommodation was in huts under the trees north of Dunwich Heath. For the enemy to gain a foothold it had to advance across a good hundred yards of open country and then negotiate the barbed wire; no easy task.

The Bromley Chain Home Low station (Air Ministry Experimental Station 24) was built four miles south of Manningtree and six miles east of Colchester between 1936 and 1939. Great Bromley village was situated in the militarily precarious position of being more or less on the boundary between two Groups of Fighter Command (11 Group and 12 Group), more specifically between the sectors known as Debden and North Weald. Bombs were dropped at Great Bromley by the Germans during the early part of the war when they were attempting to disrupt radar activity. This was abandoned when bombing seemed to have little effect on any part of the chain system. Bromley was divided into two distinct components - that of the transmitter and the receiver. The receiver site contained an earth-protected operations block, a full set of four aerial bases and over seven ancillary buildings. There was an emergency receiver block and aerial base and emergency transmission block and aerial base and a full set of four aerial bases. A standby set house, with its earthen mound, was located in the southeast corner of the site.

All of these radar stations, like Canewdon, provided long range early warning for the eastern approaches to the Thames estuary and also the general layout of the coastline, including the military installations and airstrip on Orfordness. This 'early warning' system ensured that no major airborne force could approach Britain's eastern seaboard undetected. Also, by assessing the size, altitude and direction of the approaching enemy, it enabled the RAF to organise an effective and proportional response to any major airborne threat. By the summer of 1940, this system, codenamed 'Chain Home', was fully functional and existed with no gaps from the coast of southwest England to northern Scotland. The battle for survival that lay ahead could not be fought by the pilots of RAF Fighter Command alone. By July 1940 there were 51 operational radar stations situated around the approaches to Britain. Twenty-one of these were Chain Home (CH) fixed mast stations, located around the east and south coast from the north of Scotland to Cornwall and South Wales. They could determine the range, bearing, height and strength of a hostile raid. Each CH station was capable of providing a long-range picture of the air situation at medium and high altitudes within a fixed 120 degrees arc at a range of about 150 miles at 18,000 feet from shore, but for technical reasons the CH radars could not track aircraft flying over land. When, in the early months of the war, German aircraft commenced to lay mines in the estuaries of the East Coast, it was found that the CH stations failed to detect these aircraft when flying low. Thirty smaller stations known as Chain Home Low (CHL) were constructed to provide low coverage to the estuaries of the Thames, Humber, Tyne and other rivers. CHL stations could detect aircraft flying at 500 feet out to eighteen miles and aircraft flying at 2,000 feet out to 35 miles. The first CHL station, at Fifeness in Scotland, was commissioned on 1 November 1939. In 11 Group's operational area there were sixteen coastal radar sites, eight of which were CH sites and eight of which were low-level CHL, stretching from Suffolk to Ventnor on the Isle of Wight.

But while radar was fundamental, a great deal more was involved in the air defence system. In December 1939 serious investigation of German signals had started - not a moment too soon - and in February 1940, Flight Lieutenant (later Group Captain) Scott Farnie established the first listening post at Hawkinge. Thus began the invaluable 'Y Service', which kept the Luftwaffe under permanent radio surveillance, one of the war's well-kept secrets. The ever-increasing requirement for fluent German linguists soon made it obvious that women would have to be recruited for this work as well as men. The Women's Royal Air Force had previously briefly existed at the end of World War I. The Women's Auxiliary Air Force was formed on 28 June 1939 by Royal Warrant. At the outbreak of war there were fewer than 2,000 women on strength. Its object was to replace men in the RAF where possible to free them for other active service. When war was declared, an appeal for recruits to the WAAF was broadcast over the radio by the BBC and hundreds of women immediately volunteered. The monitoring of all German signals, whether in low-grade or high-grade cipher, radio-telephony, or non-Morse transmissions, was the responsibility of the 'Y Service'. Station X, Bletchley Park, the Government Code and Cipher School, was entirely dependent upon 'Y'. It was here that brilliant academics broke the high-level encrypted German 'Enigma' radio codes and teleprinter communications.[43] The first operational break into 'Enigma' came around the 23 January 1940, when the team working under Dilly Knox, with the mathematicians John Jeffreys, Peter Twinn and Alan Turing, unravelled the German Army administrative 'Green' key. Encouraged by this success, the codebreakers managed to crack the 'Red' key used by the Luftwaffe liaison officers' co-ordinating air support for army units. Gordon Welchman, soon to become head of the Army and Air Force section, devised a system whereby his codebreakers were supported by other staff based in a neighbouring hut that turned the deciphered messages into intelligence reports. Special Communication Units were set up to feed the Bletchley Park intelligence to commanders in the field, first briefly in France in May 1940 and then in North Africa and elsewhere from March 1941 onwards. Used properly, the German military 'Enigma' would have been virtually unbreakable; in practice, shortcomings in operation allowed it to be broken.[44]

In April 1940 'Enigma' decrypts provided a detailed picture of the disposition of the German forces and then their movement orders for the attack on the Low Countries prior to the Battle of France in May. On 22 May the Bletchley Park codebreakers broke into the 'Red' Enigma' network (taking its name from the colour used to underline the unenciphered characteristics common to all messages transmitted

---

[43] In June 1941 the term 'Ultra Secret' was adopted by British military intelligence because the intelligence thus obtained was considered more important than that designated by the highest British security classification then used (Most Secret). 'Ultra' eventually became the standard designation among the western Allies for all such intelligence.

[44] German military 'Enigma' was first broken in December 1932 by the Polish Cipher Bureau, using a combination of brilliant mathematics, the services of a spy in the German office responsible for administering encrypted communications and good luck. The Poles read 'Enigma' to the outbreak of WWII and beyond, in France. In 1939 the Germans made the systems ten times more complex, which required a tenfold increase in Polish decryption equipment, which they could not meet. On 25 July 1939 the Polish Cipher Bureau handed reconstructed 'Enigma' machines and their techniques for decrypting ciphers to the French and British.

by the network) and read a Luftwaffe 'Enigma' message.[45] Decryption of traffic from Luftwaffe radio networks provided a great deal of indirect intelligence about Operation 'Sealion'. During the period of the invasion threat, 'Enigma' played a significant part in permitting the British leadership to build up a complete picture of German intentions in the Battle of Britain. In July Bletchley was decrypting prolific 'Enigma' radio correspondence from the Luftwaffe command, giving detailed information on the deployment and strength of the three German air fleets, which were preparing for massed raids against Britain. 'Enigma' intelligence kept Air Chief Marshal Sir Hugh Dowding informed of the German strategy, of the strength and location of various Luftwaffe units and often provided advance warning of bombing raids (but not of their specific targets). When, on 8 August, Göring issued his order of the day, Operation Adler ('Eagle') when the RAF should, in the Reichsmarschall's words, be 'swept from the skies' in less than an hour the decrypted order was in the hands of Winston Churchill, the Chiefs of Staff and Air Marshal Dowding. (Air Vice-Marshal Keith Park, a New Zealander commanding 11 Group, with headquarters at Uxbridge, alone of the fighter commanders was in on the secret 'Enigma' decrypts).

At first the decrypted information was sent to Fighter Command via the Air Ministry and then direct from Bletchley by teleprinter line through a Special Liaison Unit lodged in a sound-proof cubicle next to the Operations Room at the 166-year-old Bentley Priory, atop a hill at Stanmore just north of London. This had only been securely lodged underground and under concrete in March 1940. Here sat Dowding with his duty controller, the Commandant of the Observer Corps, liaison officers from Bomber and Coastal Commands, the Admiralty, the War Office, the Ministry of Home Security (air-raid warnings) and Lieutenant-General Frederick Pile of Anti-Aircraft Command. AA Command controlled guns positioned within a 25-mile-wide belt stretching from Newcastle down the East Coast, around London and southwest to Portsmouth. Included in the belt were 960 searchlights. The whole system was manned by 23,000 personnel.

A neighbouring filter centre at Bentley Priory shared the same concrete bunker where filter officers - one for each radar station - identified all the plots received from the two radar chains and the Observer Corps. Each raid was allocated a number and the filter offices checked them against 'friendly', 'hostile' or 'unknown' ('X-raids') before they appeared on the map in the

---

45 The code remained broken until the end of the war with few interruptions. Quoted in *Enigma: The Battle For The Code* by Hugh Sebag-Montefiore (Cassell, 2004).

THE DEATH RAY

Operations Room where Dowding could view the battle situation anywhere in the British Isles. This was the only place where the complete picture was available to the Commander-in-Chief 24 hours a day. Sadie Younger, a filterer at Bentley Priory during the battle, recalls: 'I can remember working flat out on the Estuary/Channel area of the filter room table. The heavy enemy attacks, meant for London, were continuous, apart from a lull at midday. Radar stations passed mass plots to plotters, working at high speed and tellers were doubled up, as there was so much information to be passed to Operations Rooms. I needed both hands to filter tracks. I even remember telling the controller on the dais that the heights on enemy raids could be anything between 15,000 and 25,000 [feet], but the weather was fine and the visibility good.'

The track of the raid would be given simultaneously to the Fighter Group controllers, who as well as the filtered radar plots from Fighter Command, received plots direct from the Observer Centres. This was the only independent source of information in the Groups, which it was their duty to pass to Fighter Command and other Groups. Balloon barrages, too, were in direct touch with Group Operations Room, which was modelled on the 'master' at Bentley Priory, but displaying on its key map only the Group area and immediately adjacent sectors. The Group Commander and his Controller could see simultaneously at any moment the exact situation on the table map of the Group area. Around the map sat WAAF girls with headphones and croupiers' rakes, moving coloured discs, which represented aircraft according to the plots received.

There was a plan in place for squadrons to use airfields of other commands if ever it became necessary to evacuate Fighter Command's main bases. The plan would never be put into practice but in 1940, 11 Group alone used 27 airfields spread across Kent, West Sussex, Surrey, Greater London, Essex and as far east as Suffolk. All Groups had several satellite fields where fighters could be dispersed. Permanent stations had an armoury, guardhouse, stores, M/T sections, workshops and modern messes, a NAAFI and modern barracks, but if they were lucky some pilots who were billeted off base were able to better enjoy the comforts of home. In August 1940, Nigel Rose, a Spitfire I pilot in 602 'City of Glasgow' Squadron, arrived at Tangmere with the rest of his squadron from Scotland. He wrote to his parents telling them that 'we live for the moment in a typical Sussex rectory (perhaps I'm not really qualified to call it that!) but there's that delightful smell of soap and flowers and new mown grass and wasps in abundance. The squadron bagged two 'certains' and three unconfirmed at tea just after we arrived yesterday.'

HITLER'S INVASION OF EAST ANGLIA, 1940

No-one understood the true nature of Fighter Command and its battle system better than Dowding, who created an air defence system without parallel based on what he would call 'science thoughtfully applied to operational requirements'. His assessment of his own and the Command's task in 1940 was clear: 'Mine was the purely defensive role of trying to stop the possibility of an invasion and thus give this country a breathing spell... it was Germany's objective to win the war by invasion and it was my job to prevent an invasion from taking place.' When the battle was joined, German listeners were amazed to find 'the air full of voices, calmly and systematically placing fighters here and there and guiding others back to base. It dawned on the listeners that this was part of a complex and smooth-running organization of great size.'

Radar stations were a tempting target. Before the start of the war, Ventnor Chain Home Station on the Isle of Wight was used to further RDF trials. Cierva autogyros were used in long-range exercises, increasing the efficiency of the radar chain. By January 1939, Ventnor was operational, with four 350-feet-high steel masts for the transmitter aerials and four 240-feet-high wooden towers for the receivers. Equipment was originally housed in wooden huts by the foot of the masts, although later it was transferred to protected buildings. On Good Friday 1939, Ventnor, along with the complete Chain Home network, began a 24-hour watch for enemy aircraft. In 1940, from 11 July, Ventnor gave effective warning of large raids. This included detecting the large force of German bombers flown on Thursday, 8th August and the even larger force sent across the Channel on Sunday, 11th August. When Monday, 12th August dawned fine and clear the first attempt was made to blind the Dowding system. It was quite obvious from de-briefing reports made out by crews who returned from the previous day's big raid in the Portland area that radar had given considerable warning of their approach and it was therefore decided after earnest representations by General Wolfgang Martini (head of the Luftwaffe signals branch at OKL) to try to put out of action all known radar stations between Portland and the Thames Estuary. The day's effort was thus designed with this aim in mind and at the same time attacks would be made upon the RAF's coastal fighter stations by taking advantage of the likely radar blackout.[46]

Ventnor was one of four radar stations as well as Portsmouth docks and several airfields targeted for attack by the force of 100 Junkers Ju 88s, 120 Messerschmitt Bf 110s and 25 Bf 109s. Hauptman Walter Rubensdörffer's Erprobungsgruppe 210 at Calais-Marck attacked the

---

46   *Battle Over Britain* by Francis K. Mason.

THE DEATH RAY

CH radars at Dover, Rye, Pevensey and Dunkirk. Dover, Pevensey and Rye were put out of action temporarily and permitted a brief but heavy attack on the airfield at Lympne but emergency measures were put into effect and all were reporting within six hours. About fifteen Junkers Ju 88s of KG 51 broke from the main formation and turned to attack the Chain Home Radar station at Ventnor. As they began their dive, Spitfires intercepted, decimating the Ju 88s before they could release their bombs. A few, however, got through. Each of the bombers was loaded with four high-explosive bombs and many added to the confusion by strafing the area with machine guns.

'In the Filter Room at Fighter Command the usual hum of activity increased as running commentaries came in from radar stations Dunkirk, Rye, Pevensey and Dover - all had reported. Then the plotting table called up to the Duty Filter Officer, Flying Officer Robert Wright: 'Ventnor's being attacked!' He threw one of the battery of switches beside him and was on the line to Ventnor, where the corporal in charge was giving a blow by blow account. 'Are you all right?' Wright asked.

'We're being properly beaten up' came the reply.

'What about the girls?'

'They're all right so far,' shouted the corporal above the din of bombs and aircraft engines, 'Blondie's yelling at us from outside. She's trying to count the buggers!'

'Poor Blondie. She never got to the end of counting those fifteen Ju 88s which were screaming down on Ventnor. When they searched later among the burning shambles she was missing.

'The radar station went off the air. In one swift blow the Luftwaffe had forced a vital breach in Fighter Command's defences. Fortunately they never realized it: by sending out impulses on another transmitter Fighter Command foxed the Germans into thinking that Ventnor was still functioning.'[47]

Despite the efforts of local firemen, who were hampered by the lack of available water on the site, most of the service buildings had been destroyed. Several delayed action and unexploded bombs were located in the site of the radar pylons, forcing the whole site to be evacuated and delaying the start of repairs. Luckily, only one soldier was injured in the attack. The radar station was put out of action, the only one in the country in the entire war to have been destroyed.

On Friday, 16th August after early morning mists had cleared the Channel coasts, the sun was shining from a cloudless sky and there was

---
47   *Duel of Eagles* by Peter Townsend.

hardly a breath of wind anywhere when the Luftwaffe again attacked Ventnor. The station had not yet been repaired since the last attack. Five of the Stukas dropped seven bombs precisely on the radar station, destroying all the below-ground buildings and all but two of the buildings above ground. Ventnor remained out of service for seven days. A mobile unit was brought up to Bembridge but its performance was so poor that its only value was in persuading the Luftwaffe that no gap existed. The reserve station at Bembridge was completed on 23 August.

After the two successful attacks on Ventnor, Germany never again attacked any of Britain's radar sites, a fact which puzzled British officers for some time. The reason behind this was that German Intelligence assumed that no serious damage had been done to any of the radar stations that were attacked. This was based upon reports from General Martini who had continued to detect transmissions from the Ventnor area after both attacks, which they assumed meant that the station was still operational. Intelligence assumed that the radar operations room and the equipment were deep underground and that further heavy bombing would be wasted. No German agent during the war learnt much about the British radar system. Had they done, German Intelligence would have discovered that the power and receiving rooms were extremely vulnerable to attack and that the raid on Ventnor had been a devastating success. It is certain that had German intelligence discovered the full effect of their attack on Ventnor, more radar stations would have been increasingly bombed, with devastating consequences. The Luftwaffe neglected strikes on the supporting infrastructure, such as telephone lines and power stations, which could have rendered the radars useless, even if the towers themselves remained intact. German intelligence also assumed that radar was not organised nationally, but on a decentralised, local level. It was believed that the RAF fighter squadrons were tied to the radio range of their home station and that the radar information was only used on a local level, a view which was wrong in every respect. In any case, the radar stations were difficult targets to attack and destroy, as the aerials themselves prevented dive bombers from accurately targeting the area without crashing into the pylons. The problem of how to target radar stations increased when, two days after the attack on Ventnor, the Stuka, which had proved so effective across Europe, was withdrawn from the war due to its high loss rate and vulnerability to RAF fighters. All of which contributed to Göring's speech of 15 August: 'It is doubtful whether there is any point in continuing the attacks on radar sites, in view of the fact that not one of those attacked has so far been put out of action.'

THE DEATH RAY

The main attack upon the RAF's defences was code-named Adlerangriff ('Eagle Attack'). Poor weather delayed 'Adler Tag' until 13 August when 'Eagle Day' opened with a series of attacks, led again by Epro 210, on coastal airfields used as forward landing grounds for the RAF fighters, as well as 'satellite airfields' (including Manston and Hawkinge). As the week drew on, the airfield attacks moved further inland and repeated raids were made on the radar chain. 15 August was 'The Greatest Day' when the Luftwaffe mounted the largest number of sorties of the campaign. Luftflotte 5 attacked the north of England. Believing Fighter Command strength to be concentrated in the south, raiding forces from Denmark and Norway ran into unexpectedly strong resistance. Inadequately escorted by Bf 110s, bombers were shot down in large numbers. North East England was attacked by 65 Heinkel 111s escorted by 34 Messerschmitt 110s and RAF Great Driffield was attacked by fifty unescorted Junkers 88s. Out of 115 bombers and 35 fighters sent, sixteen bombers and seven fighters were destroyed. As a result of these casualties, Luftflotte 5 did not appear in strength again in the campaign. By now the Luftwaffe was averaging unacceptable losses of forty-nine aircraft a day and the RAF, nineteen a day, excepting 17 August when there was no significant fighting.

The 18th of August has been dubbed 'The Hardest Day'. Luftwaffe units flew a total of 970 sorties over Britain: some 495 by medium bombers, 460 by fighters and fifteen by reconnaissance units. Of this total, about 170 of the bomber sorties were flown on the night of 17th/18th August; the remainder flown during the daylight hours that day. While British propaganda claimed 144 German aircraft destroyed the Germans admitted to losing just 36. German propaganda claimed to have destroyed 147 British aircraft, the British admitting to losing only 23, when the actual figure was around 68.[48] Following this grinding battle, exhaustion and six days of poor weather reduced operations for most of a week, gave Fighter Command a breathing space. Even so, the odds were stacked in the enemy's favour, a point forcibly made on 20th August by British Prime Minister Winston Churchill. 'The gratitude of every home in our island, in our Empire and, indeed, throughout the world, except in the abodes of the guilty, goes out to the British airmen, who, undaunted by odds, unweary in their constant challenge and mortal danger, are turning the tide of the world war by their prowess and their devotion. Never in the field of human conflict was so much owed by so many to so few.'

---

48 Other sources between them insist the RAF's losses were 27–34 fighters destroyed and 29 aircraft destroyed on the ground, including only eight fighters.

HITLER'S INVASION OF EAST ANGLIA, 1940

The recent lull allowed the Luftwaffe to review their performance. Göring may have overlooked the importance of the radar chain but there were other options available to Hitler, if he wanted them, to either destroy or raid them and steal their equipment by other means. And in England it was feared as much. One particular Home Office file of May 1940 contains the following: 'Raids may aim at the destruction of isolated points of particular importance, such as RDF stations or vital centres of communications and would probably be combined with 5th Column activity.' The same Home Office file also highlights the east coast as the most likely target for enemy landings because of its ports and open beaches. Admiralty files of the time also indicate a concern for the east coast, particularly the shoreline from Felixstowe to Hollesley Bay. Following an inspection of east coast defences, a report submitted on 1st June 1940 by Admiral Sir Frederic Charles Dreyer GBE KCB on the staff of the General Officer Commanding-in-Chief, Home Forces in 1940 as an advisor on anti-invasion measure, urged that the beaches to the north and south of Felixstowe must be well mined and obstructed with Dannart [barbed] wire and anti-tank obstacles. The Admiral also recommended mining the mouth of the River Deben and that the River Ore should be blocked at its entrance in Hollesley Bay by: 'Barges or anything else to prevent small enemy craft getting up the estuary.'

The army commanders responsible for the defence of Suffolk's beaches clearly shared Admiral Dreyer's concerns and were only too aware that the open beaches in the area, particularly Hollesley Bay, could easily be used by the enemy to land infantry, artillery and, most worrying of all, armoured fighting vehicles. Prompted by these concerns and the Admiralty report, work on coastal defences was stepped up as a matter of extreme urgency. War Office files also clearly show that extra measures were being put in place at all points of particular strategic importance, including airfields and RDF Stations. During the invasion period the overall responsibility for the defence of east Suffolk rested with the 55th West Lancashire Infantry Division and its subordinate Brigades. The war diary of the 55th for June 1940 contains a revised list of 'vulnerable points' under its control and the strength of the army units detailed to guard them. The strength of the army guard detail at Bawdsey is listed as 72, by comparison the strength at Darsham RDF station nearby is given as 36 and further up the coast at Dunwich the guard detail is listed as 18. Bawdsey's isolated position on a triangular peninsular between the North Sea and the estuary of the River Deben made the site especially vulnerable to attack by a small force of raiders which might easily be landed on the gently sloping shingle beaches within a hundred yards or so of the main installation. The overriding objective would be to put the station out of action for as long as possible, if not permanently. Carefully placed explosive charges would easily have sent the 360 feet high transmitter masts crashing to the ground. Secondary objectives would doubtless include snatching vital parts of the top secret radar apparatus, perhaps even technical personnel as well. Or perhaps such a raid would be carried out to seize the site as a strategic objective in advance of a larger landing operation - taking out the 'eye in the sky' just long enough to delay warning of the approaching airborne armada? Whatever the case, exploits such as these are usually the stuff of Hollywood.

By July a strip of coastline from the Wash to Rye in Sussex had been designated a 'defence area'. Thousands of square miles of east and southeast England had become an exclusion zone under virtual martial law, off limits to all except those who had good reason to be there. Despite these hurried anti-invasion preparations, the simple stark fact was that Britain had hundreds of miles of vulnerable coastline to defend and not a lot to defend it with. And coupled with these problems Britain's defenders also faced another entirely new threat - airborne invasion. It was estimated that five thousand enemy airborne troops could be landed on British soil during the initial stages of an invasion. There would be little warning and there was the distinct possibility that ordinary civilians would be caught up in the fighting, as had happened in the Low Countries. Church bells were to remain silent, only to be rung as a warning in the event of an airborne invasion. Any open spaces where enemy aircraft or gliders could possibly land were ploughed up and sign posts were removed in order to confuse the enemy parachutists when they arrived.

With fears of an invasion and spurred on by reports in both the press and from official government bodies of a fifth column operating in Britain which would aid an invasion by German airborne forces, calls for some form of home defence force soon began to be heard from the press and from private individuals. As the government began to intern German and Austrian citizens in the country the press baron Lord Kemsley privately proposed to the War Office that rifle clubs be formed to form the nucleus of a home defence force and Josiah Wedgwood, a Labour MP, wrote to the prime minister asking that the entire adult population be trained in the use of arms and given weapons to defend themselves. Similar calls appeared in newspaper columns; in the 12th May issue of the *Sunday Express* a brigadier called on the government to issue free arms licences and permits to buy ammunition to men possessing small arms and on the same day the

HITLER'S INVASION OF EAST ANGLIA, 1940

Sunday Pictorial asked if the government had considered training golfers in rifle shooting to eliminate stray parachutists. These calls alarmed government and senior military officials, who worried about the prospect of the population forming private defence forces that the army would not be able to control and in mid-May the Home Office issued a press release on the matter; it was the task of the army to deal with enemy parachutists, as any civilians who carried weapons and fired on German troops were likely to be executed if captured. Private defence forces soon began to be formed throughout the country, placing the government in an awkward position; these private forces, which the army might not be able to control, could well inhibit the attempts by the army during an invasion, yet to ignore the calls for a home defence force to be set up would be politically problematic. An officially sponsored home defence force would allow the government greater control and also allow for greater security around vulnerable areas such as munitions factories and airfields, but there was some confusion over who would form and control the force, with separate plans drawn up by the War Office and General Headquarters Home Forces under 63-year old General Sir Walter Mervyn St. George Kirke GCB CMG DSO the Commander in Chief of the British Home Forces. Kirke was a tough, energetic and experienced officer who had served in India and on the Western Front in World War I. In November 1939 Kirke had formulated a defence plan he dubbed 'Julius Caesar'. It was based on two assumptions: 1. any significant seaborne landing would require the early capture of a port; and 2. that it would be preceded by a heavy air offensive directed against the RAF, Home Fleet and infrastructure targets in England. Airborne participation was likewise assumed and Kirke saw the rapid elimination of enemy paratroopers as crucial. They were to be annihilated as they descended or were still assembling on the ground. Any survivors were to be hunted down by reserves of tanks and horse cavalry.[49]

The government and senior military officials rapidly compared plans and by 13 May had worked out an improvised plan for a home defence force, to be called the Local Defence Volunteers, but the rush to complete a plan and announce it to the public had led to a number of administrative and logistical problems, such as how the volunteers in the new force would be armed, which would cause problems as the force evolved.

The Home Guard was nothing new. During the First World War there had existed, the Volunteer Training Corps. The origins of the Second World War Home Guard can be traced to Captain Tom Wintringham,

---

49 *England's Final Hour? Operation Sea Lion* by James P. Werbaneth.

Wehrmacht soldiers unloading troops and supplies from a Junkers Ju 52 during the invasion of Poland in September 1939.

While Germany landed its troops in six coastal areas, at Narvik, Trondheim, Bergen, Kristiansand, Oslo and Egersund on 8 and 9 April 1940 in Operation 'Weserübung', the Royal Navy tried to oppose in the Narvik region where on 10-13 April a violent naval battle took place.

Men of Wehrmacht regroup at Oslo's Fornebu aerodrome in Norway after capturing the surrounding area during Operation 'Weserübung'.

Cheerful Danish soldiers pictured on 9 April 1940.

Luftwaffe Fallschirmjäger (paratroopers) who took part in the attack and capture of the Belgian fortifications at Eben Emael in May 1940.

Fallschirmjäger in the destroyed fortifications of the Belgian fort at Eben-Emael.

Adolf Hitler posing with Luftwaffe Fallschirmjäger paratroopers who received the award of the Iron Cross after landing by glider to capture Eben-Emael.

The blown up turret with two 120-mm artillery guns of the Belgian fort Eben-Emael.

Fallschirmjäger paratroopers carrying out a mock attack after landing in a Deutsche Forschungsanstalt für Segelflug (DFS) 230 glider.

Junkers Ju 52s in formation.

Fallschirmjäger jumping from Ju 52s.

German paratroopers jumping over Holland during the invasion in May 1940.

Above: A Dutch road block in Holland in 1939. Defences in the Netherlands proved no serious obstacle to the German Blitzkrieg tactics in May 1940.

Right: Fallen soldiers of the Dutch Army who put up a brave but futile resistance in the face of the German onslaught in May 1940.

Richard Gerken, a former German policeman, who had been recruited into the Abwehr and was assigned to Abwehrstelle Wehrkreis IV Münster Gruppe II/F in the run up to the invasion of Holland in May 1940.

A rare photograph of German Brandenburg troops in action in May 1940, masquerading as Dutch military police in the capture of the canal bridge at Roosteren. (After the Battle)

On page eight of *The Times* for 21 June 1940 there appeared a picture of a civilian surrounded by a group of German paratroops. The caption stated that the civilian was one of the many, 'fifth Columnists who had aided the parachute troops in Holland.' The same photograph has appeared in several later publications but with the apparent civilian correctly referred to as a 'Brandenburger'.

A wrecked Ju 52 at Waalhaven during the invasion of Holland in May 1940.

Wrecked Junkers Ju 52s which crash-landed in Holland in May 1940 blocking the movement of German troops advancing on a Dutch town.

Burning Ju 52s at Waalhaven in May 1940.

German paratroops en route at a crossroads in Waalhaven on the road to Rotterdam.

German paratroops rounding up defeated Dutch soldiers at Moerdijk in May 1940.

Dutch Air Force Fokker D-XXI fighters. Fitted with the Mercury engine the plane proved to be slightly under-powered for a modern monoplane fighter and was unsuitable for any high altitude interception role. However, it proved an excellent dog-fighting aircraft in close combat with the much faster Bf 109 during the many engagements in May 1940.

Dutch Air Force Fokker G.1 heavy twin-engined fighter aircraft, comparable in size and role to the German Messerschmitt Bf 110.

Dutch Air Force Fokker T-V 5 medium bomber in formation with Fokker D-XXI fighters. Wooden-winged, it had a wooden monocoque centre fuselage, a fabric covered steel tube rear fuselage and a duralumin forward fuselage. It was armed with a 20 mm auto cannon in the nose to meet the bomber destroyer part of the requirement and four defensive Browning machine guns, one each in dorsal, ventral and tail positions, with one capable of being switched between two waist positions. The bomb-bay under the centre fuselage was capable of carrying a 2,200 lb bomb load.

Bristol Blenheim Mk.IV in flight in May 1940. RAF Coastal Command Blenheims on reconnaissance early in the morning of 10 May reported eleven German aircraft crashed on the beach south of the spot where the Amsterdam Canal joins the sea and eleven Junkers on the airfield at The Hague, which was strewn the abandoned parachutes of German troops.

Oberleutnant Wilhelm Walther who commanded the Brandenburgers' 800th Special-Purpose Construction Training Battalion at the beginning of World War Two. During Unternehmen 'Weserübung' Walther's 1st Battalion of 1st Jäger Regiment performed the speedy capture of four airfields in Denmark and southern Norway. On 10 May 1940 during the invasion of Holland, Leutnant Wilhelm Walther and an eight-man team disguised as Dutch military police escorting German prisoners captured the Meuse railway bridge in Gennep intact after he obtained information about where demolition charges had been placed. On 24 June 1940 Oberleutnant Wilhelm Walther became the first Brandenburger to be awarded the Knight's Cross.

Major Theodore von Hippel, who following World War One had proposed utilizing small, elite units to penetrate enemy defences before hostilities or offensive actions had begun, commanded the First Battalion, the Brandenburg Regiment at the beginning of World War Two.

Rotterdam in ruins after the bombing raid of 14 May 1940.

Commander-in-Chief of the Dutch forces, General Henri Gerard Winkelman who decided to lay down arms, at 1650 hours on 14 May.

who returned from the Spanish Civil War and wrote a book entitled *How to Reform the Army,* in which, as well as a large number of regular army reforms, Wintringham called for the creation of twelve divisions similar in composition to that of the International Brigades which had been formed in Spain during the conflict. The divisions would be raised through a process of voluntary enlistment targeting ex-servicemen and youths. Despite great interest by the War Office, Wintringham's call to train 100,000 men immediately was not implemented but when Britain declared war on Nazi Germany on 3rd September 1939, debates began in official circles about the possible ways in which the German military might launch an invasion of Britain; in the first week of the conflict numerous diplomatic and intelligence reports seemed to indicate that there was the possibility of an imminent German amphibious assault. Many government ministers and senior army officials including General Sir Walter Kirke believed that the threat of invasion was greatly exaggerated and were sceptical but others were not, including Winston Churchill the newly installed First Lord of the Admiralty. Churchill argued that some form of home defence force should be raised from members of the population who were ineligible to serve in the regular forces but wished to serve their country; in a letter he wrote to Samuel Hoare, the Lord Privy Seal on 8 October 1939, Churchill called for a Home Guard force of 500,000 men over the age of 40 to be formed. At the same time that government officials were debating the need for a home defence force, such a force was actually being formed without any official encouragement; in Essex, men not eligible for call-up into the armed forces were coming forward to join the self-styled 'Legion of Frontiersmen'. Officials were soon informed of the development of the legion, with the Adjutant-General, Sir Robert Gordon-Finlayson, arguing that the government should encourage the development of more unofficial organisations. However, the fear of invasion quickly dissipated as it became evident that the German military was not in a position to launch an invasion of Britain and official enthusiasm for home defence forces waned and the legion appears to have dissolved itself at the same time.

In a radio broadcast on 14 May 1940, even before the decision had been taken to evacuate the BEF from France, Anthony Eden, the 42-year old Secretary of State for War, called for men between the ages of 17 to 65 who were not in military service but wished to defend their country against an invasion to enlist in the newly formed Local Defence Volunteers at their local police station. Eden had achieved rapid promotion as a young Member of Parliament and was Foreign Secretary at the early age of 38, before resigning in protest at Neville Chamberlain's policy towards Mussolini's Italy. The LDV would be the nation's 'eyes and ears', patrolling their locality watching out for and reporting the arrival of enemy paratroops, or for that matter any other 'suspicious persons'. The announcement was met with such enthusiasm that 250,000 volunteers tried to sign up in the first seven days. By July this number increased to 1.5 million. As volunteers and social groups such as cricket clubs began forming their own units, dubbed 'the parashots' by the press, in telegrams to the Lord Lieutenants of each county, it was explained that LDV units would operate in pre-defined military areas already used by the regular army, with a General Staff Officer coordinating with civilian regional commissioners to divide these areas into smaller zones. In London this was organised on the basis of police districts.

On 17 May the LDV achieved official legal status and orders were issued from the War Office to regular army headquarters throughout Britain explaining that LDV volunteers would be divided into sections, platoons and companies but would not be paid and leaders of units would not hold commissions or have the power to command regular forces. Legislation however was slowed by the preoccupation of the War Office and General Headquarters Home Forces with Operation 'Dynamo', the evacuation of the British Expeditionary Force from Dunkirk between 27 May and 4 June. Many LDV members became impatient, particularly when it was announced that volunteers would only receive armbands printed with 'LDV' on them until proper uniforms could be manufactured and there was no mention of weapons being issued to units! This impatience often led to units conducting their own patrols without official permission, often led by men who had previously served in the armed forces. The presence of many veterans and the appointment of ex-officers as commanders of LDV units only exacerbated the situation, with many believing that they did not require training before being issued weapons. This led to numerous complaints being received by the War Office and the press and many ex-senior officers attempting to use their influence to obtain weapons or permission to begin patrolling.

The issue of weapons to LDV units was particularly problematic for the War Office because re-arming and re-equipping of the regular forces would have to take precedence and so the War Office issued instructions on how to make Molotov cocktails and emergency orders were placed for First World War vintage Ross rifles from Canada and Pattern 14 and M1917 rifles from the United States. In the absence of proper weapons, many LDV units broke into museums and appropriated whatever weapons could be found, or equipped themselves with private weapons such as shotguns. Another problem was the definition of the role the LDV was to play. The War Office and the army saw the LDV because of its lack of training, weapons and proper equipment, acting as 'an armed police constabulary' which in the event of an invasion was to observe German troop movements, convey information to the regular forces and guard places of strategic or tactical importance. LDV commanders and members however, believed that they would be best suited to attacking and harassing German forces. In August, after complaints about the role of the LDV and continuing problems with having to clothe and arm them, the government responded to public pressure and redefined the role of the LDV to include delaying and obstructing German forces by any means possible. On 22 June Winston Churchill was of the opinion that one of the main causes of disciplinary and morale problems stemmed from the uninspiring title of the LDV and he wrote to Eden suggesting that it be renamed the 'Home Guard'. Despite resistance from Eden and other government officials, who noted that one million 'LDV' armbands had already been printed and the cost of printing another million 'Home Guard' armbands would be excessive, on 22 July the LDV was officially renamed the Home Guard.

Old men and adolescent boys found themselves patrolling the outskirts of towns and villages after a full day's work, or guarding makeshift strongpoints through the night. Some had been given rifles, but many were armed only with shotguns or any other old weapons they could lay their hands on, including bayonets welded into a length of pipe. With these meagre resources they were expected to put up a fight against well armed and battle hardened enemy paratroops. And the Home Guard had a number of secret roles. This included sabotage units who would disable factories and petrol installations following invasion. Three thousand members were also recruited into the commando teams of a top secret force of more highly trained guerrilla units who would act in support of the regular army if the Germans should invade.

Chapter 3

The Last Ditch

The regular defences require supplementing with guerrilla type troops, who will allow themselves to be overrun and who thereafter will be responsible for hitting the enemy in the comparatively soft spots behind zones of concentrated attack.
Statement on 2 July 1940 by Winston Churchill and the War Cabinet.

I have been following with much interest the growth and development of the new Guerrilla formations......known as 'Auxiliary Units'. From what I hear these units are being organised with thoroughness and imagination and should, in the event of invasion, prove a useful addition to the regular forces.
Winston Churchill to Anthony Eden, 25 September 1940.

In 1938 in the corridors of power in the Foreign Office in Whitehall, King Charles Street, London most everyone knew that Germany was arming for war and that Britain was largely unprepared but outwardly few refused to acknowledge the scent of danger. Chamberlain's appeasement policies had left the defence of the realm in a parlous state, although the Munich Agreement did at least give Britain valuable breathing space, at the expense of Czechoslovakia. What was needed in Britain meanwhile, was some form of improvisation should all else fail. Lieutenant Colonel (later Major General) John 'Jo' Holland, who had personal experience of the defensive against irregular warfare in India and Ireland, drew up plans to form resistance by civilians in the event of a German invasion and to carry out such tactics. (After the outbreak of war explosives and other stores were dumped around Britain but with no co-ordination, hopefully to be used by any persons willing to carry out sabotage behind the German occupation). Holland was given the task of forming a unit to study such problems.

THE LAST DITCH

He called it MI(R) - Military Intelligence (Research). Urged on by the War Office, Winston Churchill initiated the Auxiliary Units in the early summer of 1940. This was to counter the civilian Home Defence Scheme already established by SIS (MI6), but outside War Office control. The Auxiliary Units or GHQ Auxiliary Units (referred incorrectly as the British Resistance Organisation) were specially trained, highly secret units located in a coastal strip thirty miles deep extending from the north of Scotland down the east coast and round to the south of Wales, in readiness with the aim using irregular warfare to help combat any invasion by Nazi Germany. They were all at least one mile from the shore. The Auxiliary Units' purpose was to attack invading forces from behind their own lines while conventional forces fell back to the last-ditch GHQ Line. Aircraft, fuel dumps, railway lines and depots were high on the list of targets, as were senior German officers. Patrols secretly reconnoitered local country houses, which might be used by German officers, in preparation. The Auxiliary Units would fight as uniformed guerrillas during the military campaign, but were not themselves a resistance organisation (having a life expectancy of only two weeks). If defeated, then resistance units organised by SIS (MI6) would continue the struggle.

Auxiliary Units, the cover name given to the organisation, comprised of two parts. The first consisted of specially selected civilians with a good knowledge of their local area and physically capable of living rough and fighting and harassing enemy forces. The second part consisted of local wireless networks operated by Royal Corps of Signals personnel with outstations near the coast, each having a civilian operator. A system of spies and runners would supply information of enemy activity to these operators for relaying to the Signals control stations who would in turn transmit the information to the Area HQs attached to Brigade/Corps of the conventional forces. Each control station had from five to ten outstations, Southern England having a larger number as the more likely area to be invaded. Britain was the only country during the war that was able to create such a resistance movement in advance of an invasion.

Winston Churchill appointed Colonel Colin McVean Gubbins to found the Auxiliary Units and in June 1940 the selection and training of the patrol members began in earnest. Gubbins was a regular Army soldier, but due to the nature of Britain's imperial experience, he had acquired considerable experience and expertise in guerrilla warfare during the Allied intervention in the Russian Civil War in 1919 and in the Anglo-Irish War of 1919-1921. Most recently, he had returned from Norway, where he headed the Independent

HITLER'S INVASION OF EAST ANGLIA, 1940

Companies, the predecessors of the Commandos. Gubbins used several officers who had served with the Independent Companies in Norway, plus others he had known there. In July Gubbins recruited about a dozen regional Captains as Intelligence Officers who would form the backbone of the newly created Auxiliary Units. Their mission was to find thirty or so reliable men and issue them with an assortment of explosives, weapons and vital supplies. These men became known as 'dump owners'. The IO's were to help the 'dump owners' to form cells of five or six men, to train them in the use of weapons and to provide the cells with some form of hideout.

Gubbins used several officers who had just been stood down from the Independent Companies in Norway, plus others he had known in Norway. Units were localised with a county structure, as they would probably be fragmented and isolated from each other. Priority was given to the counties most at risk from enemy invasion, the two most vulnerable being Kent and Sussex. Units were quickly under wraps in Norfolk and Suffolk and Essex, with special attention being given to the area of Suffolk around Woodbridge which was felt to be a location the invaders might try to occupy first.[50]

The two best known officers from this period were Captain Mike Calvert of the Royal Engineers and 33-year old Captain Peter Fleming of the Grenadier Guards. Calvert had recently served in the 5th Battalion, Scots Guards; the famous 'Phoney Fifth', which had been formed to fight as a ski-troop in Finland. It became famous for having a couple of hundred officers masquerading in the ranks, presumably because, in the pre-war era, only officer-types would have been able to afford to learn to ski. A company of real Scots Guardsmen had the deep joy of performing any duties requiring the attention of proper soldiers.

Peter Fleming was one of four sons of the barrister and MP Valentine Fleming, who was killed in action in 1917, having served as MP for Henley from 1910. Peter and his younger brother Ian both became writers. Before the war, Peter was perhaps the better known, but after the war his brother Ian's career took off with the creation of 'James Bond'. Peter Fleming was educated at Eton and he went on from Eton to Christ Church, Oxford, graduating with a first-class degree in English. In 1932 he fell in love with the actress Celia Johnson, best known for her roles in the films *Brief Encounter* and *The Prime of Miss Jean Brodie*. They were married on 10 December 1935. Just before war was declared, Peter, then a reserve officer in the Grenadier Guards, was recruited by the War Office research section investigating the potential of irregular warfare (MIR). His initial task

---

50 *Where The Eagle Landed: The Mystery of the German Invasion of Britain, 1940* by Peter Haining (Robson Books, 2004).

was to develop ideas to assist the Chinese guerrillas fighting the Japanese. He served in the Norwegian campaign with the prototype commando units - Independent Companies - but in May 1940 he was tasked with research into the potential use of the new LDV (later the Home Guard) as guerrilla troops. His ideas were first incorporated into General Thorne's XII Corps Observation Unit, forerunner of the GHQ Auxiliary Units.

General Andrew 'Bulgy' Thorne had been Military Attaché in Berlin in the early thirties and had met the Principal of the Charlottenburg High School (the German equivalent of Sandhurst) who showed Thorne around his estates in East Prussia. Whilst there he noticed men digging holes in the ground and filling them with supplies. On enquiry he was told that they were bound to be attacked from the East and could not defend themselves. So, after the enemy had passed over, these men would be able to pop up and play hell with their supplies. Thorne used this tactic in XII Corps which he commanded after Dunkirk and was responsible for the defence of Kent and Sussex. He asked for an officer to start one of these units and he was sent Peter Fleming from the Scots Guards. Along with Mike Calvert they started to form the first of the British Resistance Organisation Units, called the XII Corps Observation Unit. It was formed on 27th June 1940 and later spread, under Colin Gubbins, to cover the whole of the UK. General Thorne also formed Battle Patrols in each Battalion with the same job as the Resistance Organisation, which was to stay behind after the army had invaded - then create havoc amongst the enemy once they had landed. Fleming recruited his brother, Richard, then serving in the Faroe Islands, to provide a core of Lovat Scout instructors to his teams of LDV volunteers. When Colin Gubbins was appointed to head the new Auxiliary Units, he incorporated many of Peter's ideas, which aimed to create secret commando teams of Home Guard in the coastal districts most liable to the risk of invasion. Their role was to launch sabotage raids on the flanks and rear of any invading army, in support of regular troops, but they were never intended as a post-occupation 'resistance' force - having a life expectancy of only two weeks.[51] Members anticipated being shot if they were captured

---

51   Both of these men were too valuable to stay long, once the immediate threat of invasion was over and both later served in Burma, Fleming in deception work and Calvert in the Chindits. Peter Fleming later served in Greece, but his principal service, from 1942 to the end of the war, was as head of D Division, in charge of military deception operations in Southeast Asia, based in New Delhi, India. In 1945 he received an OBE (Military Division) for his services. After the war Fleming retired to squiredom at Nettlebed, Oxfordshire. Fleming died from a heart attack in 1971 while on a shooting expedition near Glencoe in Argyll, Scotland. He is buried in Nettlebed Churchyard.

and if surrounded, they would need to shoot each other or blow themselves up with their own explosives rather than be taken alive.

Gubbins also appointed Captain Andrew Croft, his Intelligence Officer in the Norwegian campaign, as operational and training officer. North of the Thames the Resistance organization that was set up at the same time as Peter Fleming's in Kent and Sussex was a shade less flamboyant but Croft, the son of the Vicar of Kelvedon, in Essex had been the first Head Boy of Stowe, was an Oxford MA and had received the Polar Medal after taking part in the 1933-4 British Trans-Greenland Expedition. He had then been aide-de-camp to the Maharajah of Cooch Behar before returning to Greenland as second-in-command of the Oxford Arctic Expedition. While employed as secretary to the Director of the Fitzwilliam Museum in Cambridge, he had made a third Arctic journey, this time to Lapland with a team of ethnologists. Andrew Croft could fly a plane, was an expert skier and could make himself understood in ten languages. He held a reserve commission in the Essex Regiment and had been an early recruit to MI(R). In 1939 he led a Military Mission to the Finnish Army, moving some dozen shiploads of military supplies across then-neutral Norway and Sweden - everything from first-aid kits to crated Lysander aircraft and Crimean War surplus cannon. The supplies were to be used by a British force of 50,000 men who would fight alongside the Finns. Before this force could be raised, however, Russia and Finland came to terms and Andrew Croft was withdrawn to Norway. He was in Narvik, in uniform, on the day that the German troops landed there and from his hotel window watched them march up from the harbour. Shortly afterwards he joined up with Colin Gubbins's Independent Companies as Brigade Intelligence Officer and he was brought back to Britain in June 1940.

Towards the end of that month Gubbins sent him out to organize Auxiliary Units patrols in Essex, Suffolk and Norfolk. Because he was on his own home ground Andrew Croft needed no help in finding his first recruits. He used his father's home in Kelvedon as his base and soon the barn behind the vicarage was filled with stores of arms and ammunition, waiting to be distributed to the patrols. A lieutenant and about a dozen soldiers sent by Colonel Gubbins helped him to organize his patrols, at first only in Essex and the area of Suffolk south of Woodbridge, which seemed to him to be the part of his territory that German invaders would make for first. His patrol leaders were mainly well-to-do farmers and fruit growers. One very competent leader, at Rayleigh in Essex, was a well-known Canvey Island schoolmaster. He was also the leading local smuggler but had reluctantly to give up that lucrative sideline when France fell. Another, in Suffolk, was a distinguished Master of Foxhounds, with, naturally enough, an unparalleled knowledge of the country which he hunted.

Each patrol leader in East Anglia was allowed to nominate his own men and then Croft screened them. Recruits varied in age and occupation, from young students, factory workers in reserved occupations, miners and farmers, to professional men like doctors and accountants. Age was no barrier, as long as the recruit was fit and capable of existing under the harsh conditions anticipated. Gamekeepers and countrymen of all sorts were much sought after, as well as those with experience of Scouting and woodsmanship. The recruits were told that they were being selected for special Home Guard duties and were being 'posted' to one of three battalions, numbered 201 (Scotland and Northern Counties), 202 (Midlands) and 203 (London and Southern Counties). Whilst these men honestly believed that they were in the Home Guard, this was purely a cover and they were never officially registered as being members.

By the beginning of September Auxiliary Units patrols had been set up in all areas of East Anglia that, according to captured German plans, would have been occupied during the first phase of 'Sealion'. Since they were not enrolled as fighting men, the members of the Auxiliary Units were not strictly covered by the Geneva Convention, although their uniform may have given them some degree of protection against being shot out of hand if captured. Not only were Auxiliary Units given a life expectancy of twelve days, but they were also under orders not to be captured. Most members of the first Auxiliary Units patrols in Kent believed that after a few days or weeks they would have been flushed out by the Germans, but the Resistance men in Essex and Suffolk were more optimistic. They believed that they could have held out indefinitely, replenishing their stores of food and ammunition if necessary from the Germans' own stores.

Captain Croft held his first training sessions in the homes of his patrol leaders, but when the men had prepared their hideouts he began to hold classes underground. By the following November Croft had trained 24 seven- or eight-man groups in Essex, Suffolk and Norfolk. The first patrols were created in the areas deemed most likely for a German invasion force to land first and hence being the most vulnerable: Essex and the area of Suffolk south of Woodbridge. In the following year each of the three Counties was appointed its own Intelligence Officer. Units were localised on a county structure, as they would probably be fragmented and isolated from each other. They were distributed around the coast rather than being country-wide, with priority being given to the counties most at risk from enemy invasion, the two most vulnerable being Kent and Sussex in south east England. Croft then opted to return to Commando units.[52]

Brigadier Gubbins[53] had by then made his HQ and training centre at Coleshill House, a Palladian mansion owned by the Pleydell-Bouveries near the village of Highworth, Wiltshire, about ten miles from Swindon, with large parklands and woods very suitable for guerilla training including assassination, unarmed combat, demolition and sabotage. Recruits for Coleshill reported to the Highworth post office, from where the postmistress Mabel Stranks arranged for their collection. Every Thursday evening large numbers of Patrol Leaders and other ranks would arrive, accommodated in the large stable block, to spend the next two days receiving instruction from Specialists, Lovat Scouts and Physical Training Instructors in the use of modern explosives and weapons and unarmed combat during the day.[54] At night they were transported several miles into the surrounding countryside and required to find their way back in the dark (in the light summer evenings they wore dark eyeshields), marking tanks and aircraft hidden in the woods as destroyed, avoiding tripwires and patrolling sentries. Auxiliary Units received priority, even over the Commandoes, with the issue of plastic explosive and delayed-action chemically-activated time pencils, ideal for silent booby-traps. They were the first troops to be issued with stick pencils, a simple mine stuck in the ground and known later by Eighth Army soldiers as 'castrators', tyre-bursting mines, phosphorous hand grenades, PIAT anti-tank guns and Thompson sub-machine-guns imported from the United States. Individual members were issued with a Fairbairn Commando dagger, which was worn just above the knee, attached to the battledress trousers by five khaki buttons engaging in buttonholed tags in the top and sides of the leather

---

52 Andrew Croft so impressed on his men the necessity for keeping everything about Auxiliary Units secret that even today the majority - including the Suffolk Master of Foxhounds - deny that they ever had anything to do with Resistance activity. Fleming, Croft and Edmundson created the Resistance organizations in the three coastal areas that seemed at the time likeliest to be hit by the first wave of German invaders.
53 In November 1940 Gubbins moved to the Special Operations Executive (SOE).
54 The first courses were about 30 strong of Officers and Sergeants. The course lasted three weeks. David Stirling, who eventually formed the SAS and Fitzroy Maclean, who joined Stirling in the SAS then went to Yugoslavia to help Tito settle the Balkan problem, both attended the first course. Fitzroy attended it in plain clothes (because he was not yet in the Army, he was still in the Foreign Office). The Instructors were handpicked. David and Bill Stirling, Freddie Spencer Chapman, 'Shimi' Lovat, Mike Calvert, Jim Gavin, 'Dan' Fairbairn, 'Bill' Sykes and others. Major R. F. 'Henry' Hall MC, The Dorset Regiment.

sheath, having received instruction in silent killing based on a book by W. E. 'Dan' Fairburn, designer of the Fairburn Field Service Fighting Knife. A former policeman in the seamier areas of Shanghai, Fairburn could write with authority on all the dirty tricks that could be employed in close quarter combat, as well as on the art of silent killing and men were taught to approach German sentries silently and stab them before they had time to warn others. He and Eric Sykes, another Shanghai policeman, taught the vulnerable parts of the body - mouth slitting, ear-trapping to break ear drums, eye-gouging, the grallock (for disemboweling), rib-lifting, 'lifting the gates' - temporary dislocation of the jaw, ear-tearing, nose chopping, shin-scraping with the edge of a boot, shoulder jerking - a sharp pull downwards to dislocate the shoulder and releases to get away from any hold.' Fairbairn would always conclude every piece of advice with the injunction, 'Then kick him in the testacies.'[55] Pistols and rubber truncheons also formed part of the Auxiliaries' equipment and they wore thick rubber-soled boots, later used by the Commandos. In some units certain members were issued with a special .22 rifle fitted with a telescopic sight and silencer, capable of firing high-velocity bullets which could kill a man a mile away. It never became general issue, however, lacking the sturdiness of army rifles.

The courses were very tough. Men were wet, cold, hungry and exhausted most of the time. Anyone who grumbled, or showed a lack of enthusiasm or did not come up to the very high standard demanded, was sent back to his unit immediately. They were shot at most of the time. They were taught map reading, nutrition, hygiene, living off the land, stalking, knife and handgun work and 'Dirty Tricks' for Close Quarter Combat by Fairbairn and Sykes and Assault Landings - all by day and by night.[56]

There was an 'Attery' nearby at Hannington Hall. These sections were commanded by a subaltern with an average of sixteen regular soldiers. Their task was reconnaissance to assist the Auxiliary Unit Patrols. They would also have 'Stayed Behind'. About 3,500 men were trained at Coleshill and, with a number trained locally, a total of nearly 5,000 well-trained and armed men awaited a German invasion.

Returning to their local areas, the patrols continued their training several nights a week, often to the chagrin of regular forces. One patrol breached the security of an airfield, marking several Spitfires as destroyed. In a planned exercise on a military HQ another patrol commandeered a baker's van,

---

55 *With Britain in Mortal Danger* by John Warwicker, 2002.
56 Major R. F. 'Henry' Hall MC.

entered the main building, leaving evidence of the raid, the army commander describing the tactics as unfair, having expected an attack by conventional forces. This exercise highlighted the probability of German parachute troops destroying command HQs and security was tightened accordingly.

Operational Patrols consisted of between four and eight men, often farmers or landowners. They were usually recruited from the most able members of the Home Guard, possessed excellent local knowledge and were able to live off the land.[57] Each Patrol was a self-contained cell, expected to be self-sufficient and operationally autonomous in the case of invasion, generally operating within a fifteen mile radius. They were provided with a concealed underground Operational Base (OB), usually built by the Royal Engineers in local woodland, with a camouflaged entrance and emergency escape tunnel. Auxiliary Units hideouts were supposed to be merely the places to which Resistance men could withdraw to eat, sleep and lie low. Some of the first hideouts appeared to have been built with sieges in mind, with their own early-warning outposts several hundred yards away, connected to them by hidden telephone wires. By the end of 1940 about 300 hideouts would be in use around the country. No two were identical, but most were eventually made large enough to house six or seven men in reasonable comfort, although many at first were little more than fox-holes with log roofs, so badly ventilated that candles sputtered from lack of oxygen and the men who tried sleeping in them all night awoke with headaches. Each hideout was eventually fitted with bunks, cooking stoves, Tilley lamps and other comforts provided by the Army and each was stocked with food and water, in some cases sufficient to sustain a patrol for as long as a month. Wherever dampness was a problem the tinned foods were frequently replaced so that there was never a chance of besieged Auxiliary Units patrols being finished off by food poisoning. Most hideouts had more than enough room for the patrols' arms, ammunition and sabotage material, but in some areas subsidiary hides were dug nearby to hold these and additional stores of food. Paints were found that would resist condensation and efficient ventilating systems, often terminating above ground in tree stumps, were devised. When several senior officers from Coleshill went to the Lincolnshire fens to inspect patrols there they were invited to stay for dinner in one of the hideouts. The officers expected a makeshift meal, probably served on packing cases full of stores,

---

57 They were always intended to fight in Home Guard uniform and from 1942 the men were badged to Home Guard battalions 201 (Scotland), 202 (Northern England), or 203 (Southern England).

but when they slipped down through the trapdoor they were faced with a long dining table covered with a crisp damask cloth. The candles were in candelabra and the cutlery on the table gleamed. Many of the hideouts eventually had chemical lavatories and a few even had running water and some rudimentary form of drainage. The hideouts were so well concealed that anyone walking over them would not notice that the ground beneath their feet had been hollowed out, or that it was unusual in any way. And of course the hideouts had to be made impossible to detect from the air.

Some Patrols had an additional concealed Observation Post and/or underground ammunition store. Patrols were provided with a selection of the latest weapons including a silenced pistol or Sten gun and Fairbairn-Sykes 'commando' knives, quantities of plastic explosive, incendiary devices and food to last for two weeks. Officially they were known as 'operational bases'. The word 'hideout', the officers who ran the Resistance soon decided, suggested a more passive purpose than that for which these bases had been constructed and if overheard by the Germans or their friends, would not alert them to their intended use. Auxiliary Units hideouts were supposed to be merely the places to which Resistance men could withdraw to eat, sleep and lie low. However, some of the first hideouts in Kent appear to have been built with sieges in mind, for they had their own early-warning outposts several hundred yards away, connected to them by hidden telephone wires. And several of the hideouts in Kent were, like the one entered through the sheep trough, built primarily as lookout points.

Undoubtedly the greatest problem was that of digging the hideouts without anyone noticing - not even the members of neighbouring Resistance patrols. In most of the coastal areas the first hideouts had to be dug by the Resistance men themselves, stumbling around late at night and in total darkness. Incredibly, they usually managed to finish the job unnoticed, but anyone who happened across a half-completed hideout had to be fobbed off with some sort of story that would put an end to questions. Everything possible was done to keep the hideouts inconspicuous, the most common trapdoors on the hideouts were simply oak or elm boxes filled with a foot-thick layer of earth. Most of these trapdoors had to be lifted out and to make this easier, many of them were mounted on steel springs that, when a hidden catch was pushed, raised the tray enough for a man to get his fingers under its rim to open it. Several of the trapdoors were inadvertently discovered during the war; one of them in a wood near Great Leighs, Essex, by a courting couple. They suddenly felt the ground begin to move beneath them. When they found out why, in some alarm they notified the police who in turn notified the Army and that hideout was no longer used.

HITLER'S INVASION OF EAST ANGLIA, 1940

The usual cover story was that the hole was being dug for the storage of emergency food supplies for a secret government department - a story that did not make much sense at the time but did stop people asking questions and usually stopped them talking. Speculation about the 'food stores' still continues in some areas of Britain today and there are dark rumours about how 'They' were going to look after themselves all right.

Another major problem which faced the men who built the hideouts was that of disposing the subsoil which they had brought up. Carting this away in the dark was no easy task, especially when one remembers that a cubic foot of earth weighs just over 100lbs and the average Resistance hideout in Britain was about twenty feet long, at least ten feet wide and always high enough for its occupants to stand erect in it. Many of the methods which were worked out for scattering the spoil in Kent were taken up in other counties, but each new hideout presented new problems. Sometimes the men simply scooped away topsoil in a wood, replaced it with the spoil from their hideout, covered this with the original topsoil and laboriously replanted all the undergrowth. In Devon and Cornwall they sometimes carried out the spoil a bucketful at a time and poured it into streams. At Wickhambreaux in Kent near the mouth of the River Stour, earth from an Auxiliary Unit patrol's hideout was moved across the river on an aerial ropeway and added to a fill that had been begun by the Kent River board as an anti-flood barrier long before Auxiliary Units people appeared on the scene. Not far away, in Stocking Wood, near Baddlesmere, about three miles south of Faversham, the chalky sub-soil was so hard to hide that Norman Field hit on a particularly ingenious solution to the problem. He told his men to put the subsoil in a natural hole in the wood and he used a camouflet set to mine it. He then placed a line of the sets across the wood and, the next time German bombers flew over, detonated all the charges. What followed looked and sounded like a stick of bombs exploding and no one questioned the appearance of the chalky craters in the wood.[58]

---

58 In April 1945, when the war in Europe was drawing to a close, the War Office announced to the Press that a Resistance organisation had existed in Britain since 1940 and Sir Harold Franklyn's message of thanks to the men and women who would have been the Auxiliary Units Special Duties Section's spies was published in *The Times* on Saturday, 14 April 1945: 'I realise that every member of the organisation from the first invasion days beginning in 1940 voluntarily undertook a hazardous role which required both skill and courage well knowing that the very nature of their work would allow of no public recognition. This organisation, founded on the keenness and patriotism of selected civilians of all grades, has been in a position, through its constant and thorough training, to furnish accurate information of raids or invasion instantly to military headquarters throughout the country.'

THE LAST DITCH

Separate from the Auxiliary Units' Operational Patrols was the Special Duty Branch, originally recruited by SIS and carefully vetted and selected from the local civilian population. This group - the most 'Top Secret' of all the Auxiliary Units - acted as 'eyes and ears' and would report back to military intelligence any information they heard from 'careless talk' or from watching troop movements and supply routes. About a thousand civilians, men and women, unknown to each other and from all walks of life, acting as 'Coast Watchers', 'Observers', or 'Agents', already in action before the war, probably under MI6. They used Radio Telegraphy called 'TRD Sets' based on the 'Quench' system to ensure perfect security. They also used 'Runners' and 'Dead Letter Drops'. There were ATS Subalterns (under Beatrice Temple, niece of Archbishop Temple) and Signal personnel to back up 'the Agents'. They worked in towns as well as the countryside and came under Regional Officers and later under Auxiliary Units Special Duties Section IO's. Their HQ was at Hannington Hall until 1942 under Major Maurice Petherick, when it was relocated to Coleshill. All members were sworn to everlasting secrecy! - the civilians were unpaid! Their motto was 'Be Like Dad - keep Mum'.

The Special Duty Branch was supported by a signals network of hidden, short-range, wireless sets around the coast. The structure allowed no means of passing on such information to the Operational Patrols. It is unlikely that the wireless network would survive long after invasion and it was therefore unable to link the isolated Operational Patrols into a national network that could act in concert, on behalf of a British government in exile and its representatives still in the United Kingdom. Instead, SIS (MI6) created a separate resistance organisation (Section VII) with powerful wireless sets that was intended to act on a longer-term basis. The Special Duties Sections were largely recruited from the civilian population, with around 4,000 members. They had been trained to identify vehicles, high-ranking officers and military units and were to gather intelligence and leave reports in dead letter drops. The reports would be collected by runners and taken to one of over 200 secret radio transmitters operated by trained civilian signals staff.

Many of Britain's senior military commanders were only too aware that such techniques used in Belgium at Ében-Émael and Holland by the Brandenbergers would be used during an invasion of the UK and Bawdsey Manor's isolated position and susceptibility to a commando style raid, such as the one described, made the RDF station a particularly weak link in the radar defence chain. With the threat of imminent invasion the defence of

HITLER'S INVASION OF EAST ANGLIA, 1940

Bawdsey Manor had suddenly become a major priority and appropriate action was taken. The beaches nearby were heavily mined and covered with coils of barbed wire. Scaffolding poles and other obstacles were also erected to thwart landing craft and a net was put across the mouth of the Deben. As a defence against an airborne landing, the landward side was ringed with pillboxes. There was however a problem, barbed wire and mines may have been in relatively plentiful supply, weapons of all sizes were not. At first the best that could be done for anti-aircraft defence was two old Lewis machine guns of WWI vintage. In early September these were augmented by two 40mm Bofors guns. Even so, it was expected that in an emergency these two guns would double up as coastal artillery and fire on nearby beaches if enemy forces attempted to land. Anti tank defences were even less adequate and consisted of a solitary statically mounted 2-pounder gun, one of only two allocated to the whole of this Brigade sector.

On the RDF site itself, RAF support and technical staff were expected to fight alongside the regular army, but rifles and ammunition were sparse. If someone was killed during an attack they were to pick up his rifle and take his place. Personnel manning the radar equipment were issued with axes, sledgehammers and hand grenades and instructed to use them to destroy the equipment should the station be overrun by the enemy. They were also chillingly informed that the heavy calibre railway gun, just over three miles away at Trimley, had orders to shell the station if the Germans gained a foothold - even if RAF and Army personnel were still on site. On one occasion and quite by chance, several airmen from Bawdsey discovered that a camouflaged field gun defending the approach to the River Deben was no more than a drainpipe on an old pair of cartwheels. It is a little ironic that a vital link in Britain's radar defences, fully acknowledged as a prime target and about to play a pivotal role was being defended by fake artillery and anyone who could hold a rifle.

The dummy field gun ruse does illustrate the problems faced in the summer of 1940, not just at Bawdsey, but across the country as a whole. Recognising the need to provide vulnerable points with a higher level of protection was one thing, providing it following the disaster of Dunkirk was quite another. Any available piece of military hardware was being pressed into service. Old 6-inch calibre naval guns salvaged from warships destined for the breaker's yards were put into service as 'emergency' coastal batteries. By September 1940 over a dozen coast batteries were sited between Bawdsey and Lowestoft, including 328 Battery at Aldeburgh, 353 at Sizewell, 232 at Minsmere and 409 at Dunwich. Several were installed as part of Felixstowe's defences and just to the north of Bawdsey Manor, at Bawdsey East Lane, two old 4-inch naval guns were set up in an improvised emplacement as a temporary measure.[59] Other emergency batteries were set up elsewhere, but even these old guns were in short supply. Consequently the coastal shore batteries needed to defend a vulnerable coastline were few and far between. Given the circumstances, the very best that could be done to defend the east coast's open beaches was barbed wire and mines - defences that in reality would have posed no substantial obstacle to the Nazi invader.

---

59 The improvised battery at Bawdsey was replaced by a more permanent static emplacement (part of which still remains to this day) manned by 332 Coastal Battery, Royal Artillery. Up until being moved to Bawdsey, 332 Battery, comprising two old 6-inch naval guns, had been situated at Foulness Point, Essex. The 'Fort log book' for the new emplacement released at the PRO in 1973 contains an index of contents, listing page 21 as being a 'history of [the] site.' This, it would be expected, should contain brief details of what was on the site before 332 Battery arrived. Curiously however, the page is missing and it is clearly evident that it has been torn out.

Chapter 4

If the Invader Comes

'As soon as we beat England, we shall make an end of you Englishmen once and for all. Able-bodied men and women will be exported as slaves to the Continent. The old and weak will be exterminated. All men remaining in Britain as slaves will be sterilised; a million or two of the young women of the Nordic type will be segregated in a number of stud farms where, with the assistance of picked German sires, during a period of ten or twelve years, they will produce annually a series of Nordic infants to be brought up in every way as Germans. These infants will form the future population of Britain... Thus, in a generation or two, the British will disappear.
Richard Walther Darré (born Ricardo Walther Oscar Darré; 14 July 1895-5 September 1953), one of the leading Nazi 'Blut und Boden' ('blood and soil') ideologists who served as Reichsminister of Food and Agriculture 1933-1942. He was an SS-Obergruppenführer and the seventh most senior officer of the SS. When WWII ended, Darré was the senior most SS-Obergruppenführer, with date of rank from 9th November 1934, outranked only by Heinrich Himmler and the four SS-Oberst-Gruppenführer. At the Nuremberg War Trials Darré was sentenced to seven years at Landsberg Prison but was released in 1950. He died in a Munich hospital on 5 September 1953 of liver cancer.

In September 1939, the novelist and journalist Dennis Wheatley, then 43 years old, had offered his services to the newly formed Ministry of Information but he had been turned down and instead he threw himself into writing *The Scarlet Imposter,* a topical novel set during the early months of the war and culminating in a plot to assassinate Hitler. Wheatley had an especial interest in the threat posed by the Nazis and in the events in the Spanish Civil War. During the First World War he was commissioned as a 2nd Lieutenant into the Royal Field Artillery. He was assigned to the City of London Brigade and the 36th (Ulster) Division. Wheatley was gassed in a chlorine attack during Passchendaele and was invalided out, having served in Flanders, on the Ypres Salient and in France at Cambrai and St. Quentin. In 1919 he took over management of the family's wine business. In 1931, however, after business had declined because of the Great Depression, he sold the firm and began writing. Wheatley mainly wrote adventure novels, with many books in a series of linked works. His first book, *Three Inquisitive People*, was not published when completed, but came out later, in 1940. However, his next novel, called *The Forbidden Territory* was an immediate success when issued by Hutchinson in 1933, being reprinted seven times in seven weeks. The release in 1934 of his occult story, *The Devil Rides Out* - hailed by James Hilton as 'the best thing of its kind since Dracula' - cemented his reputation as 'The Prince of Thriller Writers'.

Overlooked by the Ministry of Information, Wheatley busied himself with another book during the winter of 1940, but his wife Joan had been recruited by MI5 and in an office in St. James Street, London had been put in charge of petrol allocation. On 27 May, the day the evacuation of Dunkirk began, she was driving Captain Hubert Stringer, an army officer engaged in counterespionage, who was certain that Hitler's next move would be to invade England. He had been tasked to think up schemes for resistance to invasion but apart from the 'routine stuff' admitted that he was having difficulty in offering anything further. Joan immediately put her husband's name forward and in due course Wheatley was a member of the London Controlling Section, which secretly coordinated strategic military deception and cover plans. He wrote numerous papers for the planning staffs for the War Office, including suggestions for dealing with a possible Nazi invasion of Britain beginning with *Resistance to Invasion*.[60]

As a child Wheatley had holidayed with his parents on the east coast of England and had spent some time as a naval cadet at Harwich with close friends in Aldeburgh and Cromer. *Dark August,* one of Wheatley's earliest novels, written in 1934, in which the plot describes an England a few years

---

60 The most famous of his submissions to the Joint Planning Staff of the war cabinet was on 'Total War' and his war papers are recounted in his works *Stranger than Fiction* and *The Deception Planners*. Wheatley invented a number of board games including *Invasion* (1938) and *Blockade* (1939). He received a direct commission in the JP Service as a Wing Commander, RAFVR and took part in the plans for the Normandy invasion.

hence about to be taken over by a group of communist revolutionaries called the 'greyshirts' who seize Scotland and Wales and march on London. A party of dedicated royalists including the prospective MP for Mid-Suffolk and a pretty young secretary flee from the panic and chaos in London to set up a last defence in Shingle Street, which is attacked and set on fire by 'a blinding sheet of flame as the projectiles struck them and then disappear, so that the remnants of the burning hamlet began to take on the appearance of a row of black and jagged teeth which were being steadily extracted.' The wounded defenders that litter the beach are only prevented from being burned alive by the arrival of counterrevolutionaries led by the Prince Regent.

In his lengthy document, *The Invasion and Conquest of Britain*, Wheatley imagined how the Nazis would plan an invasion. He believed that in the prelude to invasion the enemy would bomb both military and civilian targets and might also try to infiltrate troops disguised as parachutists, concealed in cargo ships and other vessels, supported by the activities of Secret agents and Fifth-Columnists. Wheatley was under no illusions about the lengths of brutality any enemy invasion of Britain would take, including the use of poison gas and bacteriological warfare. In an article for the *Evening News* in 1969, Wheatley said that the War Office 'had not envisaged the possibility of airborne landings designed to cut England into three sections and had placed the main landings on the coast of Suffolk. As a result, a special Committee under General Denning and Air Marshal Slessor was set up to re-examine the probabilities. My paper was studied by the Committee and afterwards Slessor told me that large parts of it had been adopted in their new and final approach. ...After the war, when the documents of the German General Staff were seized and examined, it transpired that in Operation 'Sea Lion'...I had been right in all my major assumptions! Having thoroughly frightened myself, I at once sat down to write a third paper of 12,000 words, *Further Measures for Resistance to Invasion*, which I dispatched to all those who had received my first two papers on 28 June.'

A fourth paper, *Village Defence*, soon followed.[61]

On Tuesday, 18th June 1940 the commander of the 55th Infantry Division informed Sir Will Spens the eastern Regional Commissioner that

---

61 See *Where The Eagle Landed: The Mystery of the German Invasion of Britain, 1940* by Peter Haining (Robson Books, 2004). In 1970 Haining interviewed Wheatley who 'inspired my interest in an intriguing episode of history' and dedicated his book to his memory. Dennis Wheatley died on 10 November 1977.

preparations were being made to mine all of the beaches to the north of Bawdsey Manor, right up to and including Hollesley Bay close to where the River Ore meets the North Sea. The commander of the 165th Infantry Brigade was given authority from 55th Divisional command to close all civilian access to beaches in his sector. On 4 June Winston Churchill had vowed to 'fight on the beaches'. Now it was deemed that all inhabitants save the Coastguard, including those living in the 19th century Martello tower at Shingle Street, were to be evacuated. Originally, the small isolated coastal hamlet situated within sight of the tall radar masts of Bawdsey Manor at the mouth of Orford Ness was a home for fishermen and river pilots for the Ore. The Martello tower was the most northerly of four that had kept watch over the bay since Napoleonic times when England and the coast of East Anglia had last faced the threat of invasion. The coastguards were auxiliary personnel. Like many other similar units they consisted of local men enrolled to keep watch along the coast and back up the regular coastguard, which by 1940 was under the control of the Admiralty. Up until this time, the small detachment at Shingle Street had shared beach patrols along Hollesley Bay with their colleagues from Bawdsey.

The evacuation process had been underway for several weeks, starting with precautionary measures almost immediately following the German invasion of the Low Countries on 10th May. Among those moved out in May and June were the boys from HMS *Ganges* (Shotley) and *Arethusa* (Chatham), all the London children brought to the area at the outbreak of war and most of the women and children of Sheerness, Southend, Harwich, Felixstowe, Lowestoft and Great Yarmouth. Under new security precautions control of civilian movements became much stricter. Checkpoints kept all but local residents and servicemen out of every East Coast town with a naval base and beyond half a mile from RDF stations and airfields. All the piers from Margate via Clacton and Felixstowe to Skegness were breached, except for Southend, already occupied by the Navy. All seafront cafés and hotels closed and practically all premises facing the sea were requisitioned, boarded up and sandbagged.[62] On 13 May an Ipswich Air Raid Warden noted in his diary that: 'Regulations are being tightened up around the coast, couldn't get into Felixstowe without registration cards and there are barricades on all the principle roads. Barbed wire barricades at Colchester closed at 2100.' Measures intensified over the following weeks. Divisional Army Commands in coastal areas ordered their subordinate units to accelerate all work on defences during the day and

---

62 *The Battle of the East Coast (1939-1945)* by J. P. Foynes.

man them as fully as possible by night. In June all beaches were mined, scaffolded against landing craft, entangled with barbed wire and studded with concrete obstacles.

On Saturday 22nd June, when a nationwide ban was placed on the ringing of church bells, the day was less than three hours old when a lone German aircraft, returning from an air raid over Ipswich, dropped a single bomb in fields to the west of Shingle Street. Later that same morning Sir Will Spens, acting under Defence Regulation 16(a), gave the inhabitants just 72 hours notice to pack whatever they needed and leave their isolated row of dwellings on the shore of Hollesley Bay before midnight on the twenty fifth; 'after which time no person shall enter said village except by the express permission of the Regional Commissioner, the Military Authorities, or the Police.' Spens, born in Glasgow on 31 May 1882, one of four sons of John Spens and Sophia Nicol, was educated at Rugby and King's College, Cambridge, graduating in natural sciences. Elected a Fellow of Corpus Christi College in 1907, he had spent the rest of his working life in Cambridge, apart from wartime service between 1915 and 1918 with the Foreign Office. His appointment as eastern Regional Commissioner had prompted rumours that the cellars of Corpus, which extend across (and indeed further than) the entire college campus, were to be used as the centre of operations for East Anglia in the event of a German occupation.

As a matter of extreme urgency the 165th Infantry Brigade proceeded to mine the beach at Shingle Street and block off all exit routes from the foreshore and access to the hinterland. A rudimentary gun emplacement, mounting two old 4-inch naval guns, was set up at Bawdsey East Lane to defend the exit leading off the lower end of the bay. To deny access from the beach to the 'first class' tank country beyond; work began on the construction of a wide anti-tank ditch to the rear of the bay, running its entire length right up towards the village of Hollesley. This ditch would also cut across the upper exit from the bay - the single uncategorised road that led into Shingle Street. This would in turn cut off the tiny community from the outside world and forever seal the fate of the hamlet. Despite what was said in the evacuation order, the closure of the road meant that the coastguard would also have to leave along with the rest of the inhabitants. For the remainder of the war they would be stationed in another Martello Tower roughly half a mile to the southwest. Similarly their Bawdsey colleagues would be stationed in a Martello Tower almost a mile and a half away, just to the south of Bawdsey East Lane and the emergency coastal battery. As far as is known, the two remaining towers, including the one in Shingle Street itself, remained unused throughout the war.

Early on the afternoon of 26 September, all military personnel were evacuated from the immediate vicinity of Shingle Street and the hamlet was then blasted by the howitzers of 'D' troop, 72nd Medium Regiment, Royal Artillery. Whatever the underlying reason for this act of destruction was, it was simply recorded as a 'practice shoot'. Ronald Harris, one of the auxiliary coastguard personnel had lived in a wooden, pan-tiled bungalow called 'Ronina' beside the wood, lathe and plaster walled 'Lifeboat Inn' in Shingle Street but it was damaged beyond repair. Following the order to vacate the village, he and several of his colleagues found accommodation in Hollesley village nearby. From then on they would be near their former homes only while on duty. Little did they know, but it would be almost nine years before they, or any other of the villagers would be allowed back into their homes. Harris had to wait until 1949 for a new, more permanent house to be completed. The 'Lifeboat Inn' was completely demolished.

What happened at Shingle Street was not unique; many civilians were forced out of their homes as the whole of the east coast was being prepared to face the almost certain threat of invasion. By mid June the civil authorities were overseeing the evacuation of schoolchildren from the eastern counties and a twenty mile wide coastal belt from The Wash to Rye in Sussex had been declared a 'Defence Area.' This was in effect an exclusion zone under military and police control. Civilian movement within the defence area was restricted and curfews (lasting from one hour after sunset till one hour before sunrise) were in place, leading to some towns being 'locked down' after dusk. Civilian access to beaches along the whole of the east coast had also been prohibited.

Just three days before Shingle Street's inhabitants were ordered out of their homes, the Ministry of Information had begun nationwide distribution of posters and leaflets bearing the bold heading: IF THE INVADER COMES'.

Prepared by the Ministry of Home Security under the direction of the War Cabinet, the leaflets gave proscribed instructions on 'what to do - and how to do it' when the invasion came. The double-sided flyer delivered to homes across the nation began with the reassuring lines: 'The Germans threaten to invade Great Britain. If they do so they will be driven out by our Navy, our Army and our Air Force. Meanwhile, read these instructions carefully and be prepared to carry them out.'

HITLER'S INVASION OF EAST ANGLIA, 1940

The seven concise instructions that followed were each accompanied by brief explanatory notes:

1. If the Germans come ... remain where you are. THE ORDER IS 'STAY PUT'.
2. They [the Germans] make use of the civilian population in order to create confusion and panic. DO NOT BELIEVE RUMOURS AND DO NOT SPREAD THEM.
3. The ordinary man and woman must be on watch. If you see anything suspicious, note it carefully and go at once to the nearest police ... or military officer. DO NOT RUSH ABOUT SPREADING VAGUE RUMOURS.
4. DO NOT GIVE ANY GERMAN ANYTHING. DO NOT TELL HIM ANYTHING. Hide your food, bicycles and maps. See that the enemy gets no petrol. If you have a car or motor bicycle, put it out of action. If you are a garage proprietor, make sure that no invader will be able to get hold of your cars, petrol, maps or bicycles.
5. Be ready to help the military in any way. BUT DO NOT BLOCK ROADS UNTIL ORDERED TO DO SO BY THE MILITARY OR LDV AUTHORITIES.
6. If you are in charge of a factory, store or other works, organise its defence at once. ALL MANAGERS AND WORKMEN SHOULD ORGANISE SOME SYSTEM NOW BY WHICH A SUDDEN ATTACK CAN BE RESISTED.
7. In the event of an invasion ... detailed instructions may be given to you by the Military, Police and LDV - they will NOT be given over the wireless as that might convey information to the enemy.

Remember always that the best defence of Great Britain is the courage of her men and women.

THINK BEFORE YOU ACT. BUT THINK ALWAYS OF YOUR COUNTRY BEFORE YOU THINK OF YOURSELF.

While the military and civil authorities prepared to meet the threat, the newspapers and cinema newsreels portrayed a defiant, unified nation preparing to 'defend every town, every village and every street.' Some newspapers even went as far as printing full instructions on how to use the Lee Enfield 303 service rifle and how to make petrol bombs. Other reports assured the public that the regular army was being expanded at the rate of 7000 men a day and that the LDV would soon be fully armed. Mr. Churchill himself referred to 'Britain's large and growing army and the strength of our defences' and in a speech made on 14 July, he said: 'Any plan for invading Britain which Hitler made two months ago must have had to be totally recast to meet our new position'. One popular magazine printed pictures of an imagined invasion, with enemy ships and barges heading into the jaws of a heavily defended coast. The legend beneath this picture of impending doom read: 'the defence measures [shown]... should make invasion a most perilous undertaking for the enemy.' And if other newspaper reports were to be believed, persistent RAF attacks on French and Belgian Channel ports were having a 'devastating' effect on Hitler's invasion preparations.

But the press operated under strict government controls and the defiant headlines were designed to mask the grave reality of Britain's desperate situation. The Army had lost vast stocks of weapons and equipment in France; everything was in short supply, including rifles and the ammunition to put in them. Rifles from reserves stocks were issued to the frontline units of the regular army, some of them WW1 vintage. Even so it was not enough and although units in coastal areas were being given priority the picture was bleak - as the war diaries of many units testify. The War Diary of the 46th Infantry Brigade, based in Essex, notes that at the end of June three Thompson sub-machine guns had been delivered to Brigade HQ and would be distributed: 'on a scale of one per Battalion with more to follow'. This effectively meant one 'Tommy gun' between seven to eight hundred men. The 2/4 Battalion of the South Lancashire Regiment, guarding the Suffolk coast near Dunwich, were also impressed with the acquisition of a sole Tommy gun 'firing .45 bullets', but they were still awaiting another eight anti-tank rifles to bring them up to a full complement. Reading the same page the relief can almost be felt when it is stated that 'two 3-inch trench mortars have arrived - at last!' The South Lancs were not the only infantry battalion waiting in vain for anti-tank rifles and machineguns. On 20 July General Headquarters Home Forces received a letter from C-in-C Eastern Command urgently requesting eight Bren guns and four anti tank rifles to equip an anti tank unit at Frinton. Two weeks later GHQ replied that Bren guns and anti tank rifles were being issued 'only on a priority basis' and could not authorise the order. The same scarcity of supply also applied to light machine guns and suitable anti tank rifles. Although the Boys .55 inch calibre anti-tank rifle was not a particularly effective weapon it was better than nothing and next to nothing was what many units were expected to face the invading enemy with.

HITLER'S INVASION OF EAST ANGLIA, 1940

If the supply of arms to the regular army was bad, it was far worse for the Home Guard and they were now expected to fight alongside the frontline infantry. So dire was the need for small-arms that many Home Guard units, including Felixstowe, put in requests for the loan of shotguns, but even these seemed to be in short supply. Contemporary accounts tell of shotguns being shared between two men with literally a handful of cartridges being the only ammunition available. A special 12-bore cartridge with larger shot was hastily issued in the hope that it would provide more 'stopping power.' A little later, old American manufactured Enfield PI7 rifles were issued, painted with bright red stripes around the stock to denote that they chambered non standard .300-calibre ammunition. This helped the situation to some extent, but the fact of the matter was that the shortage of small-arms was still compounded by the shortage of ammunition. The Commander in Chief Home Forces, General Ironside, assured a meeting of Home Guard commanders that gunsmiths throughout the country were being scoured for all available stocks of ammunition. In late August the regular army raised the issue of ammunition from ten rounds to fifty rounds per man, but this was still very low. By comparison, during WWI most British frontline infantrymen carried 100 rounds each in pouches and more in additional cloth bandoliers. Also, ammunition boxes containing thousands of rounds were stockpiled in the forward trenches.

The supply of arms and ammunition was no better with the bigger guns. On 13 June 355 Coastal Battery had moved its old 6-inch naval guns from Felixstowe to Sizewell. Both guns had been mounted and were ready within a matter of days, but there was no ammunition for them. A little further down the coast the 59th Medium Regiment, Royal Artillery had managed to install two more ageing 4-inch naval guns, but had not assembled their six pounders and had no proper mountings for them. They were eventually placed on emergency wooden platforms. To make up for deficiencies in coastal artillery, anti-aircraft guns along the coast were expected to engage enemy ships close to shore and also fire on the beaches. But if there was little enough ammunition of any calibre to use against the enemy there was even less to practice with. Live firing exercises were limited and many manoeuvres and schemes could only take place on paper. A typical example of this was a large scale telecommunications exercise held by the 55th Infantry Division that took place at the end of July 1940. Nineteen log sheets contain 149 messages recording the flow of communications between forward coastal units and Divisional Command HQ during an imaginary invasion. The first message, timed at 0230 on 28 July, reports that two pocket battleships and a large number of destroyers are heading for the east coast. Over twelve hours later the coastguard at Shingle Street reported that enemy troops had landed one mile to the south. The final message, timed at 18:45 the following day, reported that the enemy invading force had been successfully contained and were about to be eliminated. As a paper exercise the scheme had obviously been a success, but given the actual state of Britain's defences at this time, dealing with a real invasion force would have been nowhere near as easy.

And if a lack of weapons and ammunition was not bad enough Britain's defenders faced another problem - lack of men. Many coastal units were severely under strength, the plight of the 15th Infantry Division defending the Essex coast was fairly typical. The requirement for adequate defence of the sector to the south of Harwich was fourteen battalions. The actual strength, at least on paper, was eight, but in reality it was only six. After providing for the protection of the rear perimeter and vulnerable points against airborne attack this left only two battalions for beach defence. Further up the coast in Suffolk and Norfolk the picture was just as bleak. On 29 June the Commanding Officer of XI Corps, the higher command responsible for the defence of East Anglia, replied tersely to a GHQ Home Forces memo, stating that he had disposed his available troops as he saw fit. He finished: 'It will be realised that it is not possible to hold every beach on which [enemy] troops can be landed.' This exchange between a senior army officer and the War Office highlights the grim reality of the situation all too clearly. The fullest possible use was made of all troops on coastal defence and it was prohibited to remove men for any other duties, especially those manning coastal artillery units. Even so there was still a manpower shortage. In order to make up numbers, shore based naval units, including sailors from training establishments, were expected to take part in coastal defence and fight alongside the army and Home Guard. In Great Yarmouth, sailors from the shore base HMS *Watchful*, armed with rifles and petrol bombs, were used to man roadblocks to the rear of the town. Five hundred and fifty naval ratings from a training depot at HMS *Ganges* were to be used to defend the rear perimeter of the port of Harwich. The situation became so pressing that Coastguard personnel, including those at Shingle Street and Bawdsey were also armed. Inland, 3,500 rifles were made available to the London Metropolitan police to 'assist' the army during an invasion of the capital. It was made abundantly clear to frontline defences be they soldier, sailor or Home Guard, that positions would be held at all costs and 'there would be no withdrawal'; the older soldiers knew only too well what this order meant.

HITLER'S INVASION OF EAST ANGLIA, 1940

Emergency coastal batteries lacked ammunition and hastily constructed and improvised defences were manned by virtually anyone who could hold a rifle - if a rifle and ammunition could be found. It was under these dire circumstances that the drastic decision was made, at the very highest levels of command, to issue mustard gas shells, many from WWI stocks, to artillery units in coastal areas. Gas bombs were also issued to frontline RAF squadrons because, if the Germans landed, mustard gas would be dropped on the beaches.[63] These measures were supposed to have been used only as a 'last resort'. Although both Britain and Germany were signatories to the Geneva Protocols of 1925 banning the use of chemical weapons, this had not stopped their development and manufacture. At the outbreak of WWII both countries possessed large stocks of modern chemical weapons and delivery systems and they would have been fully prepared to use them. Spraying of Mustard gas from aircraft, referred to in Air Ministry files as S.C.I., had been under development when war broke out and was fitted to a variety of specially adapted aircraft, including Lysanders, Blenheims and Fairey Battles. Aircraft equipped to spray gas had previously been sent to France with the Advanced Attack squadrons of the RAF. During the invasion period these aircraft were stationed with the forward squadrons, ready to fly over and literally drench any beach on which the enemy landed with Mustard gas. But poison gas in itself could not compensate for the lack of weapons and equipment. There was no alternative but to improvise and given the British flair for ingenuity this led to a variety of weird and wonderful ideas being suggested or tried out.

On 13 July the Air Officer Commanding-in-Chief, Training Command was ordered to plan to make the maximum practical number of aircraft

---

63 At very high concentrations, if inhaled, mustard agent, really a liquid with the consistency of diesel oil, causes bleeding and blistering within the respiratory system, damaging mucous membranes and causing pulmonary edema. Depending on the level of contamination, mustard agent burns can vary between first and second degree burns, though they can also be every bit as severe, disfiguring and dangerous as third degree burns. Severe mustard agent burns (i.e. where more than 50% of the victim's skin has been burned) are often fatal, with death occurring after some days or even weeks have passed. Mustard agent was first used effectively in World War I by the German army against British and Canadian soldiers near Ypres, Belgium, in 1917 and later also against the French Second Army. The Allies did not use mustard agent until November 1917 at Cambrai, France, after the armies had captured a stockpile of German mustard-gas shells. It took the British more than a year to develop their own mustard agent weapon, with production of the chemicals centred on Avonmouth Docks.

available for bombing operations under the codename 'Operation Banquet'.[64] The RAF was prepared to use just about anything that would fly, excepting those in Fighter Command, including training aircraft, as makeshift bombers. In a separate initiative called Operation 'Banquet Light', 350 de Havilland Tiger Moth biplanes and other light aircraft of the Elementary Flight Training School would each be fitted with improvised bomb racks which had been designed for the DH.84M, the military version of the Dragons supplied to Iraq eight years previously. Trials were conducted at Hatfield by Major Hereward de Havilland and at the Aeroplane and Armament Experimental Establishment at Boscombe Down and the machines earned a perfectly satisfactory report. Tests were also carried out with a Tiger Moth carrying a single 240lb bomb. Modification of the relatively small number of Magister trainers were also attempted, but this proved troublesome, therefore 'Banquet Light' mostly used Tiger Moths. Flown by trainee pilots they would each drop eight 20lb bombs on any enemy invasion armada that approached the coast. Dummy bombs for training were so hard to come by that the pilots often had to use bricks on practice flights. 'Banquet' was cancelled in October 1943 having never been put into effect, which is probably just as well because the plan was virtually suicidal.

Veterans of the Spanish Civil War taught Home Guard units how to ambush and disable armoured vehicles using makeshift weapons, including the infamous 'Molotov Cocktail'. These homemade petrol bombs, used by Finnish troops against Russian tanks during the 'Winter War' of 1939 were produced in huge numbers and became standard issue to the Home Guard and regular army. In the defence areas the supply of 'Molotov Bombs' to strong points and road blocks was treated as a matter of urgency. A 'self igniting type' using phosphorous was developed, but it was difficult to store and probably downright dangerous to use. Because of the shortage of rifles, soldiers and Home Guard on airfield defence duty were issued with old sword bayonets welded into a length of pipe. This 1940 version of the 'pike', a weapon more appropriate to Tudor warfare, consequently became the butt of much derision. Other airfield defence measures included

---

[64] 'Banquet 6 Group' would see the absorption of 6 Group Pool units into the operational striking force of RAF Bomber Command. 'Banquet 22 Group' would move certain 22 group (Army Cooperation) aircraft into the operational striking force of Bomber Command and 'Banquet Alert' called for the employment of Fleet Air Arm training aircraft under Coastal Command and 'Banquet' Training which called for the absorption of aircraft from Training Command into the operational striking force of Bomber Command.

old lorries armoured with concrete for use as mobile pillboxes. There was even a plan to lay herring nets on Kent beaches to trip up enemy troops as they disembarked. And it was not just Britain's army that was preparing to launch a last ditch offensive should the invasion come.

It seemed that Britain's best hope rested in not letting the Germans set foot on British soil at all which Churchill had demanded and this task would fall to the Royal Navy. Not only was the Royal Navy larger than the German Kriegsmarine, but it had already put in place offshore defensive measures and long before there had been any threat of invasion. Within days of war being declared in September 1939 the Admiralty began laying an extensive offshore minefield to protect the east coast from German warships. By the summer of 1940 this defensive mine barrier, situated approximately forty miles or so offshore, ran practically all the way up the east coast of England. Several supposedly secret channels, including one off Aldeburgh and another opposite The Wash, ran through the barrier to allow Royal Navy warships out into the North Sea but the Germans had managed to determine the locations of these 'gaps' and both E-boats and U-boats regularly passed through them to operate close to the east coast. So frequent were these attacks that the area off the Norfolk coast near Smith's Knoll became known colloquially as 'E-Boat Alley.'[65] Nine months later, with the threat of invasion having moved from 'possible' to 'imminent', the RN proceeded to strengthen defences closer to shore. The mouth of The Wash and the approaches to some larger harbours including Great Yarmouth were mined. Other offshore anti-invasion measures were also implemented, including net obstructions to foul the propellers enemy E-boats. However, despite its size and capabilities the Royal Navy was also heavily involved in guarding Atlantic convoys, hunting enemy commerce raiders and various other duties in the far flung corners of the world. This reduced the number of warships available to protect home waters, leaving the possibility that RN forces might not be able to intercept an enemy invasion force and prevent it reaching British shores, as had happened on several occasions during WWI. Faced with this situation, the Admiralty prepared plans to use 'fire ships'. It was proposed that barges filled with fifty tons of oil and petrol should

---

65 E-boat (Schnellboot or S-Boot, meaning 'fast boat') was the British designation (using the letter E for Enemy) for fast attack craft of the Kriegsmarine. The most popular, the S-100 class, were very seaworthy, heavily armed and capable of sustaining 43.5 knots (50.1 mph) and briefly accelerating to 48 knots (55 mph). Their three Daimler Benz MB 501 marine diesel engines gave substantially longer range (approximately 700 nautical miles) than the American PT boat and the generally similar British Motor Torpedo Boat (MTB). It had a complement: of 24-30 men.

be kept moored at strategic points and in the event of an enemy landing: 'be allowed to drift down on the tide in amongst the enemy ships and then be detonated by time bombs'. As events transpired this scheme was never adopted, but the idea of fighting an attempted invasion with fire would be put into practice.

Had the Germans invaded during late June or July and established several substantial bridgeheads in southern or eastern England, in particular taking airfields, this would have given them the ability to launch a 'Blitzkrieg' on British soil. This may have created a military situation similar to that in Belgium and France just weeks before and probably with the same end result - a British armistice. During the summer of 1940 Britain's defenders were in no doubt that they faced the clear and present threat of imminent invasion and many senior military commanders were also well aware that the country was ill-equipped to defend itself against the Nazi war machine. Following Dunkirk, with the British Army unable to deploy no more than six fully combat ready infantry divisions (120,000 men), there would have been some difficulty countering any large scale campaign that followed a successful landing. This situation would improve by the early autumn, but in the interim period it was necessary for the British government to create a propaganda facade in order to mask the very desperate circumstances the nation faced and maintain both military and civilian morale. Most of this government sponsored propaganda appeared in the national press. While newspaper reports warned of imminent invasion, they also assured the public that Hitler's invasion fleet was being destroyed and that any armada that did approach Britain's shores would be annihilated. There was a grain of truth in this. The ever growing invasion armada in continental ports was being bombed by the RAF, though with varying degrees of success and certainly not with the devastating effects being claimed in the British press. But behind the reassuring newspaper headlines and cinema newsreels, those who were only too aware of the stark reality of the situation were busy preparing for what seemed to be the inevitable.

Well before volunteers began to swell the ranks of the LDV, Britain's War Cabinet had already set up the Home Defence Executive in order to co-ordinate anti-invasion preparations between the military and local civil authorities. By the end of May the government's senior intelligence assessment and advisory body, the Joint Intelligence Committee, had created its own Invasion Warning Sub-Committee (IWSC) which would scrutinise and assess every piece of available information relating to enemy invasion preparations in order to determine when and where the invasion

HITLER'S INVASION OF EAST ANGLIA, 1940

would fall. Their first report of 31st May, relating to enemy reconnaissance of the British Isles, notes the suspicious activity of a U-boat off the east coast port of Great Yarmouth, 'an unusual area for U-boats to operate'.

The general consensus of opinion in Military and Intelligence circles, at least initially, was that the invasion would fall on the coast of East Anglia. This assumption was revised later, when, from late July onwards, all the available information began to indicate an invasion across the Channel from France and Belgium. The primary evidence was the build-up of barges in Channel ports from Dunkirk to Le Havre and there was also a noticeable increase in Luftwaffe units and troop concentrations in northern France. A British Intelligence report of 29th July notes that the Luftwaffe had been ordered to avoid attacking harbours and quays on England's south coast. Just over one week later Military Intelligence reported that the Germans had ordered all leave for military police battalions to be completed by 31st August; the implication being that military police units were to be at full strength after this date, for obvious reasons. Despite all of this, the IWSC still expected the invasion to fall on the east coast and believed that the buildup of barges in Belgium and France was a decoy operation aimed at convincing the British that the invasion, when it came, would fall on the Sussex/Kent coast. The IWSC's suspicions were not totally unfounded. During the early part of July all U-boats were withdrawn from patrols in the North Sea, just as they had been prior to the invasion of Norway. A few weeks later the command of the 55th Infantry Division noted: 'the enemy has not laid magnetic mines in the following areas - The Naze and Hollesley [Bay] and Sizewell and Lowestoft. Taken with the fact that the enemy has heavily mined the sea off Orfordness which is unsuitable for a landing may possibly be an indication of his intention.' Clearly the commander of the 55th Division suspected that if the enemy had not mined the approaches to these beaches it was for a very good reason. Whether or not the IWSC was correct and the preparations in France and Belgium were a feint, will probably never be known.

'Sealion' also included plans for other diversionary measures, including Operation 'Green', a feint towards Ireland by 4,000 troops of the 4th and 7th Army Corps, embarking from western France. Another major deception, codenamed 'Herbstreise' or 'Autumn Voyage' involved a decoy force of transports and warships approaching the east coast between Newcastle and Aberdeen on the eve of the major invasion. This would draw British military and naval forces away from the 'real' invasion attempt about to take place elsewhere. Other planed deceptions included transmitting radio messages on British frequencies giving locations of non-existent invasion armadas or 'ghost fleets', once again drawing attention away from the real invasion fleet. Even before Hitler had ordered the German armed forces to prepare for an invasion of the British mainland, thousands of airborne troops were being assembled in Norway and northern Germany. Many had practised street and house to house fighting in an abandoned Polish village - specially altered to resemble an English town. They would have spearheaded the assault on Britain and using the same tactics of surprise and infiltration would capture strategic points and airfields, just as they had done in Norway and the Low Countries. Large numbers of E-boats were being gathered in Dutch and German ports. Some, armed with one twin and one single 20 mm C/30 cannon and a 37 mm Flak 42 cannon, were to be manned by specially selected crews familiar with the British coast and would be used to guide the main force. Senior military chiefs were fully aware that a large fleet of such craft could possibly land several thousand men in a 'lightening raid' on the British coast. Special 'Sturmkommando' assault units practiced seaborne landing operations on remote parts of the Baltic coast, including the Estonian Islands. Comprised exclusively of unmarried men, corporals and NCOs, their purpose would be to land covertly and form a bridgehead on the English coast. Transported to within three miles of the shoreline under cover of darkness, groups of four or five men heavily armed with machine guns, mortars and grenades would row ashore in dinghies. Having landed the Sturmkommando would secure a series of small local bridgeheads; these would then be widened into a 'connected' landing zone, allowing the landing of more troops and equipment. In order to land as many men as possible in the shortest time the commandoes would commandeer and use any available boats they found in the locality.

Several Brandenburger units, which were still in the formation stage having been formed from English-speaking foreign Germans, had also been selected to take part in operations prior to the main invasion. Since invasion never materialised, information relating to these operations is very limited and sketchy but the information that is available suggests that some companies of the First and Third Brandenburger battalions had been selected for covert operations connected with 'Sealion'. 'While the plans for 'Operation Sea Lion' were going ahead in the summer of 1940' wrote Konrad Burg, a German military historian,' several special army units - in particular the Brandenburgers - were being considered for some daring action against the enemy. Such tasks might prove risky, it was felt, but

HITLER'S INVASION OF EAST ANGLIA, 1940

whatever happened they would certainly help to educate the men for the greater task that lay ahead.'[66]

Evidence suggests that two special units were directly involved in invasion plans against England in July 1940. 'Great Britain Kommando' had been set up to operate in conjunction with the Brandenburg troops by Heinrich Himmler, the infamous head of the SS. Their purpose after the invasion was to arrest or 'take into protective custody' a list of political and public figures and, more particularly, to confiscate the valuable artefacts and paintings belonging to the Church of England and the Roman Catholic Church. Himmler made the decision to set up the undercover group of three hundred Kommandos in the week that the armistice with France was signed. The unit, who were to be led by a senior SS colonel, Standartenführer Franz Six, who in 1940 had been appointed to direct state police operations in an occupied Great Britain following invasion, were initially given the codename 'England Operation', but this was soon changed by its ambitious leader to 'GB Kommando'.[67]

The other special unit was the more elusive Pioneer Group 909, initially called the Hollmann Unit after the barracks in Berlin where it was based. These Brandenburgers were intended to land ahead of the main invasion thrust. The story of Pioneer Group 909 was first mentioned in Peter Fleming's *Invasion 1940*, in which he states that sub units of the Brandenburg Division may have attempted several reconnaissance landings on British soil before the date of the projected invasion: 'No evidence survives to show what role would have been allotted to these protean soldiers in 'Operation Sea Lion'. One of them, captured much later in the war, recalled that they were moved up the coast in August 1940, after undergoing training in 'sabotage and English etiquette'. Some of them may even have been ordered to carry out impostures.'

In early July the Brandenburgers were living in accommodation at La Chapelle near Dieppe under the watchful eye of their inspirational and hard-working leader, Major General Forster. On 2 July the First

---

66 Konrad Burg spent several years investigating the mystery of Pioneer Group 909 before publishing his findings in a series of three articles in 1965 in *Der Landser*, the long-running magazine devoted to the country's military history.

67 The war was barely over when Six, together with others like Klaus Barbie, were 'recuperated' by the US Army's CIC but in the spring of 1946 he was arrested and brought to trial in the case against the former mass-murdering Einsatzkommandos and he was sentenced in 1948 to twenty years' imprisonment. In 1951 his sentence was reduced to ten years and in 1952 he was amnestied altogether. He died on 9 July 1975 aged 65.

IF THE INVADER COMES

Battalion commanded by Major von Hippel and the Rudloff Battalion were placed on alert. Allegedly, wearing British uniforms or civilian clothes, 100 Brandenburgers in the 1st and 4th Kompanies of the First Battalion having landed with the assault troops in the Hastings area would have been part of an operation to capture Dover harbour in conjunction with other army and airborne units and bluffing their way into vital positions. The unit was to go to Dover Harbour where the British had placed a steamer which would be scuttled at the first sign of an invasion to block the harbour. They had to occupy this steamer and prevent it being used as a blockade. Then they were to switch their attention to the British coastal batteries on the cliffs. The planners envisaged that Pioneer Group 909 would use a captured British cargo ship as their means of transport across the Channel. Their short-wave radio would then be used to fool the coastal defences with messages in English until they were safely in the harbour.

The particular task of the 4th Kompanie was to prevent block-ships being sunk in the harbour entrance and neutralise coastal defences. Consequently the Brandenburg Regiment was able to report the First Battalion and the Rudloff battalion ready for action in their assigned assembly areas on the Channel Coast. The von Hippel battalion moved into the area of the 16th Army. The battalion command post was set up in Nieuwport, east of Dunkirk. III Battalion under Hauptmann Rudloff assembled in the 6th Army's sector. Its command post was located in Caen at the mouth of the Seine. I Battalion was first supposed to destroy the locks at Folkestone in an airborne operation. A second part of the battalion was to make a sea landing on the Dungeness Peninsula and knock out the locks and power plants, but especially a battery of railway guns that had been spotted there. The Third Battalion, comprising Companies 9, 10, 11 and 12 (around 600 men), was to have taken part in a lighting seaborne raid on the harbour at Weymouth as a prelude to the actual landing. It would attack some time before the main body in order to divert attention from the latter's objectives - Plymouth and Portsmouth. However, following a change in the overall plan of 'Sealion' it appears that a reduced force of just three units from the Third battalion would have been landed with the main invasion force. A 100-man-strong detachment was to land in the first wave and strike out on light motorcycles deep into the enemy rear to carry out special missions and spread confusion. The English speaking 11th Kompanie, codenamed 'Pioneer Battalion 303', had been specially kitted out with British Home Guard and police uniforms and were to neutralise a coastal battery and radar station nearby.

HITLER'S INVASION OF EAST ANGLIA, 1940

Despite initial enthusiasm, however, the plan was shelved when it was decided that coming in on a flood tide would very probably drive the captured British cargo ship onto the steep coast around Dover. Had the operation gone ahead, they would have landed with the first wave of the invasion and operated behind British lines in their disguises, infiltrating the coastal battery and radar station by stealth. It has been claimed that the radar station in question was on Beachy Head; but Beachy Head is over 500 feet above sea level and during training, which had included the use of motorcycles, usually 750cc engine BMWs, equipped with sidecars for reconnaissance, Pioneer Battalion 303 had practiced landing on open beaches.[68] The two other units in the Third battalion presumably had similar assignments. As well as these operations, it is also known that a force of twenty fast motor boats was assembled at Dordrecht for a special mission linked to the invasion. It is not beyond the realms of possibility that this would also have involved the Brandenburgers.

Two weeks later, Pioneer Group 909 was on the move again to Bussum on the coast of Holland. From here, in a captured Swedish steamer and protected by several Luftwaffe fighter aircraft, they carried out a successful trial landing on the steep coast of Heligoland intended to duplicate one in England. On the return journey to France, they were told they would invade dressed as Englishmen, according to Konrad Burg: 'At La Chapelle they were familiarised with their individual tasks. Every day there were maps to be studied and for hours they would move around dressed as Home Guards or 'Bobbies' speaking only English and practising British manners. They were to be in the first group of attackers landing to the west of Hastings to create a bridgehead. Once the defenders began retreating inland, they were to push on to the coastal batteries at Beachy Head and cut off the English there.

'On a particularly dark night in autumn 1940, a combined operation by this unit with naval personnel and the Luftwaffe was carried out. The aim was to land a small group of men on the English coast and, after taking a few prisoners, return in their landing craft to harbour. The result was worse than the pessimists had imagined. The landing craft, protected on either

---

68 The motorcycles were also equipped with a towing hook so they could tow light anti-tank or artillery weapons. However, towing strength for such a combination was low and cross country performance was poor. The Fallschirmjäger also made limited use of the Kettenrad, a semi-tracked vehicle based on a motorcycle. The Kettenrad had a motor cycle wheel in front and a track on each side of the rear. With a 1,500cc engine and a weight of 1200 kilograms it had better cross country performance and power reserves than a motorcycle but was still of limited value and difficult to load and unload from a Ju 52.

side by the navy and in the air by planes, approached to about 100 metres of the English coast when the order to land was given. Suddenly flames sprayed out through jets coming from underwater oil pipes, turning with unbelievable speed into a barrier of flames. The landing craft on which the commandos were travelling caught fire. The men who wanted to save themselves by swimming to the English shore were caught in the wall of flames. The seamen in the escort vessels could not help as they were in great danger, too. They had no option but to turn back. To complete the misfortune, English army units opened fire with their artillery and infantry weapons. And, finally, the Luftwaffe planes not only fired on the English positions, but also managed to hit some of the hapless German soldiers in the water.

'The heat from this is so great that boats will catch fire at once,' Admiral Canaris is quoted by Konrad Burg as saying, 'and even iron components start to melt. Hardly a single soldier from an invasion fleet would reach English soil. According to Burg, 'after the disaster of this experimental venture with such heavy losses, 'Operation Sea Lion' was abandoned'. No explanation was ever given. There were rumours, but these were put down with draconian methods in both the Army and in Germany generally. The Army leadership - particularly Hitler and his staff - had decided such a venture would end in catastrophe and agreed that an invasion of England was impossible.'

In a footnote to his articles, Burg also briefly quotes another version of events. According to this, Himmler had heard rumours that the English possessed a 'flame wall' defence system, but was convinced there was no truth in the stories. Indeed, so confident was he that he offered to carry out a 'sham landing' using SS troops to show such defences were non-existent. His men then set out just like those of Pioneer Group 909 - with precisely the same result.[69]

Training and preparations for these covert operations were in progress before Hitler issued Führer Directive 16 and continued unseen and unknown behind the very visible build-up in French and Belgian ports. But, as early as mid-June, one IWSC summary had concluded that: 'a seaborne expedition of a diversionary nature is probably assembling in the Trondheim/Bergen area for departure at a future date.' If this force sailed it could: 'get well into the North Sea without being observed.' Within weeks, evidence from 'reliable sources' showed that a major assembly

---

69 *Where The Eagle Landed: The Mystery of the German Invasion of Britain, 1940* by Peter Haining (Robson Books, 2004).

was taking place, with large numbers of troops, including paratroops and the assembly of shipping estimated as being 'enough to carry two Divisions.' The Admiralty was only too aware that during the invasion of Norway, German naval forces had ferried 2,000 troops on board ten fast destroyers. The RAF and Royal Navy increased their vigilance in the North Sea and along the east coast and from June onwards there was a near constant state of alert. It was quite possible that the enemy force could approach the east coast from Baltic or German ports without being detected. It had happened before, during WWI, when German warships had bombarded the English coast with virtual impunity. In late July 1940 British intelligence summaries reported that invasion exercises were taking place in Norway and that: 'preparations for a seaborne invasion of two to three Divisions 'appear complete.' From now on the preparations in the Baltic would be carefully monitored.

Emergency warning measures were introduced for all coastal units, including the coastguard. Green rockets fired by the Royal Navy or Coastguard signified that enemy ships had been sighted. Red flares or signals rockets fired by naval or army units signified an enemy landing. A little later this system was superseded by the red flare as the general alarm signal for all coastal units. In an attempt to reduce the occurrence of false alarms, the general use of flares and Very lights to within fifteen miles of the coast was prohibited for any other reason than to warn of the presence of the enemy. Troops on watch along the coast were ordered to report all sightings of warning signals to their Battalion HQs by the quickest means possible and following any warnings, all troops in forward positions were to be placed on immediate alert. Along with this, Battalion HQs of coastal units were under specific orders to bypass Brigade HQs and relay all reports of suspected landings directly back to Divisional Commands. This enabled Divisional HQs, who maintained direct contact with local RAF stations, to call in an immediate air strike against any enemy landing while it was still on the beaches.

It was also expected that a German invasion fleet might attempt to approach the coast using a large scale artificial smoke screen or natural fog bank as cover, as the Dutch had done in 1667. To counter this threat, a system of monitoring weather conditions, known as 'Volcano' forecasts was begun. On more than one occasion the heightened state of alert and the fear that a sea mist, always hazardous, might now conceal a more ominous threat led to the alarm being raised. On Sunday, 4th August an early morning heavy sea mist enveloped Lowestoft and persisted through the day. Sentries on all

IF THE INVADER COMES

coastal points were doubled and the Royal Navy positioned block-ships in the harbour. During the early hours of Saturday the 10th, coastal units were yet again required to maintain 'special vigilance' following the sighting of many suspicious vessels off the Dutch coast. The Germans had scheduled 10 August as 'Adler Tag' ('Eagle Day') when the Luftwaffe would begin their all-out assault on the RAF in order to destroy Britain's air shield and pave the way for invasion. In the event the opening attacks of 'Unternehmen Adlerangriff - Operation 'Eagle Attack' - were postponed due to bad weather and the assault began on Tuesday, 13th August when early morning low cloud base and rain cleared to a fine day with lengthy sunny periods by afternoon. The Luftwaffe would now switch its attacks from Channel convoys and coastal airfields to the main bases of RAF Fighter Command in southern England but Adler Tag was not successful. A combination of poor weather conditions and a number of errors on their part did not even put the RAF to the test. The airfields at Eastchurch, Detling, Odiham and Farnborough that the Luftwaffe was targeting were not Fighter Command airfields. German Intelligence relied on old ordinance survey maps of England and was trying to bring them up to date with information brought back by reconnaissance aircraft. During the morning the German bombers lost their fighter escort and in the afternoon a fighter escort had left France without the bombers that they were supposed to escort. Now, Göring was under the impression that all fighter squadrons in 10, 12 and 13 Groups had been sent south to 11 Group and informed Luftflotte 5 in Norway to prepare for attacks on the English north and Scotland as the time was now right. During the night of 13/14 August the Luftwaffe dropped empty parachutes, wireless transmitters, maps, photographs, lists of prominent people and instructions to supposed agents in an attempt to create the impression that an invasion was imminent and that there was an active fifth Column in Britain. Although there was some mention of this in the British press this event passed largely unnoticed. On Thursday, 15th August, large scale Luftwaffe attacks were carried out against RAF bases in southern and south eastern England, accompanied by attacks against airfields in Yorkshire and the North-East. During the afternoon RAF Martlesham Heath in Suffolk was dive-bombed by enemy aircraft in what was described as a 'determined attack.' The following day RAF Tangmere in West Sussex suffered a devastating attack by Stuka dive bombers. On Saturday, 17th August losses in Spitfires and Hurricanes over the past ten days had reached 218 (183 in combat, thirty destroyed on the ground and five in accidents). The German Government announced a total blockade of the British Isles, threatening to enforce an exclusion zone in which all ships, be they British or neutral would be sunk without warning.

A low-level attack on 18 August by nine Dornier Do 17s of KG 76 restricted the use of Kenley. In the Operations Room, the station commander, Wing Commander Thomas Prickman had watched his station's fighter squadrons being vectored to intercept high-altitude raiding forces coming in from the south-east. Then another marker appeared on the plotting table, showing the low-flyers heading across Sussex. The only fighters in his sector that were not yet committed were 111 Squadron's twelve Hurricanes, waiting at readiness at Croydon. Prickman ordered the unit to scramble and patrol over Kenley at 3,000 feet. Thanks to efficient plotting by the Observer Corps, Kenley's ground defences were at full alert. Whilst the number and type of defences varied from airfield to airfield, those at Kenley consisted of two obsolete 3-inch anti-aircraft guns, four smaller 40mm Bofors guns and about twenty .303-inch Lewis machine guns. There was also a parachute and cable installation, known as PAC which fired salvoes of rockets at any raiders at about 500-700 feet. Two Dorniers were shot down and the survivors came under repeated attack by 111 Squadron's Hurricanes. Two of the Dorniers ditched in the English Channel and two more crash-landed in France. A follow-up raid by 27 Dorniers delivered a high-altitude attack on Kenley. Altogether, three out of four hangars and several other buildings were destroyed and four Hurricanes and a Blenheim fighter were destroyed also.

Meanwhile, there had been a significant increase in pre-invasion preparations along the coast of Norway. On 13 August, following reports of German embarkations in Baltic ports, the Home Fleet at Scapa Flow had been placed on one hour's notice and orders issued that no ship was to be taken in hand for boiler cleaning or refitting until further notice. All warships on England's eastern seaboard were placed on half hour standby. The heightened state of alert was set to continue. While most eyes were firmly fixed on the ports in northern France and Belgium the Luftwaffe began to show a close interest in defences on the Suffolk coast. During the week that followed Monday, 19 August the 6-inch guns of 355 Coast Battery at Sizewell were machine gunned and 328 Battery at Aldeburgh was dive-bombed and machine gunned on the Wednesday and twice on the Thursday. These attacks coincided with two low level photo reconnaissance flights by German aircraft. On the Tuesday, while sporadic attacks were being made against several local airfields including Wattisham, an enemy aircraft flew south along the line of the coast as far as the Martello Tower

IF THE INVADER COMES

at Aldeburgh. The following day, just before 2 o'clock in the afternoon, a Dornier Do 17 carried out another low level photo reconnaissance over the same stretch of coast.

The weekend of 24/25 August culminated in a very heavy attack on Hornchurch and North Weald aerodromes, while on the Sunday evening a dense sea mist, described in some war diaries as an 'unnatural fog' and a large unidentified convoy off Beachy Head sparked a major invasion alert along the south coast. All Home Fleet units were ordered to raise steam 'with dispatch' and the Admiralty transmitted the alert to all coastal units. At 2235 and in time honoured fashion, the bugler of the 1st battalion Queens Westminster Rifles at Dover sounded the 'stand-to'. The alert turned out to be a false alarm after the convoy was identified as British. Throughout the following week the tension continued as the Luftwaffe increased its attacks on airfields, RDF stations and other military installations in southern England. At the same time there was a noticeable increase in enemy naval activity in German and Dutch ports. On Thursday, 29th August RAF reconnaissance reported a large number of merchant ships at Kiel and 350 large motor launches at Emden. Of greater concern however, was a large concentration of enemy warships and transports massed at Den Helder on the Dutch coast - directly across the North Sea from the coast of East Anglia. The following evening, as a precautionary measure, all merchant ships at sea off the east coast were ordered to the nearest port. This would also be the case on the Saturday evening. During the night the Luftwaffe carried out limited air raids over the eastern region, including Felixstowe and the surrounding area, though little damage was reported. Friday the 30th would see the most intense fighting so far in the skies over southeast England. The Luftwaffe began a forty-eight-hour assault on Fighter Command's Sector stations with attacks by 1,345 aircraft. 11 Group was threatened with being overrun by sheer weight of numbers and 12 Group was called upon to act as an airborne reserve for Park's hard-pressed squadrons.

Saturday, 31st August, which before the war would have been a Bank Holiday weekend with time to laze, remained mainly fair with haze in the Thames Estuary and the Straits of Dover. Luftwaffe attacks began early that morning with raids coming in over Kent and the Thames Estuary. The airfields at Debden, North Weald, Duxford, Biggin Hill, Manston, West Malling, Hawkinge, Hornchurch and Lympne in southern and eastern England were among the many stations attacked as well as radar stations in Kent and Sussex, several being put out of action from the afternoon until late evening. In all the Luftwaffe flew almost 2,800 sorties against London's sector airfields. Fighter Command flew 2,020 sorties, losing 39 fighters. These were the worst RAF losses of the battle so far and they brought the number of RAF pilots killed and wounded that week to 115, with 65 of the fighters downed on the 30th and 31st. Only two RAF Sector stations were still operational south of the Thames.

During the early morning, just over Bawdsey, AA machine gunners of the 2nd Liverpool Scots opened fire on a Dornier aircraft 'hedge hopping' over their positions. Another Dornier would fly over the Liverpool Scots later in the afternoon. Meanwhile at sea, in response to continuing concerns over enemy ship concentrations on the Dutch coast, four destroyers including HMS *Campbell* carried out a naval reconnaissance sweep off Texel and Terschelling, but found nothing to report. Shortly after 1630 in the afternoon, five Royal Navy destroyers rendezvoused off the Humber Light Vessel then set course through Gap D in the east coast minefield en route to a secret mission off the Dutch coast. Three hours later, the destroyers HMS *Jupiter*, HMS *Kelvin* and HMS *Vortigern* followed in their wake to patrol the eastern end of Gap D and give support if the need arose. Shortly after 2100 hours, RAF reconnaissance aircraft reported a suspicious enemy convoy off the West Frisian Islands, heading due west - straight for the Norfolk coast.

Chapter 5

The Invasion that never was

'Any person impeding the German war effort in Britain by starting hostilities will be treated as a guerilla and shot. Hostages will be taken as a 'security' measure. National laws in force before the occupation will be maintained only if they are not contrary to the purposes of the occupation. The country's state of health will be considered important only as a safeguard for the resources of the country and non-fraternization policy for the troops will be enforced on a limited scale.

In conversation with the population the utmost reserve is ordered. The enemy's intelligence service will be active and any fraternization might therefore have severe consequences. Any violence against the population and looting, will be a Military Court offence and punishable by death. Monuments will be protected. There will be compulsory acceptance of German State banknotes and coins. The rate of exchange will be 9.6 marks to the pound.

All public utilities, including gas, electricity, the railways and objects of art will be under the special protection of the Army. Sabotage will include the concealment of harvest products. The concealment of firearms, including shot-guns and other hunting arms, will be punishable by death. Severe punishment will be passed by military courts on civilians who associate with prisoners of war, make slurring remarks about the German Army of Occupation or its commanders, circulate pamphlets or organize meetings.

Industrial concerns and commercial firms, including banks, must be kept open. Closing without adequate reason will be severely punished. German soldiers can purchase what they desire. Instead of cash payment, in many cases, they can issue certificates for the value of the purchase. A military court can use its discretion in trying persons under 18, but may pass death sentence if it sees fit.

HITLER'S INVASION OF EAST ANGLIA, 1940

Listening to non-German radio broadcasts is a punishable offence. Excepted are non-German radio stations which have been permitted by the occupation army. The death sentence can be passed on persons retaining radio transmitters. A curfew will be imposed from sunset to sunrise.

The following commodities will be requisitioned: Agricultural products of all kinds, ores, mica, asbestos, precious and semi-precious stones, fuel, rubber, textiles, leather and timber. Farmers and dealers, including innkeepers, may only dispose of agricultural products in quantities necessary for the most urgent needs of consumers.

The Military Administration of England issued by the German High Command. Hitler had planned to complete the occupation of England before 9 September 1940. Weapons were to be produced under Nazi direction for the Battle of Russia. According to captured German documents, to prevent sabotage Field Marshal Walther von Brauchitsch, C-in-C of all German forces, ordered that the entire able-bodied male population between 17 and 45 should be deported to the Continent and interned as soon as possible after Britain was defeated. This represented about 25% of male citizens. The deported male population would have most likely been used as industrial slave labour in areas of the Reich such as the factories and mines of the Ruhr and Upper Silesia. Although they might have been treated less brutally than slaves from the East (whom the Nazis regarded as sub-humans, fit only to be worked to death), living and working conditions would still have been severe. Von Brauchitsch issued a directive that 'the chief task of the military administration in England will be to use all the resources of the country for the German war economy'. Britain was to be plundered for anything of financial, military, industrial or cultural value and the remaining population terrorised. Civilian hostages would be taken and the death penalty immediately imposed for even the most trivial acts of resistance. In late February 1943 Otto Bräutigam of the Reich Ministry for the Occupied Eastern Territories claimed he had the opportunity to read a personal report by General Eduard Wagner about a discussion with Heinrich Himmler, in which Himmler had expressed the intention to kill about 80% of the populations of France and England by special forces of the SS after the German victory. In an unrelated event, Hitler had on one

THE INVASION THAT NEVER WAS

occasion called the English lower classes 'racially inferior'. Had Sealion succeeded, Einsatzgruppen ('task forces' which operated as death squads) under Dr. Franz Six were to follow the invasion force to establish the New Order. Six's headquarters were to be in London, with regional task forces in Birmingham, Liverpool, Manchester and Edinburgh. They were provided with a list (known as the *Black Book*) of 2,820 people to be arrested immediately. The Einsatzgruppen were also tasked with liquidating Britain's Jewish population, which numbered over 300,000. Six had also been entrusted with the task of securing 'aero-technological research result and important equipment' as well as 'Germanic works of art'. There is also a suggestion that he toyed with the idea of moving Nelson's Column to Berlin.

On 2 September 1940 four German agents embarked at Le Touquet in a fishing boat which was escorted across the English Channel by two minesweepers. Their mission was to pave the way for the German invasion. The Nazi spies arrived on the shores of Britain under the cover of night, by rowing boat and by rubber dinghy. In one rowing boat were Jose Waldberg and Karl Meier. Waldberg, a committed Nazi, with some experience of spying in France before its fall, was born at Mainz on 15 July 1915. He spoke no English. Meier, 23, was a medical student born at Koblenz on 19th October 1916 who had studied in the United States, spoke English with an American accent, but had no experience of spying. Though German by birth he had taken Dutch nationality. He had gone into the venture with both eyes open, telling himself that a man who has an ideal must be willing to sacrifice everything for it or else the ideal isn't an ideal at all, or the man isn't a man at all, but a humble creature who deserves only pity. These two men had known each other for years and it appears that they had both been involved in illegal currency smuggling which had been discovered by the Nazi authorities. As a result they were blackmailed: either they agree to spy in England, or they would be sent to concentration camps. They chose Himmelfahrt. In the other boat were Sjoerd Pons, 28, an unemployed Dutch army ambulance driver and Charles van der Kieboom a 26-year-old YMCA receptionist from Amsterdam who was half-Dutch, half-Japanese having been born at Takarumuka, Japan, on 6th September 1914. He spoke perfect English with 'an Oxford accent'.

The two boats landed in the very early hours of the morning of 3rd September; one near Dungeness and the other by the Dymchurch

HITLER'S INVASION OF EAST ANGLIA, 1940

Redoubt. They had a wireless set and an elementary form of cipher and their orders were to send back information of military importance; they had been given to understand that an invasion of the Kentish coast was imminent. Each had with them in their suitcases £130 in £5 and £1 notes, a Morse code transmitter and receivers, a map of the British Isles, a loaded revolver, some invisible ink and about a dozen names and addresses of individuals in Britain. They also carried a pocket compass, a jack knife, chocolate, biscuits and blankets. Three had Dutch passports while the fourth had no papers. By 0530 on the same morning Sjoerd Pons and Charles van der Kieboom, although they separated on landing had been challenged and made prisoner by sentries of a battalion of the Somersetshire Light Infantry. This was hardly surprising. They were completely untrained for their difficult task; their sole qualification for it seems to have lain in the fact that each, having committed some misdemeanour which was known to the Germans, could be blackmailed into undertaking the enterprise. Neither had more than a smattering of English and one suffered, by virtue of having had a Japanese mother, from the additional hazard of a markedly Oriental appearance; he it was who, when first sighted by an incredulous private of the Somersets in the early dawn, had binoculars and a spare pair of shoes slung round his neck. They initially claimed to be refugees escaping Nazi oppression in Holland and said they planned to board a ship bound for Canada. But under questioning by an MI5 captain the men admitted being under orders to gather intelligence on British coastal defences and the morale of the British people. They had been instructed to sleep rough and mingle with the public on buses, trains and in pubs. An immigration inspector described them as being of 'refined appearance'.

In his few hours of freedom on the Kent coast, Waldberg rigged up an aerial in a tree and had begun to send messages (in French) to his German controllers. He was not caught until the following day. (Copies of three of his messages survived and were used in evidence against him at his trial). Meier gave himself away by knocking on the door of 'The Rising Sun' pub at Lydd at nine in the morning and asked Mabel Cole the landlady whether he could have a champagne cider and could he take a bath! Mrs. Cole had explained to him that this transaction could not legally take place until ten o'clock and suggested that meanwhile he should go and look at the church. She called for assistance and two members of the public stepped up to arrest him when he returned. 'You've caught me,' Maier told them 'and I don't mind what happens to me, but I don't want to go back to Germany!'

THE INVASION THAT NEVER WAS

All four spies were tried under the Treason Act 1940 in November. Pons was able to successfully argue that he had been coerced into the role, having been threatened with a concentration camp by the Germans and had always intended to give himself up. He was acquitted; the other three men were hanged in Pentonville Prison in the following month. Their trials were conducted in camera, but short, factual obituary announcements were published after the executions.

In September also, 'Hummer Nord I', an Abwehr operation to land in Scotland three spies in a He 115 seaplane possibly of Kü.Fl.Gr. 906 from Stavanger-Sola, was attempted. The three were Karl Drugge and Robert Petter, together with his girl friend, Vera Schalburg known under various aliases as Vera Erikson, Vera de Cottani, Vera di Chalbur, Vera Stravritzka and Vera de Witte, a Russian dancer he had first met in Paris before the war. Born in 1912 in Riga as the daughter of a tsarist admiral who was later killed by communists, Vera was of Danish-Russian extraction and her family had fled the Bolshevik Revolution and settled in Jutland. Later she became a ballet dancer performing, amongst other places, at the Folies Bergère and became hopelessly addicted to drugs. Still later she was recruited to the Abwehr and her career advanced rapidly under the guidance of Wilhelm Canaris, head of the German intelligence service (mostly to escape the mad and criminal White Russian aristocrat she had become involved with). Described in her documents as Madame Vera Erikson, a Dane living at 18 Sussex Place, London W11, she was to become the long-lost niece of an elderly Italian countess living in Kensington. The Germans thought this would be excellent cover for her to meet people prominent in British public life through the countess' reputation as a lavish hostess. Robert Petter, who was born in Zurich, Switzerland on 14 December 1915, was described as Werner Heinrich Walti, a Swiss subject living at 23 Sussex Gardens, London W2.

Karl Theodore Drugge, a German national who was born at Grebenstein, Hessen, on 20 March 1906 became Francois de Deeker, a French refugee from Belgium; although when he was later arrested by the British he spelled his name as Drucke. The address in his Identity Card was 15 Sussex Gardens, London W2. Petter, Drugge and Vera de Witte were taught how to launch their rubber dinghy from the floatplane; which was to take them to Scotland. The three spies were provided with English bicycles found in the cellar of the British Consulate at Bergen, on which they were ordered to cycle the 600 miles to London! They were provided with espionage equipment, radios, money and British Identity Cards and ration books.

HITLER'S INVASION OF EAST ANGLIA, 1940

On 26 September they found the Scottish coast covered in mist and rain clouds and had to return to Norway. Another abortive attempt followed, again foiled by bad weather and it was not until 30 September that the flying boat once more took off from Stavanger at 02:30. A successful landing was made off the coast at Buckie and they paddled ashore to the mouth of the Burn of Gollachy by rubber dinghy from the plane but, in the choppy sea, the bicycles were lost in transferring them to the dinghy. Without the bicycles they then had to change their plans regarding transport to London. They decided to split up, Petter going to the east and Drugge and Vera to the west. They still retained their radio transmitters which were crucial to their mission so instead of cycling inland as they had planned two of them chose to walk to Port Gordon to catch a train. Petter started off to Buckie to try to make his own way to London where they were all to meet up again. Drucke and Eriksen walked to Port Gordon railway station and arrived at seven thirty in the morning. Port Gordon had been used to strangers coming and going from the RAF camp but these two did not know where they were, they had 'strange' accents, too much money and their feet were wet. Stationmaster John Donald and porter John Geddes knew something was not right so while Geddes distracted them Donald contacted the local policeman. Vera de Witte and Karl Drucke could not even speak English. Locals described them afterwards as having guttural accents. They pretended to be refugees but when Constable Robert Grieve arrived he found their papers were wrong. They were taken to Buckie police station and a search of their luggage was enough to incriminate them. Knives, loaded Mauser automatic pistols, wireless equipment, a list of bomber and fighter stations in East Anglia, £327 in Bank of England notes, a torch saying 'Made in Bohemia' and a half-eaten German sausage!

A search by the Buckie coastguard soon turned up their dinghy and their fate was sealed. Petter however had managed to get a train from Buckie to Aberdeen and then made it to Edinburgh. He had been noticed by Aberdeen Police boarding the train to Edinburgh and when they heard of the spies at Buckie the Special in Branch were notified and arrested him in Waverley Station. Petter was eventually arrested by the Left Luggage office in Edinburgh's Waverley railway station after entering via the steps from Princes Street. All three spies were taken to London and after a trial at the Old Bailey in 1941 Petter and Drucke were hanged in Wandsworth prison. Incredibly Vera de Witte was never put on trial. The court had been told

THE INVASION THAT NEVER WAS

that 'Madame Erikson would not appear'; the assumption widely being that she had turned King's Evidence. She even managed to escape after being deported back to Germany after the war. Most of the evidence suggests she died in 1993.

Although Unternehmen Seelöwe (Operation 'Sealion'), destined to be the invasion that never was and in the view of many historians, the invasion that never could have been, had for practical purposes been cancelled before the three spies left Norway. One of them had been given, like the men in Kent, a purely tactical role connected with the invasion. According to the available evidence, the plan, in its final form, would have been a basic seaborne assault against a stretch of England's south coast from Eastbourne to Folkestone. This would have been carried out by thousands of enemy troops transported across the English Channel, most of them in converted Rhine barges. Along with the initial seaborne assault, airborne troops would have been used to capture airfields and other strategic points in Sussex and Kent.

On 2 July Field Marshal Wilhelm Keitel, chief of the armed forces high command noted: 'The Führer has decided that a landing in England is possible, providing air superiority can be attained…All preparations are to be begun immediately.' Five days later Keitel met with Count Galeazo Ciano, telling the Italian Foreign Minister that he considered a landing in England possible but extremely difficult, especially since intelligence data was meagre. On behalf of Benito Mussolini, the Italian dictator, Ciano offered ten divisions and thirty air squadrons to help with the attack. (The Germans politely declined the ground force but some of the offered air units did fly over England in the Battle of Britain). After Hitler conferred with General Alfred Jodl he made the decision by issuing Führer Directive No.16. Jodl had already put together a plan for invading England on a broad front beachhead of 160 miles, from Dover to Bournemouth, code named 'Lion'. Commander-in-Chief Field Marshal Walther von Brauchitsch called for landings across a 237-mile front, from the Thames Estuary to Lyme Bay, by thirteen divisions with 260,000 men in all. Follow up would be conducted by another 27 divisions. Admiral Raeder was as empathically opposed to the broad front as the army was for it because it was easier to protect the vulnerable vessels when they were hedged in between the minefields and the groups of U-boats seeking to protect them from the all-powerful Royal Navy and also, the Norwegian campaign had cost him half his destroyers, plus the cruisers *Blücher, Königsberg* and *Karlsruhe* and other heavy ships, including the

HITLER'S INVASION OF EAST ANGLIA, 1940

battle cruisers *Scharnhorst* and *Gneisenau* were damaged. But Raeder did believe that the Kriegsmarine could get an invasion force across the English Channel if its sea flanks could be secured.

Operation 'Sealion' originally called for nine divisions to be landed on the southern English coast in the initial main assault. Under the overall command of 65-year old Generalfeldmarschall Gerd von Rundstedt, a clear-minded and cynical man, the leader of Army Group A; four divisions of Generaloberst Ernst Busch's 16th Army would embark from Rotterdam, Antwerp, Ostend, Dunkirk and Calais, landing between Folkestone and St. Leonards. Two divisions from Generaloberst Adolf Strauss' 9th Army would leave from Boulogne and the Canche estuary to disembark between Bexhill and Eastbourne. Finally, elements of three further divisions from the 9th Army would land between Beachy Head and Brighton. These landings would be supported by 250 amphibious tanks.

The German Supreme Command realized that there would be a need for spearhead troops (paratroops and glider-borne units) in the vital opening stages of 'Sealion' and these would be followed up by the 22nd Air Landing Division. The most obvious task was to attack and secure an airfield, at Lympne, north of Folkestone on Romney Marsh. Two minutes after sunrise it was proposed that a battalion would be dropped around Hythe while other units jumped over Paddlesworth and Etchinghill. The common objective was Sandgate. While those units were moving towards the target area, the Ju 52s would be flying back to France, there to reload and to bring back another battalion. That wave of paratroops would drop around the villages of Sellinge and Postling, would reinforce the first waves and together with them would begin to surround the airfield. Encirclement would be completed and the area would be consolidated. A ground and glider-borne attack would then go in, first against the airfield and then to seize and hold the high ground beyond it. With an airfield in their possession the German forces could begin to bring in 22nd Division whose battalions would thicken the perimeter and take out new objectives. Also from the captured airfield of Lympne the Luftwaffe's advanced striking force of fighter aircraft would operate in close support of the ground forces.[70]

On 1 July 1938 the Luftwaffe High Command (OKL) ordered that the paratroop, glider and air transport units under its command be formed

---

70 *Storming Eagles: German Airborne Forces In World War II* by James Lucas (Arms & Armour Press, 1988).

into 7th Fligerdivision. Tempelhof in Berlin became the headquarters for the new formation and Major-General Kurt Student was named as the commander.[71] To assist operations on the 16th Army's open right flank, 7,000 Fallschirmjäger of the 7th Flieger-Division would drop along with the 22nd Luftlandeddivision's 3,000 glider-borne soldiers behind Beach 'B' (Folkestone-Dungeness) and capture Lympne airfield, assist XIII Corps in crossing the Royal Military Canal and develop a thrust in the direction of Dover. Landing Zone 'C' was assigned to the 16th Army's VI Corps. Its 7th Infanterie Division was to land on both sides of the Royal Military Canal in the southern reaches of the Romney Marshes, while the 1st Mountain Division seized the beaches south of Rye. The amphibious attack would take three days, during which units of 16th Army were to be ferried over from the Pas de Calais in three waves. About a week later, 9th Army, from around Le Havre, would begin its assault on Brighton Bay. Still later if conditions permitted, other forces under 6th Army would land in Lyme Bay, coming from Cherbourg.

During a period of about five days when the British were expected to be able to respond, the assault divisions would push forward to create a lodgement twenty miles deep. Then two panzer corps totalling 650 tanks would swing around to attack London from the west. Support would come from a third wave of nine infantry divisions, whereupon the Germans would have established a front across the entire length of southern England, from the River Severn in the west to the Thames Estuary near London. At the same time, eight more divisions of a fourth wave were to be landed and the campaign decided shortly after that. In *Storming Eagles* James Lucas makes the point that 'the weight and space limitations of aircraft dictated that the maximum weight which a glider could carry was one ton and this limited carrying capacity ruled out the 'lifting' of even anti-tank guns. The airborne troops holding their positions on Romney Marsh would, therefore, be without adequate support until fully armed infantry or Panzer units arrived. How long it might be before relief arrived from mainland Europe could only be conjecture and until that relief did arrive the lightly armed paras would be at a disadvantage vis-à-vis the British defenders.'

In June 1940 Germany had two regiments of paratroopers but both had suffered heavy losses during the invasion of Holland and there were probably no more than 5,000 paratroopers available that summer. There were also about 11,400 fully trained airlanding troops of the 22nd Luftlandeddivision.

---

71   James Lucas.

HITLER'S INVASION OF EAST ANGLIA, 1940

Of these forces probably no more than 15,000 could have been flown to England because of the lack of Ju 52s and DFS 230 gliders. On 11 July there were available only 400 Ju 52s and 110 gliders. By the 16th this had been increased to 1,000 Ju 52s and 150 gliders (75 per cent operational). There were also 52 Ju 89/90 transports capable of carrying between forty and fifty fully equipped men or 7,700lb of light artillery weapons. This means that the entire paratroop division, with mortars and other equipment could be drooped in one lift, followed almost immediately by part of the airlanding division, the remainder following in a second wave about three hours later. Heinkel He 59 seaplanes of the type that had been used during the invasion of Holland might well have been used against England. Special airborne units were allotted important targets such as the seizure of harbour installations and fortifications and even the Royal Family.

An attempt had been made to seize Queen Wilhelmina of the Netherlands on 10 May. First the anti aircraft and other defences would be dive-bombed and then 400 paratroopers armed with machine guns would be dropped around the palace to prevent reinforcements arriving and the occupants escaping. A hundred paratroopers would then be dropped in the palace grounds and a special team of 23 SS officers would seize the Royal Family. The Brandenburgers wearing British uniforms or civilian clothes would probably have assisted in the capture of Dover's port facilities and fortifications by bluffing their way into vital positions and 100 men were to have landed with the assault troops in the Hastings area.[72] In theory, the Luftwaffe was to use part of its bomber and dive-bomber forces to protect the 16th and 9th Armies, in addition to bombing the British coastal defences and transport infrastructure in the run-up to invasion. In practice, the Luftwaffe's support was always questionable because of Göring's uncooperative attitude, as in his cool pronouncement: 'Sealion' must not disturb or burden the Luftwaffe operations.'

Apart from providing the transport fleet and laying the minefields, the Kriegsmarine also planned to deploy ten destroyers and twenty torpedo boats to protect the west flank of the crossing, with a further thirty torpedo boats covering the east flank. Raeder's force further planned to have ten medium-sized U-boats in the English Channel west of the Isle of Wight, as well as five small U-boats.

Führer Directive No.17 dated 1 August 1940, which dealt with a landing operation in the east and south of England, began with an opening sentence

---

72 Terry Wise writing in *Airfix Magazine,* June 1975.

which left no room for doubt: 'In order to establish the conditions necessary for the final conquest of England, I intend to continue the air and sea war against the English homeland more intensively than before.' The assaults on the landing zones would have been spearheaded by the Vorausabteilung, or Advance Detachments, each of which contained 1,600 men. These hand-picked elite troops would have arrived at dawn, ahead of the main body of the fleet, having been taken close to the shore in mine-sweepers or minelayers and then transferred to fast motorboats or Sturmboote. Boats with smokescreen machines would be assigned to the advance units to help conceal the invaders, although the Kriegsmarine disliked this measure as the artificial fog also hindered navigation. The main body of the fleet would have followed in the barges towed by the tugs, escorted by auxiliary patrols and Siebel ferries. Each division in the first wave had at least two batteries of mountain or field guns, a kompanie equipped with 2cm flak guns and another kompanie equipped with 4.7-cm self-propelled anti-tank guns. In addition, the 16th Army had nine batteries with seventy-two rocket launchers. Each of the first-wave armies was allocated one artillery regiment staff, a 10cm gun detachment, a motorised heavy field howitzer detachment and a reconnaissance detachment.

Since the tugs could go no faster than six knots and many would have been slower, the fleet that sailed from Calais, heading for the landing zone between Hastings and Dungeness, would have been required to depart eight hours ahead of its planned arrival on the English coast; it would have comprised about 100 tows and extended around fifteen kilometres from the French port. The fleet sailing from Boulogne would have been even larger, consisting of tows stretching twenty kilometres from the French shore. The slow-moving armada would sail from ports between Rotterdam and Le Havre and proceed across the Channel in four lines, the pontoons and barges taking up to fifteen hours to cross even in calm conditions. Accompanying the troops of the 16th and 9th armies would be three paratrooper regiments - two to drop in the Brighton area and one to land behind Dover - with the mission to capture and hold inland targets. Maps, based on the British Ordnance Survey, were printed to show the invasion points and breakout routes from the coasts of Sussex and Kent. However, this was predicated by the absolute need to destroy the RAF so that the Luftwaffe would have aerial superiority over the Channel and the beaches.

Hitler wanted the troops of Army Groups A and B to assault southern England from the Calais-Le Havre areas in three groups. From left to right they would be: the 26th Army, the 9th Army and the 6th Army. These troops were supposed to land on the east coast of England between Norwich and Brighton. The Wehrmacht, however, preferred a broader front stretching from Margate in Kent to Weymouth in Dorset. Finally, at a conference on 26th August, Hitler sided with the navy and at the beginning of September the developed plan was to attack on a narrower front from Worthing in Sussex to Folkestone in Kent. Based on the navy's estimates of shipping capacity and current dangers von Brauchitsch was told to comply with the embarkation and landing schedules. The Luftwaffe meanwhile, had almost nothing to do with the invasion planning. Hermann Göring and his senior officers believed that 'Sealion' was just a giant bluff to scare the British into capitulating. After the victories in Norway, the Low Countries and France they suddenly came to believe that air power alone could force the issue. Hans Jeschonnek, the Luftwaffe Chief of Staff, even went as far as remarking to Major Sigismund von Falkenstein, the service's liaison officer to the armed forces high command that 'There isn't going to be any 'Sealion' and I haven't got time to bother about it.'[73]

Under the final 'Sealion' plan, 67,000 soldiers would have been operational in England within a few hours of the first landing. Within two days, that figure could have reached 138,000, rising to 260,000 within a fortnight of 'Sealion's beginning. The historian Peter Schenk, who made a detailed study of the German plans, estimated that at least 300,000 troops would have been put into the operation because the 16th Army would have been heavily reinforced.

On the last day of August, photo reconnaissance aircraft of RAF Coastal Command noticed a sudden increase in Dutch coastal and canal traffic; the invasion barges were on their way to embarkation points. 'Enigma' intercepts indicated that Luftflotte 2 was being reinforced with additional bombers. It could mean only one thing; invasion seemed imminent. In the early afternoon of 4 September Hitler gave a bombastic speech to a hysterically cheering crowd of 14,000 Berliners packed into the Sportpalast in which he announced that the attack on England was imminent. On 6 September all RAF units were placed under 'Alert No.2' meaning that invasion was considered possible within the next three days. Then on the 7th 'Alert No.1' was issued. This meant that the Germans were expected to invade within the next twelve hours. But on 3 September the projected landing date had been pushed back from 15th to 21st September. On the morning of 17 September the German general staff sent an order to begin dismantling the paratroop loading equipment at Dutch airfields.

---

73 James P. Werbaneth.

THE INVASION THAT NEVER WAS

The dispersal of the invasion shipping soon followed. The British interception of the 'Enigma' message was taken as a clear signal that 'Sealion' had been cancelled. 'Cromwell' was officially rescinded on 21st September and 'Alert No.2' reinstated. But on 22 September President Franklin D. Roosevelt telephoned Churchill to tell him 'for certain' the Germans were going to invade that day. Churchill dispatched Anthony Eden to Dover from where the Foreign Secretary reported no landing was possible due to the rough sea and fog. Roosevelt telephoned again on 23rd September to apologise. 'The codes' he said 'had got mixed.' It was Indo-China not England and Japan not Germany![74]

All seemed ready when on 12 October the Kriegsmarine received an OKW directive which stated that the landing in England was to be continued solely for the purpose of maintaining political and military pressure on England.' This marked the death of Operation 'Sealion'. The ultimate cancellation of the landing in England followed on 10 January 1941. Although the landing in England failed to take place as planned, the Brandenburgers assigned to it had enjoyed, as one of them put it, 'a lovely swimming holiday by the sea.'

On 2 October the German order of the day was issued for Operation 'Felix', the codename for a proposed German seizure of Gibraltar by the 6th Army authorized by Hitler on 24 August but the operation was destined, like 'Sealion', never to take place. Included in the Proposed German order of battle was a detachment of 150 members of the Brandenburg Regiment. 'Felix' however, never got beyond the staff study stage, even though planning continued into 1944, primarily because of the reluctance of Spanish ruler Francisco Franco to commit Spain to enter the war on the Axis side. Hitler cancelled 'Felix' on 10 December 1940. If it had gone ahead the Brandenburgers would have carried out acts of sabotage, infiltration of the defences and other specialist missions.

History's post mortem analysis of 'Sealion' has led to the almost universally accepted view that had the assault gone ahead as planned it would have ended in total failure. Even if the Germans had gained the near total air superiority they needed there would have been other limiting factors weighing against the plan: with virtually no specialised landing craft the Germans would have needed to capture a port. This would have posed problems because, at least in theory, the ports and harbours were better defended than open beaches. Even if port facilities could have been captured, the bulk of the invading army would still have been ferried across

---

74 James P. Werbaneth.

the Channel in barges. This would have limited the number of tanks and heavy artillery that could be transported and, more importantly, restricted the crossing to favourable weather conditions. It is also claimed that the unprotected barges, designed for use on rivers and canals, would have sunk in even a moderate sea swell or have been blown out of the water by the Royal Navy. Either way thousands of German soldiers would have drowned in the English Channel. General William Edmund Ironside, Commander in Chief Home Forces' first aim was to 'prevent the enemy from running riot and tearing the guts out of the country as had happened in France and Belgium.' One of his first steps had been to order the construction of a huge ring of anti-tank obstacles called the 'GHQ Line' in front of the prime objectives of London and the industrial Midlands. Still further forward were numerous fortified 'stop lines' where divisions were supposed to hold to delay and break up German thrusts before they reached the 'GHQ Line'. In other words almost half the country was to be conceded to the Germans before trying to stop them on the 'GHQ Line'. Winston Churchill was against a strategy based on mobility and counter attack and Ironside was replaced on 20 July by General Sir Alan Brooke.

In 1974 at the Royal Military Academy Sandhurst, a major war game conducted to find out what might have happened had Nazi Germany launched Operation 'Sealion' in September 1940.[75] Available troops and resources were based on known plans from both sides and weather conditions were based on contemporary British Admiralty records that had, until then, never been published. The scenario assumed that the German military had taken until September to assemble the shipping necessary for a Channel crossing and that the Luftwaffe had not yet established air supremacy. The Luftwaffe also had to continue to bomb London. As happened historically, in the main

---

75 The war game, using a scale model of southeast England, the English Channel and northern France was organized by the *Daily Telegraph* and Dr. Paddy Griffith from the Department of War Studies at Sandhurst. The British umpires were Air Chief Marshal Christopher Foxley-Norris, Rear Admiral Teddy Gueritz and Major General Glyn Gilbert. The German umpires were General Adolf Galland (air), Admiral Friedrich Oskar Ruge (naval) and General Heinrich Trettner (land). The full text of the exercise is in *Sealion* by Richard Cox. The scenario is based on the known plans of each side, plus previously unpublished Admiralty weather records for September 1940. Each side (played by British and German officers respectively) was based in a command room and the actual moves plotted on a scale model of SE England constructed at the School of Infantry. The main problem the Germans face is that are a) the Luftwaffe has not yet won air supremacy; b) the possible invasion dates are constrained by the weather and tides (for a high water attack) and c) it has taken until late September to assemble the necessary shipping.

the Germans had only converted river barges available as transport ships. The actual dispositions of the Royal Navy in 1940 were not used in the war game. However, in the pre-planning it became obvious that, had the actual RN dispositions been applied to the exercise, then it was unlikely in the extreme that any organized German forces would have reached shore at all. Consequently, as the whole idea of the game was to bring about a land battle in Southern England (this was at Sandhurst, after all!) the bulk of the RN forces were moved back in order to give the landing forces a window of opportunity to get ashore.

On 22 September the first wave of a planned 330,000 men (8,000 airborne troops and 80,000 infantry, landing in amphibious operations) hit the beaches at dawn. Elements of nine divisions landed between Folkestone and Rottingdean (near Brighton). In addition 7th Fallschirmjäger Division landed at Lympne to take the airfield. The invasion fleet suffered minor losses from MTBs (Motor Torpedo Boats) during the night crossing but the Germans lost about 25% of their unseaworthy barges. The RN had already lost one heavy cruiser and three destroyers sunk, with one heavy cruiser and two destroyers damaged, whilst sinking three German destroyers. Within hours of the landings which overwhelmed the beach defenders, reserve formations were dispatched to Kent. Although there were 25 divisions in Great Britain, only seventeen were fully equipped and only three were based in Kent, however the defence plan relied on the use of mobile reserves and armoured and mechanized brigades were committed as soon as the main landings were identified. Meanwhile the air battle raged, the Luftwaffe flew 1,200 fighter and 800 bomber sorties before 1200 hours. The RAF even threw in training aircraft hastily armed with bombs, but the Luftwaffe were already having problems with their short ranged Bf 109s despite cramming as many as possible into the Pas de Calais. During this 24 hour period the RAF lost 237 aircraft (about 23% of its fighting strength), the Luftwaffe losses amounted to 333, also about 23% of its aircraft. Naval engagements were indecisive at this stage as the Royal Navy was still assembling its main destroyer fleet to attack. The larger ships of the Home Fleet (including battleships, heavy cruisers and aircraft carriers) were not to be committed due to their vulnerability to air attack and U-boats.

22-23 September. The Germans had still not captured a major port, although they started driving for Folkestone. Shipping unloading on the beaches suffered heavy losses from RAF bombing raids and then further losses at their ports in France. The U-boats, Luftwaffe and a few surface ships had lost contact with the Royal Navy, but then a cruiser squadron

HITLER'S INVASION OF EAST ANGLIA, 1940

with supporting destroyers entered the Channel narrows and had to run the gauntlet of long range coastal guns, E-boats and fifty Stukas. Two heavy cruisers were sunk and one damaged. However a diversionary German naval sortie from Norway was completely destroyed and other sorties by MTBs and destroyers inflicted losses on the shipping milling about in the Channel. German shipping losses on the first day amounted to over 25% of their invasion fleet, especially the barges, which proved desperately unseaworthy.

The Germans managed to advance a dozen or so miles inland and even captured the ports of Folkestone and Newhaven but the docks at Folkestone had been thoroughly demolished by the British rendering the port more or less unusable. British and Commonwealth forces were moved to fully engage in the battle with the first counter attack on 23rd September, halting the advance of the Germans towards Hastings and recapturing Newhaven. German paratroops were also pinned down by long-range artillery and harassment by stay-behind forces. At this stage the Germans had few tanks and only light artillery ashore. An increasing shortage of ammunition was slowly forcing them back towards the sea. The Germans asked 'Hitler' if the bombing of London could stop and the aircraft used to support the invasion. The request was denied. By dusk on 23 September the Germans had ten divisions ashore, but most were halted by counter attacks or awaiting supplies and reinforcements.

23 September, dawn - 1400 hours. The RAF had lost 237 aircraft out of 1,048 (167 fighters and seventy bombers) and the navy had suffered enough losses such that it was keeping its battleships and aircraft carriers back, but large forces of destroyers and heavy cruisers were massing. Air reconnaissance showed a German buildup in Cherbourg and forces were diverted to the South West. The Kriegsmarine was despondent about their losses, especially as the loss of barges was seriously dislocating domestic industry. The Army and Luftwaffe commanders were jubilant however and preparations for the transfer of the next echelon continued along with the air transport of the 22nd Luftlandeddivision despite Luftwaffe losses of 165 fighters and 168 bombers. Out of only 732 fighters and 724 bombers these were heavy losses. Both sides overestimated losses inflicted by 50%. The 22nd Luftlandeddivision airlanded successfully at Lympne, although long range artillery fire directed by a stay-behind commando group interdicted the runways. The first British counterattacks by 42nd Division supported by an armoured brigade halted the German 34th Division in its drive on Hastings. 7th Panzer Division was having difficulty with extensive anti-tank obstacles and assault teams armed with sticky bombs etc.

THE INVASION THAT NEVER WAS

Meanwhile an Australian Division had retaken Newhaven (the only German port); however the New Zealand Division arrived at Folkestone only to be attacked in the rear by 22nd Luftlandeddivision, which fell back on Dover having lost 35% casualties.

23 September, 1400-1900 hours. Throughout the day the Luftwaffe put up a maximum effort, with 1,500 fighter and 460 bomber sorties, but the RAF persisted in attacks on shipping and airfields. Much of this effort was directed for ground support and air resupply, despite Admiral Raeder's request for more air cover over the Channel. The Home Fleet had pulled out of air range however, leaving the fight in the hands of 57 destroyers and seventeen heavy cruisers plus MTBs. The Germans could put very little surface strength against this. Waves of destroyers and heavy cruisers entered the Channel and although two were sunk by U-boats, they sank one U-boat in return and did not stop. The German flotilla at Le Havre put to sea (three destroyers, fourteen E-boats) and at dusk intercepted the British, but were wiped out, losing all their destroyers and seven E-boats. The Germans now had ten divisions ashore, but in many cases these were incomplete and waiting for their second echelon to arrive that night. The weather was unsuitable for the barges however and the decision to sail was referred up the chain of command.

23 September 1900 hours - 24 September, dawn. The Führer Conference held at 1800 hours broke out into bitter inter-service rivalry - the Army wanted their second echelon sent and the navy protesting that the weather was unsuitable and the latest naval defeat rendered the Channel indefensible without air support. Göring countered this by saying it could only be done by stopping the terror bombing of London, which in turn Hitler vetoed. The fleet was ordered to stand by. The RAF meanwhile had lost 97 more fighters leaving only 440. The airfields of 11 Group were cratered ruins and once more the threat of collapse, which had receded in early September, was looming. The Luftwaffe had lost another 71 fighters and 142 bombers. Again both side's overestimated losses inflicted, even after allowing for inflated figures. On the ground the Germans made good progress towards Dover and towards Canterbury; however they suffered reverses around Newhaven when the 45th Division and Australians attacked. At 21:50 Hitler decided to launch the second wave, but only the short crossing from Calais and Dunkirk. By the time the order reached the ports, the second wave could not possibly arrive before dawn. The 6th and 8th Divisions at Newhaven, supplied from Le Havre, would not be reinforced at all.

24th September, dawn - 28th September. The second wave of the German invasion which was to include tanks and heavy artillery as well

HITLER'S INVASION OF EAST ANGLIA, 1940

as supplies and men was launched on the morning of 24 September, but only the short crossing from Calais and Dunkirk to Kent. The weather calmed and U-boats, E-boats and fighters covered them. At dawn the second wave was intercepted by a Royal Navy fleet of seventeen cruisers and 57 destroyers plus Motor Torpedo Boats. At daylight the 5th destroyer flotilla found the barges still ten miles off the coast and tore them to shreds. The Luftwaffe in turn committed all its remaining bombers and the RAF responded with nineteen squadrons of fighters. The Germans disabled two heavy cruisers and four destroyers, but 65% of the German barges, three destroyers and seven E-boats were sunk for the loss of only two Royal Navy destroyers (sunk by U-boats) plus two cruisers and four destroyers damaged. Some of the faster German steamers broke away and headed for Folkestone, but the port was so badly damaged they could only unload two at a time. With the Royal Navy suffering only minor losses, the Home Fleet was ordered to stand by to sail for the English Channel. The German divisions ashore only had enough ammunition for two to seven more days of fighting. Fast steamers and ferries were pressed into service to start an evacuation of German troops from Folkestone and Rye.

The failure on the crossing meant that the German situation became desperate. The divisions had sufficient ammunition for two to seven days more fighting, but without extra men and equipment could not extend the bridgehead. 'Hitler' ordered the remaining reserves to stand down and prepare for redeployment to Poland and the Germans began preparations for an evacuation as further British attacks hemmed them in tighter. Fast steamers and motor car ferries were assembled for evacuation via Rye and Folkestone. British air and sea attacks disrupted the German evacuation over the subsequent four days. The remaining German troops in England finally surrendered on 28 September.

In the 'real' September 1940 there were in the region of seventy RN destroyers and cruisers within six hours of the Dover Straits, together with several hundred smaller auxiliaries ranging from sloops and minesweepers to gunboats, armed trawlers and armed yachts. At a meeting with Hitler, Keitel and Jodl on 20 June 1940, Raeder reported that the German navy had no suitable vessels capable of transporting an invasion force, but that it was hoped that forty five barges could be made available within the next two weeks! It would have been a very narrow front indeed.

The German plan was to land one regiment from each of nine divisions on three separate beaches separated by miles from one another with the invasion fleet leaving Boulogne, Calais and Ostend/Antwerp. The initial wave was to take approximately 96 hours to completely cross and another 72 to get ashore. That equates to *one week* just to land the first wave! This puts the equivalent of just one weak infantry division ashore on each beach. The one available parachute division was to land behind one of the beaches over a period of about two days (the Luftwaffe could only lift about half the division at a time). With no, nada, none, zip, opposition the Germans could realistically expect to lose 30 to 50% of the landing barges just through beaching them. The invasion force had little more than a motley collection of motor minesweepers, armed trawlers and small gunboats for escort with virtually nothing bigger than a 3.7cm AA gun for armament. Many of the barges would have mounted 2 or 3.7cm AA guns. The majority of the crews operating the barges had little or no sailing experience. The Royal Navy had 36 destroyers and about 400 small craft committed to immediately countering an invasion crossing. There were 26½ divisions in England of which about thirteen were fully equipped and manned. One was a fully equipped armored division. There were also six tank brigades and a number of independent infantry brigades and battalions in existence. The Home Guard numbered about 250,000 men and most had at least basic small arms and some training. The air situation was that both sides were roughly even in strength and capacity. The British early warning radar system would have given ample warning of the approaching invasion among other systems. Surprise was going to be virtually impossible for the Germans to achieve. They had nothing beyond a vague plan to return the invasion ships back to France, reload them and send a second wave across about ten days after the first wave landed. Of the ports the first wave was ostensive to capture none was capable of supporting much more than a division or two in size. Basically, from these very bare facts one can see the absurdity of the German plan. They would have tried and it would have been a catastrophic disaster.

The German navy's relative weakness, combined with the Luftwaffe's lack of air supremacy, meant it was unable to prevent the Royal Navy from interfering with the planned Channel crossings. The Navy's destruction of the second invasion wave prevented resupply and reinforcement of the landed troops, as well as the arrival of more artillery and tanks. This made the position of the initially successful invasion force untenable; it suffered further casualties during the attempted evacuation. Of the 90,000 German troops who landed on 22nd September only 15,400 returned to France; 33,000

HITLER'S INVASION OF EAST ANGLIA, 1940

were taken prisoner, 26,000 were killed in the fighting and 15,000 drowned in the English Channel.

All six umpires deemed the invasion a resounding failure. But what if an invasion had resulted in a German victory? It would have begun after success achieved by the Luftwaffe over the RAF. Hitler issued the preliminary confirmation for Operation 'Sealion' on 14 September. The decision, reached at the Führer Conference of 3rd September (which had vetoed a massive retaliation against London) in favour of continuing the bombardment of the airfields and sector stations of the southern groups of the British Fighter Command, had led swiftly to the elimination of the RAF as an effective defensive force. During the first two weeks of September, the Luftwaffe destroyed better than 300 RAF fighters, but the irreplaceable pilot losses had been the decisive factor which had finally broken the RAF's resistance.

Following the issuance of the ten day warning signal, the Luftwaffe's tasks were divided between covering the invasion's mining operations and striking at the British Channel ports to disrupt and destroy the anti-invasion destroyer flotillas. With the RAF umbrella now shattered the Luftwaffe fully developed the anti-naval mission. Among German air attacks, mining operations and U-boat actions, between twenty and thirty British destroyers became casualties, two cruisers were sunk and the capital ships, the *Rodney* and the *Repulse* were damaged during the pre-invasion assault. On 20 September the blue water diversionary force lured a British pursuit team out of Scapa Flow into the distant North Atlantic. With the issuance of the final confirmation order on 21 September, the Operation 'Herbstreise' force departed Norway to feint a landing against the east Scottish coastline. Two days later, a pair of intercepting Royal Navy cruisers were eliminated from the Home Fleet Command: one a torpedo victim, the other badly mauled by Norway-based bombers.

Incorporated into the main invasion effort, another diversionary force of a dozen empty transports departed for Lyme Bay on the eve of the German landing operation. At dawn on 'S-Tag', 24 September, while the advance detachments of Army Group A struck the Kent and Sussex beaches between Folkestone and Brighton, the Lyme Bay feint diverted the Portsmouth naval forces away from the Dover Straits assault. Throughout 'S-Tag', the Channel, the invasion beaches and the port defences at Folkestone and Dover, were continually swept by the Luftwaffe's fighters and dive-bombers. Virtually unmolested by the scant British air reserves, the Luftwaffe actions damaged or sunk another nine Royal Navy destroyers, as well as aiding the combined assault of the 17th and 7th Flieger-Division, which captured Folkestone harbour within hours of the first sea-borne landings at Beach B. 'S-Tag' saw the Germans put ashore more than 60,000 troops and although neither Dover on the right flank, nor Brighton on the left, was taken by the initial assault, the lodgement in between these end points varied between three and five miles in depth before the inland advance halted for the day.

Throughout the first three days during which the Germans solidified a seventy by ten mile bridgehead into which they poured a 125,000 man first strike force, British artillery and anti-tank fire was relatively scarce. The British infantry were holding salients against the German perimeter, as well as determinedly resisting the attacks against Dover and Brighton. On the fourth day ashore, 16th Army took Dover, but not before British saboteurs had wrecked the harbor quays and cranes and so effectively sealed the harbor entrance with sunken blockships as to prevent German debarkations at Dover for at least two weeks. At the smaller harbour at Eastbourne, the remaining echelons for the 9th Army's Brighton landings arrived on S plus 6, just in time to meet the counter-attack of the British mobile reserve attempting to break through to the beach east of the still British-held strongpoint at Brighton. The British counter-attack, spearheaded by the 1st Armored Division, came too late to penetrate the entrenched German position near Hadlow Down. By 7th October, Strauss' 9th Army, newly reinforced with the 4th and 7th Panzer Divisions, had pushed the British back across the initial lodgement line connecting to the 16th Army perimeter. The weather continued to favour the German build-up during most of October.

The assault to gain the first operational objective along the River Thames was launched on 20 October. With Dover now in operation, von Rundstedt was able to bring the four panzer and two motorized divisions of the second wave ashore to lead the German breakout operation. On 23 October the Thames was breached about fifty miles west of London at Wallingford, while Stuka dive-bombers silenced the British artillery positions north of the river. Within five days London was isolated by curving panzer formations which reached Maldon on the east coast on 28 October. The second Operational Objective, the Gloucester-Maldon line, was sealed on the thirty-fourth day of the German invasion.

On 5 November, the anniversary of the 'Gunpowder Plot,' the house-to-house fighting in London moved down Whitehall. The British die-hards

HITLER'S INVASION OF EAST ANGLIA, 1940

were there, among them Winston Churchill, cigar in mouth. A week earlier, the King and notable British lords had sailed from Liverpool to Halifax, Nova Scotia, where a free British government would meet to discredit the collaborationists' armistice announced in London on 14 November. More than 60,000 British troops would be evacuated from Glasgow between 23-30 November, leaving Hitler in control of the British Isles. The successful invasion of Britain in the autumn of 1940 led Hitler to launch Operation 'Barbarossa' in May 1941. With the Wehrmacht fully concentrated against the Russians, the Germans succeeded in capturing Moscow in early September. It appeared to be the finest hour in the thousand years of the German Reich.

Chapter 6

'The Germans have Landed'

I make no apology for saying again that invasion is certainly coming soon, but what I want to impress upon you is that while you must feverishly take every conceivable precaution, nothing that you or the government can do is really of the slightest use. Don't be deceived by this lull before the storm, because, although there is still the chance of peace, Hitler is aware of the political and economic confusion in England and is only waiting for the right moment. Then, when his moment comes, he will strike and strike hard.

William Joyce, or 'Lord Haw-Haw', as he was unpopularly known, *Germany Calling*, 6 August 1940. Joyce who was an Irish-American fascist politician and Nazi propaganda broadcaster, born on Herkimer Street in Brooklyn, New York on 24 April 1906 to an Anglican mother and an Irish Catholic father who had taken United States citizenship. His broadcasts initially came from studios in Berlin, later transferring (due to heavy Allied bombing) to Luxembourg and were relayed over a network of German-controlled radio stations that included Hamburg, Bremen, Luxembourg, Hilversum, Calais, Oslo and Zeese. In 1940 Joyce had an estimated six million regular and 18 million occasional listeners in Britain. The broadcasts always began with the announcer's words 'Germany calling, Germany calling, Germany calling'. These broadcasts urged the British people to surrender and were well known for their jeering, sarcastic and menacing tone. There was also a desire by civilian listeners to hear what the other side was saying, since information during wartime was strictly censored and at the start of the war it was possible for German broadcasts to be more informative than those of the BBC. Joyce was hanged by Albert Pierrepoint on 3rd January 1946 at Wandsworth Prison aged 39.

HITLER'S INVASION OF EAST ANGLIA, 1940

On Saturday, 31st August much improved conditions prevailed throughout the British Isles with temperatures slightly higher than the previous days and conditions were expected to remain fine with cloud periods in all Channel areas. Göring this time meant business. The Luftwaffe launched a total of 1,310 sorties against Britain in an apparent all out effort to destroy Fighter Command in one way or another. More than 22 squadrons were in action for most of the day, many of them going up to four sorties. The Vauxhall Motor Works at Luton was hit resulting in over fifty people being killed. In one of the worst days for the RAF, 39 aircraft were destroyed and fourteen pilots killed. Over fifty RAF personnel were killed (39 of these at Biggin Hill) with nearly thirty seriously injured. Two hundred civilians had been killed in the air raids and along with the radar stations of Pevensey, Beachy Head and Foreness sustaining damage, Biggin Hill was made virtually inoperable and the control of its sector was transferred to Hornchurch. The Luftwaffe lost a total of 41 fighters and bombers destroyed. As night fell, there was to be no let up. A force of 130 plus Ju 88s and He 111s of Luftflotte 3 made a night attack on the Liverpool, which was attacked for the fourth consecutive night. Do 17s and He 111s made raids on London and Portsmouth and Manchester was bombed, as was Worcester and Bristol. During the hours of darkness an oil refinery near Rotterdam and cities in Holland and Belgium and Berlin felt the brunt of an Bomber Command offensive as well.

At about 2100 hours on the clear, dark evening the heavens appeared to open up to the south of the Orford Lighthouse. Ronald Ashford, an 18-year old apprentice watchmaker and a Home Guard volunteer was on 'red alert' manning an improvised strongpoint on the outskirts of his home town of Aldeburgh. For more than three months he had spent many a long night on evening 'stand-to' with nothing to show for it. Ashford was one of thirty men of the local Home Guard platoon that had been on duty manning improvised defences on the southern outskirts of the town. The entire coast from Norfolk to Sussex was now Britain's front line and at that precise moment in time hundreds of other regular army and Home Guard units were also manning defences. But for those along the coast of East Anglia the previous two weeks had been especially anxious. There had been a continuous state of heightened alert following reports of large scale German embarkations along the Norwegian coast. All units had also received orders to be especially vigilant for a surprise landing by enemy paratroops. It seemed that despite the very obvious German preparations across the Channel, it now appeared that the invasion might fall on the east coast after all. If the enemy did arrive in the area, Aldeburgh Home Guard was expected to raise the alarm and then fight from behind a wall, firing through the loopholes they had knocked out of the brickwork. But they would have been up against the same kind of airborne troops that had conquered the Belgian fortress of Ében-Émael; elite troops to whom a brick wall with rifle slits would have posed little in the way of a challenge.

Aldeburgh platoon, like many others, had been formed in May and just like many other Home Guard units it had only recently been armed. But there was little ammunition for the few rifles they had been given and some of the men, especially the younger ones, had practically no training in the use of firearms. Many of the older men, including the commanding officer, Sir Basil Eddis, were veterans of WWI and were only too aware of the desperate situation they faced, but still managed to display some fortitude. Nevertheless, just like everyone else on the front line, deep inside they hoped the enemy paratroops they'd been told to look out for would never come. But tonight on the last day of August, as they looked to the south over the River Alde and Sudbourne Marshes, men like Ronald Ashford had reason to believe that their worst fears were about to be realised. Ashford heard tremendous gunfire and explosions in the distance and then a red glow filled the night sky over Shingle Street along the coast, which would put the fire somewhere in the Hollesley Bay area. Anxiously, he loaded a few precious rounds of ammunition into a rifle he barely knew how to use. Sporadic gunfire and the red glow lasted for several hours. Ashford said later that 'word was received that a German landing had taken place' and that 'this was later confirmed by eye-witness accounts of a shoreline littered with burned bodies. It appeared that this landing had been expected... The seabed had been laid with piping from the shore at intervals with flammable liquid.' Ashford always believed that what he witnessed that night was nothing less than an attempted German invasion on the Suffolk coast.

And he was not alone. Less than half a mile distant, away from the deserted streets of Aldeburgh and secluded behind its thick 'blackout' screens, the inside of the Jubilee Hall echoed to the sounds of a Saturday night dance. Locals rubbed shoulders with those military personnel fortunate enough to be off duty and everyone was enjoying some precious time away from the problems of daily life in a country at war and virtually under siege. Despite wartime restrictions, the weekend dance still gave younger people a chance to socialise for a few hours and leave the outside world to itself. But late in the evening, the carefree proceedings were suddenly interrupted by a brief, but curious incident and what happened would linger in the memories of some of those present like Henry Baldry long after the event. Some Army officers arrived and ordered military personnel to muster outside. They said that they needed to commandeer all available transport because 'some Germans had landed at Orfordness.' This unusual interruption lasted only a matter of minutes and when the officers left dancing was resumed. Despite the urgency of the appeal and as far as Henry Baldry recalled, for some reason the cars and soldiers were not taken after all. No one thought any more about it, little realising that they had just witnessed the opening stages of what was destined to become a wartime mystery.

While the gunfire and explosions continued in the vicinity of Shingle Street. In Felixstowe the 5th Battalion Kings Regiment fully manned all their defensive positions throughout the night and into Sunday morning following receipt of a single air raid warning at 2210, following which, 'the Battalion stood to in their posts or the reserve platoon areas'. The warning remained operative until 0310 the following morning. Though routine, it seems to be a particularly long 'stand to' for a single air raid warning, especially since there appears to be no evidence that an air raid was threatened or actually took place. There are two reports of enemy aircraft activity on 31st August. The 2nd Battalion the Liverpool Scottish diary says that 'just before 0900, the Bren gunners of No.3 Anti-Aircraft post opened fire on an enemy aircraft 'hedge hopping' towards the North'. RAF files reveal that a Dornier Do 17Z-2 was shot down by a Hurricane of 111 Squadron at RAF Debden flown by Flight Lieutenant Herbert Selwyn shortly after 0900. The final entry in the 2nd Battalion the Liverpool Scottish diary states: 'At 1500 hours a Dornier was chased over the camp by a British fighter and crashed into the sea off Bawdsey. Unfortunately it started a large fire in Tangham Forest and we rushed every available man to it'. The Dornier Do 215 had been intercepted over Cromer and then chased south pursued by three Spitfires of 66 Squadron at RAF Coltishall. It eventually crashed into the sea about twenty miles east south east of Felixstowe at 1503 hours with the loss of all four crew.

The southern edge of what was once Tangham Forest (now part of Rendlesham Forest) bordered Hollesley Heath and lay a little over two miles to the north of Shingle Street. If there was a large fire in this forest during the evening of 31 August it would almost certainly have been visible from Aldeburgh, just over eight miles away but the fire quite clearly occurred during the day. However, the first of two other reports in the 2nd Liverpool Scots' war diary referring to fires in Tangham Forest occurred on Monday, 19th August, which says, quite precisely: 'Fifteen incendiary bombs dropped at Tangham Forest started an eight acre fire... foresters put it out before dawn.' The war diary of the 165th Infantry Brigade for the same date records: '0045 hours, fifteen incendiaries dropped on Tangham Forest', (the fire seems to have been put out by the foresters themselves without any help from the army).[76] On 21 August the 165th Brigade diary reports: '18 30 hours. 55 incendiaries dropped on Tangham Forest'. This event is also reported in the diary of the Liverpool Scots, though neither diary records the extent of the resulting fire.

Not only did these events occur on dates other than the 31st, a forest fire would not explain Ron Ashford's recollections of 'tremendous gunfire and explosions that went on for several hours.' And if Henry Baldry witnessed army officers interrupting the Jubilee Hall dance in search of volunteers to fight a forest fire, why would they announce that 'some Germans had landed at Orfordness'? The only war diary that reports 'a glow in the night sky' on 31st August appears in the diary of 1/4 Battalion, South Lancashire Regiment, which was manning defences in the Dunwich area. The diary, timed at 2310, reports: 'Several miles South West glare from fire seen and as there was enemy aircraft activity at the time may have been incendiary bombs.' This exceptionally well kept and neatly typed diary records not only the time of the activity observed, but also the map reference of the observation post from which it was reported. A copy of a War Office 'purple grid' map reveals the OP to have been near the beach at Benacre Ness, just a mile and a half from Kessingland. If a line is drawn on the map directly southwest from this position it crosses over Southwold, Dunwich, Aldeburgh, Orford and Shingle Street. Therefore the source of the glow could quite possibly have been in the general direction of Aldeburgh and the coast beyond, or in Tangham Forest nearby. As the crow flies, Benacre Ness is 27 miles to the northeast of Shingle Street but the glow from a fire,

---

76 Further supportive evidence for the fire on the 19th also appears in ARP files. Intelligence Summary 703, for Monday, 19th August reports: 'No 4 Eastern Region ... a number IB (incendiary bombs) were dropped in rural areas in East Suffolk. Some trees were burned in Tangham Forest'. The only reference to east Suffolk in an ARP intelligence summary covering the evening of 31st August to the morning of 1st September, is of some bombs being dropped at Tannington, a small village near Framlingham, around fifteen miles to the northwest of Shingle Street.

even a large one, would have almost certainly been visible at that distance. A full blackout had been in operation since 2017 hours and under blackout conditions even the smallest light was visible over large distances. Just a few months earlier, during the Dunkirk evacuation, the headlines of the *Daily Telegraph* had reported: 'Fierce fighting along French coast - Midnight fires visible from England' so it is possible that a large fire could have been seen quite far away along the coast, especially if there had been cloud cover to reflect the glow.

The war diary of 327 Coastal Battery at Southwold just five miles below the 1/4 South Lancs' observation posts guarding the Suffolk coast near Dunwich does not begin until November 1940, as does 328 Coastal Battery at Aldeburgh.[77] At 2200 a South Lancs' forward observation post near Covehithe four miles north of Southwold and seven miles south of Lowestoft reported yellow flares and pyrotechnic signals fired out to sea in direction east along their battalion front. Half an hour later an OP a little further up the coast reported 'Orange flares over Kessingland'. The use of flare pistols had been strictly prohibited for any purpose other than to warn of the presence of the enemy and strict orders dictated that all sightings of warning signals be relayed to forward Battalion HQs at once by the quickest means possible. While this reporting procedure was in progress, troops in the forward beach defences were placed on 'action stations,' rifles were loaded and bayonets fixed. Bren gunners snapped a full magazine in place, adjusted settings and prepared to fire rapid bursts toward the beach obstacles. Everyone kept a sharp lookout and was ready to open fire on anything that moved out in the darkness as reports from forward observation posts continued to come in.

From Lowestoft to Sheringham there were various reports of naval gunfire, flares and explosions out to sea, continuing from 2200 until the early hours of Sunday morning. Off the stretch of coast from Lowestoft to Great Yarmouth naval gunfire was heard out to sea between 2200 and 2300 and more reports of flashes and explosions out to sea continued into

---

[77] The war diary for 355 Coast Battery at Sizewell does begin in June 1940, but the entries are sparse and there are none for the weekend of 31 August/1 September. The war diary of the 164th Infantry Brigade, the higher formation the South Lancs served under, records very little, having only one page for August 1940. The entire period from 5th August to 30th September 1940 is missing from the war diary of the 4th Battalion, Suffolk Regiment, at the time stationed in the Great Yarmouth area,. War diaries are not day to day journals in the general sense of the term and many do have gaps, but it is highly unusual that almost two whole months should be missing.

'THE GERMANS HAVE LANDED'

the early hours of Sunday morning. The earliest of the reports appearing in the diary of the 54th Infantry Brigade states: 'Naval practice-shoot off Corton at 2200-2300 hours'. Units of the 55th Infantry Brigade reported: 'various flares and explosions at sea' that continued for the following two to three hours into Sunday morning. This is also stated to have been a naval practice shoot. There are no reports of naval practice shoots in Admiralty records at this time and the Nore Command had more immediate and pressing concerns than gunnery practice. A suspicious convoy had been spotted at 2110 by RAF reconnaissance aircraft off the West Frisian Islands, steaming on a course of 270° or in plain language, heading west - straight for the Norfolk coast. As a precautionary measure, units of the Home Fleet at Scapa Flow were ordered to raise steam and reinforcements were ordered from the naval base at Rosyth. Throughout the night the light cruisers *Birmingham*, *Southampton* and *Manchester*, accompanied by destroyers, sailed at full steam towards the Humber and the light cruisers *Aurora* and *Galatea* were ordered to rendezvous with the destroyers *Jupiter*, (Captain Louis Mountbatten's 5th Flotilla flagship) *Kelvin* and *Vortigern* near the Sheringham Light Float.

Further south, destroyers from Harwich along with available reinforcements from Sheerness took up positions off the Suffolk coast. Destroyers from Harwich along with reinforcements from Sheerness took up positions off Orfordness and Aldeburgh. In London, Winston Churchill's private secretary, Sir John 'Jock' Colville, recalled in his diary published as *The Fringes of Power*: 'After dinner the First Lord rang up from Brighton to say that enemy ships were steering westwards from Terschelling. The invasion may be pending (though I'll lay 10-1 against!) and all HM Forces are taking up their positions. If these German ships came on they would reach the coast of Norfolk tomorrow morning.' At 2345 or thereabouts the Admiralty informed army coastal units from Norfolk to Essex about approaching 'enemy ships'. The entry in the war diary of the 46th Infantry Brigade at Basildon states: 'C in C Nore reported a number of enemy vessels heading for this area. They could not arrive before dawn 0500 hours.' Troops manning coastal defences watched and waited, but as events transpired the remainder of the night was uneventful - at least in south Essex.

During the two to three hours that followed receipt of the Admiralty's warning, coastal units of the 55th Infantry Brigade reported various 'flares and explosions at sea' and the 5th Battalion Royal Norfolks at Weybourne reported 'large numbers of craft twenty miles off the Norfolk coast

HITLER'S INVASION OF EAST ANGLIA, 1940

steaming westward.' (Was the diarist recording receipt of the Admiralty alert regarding the enemy convoy on course for the east coast and had he made a simple error, putting '20' instead of '120' miles?). By daybreak on the Sunday most army units had either stood down or were about to after what had been a long night. There would be one final incident for the 2nd Liverpool Scots when, at 0730, in broad daylight, AA machine gunners fired at a low flying German aircraft over Bawdsey. The war diary of 5th Battalion Suffolk Regiment recorded: 'no more developments of the message received at 2345 last night... Learnt during the day that the navy were engaged during the night about 120 miles off the Norfolk coast but no further details available.'

While army units were receiving the Admiralty's warning, *Jupiter*, *Kelvin* and *Vortigern* were patrolling off the coast listening in to the urgent exchange of radio signals between Admiralty HQ and the five destroyers off the Dutch Coast. At around 2230 the five ships of the 20th Destroyer Flotilla headed by HMS *Ivanhoe*, about to embark on a secret mine laying operation in enemy waters, received the order to locate an enemy force and make a night attack. A little over half an hour later the *Ivanhoe*, *Express* and *Esk* were approximately forty miles off the Dutch coast, with *Intrepid* and *Icarus* trailing just under half a mile behind. At 2305 a sudden and terrific explosion near *Express*'s forward magazine tore off all of the bow section, right back to the bridge. Miraculously the destroyer managed to stay afloat. Minutes later, while manoeuvering alongside the *Express* to render assistance, *Ivanhoe* also was damaged by a severe explosion. In the following confusion and in the belief that the order to abandon ship had been given, sailors from both ships took to the life boats and rafts. Almost simultaneously the unfolding disaster reached its dreadful climax when HMS *Esk* suffered two successive and violent explosions and sank almost immediately. Lieutenant Commander R. J. H. Crouch and his entire crew except one were killed.

At 2313 hours in the very midst of the catastrophe, the destroyers received a second, more urgent radio communication from C-in-C Nore Command to 'jettison mines immediately with safety pins in and attack enemy.' This was an order that fate had already prevented from being carried out. The whole tragedy from beginning to end had lasted just twenty minutes. *Ivanhoe*, still afloat but with her engines out of action, ordered the *Express* to proceed westward to England. *Intrepid* and *Icarus* retired from the area having managed to escape the carnage unscathed. At one minute to midnight HMS *Intrepid* sent a signal to Admiralty HQ Whitehall

'THE GERMANS HAVE LANDED'

giving the bleak details of the situation and that along with HMS *Icarus* she was returning to the Humber. As they turned about army units along the coast from Norfolk to Essex were receiving the news that enemy ships were heading their way. Troops fully kitted out in all their equipment including respirators were immediately placed on full alert.

Shortly after midnight some distance northeast of Sheringham, *Jupiter* received reports that the *Express*, *Ivanhoe* and *Esk* had hit mines. Realising that assistance was required the three destroyers set a course eastwards and made for Gap D, the nearest gap in the east coast defensive minefield. Shortly after getting under way lookouts reported very large flashes to the southward at sea off the coast. Assuming that this might be an action involving an enemy invasion force the destroyers altered course and in the words of Captain Louis Mountbatten, *Jupiter*'s Captain, proceeded to 'March to the sound of the guns.' At 0210 hours *Jupiter*'s searchlight 'illuminated a darkened ship whose character at first appeared doubtful'. It also attracted the attention of a Fairey Swordfish aircraft of 812 Squadron Fleet Air Arm at RAF North Coates which was low on fuel after a raid on the Vlaardingen oil tanks near Rotterdam. It subsequently ditched in the sea and all three crew were rescued. The destroyers completed the 44 mile journey through Gap D and by 0500 on Sunday morning had passed through the east coast mine barrier. They then proceeded to search for the damaged *Ivanhoe* and *Express*.

At dawn on the 1st HMS *Ivanhoe*, with its main engine still out of action, was spotted some distance east of their position by a RAF Coastal Command Hudson aircraft from North Coates which signalled that four MTBs were coming from Felixstowe to take on the wounded. At 1100 hours they arrived. Some of the first to be rescued were 25 men in one of *Ivanhoe*'s whalers. MTB 15 remained with the destroyer and a skeleton crew strayed on board to continue with an attempt to get the ship back to England. (Lifeboats and rafts from *Ivanhoe* and *Express* would be located over the following two days but many survivors drifted helplessly toward the Dutch coast and were taken prisoner). By 0900 the *Express* had been located and HMS *Kelvin* began the long and hazardous task of towing her back to the Humber, stern first. Two hours later the tow broke and *Jupiter* took over for a while, leaving *Kelvin* free to proceed to the assistance of the stranded *Ivanhoe*. By the early afternoon *Ivanhoe*'s skeleton crew had finally given up and been taken off by MTB 15. The abandoned destroyer drifted for nearly two hours before being located by HMS *Kelvin* and scuttled with a single torpedo.

HITLER'S INVASION OF EAST ANGLIA, 1940

The rescue operation would continue through the night and on into Monday, 2nd September with MTBs and RAF aircraft continuing the widespread search for lifeboats. Some survivors told of seeing 'suspicious motorboats' during the early hours of Sunday morning. Late that afternoon the Admiralty received intelligence from 'reliable sources' (Alpha intelligence - an 'Enigma' decrypt) reporting that an important German formation, type unknown, would be at sea that night, operating between Dutch and English coasts and would enter Dutch ports Monday early morning. Coded messages were immediately sent to C-in-C Nore Command and the War Office and Air Ministry were also made aware of this important information. At 0350 on Monday morning it was reported that '40 vessels, motor cruiser type, 60' long 53° 04^ 3° 48'E, lights on masts three unidentified vessels fired on our aircraft' a little over ninety miles due east of Great Yarmouth, heading in a south-westerly direction. Admiralty intelligence had estimated that a large fleet of motor boats could land several thousand men in a lightening raid on the British coast and this, by any estimation, was a large fleet. This force was larger than the convoy spotted on 31st August, yet their presence, closer to the Suffolk coast and larger in number than the one reported on the Saturday evening, does not appear to have sparked a similar alarm. Could it be that the RN knew there was no threat from this force, which might have been in the process of returning to Dutch ports, possibly because the planned operation they were due to take part in had been called off?

By mid-morning on Monday, 2nd September many of the larger Royal Navy ships were back in port and it was left to the MTBs to continue the search for any remaining survivors. The *Express* finally reached the Humber in the late afternoon, just as the last group of survivors was being picked up in the North Sea. They would eventually arrive at Great Yarmouth around midnight on 2nd September, bringing the operation to a close. During the next few days the survivors were landed at several east coast ports, including Great Yarmouth, from where some were transported inland to Norwich. All told the death toll on the three destroyers was almost 300 but with wounded and prisoners, the full casualty figure was well over 400. Only during Dunkirk did the Nore Command suffer worse losses in a single day.[78] Pat Barnes, a schoolgirl

---

78 *The Battle of the East Coast (1939-1945)* by J. P. Foynes. The true scale of the Royal Navy's loss was revealed when, on Friday, 13th September *The Times* published the full casualty lists for *Esk*, *Ivanhoe* and *Express*.

'THE GERMANS HAVE LANDED'

living on a poultry farm in Spixworth, north-east of the city recalled: 'For two days a convoy of army ambulances occupied Crostwick Lane, travelling slowly, the drivers very grim-faced. We used to get lots of army traffic through the lane but nothing like this. Occasionally an army lorry would stop for eggs or apples and so the next time my mother asked what was going on two weeks before. She was told that they contained the dead bodies of Germans washed up on the beach, as an invasion had been attempted. But that was all we were told.'[79]

On Monday, as the crippled *Express* was being towed stern first into the River Humber and long before the Admiralty made any public statements about the *Express*, *Esk* and *Ivanhoe*, reports appeared in several newspapers suggesting that the Royal Navy had lost both ships and men in some sort of action. The Ipswich *Evening Star* said that 'reports, coming from Berlin via neutral sources, claimed that on the previous Saturday night German U-boats had sunk two British destroyers in the North Sea.' Both the *Evening Star* and the Norwich *Eastern Evening News* reported: 'Nazis Claim 5 Destroyers Sunk.' As well as the two previously unnamed destroyers sunk by U-boats, three 'modern' destroyers, *Express, Esk and Ivanhoe* had also been sunk. The *Express* of course had not been sunk, but the fact that the three destroyers had been named by the Germans before the Admiralty had released any details to the British public was unusual. The German claims were reported on the front page of Friday's *Daily Mirror* beneath the heading 'Destroyers *Ivanhoe, Esk* and *Express* reported sunk'. (The *Eastern Daily Press*, quoting from a released Admiralty communiqué later, accurately reported the loss of the *Ivanhoe* and *Esk* as being sunk by 'torpedoes or mines' and that the *Express* had been damaged but was safely in port). The German claims also made the front page of the *News Chronicle*, while the successful sinking of the German troopship by a 'British submarine' on Monday, 2nd September was relegated to page 6. (HMS *Sturgeon* had torpedoed and sank a German troopship off the coast of Denmark,

---

[79] *The Bodies On The Beach* by James Hayward. On Saturday, 7th September, German E-boats attacked a merchant convoy off Great Yarmouth in broad daylight sinking four small merchant vessels and damaging a fifth. Hit and run attacks such as this, carried out by fast German 'sea raiders' had been a regular occurrence off the coast of East Anglia since the outbreak of the war, although they were rarely, if ever, reported in the press. News that enemy naval forces were operating just off the east coast and with virtual impunity would not have made comfortable reading. As in many other cases, the public remained unaware that another four merchant ships had just fallen prey to the hunters of 'E-Boat Alley'.

drowning an estimated 3,000 enemy troops).[80] Within days the Swedish press had named the ship as the *Marion* or *Barion* [sic] and reported that 'much wreckage and corpses had been washed ashore on the Swedish coast.' No German troopship named the *Marion* was known to exist and Admiralty reports identified the ship as the *Pionier* which was destined to become inextricably linked with stories that would soon emerge of German bodies on English beaches.

The Admiralty enquiry into the incident off the Dutch coast, which drew upon eye witness accounts and records of naval signals traffic for the night of 31st August concluded that the destroyers had hit mines having changed course to intercept a reported enemy convoy and that no other enemy forces had been involved. From the available evidence it seemed probable that the mystery armada was a mixed force of minelayers, auxiliary minesweepers and torpedo boats escorted by three destroyers, the *Erich Steinbrink*, *Paul Jacobi* and the *Karl Galster*; all in all a force of about fourteen ships. German sources reveal that the mine laying mission and long voyage from Cuxhaven down the Dutch coast to Rotterdam was uneventful. While it is acknowledged that the flotilla was spotted by RAF reconnaissance aircraft there is no mention of sighting let alone action against any British warships. It is apparent however that the Germans had intercepted RN signals traffic during the night and were aware of the fate that had befallen the British ships.

Whatever the cause of the night's activity, things had quietened down by dawn on the Sunday morning. Over the following days word spread amongst local troops that the German's had attempted a landing on the Suffolk coast. Stories on the 'grapevine' told of beaches littered with German dead, some of them, it was said, wearing British uniforms. It was whispered that an invasion had been stopped by 'setting the sea on fire' or that an armada of enemy ships had been destroyed by the RAF and Royal Navy; the

---

80   At the time this success for the Royal Navy was the exception rather than the rule. Until the spring of 1940 the war at sea had gone steadily in Britain's favour. Even the Germans' victorious campaign had cost the Kriegsmarine one-third of its cruisers and almost half its destroyers. However, in the period between June and October, when U-boats sank 282 ships with only seven U-boats lost to all causes, became known to the U-boat crews as the 'Happy Time'. At first the U-boats attacked shipping in the South-West Approaches. During June sinkings by U-boats peaked at 63 ships. By August they became bolder, following up on the surface during the day and delaying closing in on convoys until nightfall. To escape detection by the Asdics they remained on the surface and attacked under cover of darkness. Coastal Command did not have an answer to such tactics and from the beginning of June to the end of 1940 over 300 million tons of Allied and neutral shipping was sunk.

outcome of either ending with hundreds of dead German soldiers being washed up on east coast beaches. An RAF pilot told of being scrambled from an aerodrome in the south of England during the invasion alert. Flying a Blackburn Roc he had orders to drop incendiaries and ignite an oil/petrol mixture which had been spread on the surface of the sea. Later in the war Ronald Ashford said that a refugee from Belgium, who had joined the British armed forces in 1944 and was now based in Suffolk, claimed to have known about the invasion attempt on the night of 31st August/1st September 1940. The Belgian, who had been living in the Belgian port area at the time in question, said that he had witnessed survivors landing at the port - 'some badly burned - and bringing many bodies with them.' Ashford believed, along with many others, that all reports of this event were immediately suppressed by Britain's wartime government. The spreading rumours were discussed in the corridors of government and vague reports appeared in some newspapers. But behind the whispers and denials, on the east coast Ron Harris and the other coastguards at Shingle Street received written orders to 'look out for charred bodies.'

Chapter 7

Caught like Fish in a Frying Pan

'We were caught like fish in a frying pan,' was the way a German soldier who escaped from the debacle described it to a French nurse. Only a few thousand Germans succeeded in reaching the French coast. The others perished in the sea or were burned to death... The fact is that hospitals in occupied France are filled with Nazi soldiers, all of them suffering from severe burns. Thousands of dead Germans have been washed ashore.
According to a 15th December report in the *New York Times* by one Boris Nikolayevsky, no doubt issued from the BSC office on Rockefeller Plaza.

On the afternoon of 5 July 1940 Major General Sir Thomas MacDonald 'Donald' Banks KCB DSO MC TD, recently returned from active service in France with the 50th Northumbrian Division, met with Mr. Geoffrey Lloyd, the MP for Birmingham Ladywood and newly appointed Secretary of State for Petroleum, a position he would hold until 1942. Born in St Peter Port, Guernsey on 31 March 1891, Banks saw service in the First World War as Commanding Officer of the 10th (Service) Battalion Essex Regiment and the 8th Battalion Royal Berkshire Regiment. As a result of his actions, he was awarded the DSO, Military Cross, the Croix de Guerre and was mentioned in despatches twice. After World War I he continued with the Territorial Army and commanded the Kensington Regiment from 1927 to 1931. He was knighted in the New Years' Honours List of 1935. In 1936, he transferred to the Air Ministry, where he was appointed Permanent Secretary, in 1938 becoming first Permanent Under Secretary of State for Air. He was responsible for setting up the Empire Air Training Scheme and travelled to Australia and New Zealand to discuss the manufacture of aircraft there. In the Second World War he returned to military service and was Adjutant and Quartermaster General of the 50th (Northumbrian)

Division. He served in the British Expeditionary Force (BEF) in 1940 and was mentioned in despatches. He became a Major-General in 1943.[81]

The government minister outlined the dilemma he faced: the vast stocks of petroleum in Britain's refineries and depots, either risked destruction by enemy bombing or, in the event of an invasion, would have to be destroyed to prevent them falling into enemy hands. However, the Secretary of State had an idea of how they might be better used in the country's defence and gave Sir Donald the responsibility of heading a new department tasked with the development of flame warfare. And so it was that on 9 July, according to its history, the Petroleum Warfare Department officially came into being, having been created with the specific purpose of developing offensive and defensive petroleum flame weapons. Lloyd would claim later that his initial interest in the possibilities of flame warfare had been inspired by reports of British soldiers: 'who'd seen a blazing petrol lorry hold up some advancing Germans during the Dunkirk retreat.' This may well be true, but the PWD had been jointly conceived by Lloyd and Lord Hankey, Chancellor of the Duchy of Lancaster and a leading government advisor, who had a long standing interest in flame warfare dating back to WWI. Both men shared the same vision of using Britain's considerable petroleum stocks to create an impenetrable ring of fire around the nation's shores; a ring of fire that would 'swamp the invader in a sea of flame.'

American intelligence chief, Colonel William Donovan, a millionaire Wall Street lawyer and an influential Republican, had worked with MI6 on an occasional basis since 1916. In July 1940 Donovan was invited to visit Britain to assess the military situation first hand and to counteract the gloomy reports sent back by Joseph P. Kennedy, a

---

81 From 1940 to 1945 he was Director-General of the Petroleum Warfare Department, which developed innovative applications for petrol during the conflict, including FIDO, (fog dispersal at airports) and PLUTO (pipeline under the ocean taking fuels from England to Europe during and after the Invasion build-up). In 1946 he was awarded Legion of Merit, Degree of Commander by the President of the United States of America. The citation reads: Major-General Sir Donald Banks, British Army Director General, Petroleum Warfare Department, Ministry of Fuel and Power, performed outstanding services in the ETO from March 1943 to November 1944, by assisting in the production and manufacture of an improved American flamethrower fuel. His department cooperated fully with the American Forces and adapted the Crocodile mechanical flamethrower to the Sherman tank and trained American personnel in its operation and maintenance. He also provided the US 9th Air Force with a field mixing unit which was employed during the Normandy campaign. General Banks cooperation and keen understanding of the problems involved, contributed substantially to the successful prosecution of the war.

HITLER'S INVASION OF EAST ANGLIA, 1940

self-made millionaire of Irish stock and America's defeatist ambassador in London.[82] Donovan arrived on 17th July and spent a whirlwind tour of just over two weeks, meeting King George VI, Winston Churchill and the heads of MI6, MI5 and SOE, as well as other assorted senior intelligence figures. Much of what Donovan saw was an elaborate deception to persuade him that Britain possessed the means to continue the fight.[83] He was shown things no American had seen before: their top secret invention of radar, their newest interceptor planes, their coastal defences. He was made privy to some of Britain's ingenious propaganda devices, including the carefully planted rumour that a system of underwater pipelines could turn every beach and cove into a sea of flaming oil in case of German landings. They unlocked their safes and initiated him into the mysteries of the SIS and the techniques of unorthodox warfare. He was particularly intrigued by their use of captured German spies as counter-agents and playbacks.'[84]

It is the generally accepted view that Britain's foray into flame warfare began with the setting up of the PWD and this would ultimately lead to the development of the Flame Barrage, the wonder weapon that could literally

---

82 His term as ambassador and his political ambitions ended abruptly in November 1940 with the publishing of his controversial remarks suggesting that 'Democracy is finished in England. It may be here, [in the US].' Kennedy resigned under pressure shortly afterwards.

83 Before the end of the year American journalist Ralph Ingersoll, after returning from Britain, published a book concluding that 'Adolf Hitler met his first defeat in eight years' in what might 'go down in history as a battle as important as Waterloo or Gettysburg'. The turning point was when the Germans reduced the intensity of the Blitz after 15 September. According to Ingersoll, '[a] majority of responsible British officers who fought through this battle believe that if Hitler and Göring had had the courage and the resources to lose 200 planes a day for the next five days, nothing could have saved London'; instead, '[the Luftwaffe's] morale in combat is definitely broken and the RAF has been gaining in strength each week.'

84 *Donovan of OSS* by Corey Ford. On the basis of the opinions he expressed on his return, President Roosevelt agreed to enter into Lend-Lease negotiations with Britain which resulted in the delivery of desperately-needed equipment. Donovan is best remembered as the wartime head of the Office of Strategic Services (OSS), a precursor to the Central Intelligence Agency. He is also known as the 'Father of American Intelligence' and the 'Father of Central Intelligence'. On 11 July 1941 Donovan was named Coordinator of Information (COI). In 1942 the COI became the Office of Strategic Services (OSS) and Donovan was returned to active duty in the US Army in his World War I rank of Colonel. He was promoted to brigadier general in March 1943 and to major general in November 1944. Under his leadership the OSS would eventually conduct successful espionage and sabotage operations in Europe and parts of Asia.

set the sea on fire. This however is not quite true. Britain's development and use of flame weapons, including experiments to create fire barriers by burning oil on water, had begun almost twenty five years earlier during WWI. Following the use of flamethrowers by the Germans in July 1915 the British army carried out a number of trials at its Wembley Experimental Station aimed at devising their own flame weapons. Following the success of these trials a number of large flamethrowers were developed and sent to France to be used on the Western Front. The larger British flamethrowers were designed to be mounted in static positions along the frontline trenches. One of the earliest types in service, the 'Livens Gallery Projector', had a series of pipes fed from a single high pressure reservoir, each nozzle being capable of throwing a jet of burning oil 100 yards or more. A later type, the more fearsome 'Vincent', had a range of 130 yards. Winston Churchill as First Lord of the Admiralty witnessed a demonstration of a gallery flame projector in 1916. It seems Churchill was suitably impressed and this undoubtedly led to the Royal Navy carrying out its own trials with flamethrowers. Following these trials, Liven's Gallery Projectors were fitted to several warships, one was mounted onboard the cruiser HMS *Vindictive* when it took part in the Zeebrugge raid on 23rd April 1918. The end of hostilities brought with it an end to the development of the flamethrowers and many were simply scrapped, though some did survive.

The Admiralty however, had also carried out other flame warfare experiments, including burning oil and petrol mixtures on water as a possible harbour defence. Early experiments showed that the concept was feasible and work continued even after the end of WWI with at least one successful trial taking place in the late 1920s. It is no surprise therefore that in 1937, when Colonel Colbeck of the Royal Engineer and Signals Board had the idea of using petrol to defend beaches against enemy landings his first port of call was the Admiralty. Colbeck proposed two systems, the most basic of which was an offshore minefield of small submerged petrol drums that could be fired electrically from the beach. Upon detonation the drums would blast their flammable contents to the surface creating pools of fire that would spread over the water. A second, more sophisticated system, delivered fuel through underwater pipes that ran offshore; the fuel then rose to the surface and spread out to form pools of inflammable liquid that could be ignited using flares. The Admiralty became sufficiently interested in the proposals to organise trials at Weymouth later in the year. Evidently the Admiralty's expertise in this area was very much in demand. At around the same time as the Weymouth trials, the Royal Navy was involved in similar tests carried out by the Air Raids Precautions department at Shoeburyness. Unfortunately little evidence of these or any other earlier trials appears to exist. However, one Admiralty file of August 1940 does contain a passing reference to previous experiments, stating that: 'the petroleum mixture [is] based on Lord Hankey's experiments of many years ago'. Lord Hankey's experiments of 'many years ago' had in fact taken place at Sheerness and on the River Ore in Suffolk. The River Ore runs out into Hollesley Bay and the North Sea just above Shingle Street, therefore and as tenuous as it is, in modern parlance Shingle Street and flame warfare 'have a history.'

Just three years on from Colonel Colbeck's proposals and with Britain now at war, the Admiralty's experimental work with offshore flame barriers was still in progress. On 16 April 1940, just one week after the Germans invaded Norway and the 'Phoney War' came to an abrupt end, the Royal Navy carried out a test that involved discharging two tons of petrol from the ballast tanks of a submarine. In this initial experiment the petroleum slick that formed on the water's surface could not be ignited. However, a second trial carried out on 22nd April that used specially manufactured incendiary candles was successful. Another method considered was laying a trail of fire on the surface of the sea by towing a long gigantic burning wick behind an oil tanker. The 350-ton *Ben Hann* was fitted with special apparatus to carry out an initial trial on the Clyde. Although the test run was marginally successful the idea was taken no further, but the trail of flames in the tanker's wake, half a mile long and 40 feet high, must have looked impressive. As well as these efforts, private individuals had also approached the Admiralty with their own ideas for creating defensive flame barriers. Concerned that German sea planes might attempt to land on the Norfolk Broads, Sub Lieutenant Friggens of the Royal Naval Volunteer Reserve, proposed using a series of oil drums anchored just below the surface of the water, each with a small explosive charge that could be detonated electrically from the shore. The 'Wroxham Roasters', as they became known, were similar to the submerged petrol drums proposed by Colonel Colbeck and like Colbeck's device there is some evidence to suggest they were tested with workable results.

By May 1940 attempts to create defensive flame barriers on the surface of the sea had gone no further than the aforementioned tests, some of which had been relatively successful. Following Dunkirk and now faced with imminent invasion, just about anything that could defend Britain's shores was being considered, including the Royal Navy 'fire-ships' mentioned in the previous chapter. In late June, following a defence measures conference at Deal, it was decided to carry out further experiments to flood the sea with ignitable mixtures. A number of methods would be investigated, including Colonel Colbeck's earlier proposals of oil drums anchored to the seabed and the pipeline delivery system, which would of course develop into the 'flame barrage'. More importantly, it was decided that all the separate work on flame defences being carried out by the Admiralty and others would now be united into a single effort. Within two weeks of this decision the PWD had been formed. On 8th August a successful attempt at burning oil on the surface of the sea took place at Shoeburyness when a barge containing fifty tons of petroleum was blown up with spectacular results. Work progressed quickly and the first successful trial of an offshore flame barrage took place on 24 August near Titchfield on the northern shores of the Solent when a steady supply of a petrol/oil mixture was pumped down pipes to emission points set below the surface of the water. As the mixture rose to the surface and spread out over the sea it was ignited using either Admiralty flares or a sodium and petrol pellet ignition system.

In *Invasion of England 1940* German historian Peter Schenk refers to a German Naval Operations Office report of 10 August 1940 that states: 'The British might use burning oil on the sea as a coastal defence' and 'just over a week later on 18 August, at Wilhelmshaven, the German Navy not only successfully replicated a flame barrage but had also developed countermeasures to deal with them.' One solution was to surround the patch of blazing oil with a chain of floating logs and simply tow it out of harm's way. If this is correct and there is no reason to doubt it, the German Navy were aware that the British might use burning oil as a coastal defence but how was it possible that the Germans had tested countermeasures to a weapon that the British had not yet developed? It has been suggested by many, including Geoffrey Lloyd and Sir Donald Banks, that German aircraft probably flew over and reported early flame barrage trials while they were in progress. In support of this is the often told story of a German air raid on Portsmouth that took place while the Titchfield trial was in progress and 'clouds of black smoke hung over the Solent.' The Germans, it is supposed, saw the burning waters of the Solent and a Luftwaffe communiqué the next day reported that: 'South coast towns had been attacked with excellent results and large scale fires had been observed in the vicinity of Portsmouth.' This incident is undoubtedly true, but it took place on 24 August, after the Germans had begun their experiments with countermeasures. The curious fact remains that the Germans were not only aware of the PWD's secret trials, but had successfully investigated counter-measures before a fully functioning flame barrage had been perfected, let alone installed. Could the Germans have been acting on other information besides aerial reconnaissance? Other trials with flame barriers had been carried out well before the Titchfield test took place, well before the PWD had been formed. As well as offshore flame barriers, work had also been in progress on a variety of other improvised flame weapons for beach and airfield defence.

These devices ranged from the crude but effective to the downright dangerous. One idea, suggested for the defence of Harwich against enemy landing craft, involved hurling canisters of petrol that would ignite on hitting the water and spread a sheet of flame over the sea. Other ideas included: igniting 4-gallon drums of petrol in a row across a road, throwing 2-gallon drums over cliff tops, using a blazing automobile as a mobile 'fire-car' and flooding a road with petrol through perforated pipes fed from a 200 gallon tank. Even more basic was a scheme to fill anti-tank ditches with petroleum impregnated peat, when ignited this created a spectacular wall of flame that generated a fierce heat. Churchill himself witnessed a demonstration while on an inspection tour of east coast defences and was forced to retire to a safe distance from the flames while mopping the sweat from his brow. Apparently he was suitably impressed and expressed his satisfaction with some well chosen words. Undoubtedly many of these early devices would have been more dangerous to their operators than an attacking enemy and were taken no further than initial experiments, but two extensively used weapons did come out of all this. The defile trap typically consisted of a series of pipes laid either side of a track or narrow road leading inshore from a beach. The pipes, connected to storage tanks, were pierced to spray oil over the whole area and when fired the road became a raging furnace. However, it was the Flame Fougasse that was the most widely used of the early devices. This simple but effective 'fire breather' usually consisted of a 40-gallon drum containing a petroleum mixture attached with an explosive charge. The Fougasse was normally buried on its side in sandbags or earth with the top face, or 'business end' free from obstruction and ready to discharge its lethal contents. It was basically a surprise or ambush weapon, upon detonation of the explosive charge a tongue of flame saturated the immediate frontal area with burning petrol. Flame Fougasses were installed in large numbers at exits from beaches and any other defensive position deemed strategically important. They were also often mounted side by side in batteries and when fired simultaneously the results were

Bawdsey radar station viewed from the jetty for the Felixstowe Ferry before the war. The presence of highly conspicuous pylons dotted around Britain's coast was almost certainly photographed by the airliners of Deutsche Lufthansa as they purposely crossed the Suffolk coast over Bawdsey, en-route from Germany to Croydon and, in August 1939 by the re-commissioned German airship LZ130 *Graf Zeppelin*.

Robert Watson Watt, British radar pioneer.

WAAF radar operator Denise Miley plotting aircraft on a cathode ray tube in the Receiver Room at Bawdsey Chain Home station later in the war, in May 1945.

The Debenham, Suffolk Auxiliary Unit, one of scores of units in Churchill's 'Secret Army' prepared to help thwart any invasion attempt on the east coast of Britain in 1940.

Auxiliary Units were taught close quarters combat, armed with a variety of weapons including the classic Commando fighting knife, the architects of which were two retired Shanghai Police officers Major William E. 'Dan' Fairbairn (left) and Major Eric A. 'Bill' Sykes (right). (the late Peter Robins Collection)

Vera de Witte, one of three captured German spies, two of whom who were put on trial at the Old Bailey in 1941 and were hanged in Wandsworth prison. Incredibly Vera de Witte was never put on trial and it was assumed that she had turned King's Evidence. She even managed to escape after being deported back to Germany after the war. Most of the evidence suggests she died in 1993.

Tethered barges in harbour in preparation for Operation 'Sealion', the proposed invasion of Britain in September 1940. On 8 July Bristol Blenheims made a daylight attack on barges in Dutch canals; some of the bombers attacked from a height of less than 1,000 feet and their crews saw some of the barges alight and the wreckage of others floating on the water. On the same day a canal south of Furnes in Belgium was reported to be packed with barges over a distance of ten miles. On 11 July, the day the Battle of Britain began, large concentrations of barges, tightly packed together were seen on the canal between Dunkirk and Furnes while just south of Furnes there was only a small concentration of barges. Blenheims were now out as often as possible attacking barges in the Dutch and Belgium canals.

German troops manhandling an artillery piece ashore during an invasion exercise.

German troops bringing horse drawn vehicles ashore during an invasion exercise. These laborious methods would have resulted in their total destruction by RAF aircraft had the invasion force got ashore in southern England in the summer of 1940.

A graphic demonstration of the British 'Setting the sea on fire' to 'catch any potential enemy invasion 'like fish in a frying pan'.

Thirty-six year old American journalist William Lawrence Shirer, seen here at Compiègne in Northern France in 1940 who reported the rumours and disturbing sights that fed the story of the burning sea in September 1940.

RAF fighter pilots at readiness.

London docks burning on Sunday, 8th September 1940.

Bawdsey radar station photographed in 1942 by a German reconnaissance aircraft. Bawdsey's isolated position on a triangular peninsular between the North Sea and the estuary of the River Deben made the site especially vulnerable to attack by a small force of raiders which might easily be landed on the gently sloping shingle beaches within a hundred yards or so of the main installation.

Reichsmarschall Hermann Göring, seen here inspecting Fallschirmjäger that would feature prominently in any airborne operations over England in 1940, believed that 'Sealion' was just a giant bluff to scare the British into capitulating, but though the Luftwaffe's support was always questionable because of Göring's uncooperative attitude, he enthusiastically embraced any attempts by his beloved Luftwaffe in 'small invasions that might go a long way'.

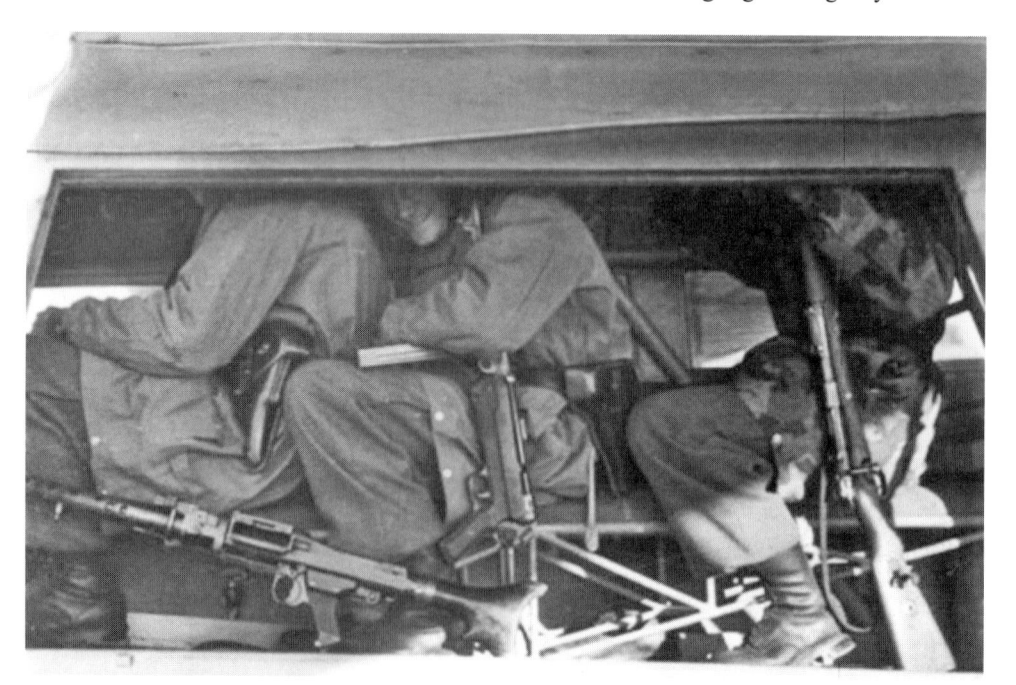

The transportation of Fallschirmjäger paratroopers in the highly uncomfortable and cramped DFS 230 gliders during landings on enemy positions was of short duration but normally effective.

Fallschirmjäger paratroopers prepare to board their Ju 52 troop transports.

Fieseler Fi-156 Storch ('Stork')-93 favoured by the Brandenbergers. In early May 1940 in the southern Ardennes, Fieseler Storch light reconnaissance planes dropped members of the Brandenburg Regiment on the bridges immediately to the south of the 10th Panzer Division's route of march.

The gun house at the Minsmere battery on cliffs near the remotely sited Chain Home Low (CHL) radar station at Dunwich just north of Aldeburgh in Suffolk pictured in 1941. Britain's highly prized radar stations were protected by fortified installations such as these.

Dunwich radar station, which became operational on 1st January 1940, with the 185 feet tall wooden radar tower (left) and the Fisherman's Cottages (now a National Trust site, centre). By July 1940 there were 51 operational radar stations situated around the approaches to Britain.

Overall view of the Dunwich area.

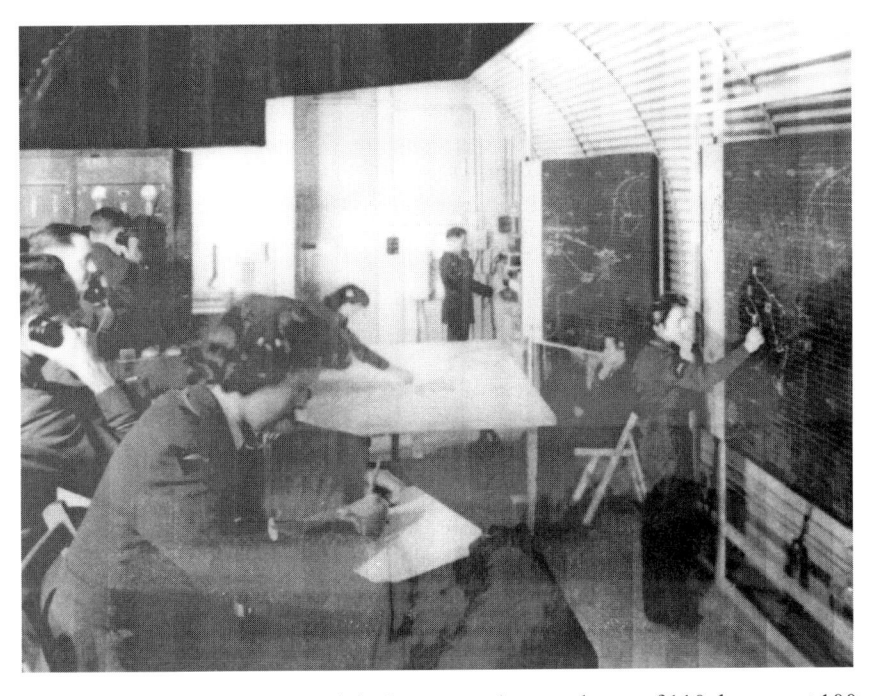

The Greyfriars control room at Dunwich. Over a south-easterly arc of 110 degrees at 100 miles range this Type 16 range installation just covered all the North Sea to the Belgium and Dutch coast and on 200 miles, reached beyond Amiens and Brussels. The transmitter controls are at the back. The plan of the operation was plotted on one wall chart whilst the actual radar plot was plotted on the other, so that the controllers could see if the plan was being followed.

The SS *Freden,* like its contemporary, the *Lundby*, an ordinary Swedish tramp steamer, was attacked by two U-boats in the spring of 1942 but survived both unscathed. At the start of WW2 *Lundby* was owned by a Danish company and was seized after the German invasion and put to work by the Nazis. On 20 September 1941, *Lundby,* now US-owned and re-named *Pink Star*, was part of an Allied convoy that was attacked by U-552, under the command of Erich Topp who fired a spread of torpedoes into the convoy, hitting only *Pink Star,* which quickly sank.

Any land and seaborne invasion attempts could be expected to be supported by Schnellboots of the German Kriegsmarine like this one (S 204) seen surrendering off Felixstowe on 23 May 45. In 1940 Felixstowe was potentially one of several targets for any enemy amphibious operations on England's vulnerable East Coast.

German support troops seen here coming ashore would follow any invasion attempts or guerrilla 'tip-and-run' raids, however small, on Britain's East Coast.

A Fallschirmjäger paratrooper making the characteristic 'spread-eagle' parachute jump into action.

British Army and Special Forces were trained to rigorously defend key points on the East Coast in the event of land and seaborne invasion attempts by German forces by all means possible, whether it was hand-to-hand-combat or even setting the sea on fire. There were no rules when it came to Britain's survival.

Captured Fallschirmjäger paratroopers.

No pictures seem to exist of captured DFS 230 gliders on British soil but this one is of a Fallschirmjäger battalion 500 glider that was captured during an airborne assault in Yugoslavia.

The Würzburg radar installation at Bruneval in northern France whose successful capture and removal on the night of 27/28 February 1942 showed just what could be achieved by a well-planned and executed combined operation on a remotely sited coastal location by a small but determined force of troops supported by highly effective airborne force.

The Battle of Crete, which began on the morning of 20 May 1941 was the first occasion where Fallschirmjäger were used en masse, the first mainly airborne invasion in military history, the first time the British made significant use of intelligence from decrypted German 'Enigma' messages and the first time German troops encountered mass resistance from a civilian population. Planning was rushed and much of Unternehmen (Operation) Merkur ('Mercury') was improvised, including the use of troops who were not trained for airborne assaults and German losses were high. That the Fallschirmjäger, formerly a weapon of surprise, which was now lost to them, finally triumphed, was due in no small part to the defenders' failures - their ultimate defeat being snatched from the jaws of victory. Thankfully, no such fate befell this country in 1940 when the outcome could have been the same.

spectacular. Existing film footage of a Fougasse battery in action shows a beach being engulfed in a sea of flame.

It seems highly likely that coastal flame defences, albeit crude ones were in place during the late summer of 1940. Furthermore it was not only the Royal Navy and the PWD who could set the sea on fire. The war diary of the 1st London Infantry Brigade of 10 August mentions the completed installation of a 'petrol flame producing device' at Seasalter near Whitstable (this was just two days after the Shoeburyness test). Another official report later that same month states: 'At the present time the location of seventy static flame traps in various parts of England has been settled and twenty of them are already completed.' There is also evidence that other flame weapons awaited the arrival of German troops on English beaches. In his book *East Anglia at War*, Derek Johnson makes an interesting reference to a 'flame gun' at Felixstowe. The reference itself is actually in a passage concerning King George VI's inspection of Felixstowe's coastal defences on 11 July 1940: 'one thing he must have been impressed with on his tour was the novel flame gun ... a series of giant flame throwers had been built into several strategically placed cliff faces around the east coast. If invasion barges did breach the Channel they would be met with a sea of blazing oil'.[85] Could these heavy flamethrowers and the Felixstowe 'flame gun' be equipment that survived from the First World War? This was a time when no stone was being left unturned in the search for any usable military hardware. Large calibre naval guns of WWI vintage and older were definitely used in rudimentary emergency coastal batteries. Therefore, it is not beyond the realms of possibility that any leftover Gallery Projectors or naval flamethrowers could also have been pressed back into service.

Sefton Delmer of the Political Warfare Executive wrote of his radio broadcasts in September 1940 that: 'The line about burning in the Channel fitted in perfectly, as of course it was intended to do, with the information which our deception services had planted on Admiral Canaris...' Denis Sefton Delmer was a Jewish-British journalist of Australian heritage and propagandist for the British government. Born 24 May 1904 in Berlin he was fluent in German and in the 1930s he became friendly with Ernst Röhm

---

85 The King's visit is verified in the war diary of the 165th Infantry Brigade; unfortunately the report does not go into any great detail. However, there are other sources that refer to flame throwers being installed as part of Britain's wartime coastal defences. *The Times* of June 1945 carried an interesting article about the earlier work of the PWD and the flame defences that had awaited the Germans in 1940. There is an accompanying photograph showing flame defences in operation, the caption reads: 'Heavy flame-throwers, installed for the defence of Channel ports in 1940 being tried out.'

who arranged for him to interview Adolf Hitler. During the war he led a black propaganda campaign against Hitler by radio from England, sufficiently successful he was named in the Nazis' Black Book for immediate arrest after their invasion of England. In September 1940 Delmer was recruited by the Political Warfare Executive (PWE) to organize black propaganda broadcasts to Nazi Germany as part of a psychological warfare campaign. Cleared to work for the Political Intelligence Department of the Foreign Office, he was based at Wavendon Towers in what is now Milton Keynes new town. The operation joined a number of other 'Research Units' operating propaganda broadcasts. The concept was that the radio station would undermine Hitler by pretending to be a fervent Hitler-Nazi supporter. 'Our rumour agencies, too, had been busy spreading it everywhere' continued Delmer. 'The mean murderous British, it was said, had apparatus in readiness in which they were going to set the Channel and the beaches on fire at such time as Hitler launched his boats. This was a lie. But it went over so well that it is believed by many Germans to this day.'[86]

On Friday, 27th September a select group of civil servants and military officers, known as the 'Underground Propaganda Committee' had gathered for their usual weekly-meeting in room 207 at Electra House on London's Victoria Embankment. The UPC (also referred to as Department EH) had been formed in the early days of the war with the express purpose of waging psychological warfare against Nazi Germany. This small committee, secretly funded by the Foreign Office, would pursue a propaganda campaign of whispers, rumours, disinformation and downright lies, all calculated to undermine the morale of the enemy. This was to be a war of words where 'inspired rumours', or 'Sibs' (a rumour, after the Latin word sibilare', meaning to 'hiss') would be fed to the correspondents of the neutral press, or broadcast over the airwaves - much in the same way that the notorious 'Lord Haw Haw' broadcast German propaganda to Britain.' With the threat of impending invasion now hanging over the UK, the UPC desperately turned its talents

---

[86] In France in early October, one Marie Bonaparte claimed that '350,000 men were burnt alive by fuel oil spread on the sea. The British collected the corpses, identified them by their identity discs, loaded them in planes and dropped each corpse in its own village to strike terror into their families and undermine German morale... From Calais to Honfleur the German soldiers could be seen swimming ashore upright. It was an army of the drowned. Their heavy equipment had slipped to their feet and so they were kept upright... The Germans are in such terror of embarking for England that they have to be driven aboard with machine-guns at their backs and their hands tied, to prevent them committing suicide. Quoted in *Myths & Legends of the Second World War* by James Hayward, Sutton Publishing 2003.

CAUGHT LIKE FISH IN A FRYING PAN

to the creation of 'anti invasion rumours', false information that would, hopefully, deceive the Germans into believing Britain was better defended than it actually was. The minutes of the meeting record the proposal of two new anti invasion 'Sibs'. The first and more imaginative of the two, suggested spreading a rumour that Britain has a new, top secret anti-invasion weapon: 'a mine to be dropped from aircraft. In distinction from other mines it does not explode, but spreads a very thin film of highly inflammable and volatile liquid over the surface of the water for an enormous area. The mine's further action then ignites provoking a terrible flame.' The available evidence indicates that the 'terrible flame mine' was considered by the Joint Intelligence Committee (JIC) at a meeting on Monday, 7th October. Exactly two weeks later, the UPC received a memo from the JIC stating the following: 'Reference to anti-invasion rumour submitted by Department EH for consideration by the JIC on 7 October, concerning mine dropped from aircraft capable of spreading a thin film of inflammable liquid. To produce and maintain a 'terrible flame', however, for any useful period would demand such enormous quantities of aircraft and bombs as to make the proposal impracticable. We therefore consider it inadvisable to proceed with this rumour.' Following the doubts cast by the JIC the flaming mine 'Sib' was subsequently shelved, at least for the time being.

It was also proposed that reports should be published suggesting that: 'Small scale attempts at invasion have been made and beaten off with devastating losses. In fact none are alive to tell. Thousands of floating German corpses have been washed ashore.' Following the established procedure, both these 'inspired rumours', being of a military nature, were ultimately forwarded to the Joint Intelligence Committee for assessment before being deemed suitable for use. (Just three weeks later and after the 'invasion Sib' had been 'rubber stamped' by the JIC, there are 'guarded' claims from the Air Ministry, quickly followed by press reports suggesting the RAF had surprised and bombed an 'invasion dress rehearsal'). This 'Sib' was evidently more successful than the imaginary 'flame weapon'. Evidence from UPC files reveals that after consideration by the JIC, the rumour was eventually passed to the Secret Intelligence Service (MI6) and another recipient referred to as 'AGENCY X'. Whether or not this 'inspired rumour' was ever actually used as intended is unknown but weeks before this 'Sib' had been proposed, let alone accepted, an almost identical rumour was already in widespread circulation and government sources had strenuously denied that there was any truth in these rumours. It seems strange, if not bizarre, that the UPC should want to create an anti-invasion rumour identical to the rumours already in circulation and moreover a rumour that other official sources had fervently denied as being without foundation? It is also curious that this anti-invasion 'Sib' should be created with official backing at a time when Britain's leaders knew that the threat of invasion had diminished.

A 'Short Invasion Phrasebook' dropped in large quantities by the RAF over the enemy coast in late September held that British submarines had spread oil on the water and it made explicit reference to seas of petrol and burning comrades. In October propaganda leaflet (EH 473) dropped over occupied Europe by the RAF parodied a German marching song *Wir Fahren Gegen Engelland* and included references to a 'burning sea' while the BBC's German service offered similarly mordant language lessons on the radio and warned German troops that a 'warm' welcome awaited them.

The RAF certainly had the means to 'rain down fire from the skies'. When desperate measures were called for by Bomber Command on 4 September Intelligence Officers told crews they would be despatched to the Black Forest, where the Germans were massing heavy armament. They were to carry a new incendiary device called 'Razzle'. This consisted of a wad of wet phosphorous placed between two pieces of celluloid, which ignited to produce an eight-inch flame when the phosphorous dried. 'Razzles' and 'Deckers' consisting of small phosphorous pellets in celluloid strips were dropped through flare chutes to start fires among crops and in forest areas. The incendiary devices had to be kept in tins of alcohol and water until dropped so that they would ignite when they dried out. Wellingtons of 149 Squadron had first tried an experiment on the night of 11th/12th August, carrying fifty biscuit tins each filled with up to 500 examples but Churchill, fearing that such tactics could lead to German reprisal raids, had ordered the scheme to be postponed. Bob Shepherd of 75 Squadron RNZAF recalls. 'I took the lids off the tins and there were wads swimming about in a solution. I opened the flare chute and one by one, tossed out the contents of three tin loads from about 10,000 feet. We also dropped a full load of incendiaries and six 250 pounders. There was hardly any flak at all.'[87]

The Air Ministry also developed larger types of bombs that contained a variety of flammable fillings, including mixtures of petrol, Benzol, crude rubber and phosphorous. These devices were technically very similar to the German 'oil bombs' that were used with frightening effect in the 'Blitz' on British towns

---

87 On the night of 16th/17th October some aircraft dropped incendiary devices into the Harz forests.

and cities, most notably Coventry. The larger incendiary devices were primarily intended for use against large forested areas, but the RAF had also carried out earlier experiments with the intention of spreading fire on enemy waterways. These experiments involved the development of the RAF's most intriguing fire raising weapon, the curiously named 'Aumonier's Cough Mixture.' When dropped from the air this chemical compound could spontaneously ignite oil slicks that had formed on the surface of the sea. The 'Mixture' probably contained Triethylborane (TEB), a liquid with a pungent odour reminiscent of ether and capable of igniting spontaneously in air. It is not known if this weapon was ever deployed in action. However, there are examples of oil from vessels being deliberately ignited by enemy aircraft during an attack. One such incident was the sinking of the French destroyer *Bison* during the Norwegian campaign. Sailors onboard HMS *Afridi* who witnessed the attack, reported that German aircraft had deliberately ignited oil from the stricken vessel with incendiary bombs causing many casualties. Survivors of the catastrophic sinking of the British troopship *Lancastria* also claimed that German aircraft had dropped incendiary bombs to ignite oil leaking from the sinking ship. Many of the men who were struggling to swim away as the ship went down perished in the flames or were severely burned. The two incidents described are proof enough that such terrible things could and did happen. There is some evidence that RAF aircraft were ready and waiting to drop incendiary bombs on oil/petrol mixtures that had been purposely spread on the surface of the sea.

At a time when there was a desperate need to defend Britain's shores, measures were handicapped by a lack of resources; hence the improvisation that led to flame weapons. Although the official history tells us that the PWD did not actually begin to install flame barrages until 1941, there is other evidence showing that various improvised methods had been considered, tried, or were actually in place at the time in question - the Flame Fougasse and burning anti tank ditch to name but two. And if a 'Flame Gun' or guns, were installed on the cliffs at Felixstowe in July 1940 then at least one flame defence measure was not all that far from Bawdsey Manor and Shingle Street at that time. Cryptic references to these supposedly secret weapons even appeared in the press. Beneath the headline 'Hidden death waits where invaders might try landing', the *Daily Herald* of 3 September published a report on south coast defences that ended with the words: 'Narrow roads leading into the country, [from the beach head]... would be under fire and flame.' This is obviously a veiled reference to defile traps and other flame defences that were, according to all the available records, supposedly still in the early stages of development. Perhaps most astonishing of all is that the German Navy had begun to experiment with countermeasures six days before the first successful trial of a flame barrage took place on 24 August.

It has been stated by the MoD that there were no flame defences on the Suffolk coast in 1940 (it must therefore be assumed that request made by the 165th Infantry Brigade in September of that year was denied). Although there is scant evidence, it is not beyond the realms of possibility that flame defences may have been in place at certain locations, particularly those that had been identified as strategically important and at high risk of attack. Given the circumstances, had the 'Wroxham Roasters' or any other device, no matter how crude, proved workable, would they have been shelved while precious time was wasted on attempts to develop something better? Or would they have been hurriedly put to use in the defence of a highly vulnerable but essential coastal RDF station, soon to be vital to Britain's survival? Anything was better than nothing given the desperate circumstances of the time. It seems likely therefore that some form of flame defence could have been in place at Bawdsey Manor, or indeed other vulnerable points along the coast. Perhaps submerged petrol drums or a beach barrage, or even the anti-tank ditch to the rear of Hollesley Bay may have been flooded with a petroleum mixture. Any one of these devices, if activated, could have caused the red glow in the night sky witnessed by Ron Ashford. And if they had been used they would also have needed replenishing or replacing. Could this have been the reason for the 165th Infantry Brigade request; to replace a spent improvised device with a more substantial flame barrage? If flame defences of any kind were in place and had been used, were they activated accidentally during a mock invasion exercise incinerating British troops? Or were the scorched bodies German invaders in British uniform?

Chapter 8

'Even a Small Invasion might go a Long Way'

'I hear from Lancaster in the flats who has just been to Wickham Market in Suffolk, that on Saturday night and again on Tuesday invasion was attempted. Not one Nazi returned. Their bodies are still being washed up along our shores. That is the end of all Nazis who seek to molest our freedom - death.

Diary entry on 14 September by London schoolboy, Colin Perry.[88] **By a curious irony it was a quarter of a century before, on 8 September 1915 that Zeppelins had made their first big raid on London.**

On Saturday, 7th September after a bath and a quick change into a respectable uniform a small party of fighter pilots of 242 Squadron at Coltishall in Norfolk were soon jammed into an ancient car and bounced along the narrow, winding road which leads to Norwich. Some hours later they were still wedged together in the crowded, stuffy bar of the 'Bell' when a posse of Service police stalked in and announced that all RAF personnel were to report back to their airfields at once. At Coltishall Pilot Officer 'Johnnie' Johnson and his fellow pilots found that Alert No. 1, 'invasion imminent and probable within twelve hours', had been declared by the responsible authorities and the defences were to be brought to the highest state of readiness. The scene in the mess could only be described as one of some confusion. Elderly officers, mobilized for the duration, darted about in various directions. Their CO was not to be seen and the pilots tried to get a coherent explanation of the situation. They soon heard half a dozen different versions, the most popular of which was that the invasion was under way and some enemy landings were expected on the east coast.

---
88 Later published as *Boy in the Blitz*.

HITLER'S INVASION OF EAST ANGLIA, 1940

Perhaps the CO and the flight commanders were already at dispersal and Johnson left the ante-room to make a telephone call from the hall. As he hastened along the corridor he almost collided with a squadron leader who stumped towards him with an awkward gait. His vital eyes gave Johnson a swift scrutiny, at his pilot's brevet and the one thin ring of a pilot officer.

'I say, old boy, what's all the flap about?' he exclaimed, legs apart and putting a match to his pipe.

'I don't really know, sir,' Johnson replied. 'But there are reports of enemy landings.'

The squadron leader pushed open the swing doors and stalked into the noisy, confused atmosphere of the ante-room. Fascinated, Johnson followed in close line-astern because he thought he knew who this was. He took in the scene and then demanded, in a loud voice and in choice, fruity language, what all the panic was about. Half a dozen voices started to explain and eventually he had some idea of the form. As he listened, his eyes swept round the room, lingered for a moment on his pilots and established a private bond of fellowship between them.

There was a moment's silence whilst he digested the news. 'So the bastards are coming. Bloody good show! Think of all those juicy targets on those nice flat beaches. What shooting!' And he made a rude sound with his lips which was meant to resemble a ripple of machine-gun fire. The effect was immediate and extraordinary. Officers went about their various tasks and the complicated machinery of the airfield began to function smoothly again.[89]

Vera Shaw, a plotter at 11 Group Headquarters, Uxbridge, wrote: 'Early duty. Lovely day dawning, though trouble expected. Around 0800, warning from Command of a big raid. It came! 250-plus aircraft approaching Dover. Plots came thick and fast. Soon table covered with raids. Noise indescribable - why must everyone shout so? Squadron board shows all squadrons in combat. By midmorning the King and Mr. Churchill appear in the Controller's room. At one stage, Mr. Churchill asked if we had any more squadrons to call on. 'No,' said the Controller.'

At 1554 hours the first track plotter at Bentley Priory reached forward to place an initial raid counter on the table map. Showing twenty-plus over Pas de Calais, it was quickly followed by others of growing size, until Dowding realised that this was the largest raid he had yet faced. As the full situation was flashed to Group and sector controllers, fighters of all three southern Groups were frantically brought to state. The first coastal Observer Corps

---

89 Adapted from *Wing Leader* by James Edgar 'Johnnie' Johnson.

'EVEN A SMALL INVASION MIGHT GO A LONG WAY'

report of the enemy formation reached the Maidstone centre at 1616 hours and told of many hundreds of aircraft approaching the coast between Deal and the North Foreland. Half an hour before, Hermann Göring, ridiculously bedecked in pale blue and gold had stood on the cliffs near Calais and watched wave upon wave of his bombers and fighters set course for London. Göring had launched 348 bombers and 617 single-and twin-engine fighters in the greatest aerial armada yet seen in the first of German 'reprisal' attacks on the capital following raids by RAF Bomber Command on Berlin. Hitler had seemingly snatched defeat from the jaws of victory by diverting Luftflotten (Airfleet) 2 and 3 from their attacks on the RAF sector stations to attack London. He wanted retribution for the raids on Berlin and in the process changed the entire nature of the battle. The German Airfleet commanders, Generalfeldmarschall Hugo Sperrle and Generalfeldmarschall Albert Kesselring were divided on how to defeat RAF Fighter Command. Against his wishes, Kesselring had been discharged from the army on 1st October 1933 and appointed head of the Department of Administration at the Reich Commissariat for Aviation (Reichskommissariat für die Luftfahrt), the forerunner of the Reich Air Ministry (Reichsluftfahrtministerium), with the rank of Oberst (colonel). Kesselring had become Chief of Staff of the Luftwaffe on 3rd June 1936 and he oversaw the expansion of the Luftwaffe, the acquisition of new aircraft types such as the Messerschmitt Bf 109 and Ju 87 and the development of paratroops. Like many ex-Army officers, he tended to see air power in the tactical role, providing support to land operations. On 1st October 1938 he was promoted to General der Flieger (air general) and became commander of Luftflotte 1, based in Berlin. While Sperrle wanted to continue the attacks on the fighter stations Kesselring argued that it was a waste of time as RAF Fighter Command could simply withdraw out of range to the north of London. 'We have no chance of destroying the English fighters on the ground' he said. 'We must force their last reserves of Spitfires and Hurricanes into combat in the air.'[90] To do so he needed to attack London. An OKW Directive on 16 August had already said as much: 'On D-1 day the Luftwaffe is to make a strong attack on London, which should cause the population to flee from the city and block the roads.'

It did nothing of the kind. Peter Wood, who was living in Tulse Hill in south London and working in the City for a shipping company was playing football near Crystal Palace when he heard some unseasonal thunder. He looked up to see the sky full of German bombers - but the game went on. 'Literally dozens of Germans, accompanied by smaller aircraft which

---

90   *Operation Sea Lion - Myth or Reality* by A. R. Tucker.

HITLER'S INVASION OF EAST ANGLIA, 1940

I took to be fighters, were going over at about 500 feet. There didn't seem to be any gunfire from our defending forces at all. Fortunately for us, they overflew us, because they were obviously heading for the docks, for what was, as we know now, the first bombing of the docklands at that time. We shrugged our shoulders and carried on to finish our game of football. After that the bombing of London increased in volume and the routine was to sleep in a reinforced cellar where my wife's family lived in Tulse Hill and when the all-clear went in the morning, you just got up, washed and dressed and went to work.'

This vast aerial armada, the greatest yet seen, had assembled 88 miles away over the Pas de Calais and headed towards the Thames Estuary on a twenty mile front stepped up from 14,000 feet to 23,000 feet. The more than a mile and a half high formation covered an astonishing 800 square miles, a sight which must have sent shock waves throughout Fighter Command when the radars first picked up the mass formation. At 1617 hours Air Vice-Marshal Park ordered eleven RAF fighter squadrons into the air and six minutes later all remaining Spitfires and Hurricanes were brought to Readiness. By 1630 all twenty-one squadrons stationed within seventy miles of London were in the air or under take-off orders. Take-off orders were passed to the pilots by the sector controller by telephone or loudspeaker. Flight Lieutenant Denis Robinson of 152 Squadron at Warmwell recalled: 'The worst time was just waiting. When the phone rang the orderly would shout 'Squadron Scramble - Angels 15 [15,000 feet].' In an instant we were running to our aircraft, grabbing the parachute off the wing, buckling it on as you scrambled into the cockpit. Then pull on the helmet already attached to radio and oxygen supply, whilst somehow starting the engine. It was a grass field without runways, so it's a matter of getting into the wind, keeping a sharp look-out for other aircraft, full throttle and away we go.' Further instructions followed over the aircraft radio after take-off.

The RAF pilots who were sent up to intercept became embroiled in melees and attacks that might begin and be pressed home at any height from 25,000 feet down to near the ground. One moment there could be as many as 140 separate fights going on at the same time, the next pilots were seemingly alone. It was a situation that must have frozen the blood of even the bravest of men, if they had time to dwell on it. The situation demanded the utmost alertness and once sighted, the RAF pilots opened fire at an average of 200 yards, closing sometimes to less than fifty yards. As the first four squadrons of RAF fighters attacked the southern flank of the huge formation it was soon apparent to Dowding and Park that the Luftwaffe was

'EVEN A SMALL INVASION MIGHT GO A LONG WAY'

heading for London and not the precious Essex and Kentish fighter airfields. Breaking out of a layer of haze east of Sheppey, fighter pilots found themselves on the edge of a tidal wave of aircraft, towering above them rank upon rank, more than a mile and a half high and covering 800 square miles, all heading for the capital. The full force of the raid was destined to fall on the east end of the city and the docks at Rotherhithe, Limehouse and Millwall and the Surrey Docks and those hard by Tower Bridge. The vast gasworks at Beckton and the West Ham Power Station shook and erupted under the storm of explosive. Two hours later fires were raging for almost ten miles down the banks of the River Thames. By 17:45 hours the German formations had turned south and east for home, scattered and disordered but still largely intact.

From 2010 hours until 0430 hours on Sunday morning a second wave of bombers - 318 Heinkels and Dorniers, their bomb loads composed of a high proportion of incendiaries streamed in from the east, stoking the fires which now raged scarcely checked along nine miles of waterfront, turning the already blazing fires into a raging inferno. Fire crews struggled to subdue firestorms. The devastating attack left 306 killed and 1,337 seriously injured in the capital itself and a further 142 killed in the suburbs. Despite the spirited and strong resistance put up by the fighter squadrons, not least the Poles of 303 Squadron, many of the bombers had a clear run over the capital, which was heavily bombed. Nineteen Fighter Command pilots were lost from the 28 fighters shot down and 41 German aircraft were destroyed.

At the height of the raid and in the belief that the large scale air attack on the nation's capital heralded the invasion, GHQ Command Home forces issued the invasion imminent alert, code word 'Cromwell' to all army units in southern and eastern areas. The warning signified that an invasion attempt was expected at any time within the next 48 hours. Army units from Division down to Battalion level recorded receipt of 'Cromwell' between 2100 to 2130 hours. Throughout the following hours all units took up positions ready for immediate action, essential telephone and telegraph lines were taken over and in coastal areas, harbour authorities stood by ready to immobilise dockside facilities on receipt of more definite orders. The Home Guard were called out in parts of southern and eastern England and in many cinemas feature films were interrupted by onscreen notices advising military personnel in the audience to return to their barracks. Corporal Bunty Walmsley, a locally recruited WAAF who worked in the Operations Room at Stratton Strawless Hall on the Norwich to Aylsham road not far from RAF Coltishall on a six on-twelve off shift pattern in three watches, recalled that she with other members of her watch were suddenly roused from their beds and told to immediately assemble outside to be addressed by the WAAF Commanding Officer. Garbed in various forms of night attire, they all staggered outside looking the worse for wear. The next moment their Commanding Officer appeared, dressed in full uniform and, to their amazement, proceeded to inform them that the Germans had invaded the south coast and that further landings were likely. She went on to say that if Coltishall should be involved, she expected each one of them to defend the station by any means possible. Bunty's only weapon was a poker allocated to her billet! In the morning, they were all due to report for their watch at 0800 hours. On meeting up with some of the RAF section of her watch, the WAAFs discovered that none of them had been disturbed and were equally unaware of an invasion.

242 Squadron had spent another frustrating day at readiness at Coltishall waiting for 11 Group's call. To them 7th September must have seemed like another opportunity missed as the squadron spent most of the day kicking its heels as reports filtered through of waves of German bombers attacking London. Finally, at 0445 hours, Operations rang and Bader and his pilots, straining at the leash, at last got the order to scramble. Once airborne 'Woody' Woodhall the sector controller at Duxford calmly told Bader that there was some 'trade' heading in over the coast. Wing Commander Alfred Basil 'Woody' Woodhall was a South African who in 1914 had been a lance corporal in the Witwatersrand Rifles before joining the Royal Marines. During the early 1920s, he had flown biplane torpedo bombers before transferring to the RAF in 1929. When war came, Woodhall had a desk job at the Air Ministry and he was posted to Duxford on 12 March 1940 as senior controller. When the sector controller directed his fighters to intercept a hostile raid a simple code was used between them: 'Scramble', take-off; 'Angels (ten)', height (10,000 feet); 'Orbit', circle (a given point); 'Vector' (one-eight-zero), steer (course of 180 degrees); 'Buster', full throttle; 'Tally-ho!', enemy sighted; 'Pancake', land. The South African asked Bader to 'Orbit North Weald. Angels ten' and added, 'If they come your way you can go for them.'

Bader climbed to 'Angels 15'. Nearing North Weald Woodhall called Bader again. 'Hallo, Douglas. Seventy-plus crossing the Thames east of London, heading north.' In the distance Bader saw black dots staining the sky. They were not aircraft. They were anti-aircraft bursts. This could mean only one thing. Over the radio Willie McKnight called out, 'Bandits. 10 o'clock.' Bader recalled, 'We had been greatly looking forward to our first formation of 36 fighters going into action together, but we were

'EVEN A SMALL INVASION MIGHT GO A LONG WAY'

unlucky. We were alerted late and were underneath the bombers and their fighter escorts when we met fifteen miles north of the Thames.' All Bader could do was attack the formation of about seventy Dorniers of KG 76 and Bf 110s of ZG 2 heading for North Weald as best they could while eight Spitfires of 19 Squadron tried to hold off assaults from the Bf 109s flying high cover. When the claims were totted up they totalled eleven enemy aircraft and two probables; all for the loss of two Hurricanes and one pilot killed. On landing Bader rang the Operations Room in a fury to be told that they had been sent off as soon as 11 Group had called for them from Duxford. This was one of the recurring problems during this heavy last period of the battle. Next morning, 242 Squadron flew to Duxford where Bader and his pilots again spent a frustrating day waiting in vain to be summoned by 11 Group as the German bombers returned to bomb London.

When the belief that the large scale air attack on London heralded a German invasion, GHQ Command Home forces issued the invasion imminent alert, code word 'Cromwell' to all army units in southern and eastern areas. The warning signified that an invasion attempt was expected at any time within the next 48 hours. The war diary of the 2nd Liverpool Scots for Sunday, 8th September, records: '10:20 hours Code word 'Cromwell' called off, just another jittery flap. In some parts of the country they even rang the church bells.' The ringing of church bells was the signal for an airborne invasion, causing several instances of mild panic. Very quickly the alarm was relayed to other counties and, before it could be countermanded, in various places actions began to be taken. In Lincolnshire, possibly owing to faulty communications, the local defence forces believed that the signal had been given because an unidentified boat had been seen off the coast and a motor-cycle dispatch rider raced from church to church in the city of Lincoln. While the bells of five of the churches began to ring out across Lincolnshire, warning the outlying villages that the Germans were coming, two Royal Engineer officers arrived at Lincoln railway station, reported to Mr L. J. Stephens, the District Superintendent and told him that the Germans had landed and therefore they had brought along explosives with which to destroy his railway yard. Stephens, a cautious man, insisted on telephoning the London and North Eastern Railway's Southern Area Central Control. He found out the true situation and so Lincoln's railway station was saved. But before the 'Cromwell' order was countermanded, several small bridges in Lincolnshire were destroyed by zealous sapper officers.[91]

---

91 *The Last Ditch* by David Lampe.

HITLER'S INVASION OF EAST ANGLIA, 1940

Although the invasion imminent warning should have remained operative for two days, it was called off by 1000 hours on the Sunday morning and virtually all units had been stood down. The diary of the 5th Battalion Kings Regiment at Felixstowe reported that all troops had 'stood-to' until 0915 and that there had been 'no activity during the night'. The following entry also notes that officers met later in the morning to, 'discuss [the] previous nights happenings.' Army units along the east coast generally reported a quiet night, at least quieter than the previous Saturday night. Though the invasion alert was a false alarm, curious rumours of a real invasion attempt were already spreading through the eastern counties. The 165th Infantry Brigade received a letter from Divisional command saying that 'the troops must be persuaded to think that the invasion threat is not over'. This directive was passed to all the Brigade's subordinate Battalions, including the men of the 2nd Battalion Liverpool Scottish at Shingle Street. Why senior army officers were insistent that the ordinary soldiers defending the Suffolk coast needed to be told that the threat of invasion was not over (or needed reminding that it still existed) is difficult to understand especially given what happened later that same evening. And curiously, just weeks later these denials were being contradicted by Air Ministry bulletins suggesting an invasion attempt had been broken up by the RAF sometime during September. It was also reported that the RAF had bombed a large scale enemy invasion practice causing huge losses and it was claimed that the bodies of German soldiers had been washed up on shores from France to Norway - but there was no official mention of any on English beaches, at least not at first.

The press had been quick to play down the events of 7 September and douse any speculation that may have existed amongst the civil population that an invasion was imminent, following massive air raids on east London. On Monday, 9th September, the *Daily Mail* gave front page coverage to an explanation of the weekend's events beneath the heading: '3 MORE INVASION SCARES'. The *Daily Herald* and several other national dailies also carried similar reports. Readers were assured that the authorities were making urgent inquiries into the ringing 'by mistake' of church bells in several areas of Britain. According to the reports the invasion alarm had been sounded from Hampshire to the Northeast of England and also in parts of Scotland. It was stated that the Home Guard had been called out in parts of southern and eastern England and off duty military personnel had been ordered back to their barracks. The *Daily Herald* also reported that on the Sunday morning, the residents of Basingstoke had milk delivered to their doorsteps by Home Guard milkmen still in their uniforms and carrying rifles. The 'false alarm' stories would continue to appear over the following two days but they were quickly displaced from the front pages of the newspapers by official warnings of 'imminent invasion'. The situation appeared to be so grave that the prime minister made a personnel radio broadcast to the nation, during which, referring to the invasion preparations across the Channel, he said: 'We cannot tell when they will try to come. We cannot be sure in fact they will try at all, but no one should blind himself to the fact that a heavy, full-scale invasion of this island is being prepared with all of the usual German thoroughness and method and that it may be launched at any time now upon England, upon Scotland, upon Ireland or upon all three. If this invasion is going to be tried at all it does not seem that it can be long delayed ... Therefore we must regard the next week or so as a very important week in our history.' Churchill's detailed delivery went on to condemn the Luftwaffe's attacks on London and other cities and praise their defenders. He also reassured the nation that: 'Our fleets are powerful and numerous, our air force is conscious of its proved superiority, our shores are well fortified and strongly manned... we have a larger and far better equipped army than we have ever had before - and a 'million and a half men of the Home Guard, just as much soldiers of the regular army in status as the Grenadier Guards.' But in reality the prime minister's words masked the true facts; Britain's shores were not particularly well fortified or manned and the Home Guard was poorly armed. Nevertheless, the essence of his stirring and defiant speech was reported in the press beneath a variety of headlines, always accompanied by ominous warnings.

On Wednesday, 11th September, the same day that the military authorities formally requisitioned Shingle Street, the front page of the *New York Sun* carried the headline: 'Churchill Warns That Hitler Is Assembling Craft and Troops for Invasion of England'. It further stated that 'the next week may be the most critical in England's history.' Another, shorter report, suggested that the Germans had already attempted a landing on the English coast. On Thursday, 12th September it was cloudy in the Channel and there were only small raids in the south of England and even a reduced effort by the German raiders at night when the main force raided the capital. Several provincial newspapers in the UK reported details of what was claimed to be a failed attempt by German forces to land in England. The story upon which their reports were based had originated in the USA, having appeared in the previous day's edition of the *New York Sun*, beneath the headline: 'French Report Hitler has tried Invasion Already.' The *Sun*'s report was supposedly based upon information received from 'French residents and

HITLER'S INVASION OF EAST ANGLIA, 1940

independent sources', claiming that an attempt by Nazi forces to land in England had 'failed disastrously.' It was stated that the invasion force had set out from the French port of St. Malo with the intention of landing on the west coast of England. The newspaper added that the French informants had been 'reticent about details' but believed the story had already been reported in the British press [sic].[92] The very few British newspapers that reported the story on the following day simply gave the basic details and echoed the *Sun*'s assertion that the failed attempt had been 'nothing short of suicide.' The *News Chronicle* reported that German ships were 'Massing from Hamburg to Brest', while the *Daily Telegraph* warned: 'Next week likely to be most fateful.' The following day's edition of the *Telegraph* went as far as quoting reports from Berlin, stating that 'Invasion Day is Monday.'

On Friday, 13th September Mr. Richard Brown, an Air Raid Warden in Ipswich had heard rumours among work colleagues and recorded them in his diary. 'New York now has rumours that Jerry corpses are being washed up on the Yarmouth beaches in quantities.' His comments are curious; the story that had appeared in the *New York Sun* had not mentioned bodies, or Yarmouth. Neither had the very few British newspapers that repeated the story - they would not have been allowed to. On the following Monday, beneath the heading 'Too Busy Tongues', the editor of the Leicester *Mercury* commented: 'Despite warnings and exhortations, it seems the spate of rumours flows more strongly than ever.'

Within days the Leicester MP and Assistant Post-Master General, Captain Charles Waterhouse, told the audience at a public meeting that: 'there was no foundation for a rumour that an attempt had been made by the Germans to invade this country.' More stories of a German invasion attempt appeared in several provincial newspapers. Once again the stories originated from America, claiming that a small scale invasion attempt had failed having been: 'beaten off with heavy losses.' These new stories mirrored the already established and still spreading rumour. The report that appeared in the Northamptonshire *Evening Telegraph* was typical, intimating that the invaders had been annihilated and it ended with the words: 'no German remains alive to tell.' Whatever its origins, the content of the rumour and the rapidity with which it had spread, are indeed extraordinary, given that this was a time when spreading this type of rumour would lead to a charge of causing 'Alarm and Despondency'. An offence that if proven would incur severe penalties under Defence Regulations. However, the fear of punishment seems to have had little effect on the spread of the invasion

---

92 This was not the case - the British press was under strict censorship.

rumour and the stories continued to circulate on the 'grapevine' through the remainder of September. In the meantime the press reports also continued, some claiming that a Nazi invasion armada had been 'scattered and destroyed' by a combination of Channel gales and RAF raids.

Over the weekend of 14/15th September the Operational Record Books of many RAF squadrons reported that aircraft were grounded due to bad weather in the Channel but, bombed dress rehearsal or otherwise, could a number of bodies, no matter how many, float en masse all the way across the English Channel or the North Sea, some ending up on Suffolk beaches? During the Dunkirk evacuation there had been substantial loss of life when the Luftwaffe bombed boats and ships as they rescued the BEF from the beaches. On 28 May when the destroyer HMS *Wakeful* was torpedoed and sunk by a E-boat only one of the 640 allied troops and 25 of *Wakeful*'s crew survived. Nineteen crew and 275 troops were killed when the minesweeper HMS *Skipjack* was bombed by Stukas off La Panne beach on 1st June. It has been estimated that around 2,000 troops had lost their lives before Operation 'Dynamo' came to a close on 4 June. And yet there appears to be no contemporary reports of British or French bodies being swept across the Channel to the shores of Kent and Sussex. Coastguards gave the considered opinion that it is theoretically possible for a body to float all the way across the North Sea, but unlikely based on the mechanics of the east coast tides. If a body was washed ashore on the east coast it had in all probability gone into the sea relatively close to the shore. Furthermore, if the body went into the sea when the tide was going out it would be washed down the coast and if it went in to the sea when the tide was coming in, it would be washed up the coast. Records relating to bodies washed ashore along the east coast during WWII appear to support the coastguard's expert opinion:

'The body of German airman Eric Kotulla, a crewmember of a Dornier shot down off Brancaster on 21 August, drifted 25miles down the Norfolk coast before being washed ashore at West Runton on 2 September.[93] Although it is possible that the bodies of German soldiers may have floated across the Channel or North Sea, it is also possible that they could have gone into the sea much closer to the shore and were then dispersed along the coast to be washed ashore elsewhere days or even weeks later.

---

93 The body of Wilhelm Stocker, the crewmember of a Do 217 that crashed into the sea off Lowestoft on 11 May 1941 was washed up on the town's north beach seven weeks later on 29 June. The body of Lieutenant Irwin Roth USAAF had been in the sea for over twelve weeks when it was brought into Felixstowe on 9 May 1945. His B-17 had crashed at Ramsholt on the north bank of Deben on 20 February.

HITLER'S INVASION OF EAST ANGLIA, 1940

On Saturday, 14th September several British newspapers printed short extracts from a story that had appeared in the same day's edition of the *New York Times*. In the American report, Dr. Charles Bove, the former head of the American Hospital in Paris, just returned to the US from France, claimed that: 'Germany has already tried to invade England and has failed at high cost.' He backed up his claims by stating that he had seen the bodies of German soldiers floating in the Channel following a failed invasion attempt: 'There were hundreds in the water off Cherbourg.' The *New York Times* also quoted British military sources as saying: 'there has been absolutely no attempt at invasion in any shape size or form.' But, even as these brief reports appeared in the British press, rumours that a German invasion attempt had actually taken place were already in widespread circulation. And in the word-of-mouth stories spreading throughout the eastern counties of England, the attempt had been destroyed and the bodies of German soldiers had been washed up on east coast beaches. In one version of the rumour, an enemy invasion fleet had set out but had been destroyed by the RAF before it reached British shores. Another maintained that a small enemy force had landed but had been immediately 'overcome' and annihilated. There were also accompanying tales of mysterious night time convoys of lorries and ambulances going to and from beaches.

Due to the failure of the Luftwaffe to establish air supremacy, Hitler chaired a meeting with the OKW staff on 14 September at his headquarters. Hitler concluded that air superiority had not yet been established and 'promised to review the situation on 17 September for possible landings on 27 September or 8 October.' Hitler even asked 'Should we call it off altogether?' General Hans Jeschonnek, Luftwaffe Chief of Staff, begged for a last chance to defeat the RAF and for permission to launch attacks on civilian residential areas to cause mass panic. Hitler refused the latter, perhaps unaware of how much damage had already been done to civilian targets. He reserved for himself the power to unleash the terror weapon. Instead political will was to be broken by destroying the material infrastructure, the weapons industry and stocks of fuel and food. Göring was in France directing the decisive battle, so Erhard Milch deputized for him. Milch, now with the rank of general, commanded Luftflotte 5 during the Norwegian campaign. Following the defeat of France, Milch was promoted to Generalfeldmarschall and given the title Air Inspector General. As such, Milch was in charge of aircraft production. Milch had been amazed by the wreckage at Dunkirk and fearing that Germany 'had no time to waste' on 5 June had formulated a daring scheme to invade Britain immediately with

'EVEN A SMALL INVASION MIGHT GO A LONG WAY'

paratroopers spearheading a landing in southern England under cover of heavy bombing. The paratroopers were to seize two airfields which would be used to bring in fleets of Ju 52s carrying ammunition and weapons. Once a bridgehead had been established, ten infantry divisions could then he transported across the Channel to finish off Britain's weakened forces. Milch had put the plan to Göring but he told him that 'it could not be done.' Göring however, changed his mind and the following day visited Hitler in Brûly-de-Peche, the Belgian village where Hitler based himself during the final stages of the French campaign and outlined Milch's scheme, which the Reichsmarschall claimed 'was a blueprint for victory'. But the Führer was unconvinced.

In London on Sunday, 15th September Raymond Lee the United States Military Attaché wrote: 'This is the date after which I believe Hitler's chances will rapidly dwindle. The weather holds good in a miraculous manner but there are faint premonitory puffs of wind from the South-West and a chill in the air. Dispatches received through Switzerland say that there are the beginnings of a press campaign in Germany breaking the news to the people that England is to be subdued by blockade and bombing. If this is true, Hitler is on the downgrade. I can't for the life of me puzzle out what the Germans are up to. They have great air power and yet are dissipating it in fruitless and aimless attacks all over England. They must have an exaggerated idea of the damage they are doing and the effects of their raids on public morale... Just as I finish writing this, the heavy guns commence giving tongue and the little Irish maid comes in to turn down the bed. She went over to Victoria to see the plane which crashed there and is very pleased because she saw the dead German crew extracted from the wreckage.

The large scale attack on London on 15 September failed to break the back of Fighter Command. Squadron Leader Walter Myers Churchill DSO DFC Commanding 605 (County of Warwick) Squadron recalled: 'The day dawned bright and clear at Croydon. It never seemed to do anything else during those exciting weeks of August and September. But to us it was just another day. We weren't interested in Hitler's entry into London; most of us were wondering whether we should have time to finish breakfast before the first blitz started.' The first big attack came in the morning at 1100 hours. A wave of about 100 German aircraft was spotted heading over the Kent coast towards London followed by a second wave of about 150 aircraft. Spitfire and Hurricane squadrons were sent to meet them and many German planes were reported to have turned away without dropping any bombs.

HITLER'S INVASION OF EAST ANGLIA, 1940

At about 1400 hours another wave of about 150 German aircraft crossed the coast near Dover - again followed by a second wave of 100 aircraft. They appeared to be heading for targets in south London and railways in London and Kent. Fighter patrols were again ready to meet the enemy and only seventy or so enemy planes reached central London where there were a series of dogfights. The attacks continued with smaller raids on Portland and Southampton. Again the enemy aircraft were successfully driven off by the RAF fighters. As darkness fell, the raids continued on London inflicting major damage on targets in the south of the city.

At 2000 hours on Sunday night, Winston Churchill, who had returned to 10 Downing Street, was awoken. He received bad news from the Navy. In the Atlantic sinking of shipping had been bad, but his Secretary informed him that all had been redeemed in the day's air battle. He was told that the RAF had downed 183 enemy aircraft for less than forty aircraft lost. (The true figure was 56 German aircraft shot down for the loss of 26 RAF fighters but thirteen pilots were saved). By the time that most people had either emerged from their Anderson shelters or had risen after another rather uncomfortable night's sleep, the daily newspapers were busy informing them of the events of the previous day. The *Daily Telegraph* stated that 'Of the 350 to 400 enemy planes launched in two waves against the capital and south-east England, 175, or nearly 50 per cent were shot down according to returns... The Germans loss yesterday was their highest since 15 August, when 180 were shot down. On 18 August they lost 153. In personnel their loss yesterday was over 500 airmen against twenty RAF pilots.' The *Daily Herald* told a similar story, but added that AA gunfire had brought down four of the 175 German aircraft. On the subject of the RAF victory, they went on to say that in both of the raids, the gallant pilots and squadrons of the RAF harassed the bombers so much that those that were not shot down, were harried and chased right back to the Channel. The Germans had encountered their most gruelling reception so far.

As a British flying boat arrived in New York delivering news of a 'record bag' of 185 enemy aircraft the German Embassy tried in vain to correct the total but they were ignored and the *New York Times* ran several excited stories calling for a military alliance with Britain and her Commonwealth. Belatedly the Nazi Party newspaper *Völkischer Beobachter* announced that attacks on London had caused considerable damage. It claimed the Luftwaffe destroyed 79 RAF aircraft for 43 losses. Actual RAF losses amounted to 29 fighters.

Göring called a conference to inform the Luftwaffe that the German fighters had failed. He informed his Luftflotten commanders that,

'EVEN A SMALL INVASION MIGHT GO A LONG WAY'

'The British air force is far from finished, their fighters proved that yesterday. Their bombers are continually attacking our barge installations and although we must admit they have achieved some form of success, but I will only say and repeat what I have said before and that is our orders to attempt full scale attacks on London, instead of the destruction of their air force will not achieve the success we need, it will only act as our demise.' The Luftwaffe's losses had been brushed aside by the Reichsmarschall who still maintained that RAF Fighter Command would be annihilated 'in four or five days' but ordered a resumption of attacks on Fighter Command and the factories supplying it. German Intelligence however, had failed to appreciate that on the morning of Monday, 16th September no less than 160 new Hurricanes and Spitfires were available as replacements with upward of 400 aircraft available elsewhere for delivery within one week.

If Göring was disappointed, Hitler was furious. London was supposed to have been flattened and in flames and the people supposed to have been bombed almost into submission.[94] Göring ordered the air fleets to begin a new phase of the battle. Hitler hoped this might result in 'eight million going mad' (referring to the population of London), which would 'cause a catastrophe' for the British. In those circumstances, Hitler said, 'even a small invasion might go a long way'.

We can only speculate what this 'small invasion' or possibly as many as three invasions might have been.

---

[94] Göring remained as commander-in-chief of the Luftwaffe until the final days of World War II. In 1941 Hitler designated Göring as his successor and deputy in all his offices. At the Nuremburg War Trials in 1945 Göring was found guilty on all four counts and was sentenced to death by hanging but he cheated the hangman by committing suicide with a potassium cyanide capsule the night before he was to be hanged.

Chapter 9

Unternehmen Brandenburg Concerto

There have been at least two attempts by the Germans to invade England from the French coast and in both instances the Nazis were literally consumed by fire. This was the story told in France by workers from the occupied area along the Channel coast and confirmed by nurses who worked in hospitals attending German soldiers who had escaped from the British flames. The first invasion attempt was made in August, the second early in September, over another route. Both failed when British planes dropped incendiary bombs and set afire tanks of oil and gasoline in the Channel. As disclosed by Frenchmen in a position to know, the British sowed the Channel with oil tanks sufficiently beneath the surface to be hidden from view. Parallel with these the British anchored thousands of gasoline tanks. Then they waited for the Germans... People in the occupied French ports estimate that perhaps as many as 80,000 German troops perished in the two attempts. The fact is that hospitals in occupied France are filled with Nazi soldiers, all of them suffering from severe burns. There was a wave of mutinies in the German Army in September, many of the troops declaring that they would not face again the 'burning sea' when they learned that a third attempt at invasion of England was being planned.

Boris Nikolayevsky, 'a distinguished Russian publicist and historian' resident in France before his recent arrival in New York, with 'particularly close contacts with French political circles' writing in *The New York Times,* **15 December 1940.**

On Saturday, 7th September early high cloud gave way to light cloud but remained fine throughout southern England. In the Channel the early morning haze quickly disappeared, leaving clear skies. *Lundby,*

UNTERNEHMEN BRANDENBURG CONCERTO

the apparently ordinary Swedish tramp steamer, with an extraordinary Luftwaffe escort, neared the Suffolk coast after her long sea journey across the North Sea. Seamen lived in dark, confined, damp, poorly ventilated and often rusty dormitory accommodation with wooden board bunks three or more high, without running water and lacking heating. Each man was provided with one or two blankets at best and was expected to bring his own 'donkey's breakfast' - a sack cloth bag containing straw which was to serve as a mattress. In the pre-war years seamen competed to sign on aboard vessels owned by shipping lines which were known as 'good feeders' due to their staple diets being superior while others would be avoided for providing poor food. Usually the food was coarse and poor. Any frozen food available was from a refrigerator and after the ice melted salt meat from brine tubs and butter from tins provided much of the staple diet. Fresh eggs, fruit and vegetables might or might not be provided on arrival in port dependent on the budget held by the Chief Steward which was spent only with permission from the Master who was there to ensure the success and profit of each voyage.

Below decks, almost to a man the one hundred English speaking Germans of number 11 Kompanie, 3rd Battalion Brandenburger commandoes were glad they had been provided with the rather uninspired combination of processed meats and cheeses, 'ersatz' instant coffee and dry 'rusk' type biscuits/crackers. Many enjoyed the combat issues of rum and brandy while others took dextrose thirst quenching tablets. They wanted to rid themselves of their British police and Home Guard uniforms but after rendezvousing with troops and combat engineers of the 7th Flieger-Division, the Brandenburger commandoes were to raid Felixstowe docks and also infiltrate and capture the important radar station at Bawdsey Manor nearby. Unternehmen 'Grün' or 'Fall Grün' ('Case Green') as it was codenamed would be the second of Hitler's 'small invasions' that might go a long way'. The Brandenburgers hoped that it would prove more successful than three separate military operations of the same name, all of which had been cancelled. 'Fall Grün (Czechoslovakia)', the planned invasion of Czechoslovakia, was to have been carried out in September 1938. Operation 'Green' had been planned as an invasion of Ireland in support of the invasion of Britain. Operation 'Tannenbaum' was the planned invasion of Switzerland.

The Brandenburgers had heard many rumours following the failure of 'Fall Weiss 2' ('Case White') the previous attempt to raid Bawdsey Manor

HITLER'S INVASION OF EAST ANGLIA, 1940

on 31st August.[95] At first, all had seemed to go as planned and the weather augured well. Much improved conditions prevailed throughout the British Isles, temperatures were slightly higher than the previous days and conditions were expected to remain fine with cloud periods in all Channel areas as six Heinkel He 59B-1 seaplanes of Staffel Schwilben, attempted to land a force of sixty infantry and combat engineers of the 22nd Luftlandeddivision on the coast of Suffolk. But the Heinkels, left over from the attack on the River Maas during the invasion of Holland on 10 May, were in poor condition and three of the obsolete aircraft had been forced to abandon the mission, leaving the three others to continue on alone without escort to the Suffolk coast. A fourth He 59 was lost when it alighted on the rough sea, toppled over and crashed, drowning everyone on board. Although many of the 'Fall Weiss 2' attack force managed to get ashore they too were killed and mortally wounded when the sea was set on fire. Those that survived were hunted down and shot and killed. There were no survivors.

The attendant flotilla of twenty fast E-boats from Dordrecht in the western Netherlands, their cover now blown, decided that discretion was the better part of valour and fled as the mangled and burned bodies of the 22nd Luftlandeddivision were swept upstream by the strong current to be washed up on the shore near Shingle Street. The two surviving He 59s were beached off shore but they and two E-boats, which had got too close, were quickly consumed by fire when the sea was set alight. Some of the infantry and combat engineers managed to escape the conflagration by getting into their rubber dinghies but their respite was short lived in the burning sea and their charred bodies and those of the Kriegsmarine were added to the scene of carnage as tremendous gunfire, explosions, searchlight beams and pyrotechnics rent the air and then a red glow filled the night sky over Shingle Street.

At Darsham approximately four miles north east of Saxmundham and about five miles from Dunwich in Suffolk on 7 September, in an underground chamber beneath a mass of dead branches and a carpet of leaves in remote woodland, an anxious Auxiliary Unit 'cell' - No.34 - waited attentively for their instructions from the Special Duty Section at Great Glemham. Women manned the Special Duties Section, the

---

95 'Fall Weiss' ('Case White') was the Nazi strategic plan for the invasion of Poland. The German military High Command finalized its operational orders on 15 June 1939 and the invasion commenced on 1 September. In 1943 'Fall Weiss' was used once again when a combined Axis operation was made against the Yugoslav Partisans throughout occupied Yugoslavia.

secret communications arm of the Auxiliary Units and transmitted on their secret TRD Sets intelligence gathered by the Auxiliary Units, being given their information through a series of dead letter drops. The cell had six months rations and ammunition and they met in secret at an empty house in the local area. Secrecy was all important and each cell was not known by name to any other cell just in case of interrogation or collaboration. Each member of a cell wore standard 1940 pattern battle-dress blouse and trousers, with the Field Service side cap. The trousers were tucked into black or dark brown leather anklets over standard black ammunition boots. No equipment was worn, other than a webbing or leather waist belt, supporting a revolver holster. Some Auxiliaries wore better quality Army issue uniforms 'acquired' from friends or relatives in the Forces. The men carried an American 45 automatic pistol, a Thompson 'Tommy' sub-machine gun, a Mills Bomb, a Fairbairn dagger and a sabotage manual disguised to look like 'The Countryman's Diary'!

The Auxiliary Units' job was not to engage the enemy but to be behind the German lines after they had landed and moved inland. They could then engage in sabotage, blowing up bridges, railway lines and aircraft. In addition to their Commando daggers and machine guns, they had nitro-glycerine 'sticky' bombs for slapping on the side of advancing tanks. They were issued with plastic explosives rather than traditional gelignite which was inclined to 'sweat' if not properly stored and became dangerous. Their grenades came with four-second fuses, unlike the standard seven-second variety used by the regular Army (greatly increasing the risk to the thrower but reducing the prospect of one being thrown back). And every unit was issued with one extra, unusual piece of kit: a gallon of rum. This was not for recreational use. Not only were Auxiliary Units given a life expectancy of twelve days, but they were also under orders not to be captured. They were given three morphine tablets; one to ease the pain if injured, two to knock them out and three to kill themselves. The rum might help.

3 Group, one of five Groups in Suffolk, with a HQ at the Mill House in Cransford near Framlingham was led by Captain George Scott-Moncrieff with LWO Turner as his 2nd Lieutenant. Cell 34 at Darsham, was one of over thirty Patrols in the county. Lieutenant 'Charlie' Spencer, a local vicar (who used the lightning conductor on his steeple as a radio antenna) was the Patrol leader. He had been a captain on the Western Front in World War One but war in the trenches was more than enough for most men and he had turned to the cloth during the thirties. Each Patrol leader recruited his 'five desperate men', often from among existing networks of family

and friends. Most were very young - too young to have been called up for army service - or members of reserved occupations. Their observation post was built by the Royal Engineers and was very well hidden. There was a hollow tree stump to cover the door into the bunker. To open the hatch there was a drainpipe with a wire through it. When the wire was pulled it released the catch which opened the hatch. Ammunition, bombs and various items of equipment were stored there. One night during a night training exercise, Spencer came across his men standing about twenty yards from the underground base. When he asked them why they had not gone in he was told that they couldn't because a courting couple were making love on the 'roof', totally oblivious to was actually below them! The unit only knew the men in their own group so that they could never give the game away as to the whereabouts of others. Spencer was a heavy drinker and if the invasion came, Sergeant Herman Perry, a local farm labourer, was going to kill him. As group leader Spencer was the only one who knew all the locations of the Patrols. So Herman would have had to do it, see?' He had no qualms about killing his own people. Perry would not have shot 'em, he would've garrotted 'em, using his home-made 'cheese-wire' used for garrotting sentries, which consisted of a two-foot length of thin piano wire with a short broomstick handle at each end.

Private Herbert 'Bert' Beaumont, an apprentice motor mechanic, born in 1924, had joined the Home Guard in 1940. Then he was called into the CO's office at his Drill Hall where a panel of officers asked him lots of questions, staring with his age. He said '16'; no, I mean 18'! I thought that's what you said' commented one of the officers. Then they asked him if he wanted to join a special organization. As he had to sign the Officials Act, it sounded more exciting than the Home Guard. It seems that he had already been security vetted by the police and MI5 and his family background had been investigated. He was recruited as an observer for the Auxiliary cell and he knew what could be required of him at any minute. Like all Auxiliaries he had been sent for training in martial arts, sabotage and silent killing at Coleshill House in Wiltshire. Yet men like 'Bert' had to endure taunts - and even the odd fight - from those who objected to the sight of a healthy young man not 'doing his bit'. His mother and father scolded him for his constant late nights. They believed he was in the Home Guard as he always wore Home Guard uniform and flashes which were a cover for all his secret activities, such as getting through airfield security at local air bases and then 'blowing up planes'. He had a .45 Thompson sub-machine-gun or 'Tommy gun', a .22 Winchester sniping rifle with telescopic sights and silencer, which was intended to takeout sentries and guard dogs and, possibly under operational conditions, collaborators (and informers, although these intentions were unspoken); a .455 Webley Mk VI revolver and a Fairburn dagger. Some of these he kept hidden in his wardrobe. His identity card enabled him to travel wherever he was needed and his girlfriend Dorothy became exasperated by his refusal to attend Saturday night dances. In fact, he was just training. Many Auxiliaries had the same experience but they all were forbidden to talk about it.

Lance Corporal Ivan Potter, a worker in a crane factory - a reserved occupation - was exempt from army service, but had proved himself a resourceful member of the Patrol. He was one of the few Auxiliaries who had acquired a German Mauser which accepted the 9mm Sten gun ammunition. Each Auxiliary received training in the basic principles of making and using explosive charges but Potter was particularly adept at improvising with their basic supplies, building his own roadside bombs and a 'carpet-sweeper' device for blowing up pillboxes. One of his improvised explosive devices looked like any old tin of tobacco, left on the side of the road. But if anyone opened it, 'well', he said 'there was a little surprise, ain't there!' The tin contained a brass rod and wire detonator. 'Boom! Have a man's hands off with that, you would. Maybe an arm, if you were lucky!' He even provided every member of his Patrol with a custom-made brass knuckle-duster with a six-inch knife at one end and a razor blade at the other. 'That was for cutting the artery here,' said Ivan, drawing his thumbnail down the side of his neck. 'Quickest way to kill a man, that.' Collaborators or anyone threatening the security of the Patrol were to be dealt with swiftly.

Corporal 'Mick' Small, a gamekeeper, was really a poacher. His wife Edith knew nothing of his activities in the Auxiliary Units but once, when he returned from a weekend course, he did not get back until four on the Monday morning and there was an air raid. Edith had not gone to bed but had slept in a chair in the living room. Small arrived home with his face all blackened and when he opened the door his wife woke up and he frightened her to death! Small was not frightened about the Germans coming and felt confident as a result of his training but his main concern was for Edith because once it was realised that her husband was operating behind German lines following an invasion, the wives would be prime targets.

Private 'Sid' Warwick, a sixteen year old plumber's mate and Private 'Ernie' Wentwood, a 16-year old jobbing carpenter who worked on a building site erecting barracks for RAF airmen and soldiers in the regular army made up the other members of the 'cell'. Warwick and Wentwood were the youngest and often on the end of good-natured banter from the older members like Mick Small and Herman Perry. 'He'd have been shot forty times by now, lighting the fuse like that!' Mick Small once exclaimed. 'Oh, you don't want to hold the Sten by the magazine!' Herman muttered, shaking his head. Although he did not always show it, Small was apprehensive. He believed the cell could cause problems to start but the Germans would have soon snuffed them out and it would not make any difference. The only thing that might was if they could blow a bridge or tunnel in their area. 'They'd have a bloody hard time fixing it', Small said.

Hermann was more confident. He knew that his cell had the main Ipswich to London railway line passing by. All they had to do was pull out the keys on the main line, on the outside of the curve, loosen the bolts and the speed of the train would roll it over the embankment. Wouldn't even need any explosives! Plastic High Explosive (PHE) was only then becoming available but the more common explosives were gelignite (which if handled with bare hands could produce a headache equal to a first class hangover!), blasting gelatine and Nobel's Explosive 808, with its distinctive smell of almonds. Hermann's Patrol had supplies of white 1lb guncotton slabs, about the size of a thick paperback book. These had a central circular hole for the insertion of a purpose-made primer and detonator. During training he had practised his skills on disused railway lines and derelict vehicles. Spencer's cell's main objective in the event of an invasion would be the clutch of operational airfields and others under construction in their immediate vicinity. They would have to penetrate the heavily reinforced outer perimeters, avoid contact with German paratroopers and blow up any Ju 52 transports before they could take off again. Ivan Potter for one could not wait 'for the buggers to invade!' He once admitted that at their age you're mad for anything, aren't you? I thought it was wonderful!' 'It was a game for us,' 'Bert' Beaumont agreed. 'We were doing our bit and were allowed to do more than our bit because we had these special duties.'

At Great Glemham Out Station in a typically attractive Suffolk village roughly equidistant between Framlingham and Saxmundham, Barbara Jenkins manned her radio. She was already serving in the women's Auxiliary Territorial Service when she was approached to join the special duties section. When called in to see a senior officer she had been told that the War Office urgently wanted volunteers for a secret and dangerous job and that she should go for it. So Barbara did. She was only fourteen when she was enrolled in the special duties section. Colonel Harry Blenkinsop, the army organiser for the area had asked her father if he thought she would fold up at the sight of a German. Her father told him Barbara did not fold up at anything - horses, bulls, schoolmistresses - so the colonel recruited her. He thought a kid on a horse was unlikely to be suspected of anything. So she was to ride out and spot any choice targets, in terms of troops or supply dumps.' Barbara had two horses, one chestnut, for riding during the day and one black, for night exercises when she would ride cross-country. It was just one big adventure but then her brother George was killed in action flying from Malta and she began to think more seriously about it and wanted to have a go at the Germans however she could. The job was to travel around the country establishing networks of radio operators. Barbara had to sit there all day sending and receiving messages. Once the messages were all coming in loudly and clearly, someone else was brought in to operate it and Barbara would go off and start all over again. In between times, Barbara had to listen out for enemy agents broadcasting to Berlin. They noted times, voice, the language if possible and where it was on the range. She had heard agents broadcasting. Barbara was trained to use a rifle and a pistol, but was never issued with either. She did have cyanide pills however and in the event of an invasion, she and others like her would be operating the radio posts until the Germans 'got them'.

The men of Cell 34 too, were ready. They had left their families suddenly and with little explanation just disappeared into the night. They had to sign the Official Secrets Act and swear they would not tell anyone, not even wives and friends, for fifty years! They just said, 'Sorry, Mum and Dad, I'm off now. The Germans have arrived and I've been told to go somewhere.'

But the Germans did not arrive and no instructions were transmitted from the Special Duty Section at Great Glemham. They were not to know that Unternehmen 'Grün', the operation of 7 September using troops and combat engineers of the 7th Flieger-Division and members of the Brandenburg commando detachments embarked on the *Lundby*, had faired equally as badly as 'Fall Weiss 2' had done on 31st August. When finally, 'Fall Grün' went ahead on 7th September, it was much the same scenario as that planned for 'Sealion' except that an attack on the port of Dover and a raid to neutralise a coastal battery and nearby radar station had been replaced by Felixstowe and Bawdsey respectively. Should the River Ore be blocked at its entrance in Hollesley Bay by barges or anything else to prevent small enemy craft getting up the estuary the 4th Kompanie Brandenburger commandoes were to clear it. Also, they were to clear the beaches to the north and south of Felixstowe of mines and barbed wire and anti-tank obstacles. The objective of the 11th Kompanie, codenamed 'Pioneer Battalion 303' was the Bawdsey radar station and the 332 Coastal

Battery. The manpower of a two-gun coast battery like '332' ranged from about seventy to 150. Since only about six to eight men were needed to work a single gun at a given moment, this seems a high figure but each battery had a 'BOP' (Battery Observation Post) - a concrete tower with steel shutters for lookouts and range finders, two searchlights, one or two sentry posts for inland defence and security, a magazines, an electric generator room and machine guns for local (including anti-aircraft) defence and all these needed relief watches.[96]

The No.3 Naval Detachment at Bawdsey East Lane just four miles along the coast from Felixstowe, which came under the overall command of the 165th Infantry Brigade, fired only a few rounds from their two improvised old 4-inch naval guns before being overrun, but both the 332 coastal battery and the 72 soldiers on guard detail put up stiff resistance. Minefields on the beaches to the north of Bawdsey Manor, right up to and including Hollesley Bay also inflicted heavy casualties on the raiders. Setting the sea on fire completed the rout. Part of the base's defences consisted of drums of petrol chained to concrete blocks under the sea and wired to detonators. When the enemy assault from the sea began, the drums were blown and the petrol rose to the surface, where it was set alight using tracer rounds. The conflagration engulfed the raiders and choking acrid black smoke and the nauseous smell of burning flesh permeated the air over a large area of sea. Death was slow and horrible but Britain, its backs to the wall, felt no remorse. The Brandenburgs attired as they were in Home Guard and British army uniforms, were dispatched on the spot, their bodies then taken away and later buried in anonymous graves in East Anglia and further afield.

At Felixstowe the defences had also proved insurmountable. Defenders of harbour areas in particular had been told to do everything in their power to deny them to the Germans. Standing orders were of the following kind: 'The Felixstowe battalion will defend the battalion area against any form of attack, with every means at its disposal and with the cooperation of all supporting arms and to the last man and the last round. There will be NO withdrawal.'[97] The Fixed Defences sites which originated from Tudor times had been repeatedly rebuilt since to resist the threat of Holland, France and Germany in turn, sprawled across sizeable areas. The Landguard compound, occupied

---

96 *The Battle of the East Coast (1939-1945)* by J. P. Foynes.
97 212 Brigade War Diary (PRO WO 166/1065). *The Battle of the East Coast (1939-1945)* by J. P. Foynes.

UNTERNEHMEN BRANDENBURG CONCERTO

by 1,500 men of 515 Regiment, was over a mile long. Landguard Fort, a great Victorian brick pentagon aptly known as 'The Tomb' was an important headquarters for the Harwich area. It housed Fixed Defences HQ and initially the Operations Room for the AA guns, until this was transferred to the even older Q Tower, a Martello Tower in Felixstowe Town.[98] The series of giant flame throwers installed on the cliffs at Felixstowe created a sea of blazing oil which engulfed the raiders in a devastating agony of death. The few survivors were quickly mopped up by the 55th West Lancashire Infantry Division's 164th and 165th Brigades[99] and the three Felixstowe-based motor torpedo boats. The *Lundby* left the scene and headed slowly back to Norway.[100]

The Führer was enraged when details of the failures of both 'Fall Weiss 2' and Unternehmen 'Grün' reached him at his residence at the Berghof. The news of the failure of 'Fall Weiss 2' had deliberately been kept from the Führer by a combination of fear and inter-service politics and rivalry. When eventually he was informed, the Führer immediately blamed the debacle on his army chiefs Field Marshal Walther von Brauchitsch and General der Artillerie Franz Halder and OKW Chief of Staff Alfred Jodl and Grossadmiral Erich Raeder and the German Kriegsmarine and Reichsmarschall Hermann Göring and the Luftwaffe in particular for the 'confused and muddled thinking', 'flawed planning' and 'poor execution'. The three services often followed their own agenda, as had happened on 7 July when the inability of the three units that made up the German military to either work together or support one another during discussions about the dispositions and objectives of the attack on England had manifested itself.

---

98 *The Battle of the East Coast (1939-1945)* by J. P. Foynes.
99 Infantry divisions, subdivided into brigades and battalions had field and anti-tank artillery regiments attached. *The Battle of the East Coast (1939-1945)* by J. P. Foynes.
100 On 12 July 1941 *Lundby* was taken over as an idle foreign vessel in United States ports and ownership was transferred to the US War Shipping Administration. In August 1941 she was assigned to the United States Lines Inc., renamed SS *Pink Star* and registered in Panama. On 3rd September *Pink Star* sailed from New York loaded with general cargo under the command of John S. MacKenzie as part of Convoy SC-44, bound for the United Kingdom. Due to provisions of the Neutrality Act prohibiting US flagged vessels or citizens sailing into war zones, the crew was composed of Canadians, Dutch, British, Belgians, Chinese and one each of Polish, French, Portuguese, Irish, Danish and Ecuadorian nationality. At 0151 on 20 September, U-552, under the command of Erich Topp fired a spread of torpedoes into the convoy. Only *Pink Star* was hit and quickly sank. Of her crew of 35 men, 13 died with the ship. The sinking came seven days after the US had warned Germany concerning attacks on shipping in the Western Atlantic and three days after Secretary of the Navy Knox announced the Navy would take protective measures.

HITLER'S INVASION OF EAST ANGLIA, 1940

Equally, Hitler's seeming refusal to listen to his military commanders and wanting things done his way, which came out of the success the military had against Poland and the nations of Western Europe - countries attacked without the overwhelming support of the military but attacked because Hitler instinctively knew that they would win - or so he believed played its part.[101]

The Führer anticipated that his three services would be at constant loggerheads over the details for landing troops in East Anglia, just as they had when announcing the build up to 'Sealion'. To guard against inter-service bickering and possible outright failure, he had ordered that plans be formulated for three 'small invasions' in total. In the continued absence of Reichsmarschall Göring, he had turned to General Milch. The Führer had decided that even though air superiority had not yet been established, he ordered that preparations be made for Unternehmen 'Brandenburg Concerto', the third attempt to land his forces on the British beaches, to begin. Whereas the two seaborne attempts had failed Unternehmen 'Brandenburg Concerto', which would go ahead on Monday, 16th September would use Ju 52/3m transports towing DFS 230 gliders filled with Luftwaffe Fallschirmjäger paratroops and glider-borne troops respectively, as well as Brandenburgers. Having given up on Bawdsey and the dangers that an assault from the sea presented and after studying maps and intelligence reports the Führer decreed that the transport aircraft would drop the paratroopers behind the Minsmere Cliffs at RAF Dunwich and assault the radar station and Battery 409 nearby. The assault teams in the gliders would cast off to land on the radar station itself. The Führer had deluded himself into thinking that 'Brandenburg Concerto' would be just as successful as the assault by gliders on the Belgian fortress of Ében-Émael on 10 May.

The plan for Unternehmen 'Brandenburg Concerto' removed the need for the Gebirgsjäger to be involved, assault boats could be dispensed with and Pioneer Battalion 303 had no need to practice landing on cliffs because the airborne attack force would leapfrog the beaches. As the DFS 230s required very little landing space they could land directly on the objective (although German intelligence overlooked that fact that anti-glider trenches had been dug on Dunwich Common). The threat of the high cliffs ideally suited for enfilade fire was therefore removed: besides which it was only a 'river crossing' after all? Why, the Pioneer Battalion could even use their motorcycles! In the build up for 'Sealion' it was claimed that the target for the Brandenburgers was the radar station on

---

101 Peter D. Antill BA (Hons) MSc (Econ) PGCE (PCE).

UNTERNEHMEN BRANDENBURG CONCERTO

Beachy Head; but Beachy Head is over 500 feet above sea level and during their actual training, which had included the use of motorcycles, Pioneer Battalion 303 had practiced landing on open beaches. Although no further information exists, the two other units from the Third battalion presumably had similar assignments.

Having removed what the Führer believed were the major risks for failure, it was generally known that Unternehmen 'Brandenburg Concerto' was almost suicidal and no-one expected many men to return. Even if the troops accomplished their tasks successfully they would then have to take to their dinghies and paddle their way to E-boats waiting off shore to transport them to Holland. The original commander of the operation protested that he had not been given enough time to prepare the mission and that the paratroopers had never before dropped at night;[102] nor had they enough time to establish any unit cohesion or train together, but his protestations had proved in vain and had been dismissed. The Führer's operational staff did not dare voice their opinions in open discussion but they did take pains to remind their leader that each lumbering Ju 52/3m was capable of carrying just twelve fully equipped paratroopers and the DFS 230 wooden gliders, only eight troops. At least 240 assault troops would be needed to ensure some semblance of success and to carry less would be suicidal. To achieve this total, a dozen Ju 52s had been found and it was suggested that each would tow a DFS glider behind them but three of the transports were required to carry additional heavy equipment making towing a glider at night too cumbersome and dangerous so only nine gliders would be used. Not only did this limit the overall number of assault troops to just 216 men, it also reduced fire power because each glider was armed with a MG34 to cover the assault by the eight storm troopers in each DFS 230. The operational staff wanted more transports and troops as a mobile reserve but the Führer insisted that no additional Ju 52s could be spared because of the losses sustained in the May 'Blitzkrieg' and the build up for 'Sealion', which had priority. Seizing on Milch's earlier proposal the Führer added that once a bridgehead had been established, ten infantry divisions would need to be transported across the Channel in a fleet of Ju

---

102 Officially, Operation Stösser (Operation 'Auk') a paratroop drop into the American rear in the High Fens area during the Battle of the Bulge was the German paratroopers' only night-time drop during World War II. Their objective was to take and hold the Baraque Michel crossroads until the arrival of the 12th SS Panzer Division. The operation was led by Oberst Friedrich August Freiherr von der Heydte. He was given only 8 days to prepare the mission. The majority of the paratroopers and pilots assigned to the operation were undertrained and inexperienced. The mission was a complete failure.

HITLER'S INVASION OF EAST ANGLIA, 1940

52s to finish off Britain's weakened forces. And after two airfields had been seized, they would be used to bring in more Ju 52s carrying ammunition and weapons. But when it was pointed out that after the gliders had cast off the Ju 52s could land at RAF Woodbridge or even Bentwaters where an airfield was under construction, to give support, the Führer contemptuously dismissed these suggestions with a swift sweep of his hand. During the invasion of Holland hadn't Ju 52s become stuck in the soft soil and mud when attempting to land on the uncompleted airfield of Valkenburg, while Dutch fighters strafed and destroyed many more transports that had landed on the beach north of The Hague?

Hitler sanctioned the use of two Fieseler Fi-156 Storch light reconnaissance aircraft to enable members of the Brandenburg Regiment to land with Empfänger Blind landing transmitters as near to the objective as possible. Each Ju 52 would carry an Empfänger Blind landing receiver and the information received would pinpoint exactly the spot for the paratroopers to land. The Storch had proved successful in Brandenburger operations to take the bridges immediately to the south of the 10th Panzer Division's route of march in the southern Ardennes during the invasion of France in May. The Führer, much encouraged, believed success was assured and the English would not set the sea on fire to prevent the assault. The crucial element for the assault force was time. It was believed that the combination of a noiseless approach by the gliders used by the assault force would give the attackers the element of surprise. However, German estimates were that this would last, at the most, for sixty minutes, after which the superior numbers of the forces defending the radar station, as well as any reinforcements sent to the area, would begin to come to bear against the relatively small number of lightly armed airborne troops. The German plan, therefore, was to eliminate within those sixty minutes as many defending positions and soldiers as was possible. The destruction of these was expected to be completed within ten minutes; within this time the airborne troops would have to break out of their gliders, cover the distance to the objective, fix the explosive charges to the radar masts and detonate them, all while under enemy fire. Unfortunately for the Germans, 'Enigma' decrypts had already allowed Britain's defences; not least Fighter Command and the Royal Navy, to build up a complete picture of German intentions and the element of surprise had already been lost. With the 'Enigma' code broken they knew what was to be expected and were able to prepare the defences accordingly.

UNTERNEHMEN BRANDENBURG CONCERTO

All along the East coast Army and Home Guard units, naval bases and coastal artillery positions were brought to readiness and all leave was cancelled. The seven Auxiliary Unit members of Cell 34 about five miles from Dunwich thought, wrongly, that RAF Darsham was the target but got ready nonetheless. There were three states of readiness, short of actual combat: 'Normal', 'Alert' and 'Invasion Imminent'. Typically, one fifth of defenders manned their posts under the first. At naval bases the rest were at two hours' notice by day (primarily for beach landings) and half an hour by night (mainly for harbour raids and parachute drops). 'Alert' meant a two-fifths manning, with notice for the rest cut to half an hour. 'Invasion Imminent' meant the total manning of defences in misty weather, three quarters by night and half in daylight. By night the defence perimeters were continuously patrolled by troops equipped with indispensible maps of the minefields and with pyrotechnics for signalling, while motor boats did likewise on the estuaries and creeks. A green rocket meant 'I have sighted enemy ships'; a Golden Rain, 'SOS, enemy landing; a red 'Enemy have landed' and a white 'I require assistance'.[103] The Führer had miscalculated and not for the first time.

At Waalhaven airfield near Rotterdam just after midnight on 16 September, the two overloaded Fieseler Fi-156 Storch light reconnaissance aircraft with the members of the Brandenburg Regiment and the Empfänger Blind landing transmitters took off first. In flight, the main landing gear legs hung down, giving the aircraft the appearance of a Storch, which gave the aircraft their unique nickname. Soon after, at airfields in the area of Laon in Hauts-de-France, northern France squads of the 7th Fallschirmjäger Division began boarding the Ju 52s and DFS 230 gliders During the morning of 10 May Major (later Colonel) Hermann Goetzel's Anti-tank Company, equipped with the 3.7cm Pak, had paraded on the airfield at Paderborn waiting to be flown into Holland with 22nd Division's second-wave units. In the weeks immediately following the campaign in France, on 7th or 8th September Major Goetzel, now of HQ 7th Flieger-Division was concerned with the raising of new airborne formations and their equipping. His orders were to undertake a reconnaissance with two other paratrooper captains to select airfields in Belgium and northern France from which the airborne troops could take off for 'Sealion'. Travelling in a light truck the three officers not only found eight suitable airfields, chiefly in the area of Laon, from which the operations could be flown, but also a building near Laon which could

---

103 *The Battle of the East Coast (1939-1945)* by J. P. Foynes.

serve as a Para supply base. Within days Goetzel was ordered to prepare the airfields for the arrival of the paratroops. The glider group, which would be carrying a battalion of the Assault Regiment in the opening attacks, was to be brought by glider to the advanced airfield ready for the dawn take-off. Shortly after the movement orders were issued the advance parties were suddenly to move quite openly, into the departure areas of northern France. Goetzel had formed the opinion that 'Sealion' had certainly been postponed if not cancelled altogether. It was obvious that the open concentration of paratroops in northern France had nothing to do with the preparation for an airborne assault.[104]

Now, that was all about to change. This time no specialist badges were worn, all distinctive uniform was packed away and no paratroop songs were to be sung, so that British Intelligence should not learn that the airborne units were preparing for action.

Each trooper wore a beige jumpsuit, thick fur-lined black leather boots, jump gloves and a Luftwaffe Model 1935 Stahlhelm steel helmet, which incorporated a more substantial leather liner and chinstrap design which provided far more protection for German airborne troops.[105] The paratroopers wore, over their uniforms, Rückfallschirm, Zwangablösung or 'Backpack Parachute, Static Line Deployment', based on the Italian 'Salvatore' design suspended from the harness via one single riser. This meant that the paratrooper had much less control and also, the descent speed was too fast in many cases. Paratroopers had to throw themselves forward out of the Ju 52, jumping in spread-eagle exit position and in the resulting face-down position when the chute opened, control was nearly impossible. The opening shock of this canopy first parachute was also very harsh but the chute would fully deploy in under forty metres, which meant a lower drop altitude and less time dangling helpless in the air. The chute was attached to the harness with four clips which were difficult to undo when under fire or when the trooper was being wind dragged. To remove their parachute harness required the paratrooper to stand stationary upright for up to eighty seconds. The necessity of landing on knees and elbows reduced the amount of

---

104 *Storming Eagles: German Airborne Forces In World War II* by James Lucas (Arms & Armour Press, 1988).

105 As a consequence of the heavy casualties inflicted on German armed forces in Russia later in the war the Luftwaffe produced a camouflaged parachute jump smock for the Luftwaffe Fallschirmjäger nicknamed the Knochensack (bonesack) which was designed to wear over a paratrooper's equipment. They were made in a variety of camouflage patterns and made from tough cotton material.

equipment the trooper could carry and even with pads, significantly increased the chance of injury. As a result, they jumped armed only with a holstered pistol (the Fallschirmjäger readily employed the best of several foreign-made small arms including the Italian Beretta Modello 38 9mm submachine gun and the FN Browning P-35 9mm pistol) and a small Fallschirmjäger-Messer 'gravity knife'. A blade contained in its handle was opened by the force of inertia or gravity, the main purpose being that it allowed opening and closing to be done one handed, in situations where the other hand is occupied. Parachutists could use it to cut off their parachutes when tangled in a tree or similar.

Except for pistols, grenades and the occasional submachine-gun, German paratroopers had to rely on separate containers or Abwurfbehälter für Nachschub (Dropping container for supplies) five feet long and sixteen inches square for their main combat equipment. The container had a screw-on, corrugated metal-alloy cushion at one end to absorb the impact of landing and the parachute was connected at the other end. Some containers were equipped with a pair of small wheels and a towing bar that could be clipped onto the container after the drop to allow the container to be towed from the drop zone. A single forty-man-plus platoon of Fallschirmjäger needed no less than fourteen containers just for weapons and a basic ammunition supply. The containers were carried either under the wings of the Ju 52 or in the rear of the fuselage. Each container could hold over 200lbs of equipment and the maximum loaded weight was 260lbs. The Fallschirmjäger had access to the best weapons of the German military and were equipped with what were undoubtedly the best light machine-guns of World War II. Also, they were among the first combat units to use assault rifles and recoilless weapons in combat. The FG 42 automatic rifle, which combined the firepower of a machine gun with the lightweight handling characteristics of a standard infantry rifle, had been developed specially for the paratroopers. Each German infantry squad (ten to twelve men at full strength) was equipped with one MG-42 light machine-gun and this went a long way toward overcoming the relatively slow firing rate of the bolt action Mausers.

For assault rations the Fallschirmjäger troopers were provided with the same rather uninspired combination of processed meats and cheeses, 'ersatz' instant coffee and dry 'rusk' type biscuits/crackers that the Brandenburgers had carried with them aboard ship on the *Lundby* on 7 September but at least they had received their combat issues of rum and brandy and dextrose thirst quenching tablets. Provision was made on board the Ju 52s for the standard German Army 'Esbit' folding, solid fuel cookers, little larger than a packet of cigarettes that opened up to one of two positions. The cooker could support anything from a pot to a cup. When closed, the stove held the solid fuel supply.

Much cooler conditions were coming in from the North Sea on 16 September. Most areas could expect heavy cloud cover and rain in all districts that was expected to be heavy at times. The thought of any major raid on Britain was obviously out of the question. Conditions were in fact disastrous and only a few small feints were intercepted and the odd reconnaissance aircraft. The largest was an impending raid towards North Kent targets, but nothing really developed. 0730 hours: Radar picked up a medium plot coming in from the Channel and spread out along the Kent coastline. This was confirmed as 100 plus, but turned out to be Bf 109s, probably looking for targets of opportunity rather than any pre-planned raid.

The armada of gliders and transport aircraft began taking off from Waalhaven at around 0100 hours, turning north towards their objective. The troopers in the gliders sat in line down the centre, straddling a bench. The last four men faced the rear of the glider. The only door was in the port rear but 'kick out' panels on either side of the fuselage could be removed for a quick escape. Some of the Ju 52 pilots were so inexperienced at flying at night that they flew with their navigation lights on. Strict radio silence was maintained, forcing the pilots to rely on timed intervals to point them towards the Suffolk coast. The radio silence also ensured that senior commanders of the assault force could not be informed that the tow-ropes on one of the gliders had snapped soon after take-off when another Ju 52 passed so close to the DFS 230 that the towing cable broke and the glider was forced into a wild manoeuvre. Within seconds the wings had disintegrated and plunged all nine men to their deaths when the glider crashed into the sea off the Dutch coast. The five remaining gliders released their tow-ropes twenty miles away from their objectives at an altitude of 7,000 feet, which was deemed high enough for the gliders to land by the radar station and on top of the objective and also maintain a steep dive angle to further ensure they landed correctly.

British anti-aircraft artillery positions detected the Ju 52s and opened fire. This alerted the defences in the area to the presence of the gliders. Searchlights at 409 Coastal Battery were switched on and began sweeping the sky. Up went 'Golden Rain rockets signalling the enemy landing and they were joined by red 'Enemy have landed' pyrotechnics. A few white 'I require assistance' rockets followed. The gliders were engaged by heavy anti-aircraft fire as they landed, causing one of the gliders to stall in mid-air. The resulting crash severely wounded all eight airborne troops. The pilot of a third glider released his tow-rope prematurely and was unable to land near the objective. Due to a navigation error by the pilots of the transport aircraft towing the gliders, a fourth glider was dropped in the wrong area. As the glider pilots began dropping their wheels in flight so that landing could be made on a ventral central skid, a fifth was hit by anti-aircraft fire and crashed into the ground killing most of the occupants. The remaining glider utilized its arrester-parachute to slow the descent and rapidly bring it to a halt before the Fallschirmjäger emerged and broke down fences and hedges obstructing the glider before moving on to attach their primitive unlined shaped charges to the radar masts. It had been assumed that the weapons at the radar station could not stop the airborne assault, but this assumption was found to be false when the weapons opened fire, forcing the airborne troops in the area to go to cover. At Ében-Émael at this juncture air support had been summoned but there were no Stuka squadrons or motorised reserves that could come to the rescue this time. And until the rifles and other weapons that were dropped in separate containers were recovered, the German troopers were relatively poorly armed. The number one priority of the troops upon landing was to find their containers. Coloured bands or other markings aided retrieval by the correct units and to indicate which items the container carried. Only 20% of the men dropped were trained to jump with their weapons and equipment. This disadvantaged the mission as a very high percentage of the weapons and supply containers were never recovered. British riflemen inflicted many casualties.

With a radar station and a coastal battery to protect, Dunwich Heath was covered with infantry positions and defences. The 2/4 Battalion of the South Lancashire Regiment had two 3-inch trench mortars, a Tommy gun and several anti-tank rifles. A spigot mortar pedestal lay concealed in the heather. The spigot mortar was a weapon that fired a 20lb projectile that could be used against infantry or armoured vehicles. When used in a static role, a surrounding pit was dug for the crew of three to five men, which was reinforced with concrete and provided lockers for the ammunition. The spigot mortar post was combined with other defences such as concrete pillboxes, trenches, anti-tank blocks and barbed wire. These defended both the battery and the radar station. On the heath itself, anti-landing and anti-tank ditches were also dug to protect the cliff from German troops who had landed elsewhere and who were expected to attack from the west. The mortar teams displayed their preparation

HITLER'S INVASION OF EAST ANGLIA, 1940

by accurately sending mortar shells to glider landing sites, destroying several gliders before the German troops were even able to get out after landing. Survivors were mopped up by soldiers of the 55th (West Lancashire) Infantry Division's subordinate Brigades. They were supported by 36 men of a Home Guard unit, of whom the youngest was 16 years of age and the oldest, sixty. Some of them, including the CSM (Company Sergeant Major) an ex-WW1 machine gunner who had served in the Machine Gun Corps from 1915-1918, had previous military experience, which was put to good use. Ten more would transfer to the regular forces by the end of 1940.

As the Fieseler Fi-156 Storch aircraft appeared overhead the two man teams of the Brandenburg Regiment got ready to set up the Empfänger Blind landing transmitters. With its very low landing speed, the Storch often appeared to land vertically or even backwards in strong winds from directly ahead and this arrival proved no exception. Their pilots skilfully landed in just 30 metres (100 feet) in fields near the radar station and the Brandenburgers deplaned immediately. 'Tough as leather, as hard as Krupp steel' went the fanatical German parachutist's creed but though they were 'tuned to the topmost pitch' they forgot to 'keep their eyes wide open' and never got the chance to set up the transmitters or the opportunity to 'fight with chivalry nor extend any quarter to a guerrilla, their hardened adversary now.

The pair of three-man teams led by Lieutenant Charlie Spencer and Sergeant Herman Perry of 34 Auxiliary Unit moved stealthily through the undergrowth towards the long-legged, big-winged Storks. As soon as Perry saw two Germans curiously wearing Home Guard uniforms emerge from the first Storch he crept forward with his home-made two-foot length of thin piano wire with the short broomstick handle at each end and garrotted the smaller of the two men. Lance Corporal Ivan Potter slit the throat of the second German with his Fairburn dagger. A few hundred yards further on Lieutenant 'Charlie' Spencer crouched down near the second Storch holding his .455 Webley Mk. VI revolver but he had no need to use it on the two Germans inside. 'Bert' Beaumont silently shot one of them with his .22 Winchester sniping rifle and Corporal 'Mick' Small, stalking his prey like the pheasants and partridge he had caught napping on more occasions than he could remember, dispatched the other by slitting his mouth with his Fairburn after breaking his ear drums and gouging out his eyes. Herman Perry slapped two nitro-glycerine 'sticky' bombs against the side of the first Storch and blew it to pieces. 'Charlie' Spencer destroyed the second Storch by tossing two grenades with four-second fuses into the open window of the aircraft. The Patrol's two 16-year old privates, 'Sid' Warwick and 'Ernie'

Wentwood, were killed in a firefight after engaging the occupants of the glider that was dropped in the wrong area but they did manage to kill three of the troopers with their 'Tommy Guns' first.

The loss of the two Empfänger Blind landing transmitters caused pandemonium as the Ju 52s flew in. Some of the pilots began panicking and several revealed their indiscipline by abandoning any attempt to find the intended drop zone. Their only priority now was to drop their cargoes of men and materials as quickly as possible and leave the area immediately. Some Fallschirmjäger jumped from 250 feet, with appalling results. They suffered broken limbs or worse as a result of landing on knees and elbows and many others were swept away into the night and perished in the sea after it was set alight by the defenders. At least one kompanie was dropped in the wrong place, some men perished due to being dropped into the sea. This was blamed on the lack of experience and courage of the jumpmasters on the Ju 52 transport aircraft. Luck was not with one stick of paratroops that landed in a line of railings where all the men were impaled on them; whether this could be blamed on the jumpmaster or the parachute design which gave the paratroopers hardly any control was uncertain. The fact is many men perished due to being incorrectly dropped. Strong winds deflected paratroopers whose aircraft were relatively close to the radar station and made their landings far rougher. Only a fraction of the force landed near the intended drop zone. Since many of the German paratroopers were very inexperienced, some were crippled upon impact and died where they fell.

A few of the Ju 52 aircraft carried on for 25-30 miles and dropped straw filled dummies to try to deceive the British that they were being attacked from the rear. Unfortunately for them, they were shot down by mobile guns that had been brought up to cover particularly important stretches of coast during the invasion threat or the anti-aircraft defences. Beyond the cliffs at the radar site several Brandenburgers wearing Home Guard uniforms were shot after surrendering. Those that survived cut and ran before scrambling down the cliffs to the beach below. As soon as they began paddling their rubber boats the sea was set on fire and the coastal batteries at Aldeburgh, Sizewell, Minsmere and Dunwich opened up. The burned bodies and those who had been shot while wearing Home Guard uniform who were pushed over the cliffs and into the sea, drifted onto beaches all along the coast to be picked up later and their remains buried in unmarked graves.

The coup de grace for the German raiders occurred when the second wave of Ju 52s was intercepted off the coast of Kent by Blenheim Mk.Ifs of 600 Squadron at RAF Manston equipped with AI Mk.III (airborne

HITLER'S INVASION OF EAST ANGLIA, 1940

interception radar). The Blenheims opened up with their ventral pack of four .303 inch Browning machine guns and one fixed forward-firing .303 inch gun and a second .303 in a dorsal turret. Several Ju 52s went down before the rest aborted and headed back towards Holland. Historians have since written that: 'It is difficult to ascertain as to who shot who down on this day. Besides a few squadrons on training flights, only two RAF squadrons were reported to have flown on operational duty. Yet statistics indicate that nine German aircraft were shot down.'

Hitler had been against cancelling the invasion as 'the cancellation would reach the ears of the enemy and strengthen his resolve' but on 17 September it was announced: 'The enemy air force is still by no means defeated: on the contrary it shows increasing activity. The weather situation as a whole does not permit us to expect a period of calm. The Führer has therefore decided to postpone Operation 'Sealion' indefinitely.' On 19 September Hitler ordered that no further barges were to be added to 'Sealion' ports, but those under assembly were to continue.[106] The invasion forces were broken up and moved East on the understanding it could be reassembled with only three weeks' notice. As summer gave way to autumn and worsening weather conditions, the Germans realised the RAF could not be beaten in 1940 (from August to September the Luftwaffe lost 1,140 aircraft) and as Germany was preparing to attack Russia, Operation 'Sealion' was cancelled. Field Marshal von Rundstedt best summed up the reasons for the cancellation: 'The German navy would have had to control the North Sea as well as the Channel and was not strong enough to do so. The Luftwaffe was not sufficient to protect the sea crossing on its own. While the leading part of the forces might have landed, there was the danger that they might be cut off from supplies and reinforcements.'

'Sealion' was dead in the water - literally.

---

106 Four years later, during the Normandy Landings, the Royal Navy would successfully use hundreds of Thames lighter barges, adapted in much the same way as their German counterparts.

Chapter 10

Went the day Well?

Went the day well?
We died and never knew.
But, well or ill,
Freedom, we died for you.
Epitaph written by the classical scholar John Maxwell Edmonds which originally appeared in *The Times* **on 6 February 1918 under the heading 'Four Epitaphs'.**

Thirty-six year old American journalist William Lawrence Shirer, writing cautiously from Geneva on 16 September 1940, described the rumours and disturbing sights that fed the story of the burning sea: 'The news coming over the nearby border of France is that the Germans have attempted a landing in Britain, but it has been repulsed with heavy German losses. Must take this report with a grain of salt.' Born in Chicago in 1904, Shirer was raised as a Protestant and attended Washington High School and Coe College in Cedar Rapids, Iowa. He graduated from Coe in 1925. Working his way to Europe on a cattle boat to spend the summer there, he remained in Europe for fifteen years. He was European correspondent for the *Chicago Tribune* from 1925 to 1932, covering Europe, the Near East and India. In India he formed a friendship with Mohandas K. Gandhi. As a print journalist and later as a radio reporter for CBS, Shirer covered the strengthening one-party rule in Nazi Germany beginning in 1933, reporting on Adolf Hitler's peacetime triumphs like the return of the Saarland to Germany and the remilitarization of the Rhineland. Since 1934 he had lived and worked in Germany during the era of the Third Reich and had became well known for his broadcasts from Berlin, from the rise of the Nazi dictatorship until 1940. In his article entitled *Berlin Diary* he wrote of the bombing of the Channel Ports: 'From what I saw of these bombings myself and from what I have been told by

HITLER'S INVASION OF EAST ANGLIA, 1940

German airmen, I think it is highly improbable that the German Army would ever be able to assemble in the ports of Boulogne, Calais, Ostend or on the beaches, enough barges or ships to launch an invasion in the force that would be necessary.'

In 1934 Shirer was hired for the Berlin bureau of the Universal Service, one of William Randolph Hearst's two wire services. In *Berlin Diary*, Shirer described this move, in a self-proclaimed bad pun, as going from 'bad to Hearst'. When Universal Service folded in August 1937 Shirer was first taken on as second man by Hearst's other wire service, International News Service and then laid off a few weeks later. On the day when Shirer received two weeks' notice from INS, he received a wire from Edward R. Murrow, European manager of Columbia Broadcasting System, suggesting that the two meet. A few days later in Berlin, Murrow told him that he could not cover all of Europe from London and that he was seeking an experienced correspondent to open a CBS office on the Continent. He offered Shirer a job subject to an audition - a 'trial broadcast' - to let CBS directors and vice presidents in New York judge Shirer's voice. Shirer feared that his reedy voice was unsuitable for radio, but he was hired. As European bureau chief, he set up headquarters in Vienna, a more central and more neutral spot than Berlin. Shirer was in Vienna on 11th March 1938 when the German annexation of Austria (Anschluss) took place after weeks of mounting pressure by Nazi Germany on the Austrian government. The only American broadcaster in Vienna, Shirer had a scoop but occupying German troops controlling the Austrian state radio studio would not let him broadcast. Shirer flew to London via Berlin, the direct flight being filled with Jews trying to escape from German-occupied Austria. Once in London, Shirer broadcast the first uncensored eyewitness account of the annexation. Early in his career he expressed disappointment at having to hire newspaper correspondents to do the broadcasting; at the time, CBS correspondents were prohibited from speaking on the radio. Shirer was the first of 'Murrow's Boys,' broadcast journalists who provided news coverage during World War II and afterward.

As the summer of 1940 progressed, the Nazi government pressed Shirer to broadcast official accounts that he knew were incomplete or false. As his frustration grew, he wrote to bosses in New York that tightening censorship was undermining his ability to report objectively and mused that he had outlived his usefulness in Berlin. Returning to Berlin from Geneva on 18 September where his wife of nine years, Theresa 'Tess'

WENT THE DAY WELL?

Stiberitz, an Austrian photographer, was working, Shirer wrote: 'The train arrived at the Potsdamer Bahnhof right on time. I noticed several lightly wounded soldiers, mostly airmen, getting off a special car which had been attached to our train. From their bandages their wounds looked like burns. I noticed also the longest Red Cross train I've ever seen. It stretched from the station for half a mile to beyond the bridge over the Landwehr Canal. Orderlies were swabbing it out, the wounded having been unloaded, probably, during the night. The Germans usually unload their hospital trains after dark so that the populace will not be unduly disturbed by one of the grimmer sides of glorious war. I wondered where so many wounded could have come from as the armies in the west stopped fighting three months ago. As there were only a few porters I had to wait some time on the platform and picked up a conversation with a railway workman. He said most of the men taken from the hospital train were suffering from burns. Can it be that the tales I heard in Geneva had some truth in them after all?

The next day he recorded: 'Returning to town we noticed a large crowd standing on a bridge which spanned a railroad line. We thought there had been an accident. But we found the people staring silently at a long Red Cross train unloading wounded. This is getting interesting. Only during the fortnight in September when the Poles were being crushed and a month this spring when the west was being annihilated have we seen so many hospital trains in Berlin. A diplomat told me this morning his legation had checked two other big hospital trains unloading wounded in the Charlottenburg railroad yards yesterday. This makes four long trains of wounded in the last two days that I know have arrived here. 'His wife Theresa and their daughter Eileen 'Inga' left Geneva in October. After 'a rather harrowing trip through occupied France en route to Lisbon' they were living in New York. Shirer was subsequently tipped off that the Gestapo was building an espionage case against him, which carried the death penalty so he began making arrangements to leave Germany. Shirer's ship steamed out of Lisbon on 13 December for the United States.

A little over two months earlier, on Saturday, 21st September the *New York Times* reported that 'Robert Solberg, described as the vice-president of a steel company', returning with his wife and daughter after twenty years of residence in France, said the Germans were holding invasion practice off the French coast and that British bombers had taken a heavy toll. It is clear that several passengers arriving in New York from Lisbon on liners

HITLER'S INVASION OF EAST ANGLIA, 1940

such as the *Exeter* were primed by British intelligence. Robert Solberg, a former Tsarist cavalry officer who fled the Bolshevik revolution in 1917 and who had acquired American citizenship prior to the outbreak of the Second World War, was one of these. Solberg added that he had definite information that the Germans had attempted no actual invasion of England. He said the British, tipped off by the Dutch and French, waited for the barges with planes and submarines and that 'thousands of Germans have been lost in this fashion. Solborg was quoted as saying that he recently visited a French Channel port where bodies of German troops were being washed ashore daily.'

On the same date, a *Daily Mail* correspondent in New York gleaned further details from Mr. Solberg, 'The British sent submarines and planes and sank the barges. It is estimated that at least 10,000 Germans lost their lives. Many of the German troops are refusing to continue the practice and hundreds are being transported back to Germany with their hands tied behind their backs.'[107] A later report in the *Daily Mail*, referring to the RAF action 'a week ago today', put enemy invasion losses at 50,000 troops. Doctor Paul Schiff, a general practitioner from Paris who owned a villa on the coast between Gravelines and Dunkirk, returned at the end of July to find out whether his holiday home was still standing. A few hundred yards from the beach, a German roadblock prevented him from seeing the villa. He recalled later in a letter to a relative: 'I went back to Dunkirk and spoke to a friend who was the manager of the Le Seur works. He told me that the road to the beach was being guarded night and day by German soldiers with fixed bayonets who had orders to shoot anyone who tried to go any further. My friend said that there were lots of bodies that had been washed up onto the beach. They were all apparently blackened and burned. The Germans were burying them in the sand.'

Madame Pauline Lozère, who ran a shop in Gravelines near Dunkirk and kept a diary throughout the German occupation, wrote 'Some German officers told me and my friends – so that I had it from three different sources - that the Germans had made an attempt to land in England starting from Calais and Brest. They had used rubber canoes like those used for crossing streams and rivers, but the attempt failed. No one knows how many were killed. The soldiers could be seen washed ashore upright. It was like an army of the drowned. Their heavy equipment had slipped to their feet so they were kept upright.'

---

107 In December 1940 Solberg was recruited by American military intelligence. In October 1941 he was posted to London to liaise with SOE, reporting directly to Colonel William Donovan, the OSS chief.

WENT THE DAY WELL?

An 11 Corps summary of 'rumours and indiscreet talk' on 25 September stated that '15 Division report the currency in their area [north Essex] of a rumour that the bodies of thousands of German soldiers have been washed up on the beach at Clacton. The source of this cannot at present be traced. An intelligence summary from the 45th Infantry Brigade In the same sector reported: 'Rumours of a spectacular nature have been very widespread. The following were the principal ones noted: (i) 'Nearly all troops in the Sub Area have heard the rumour that thousands of bodies of German troops were washed up on the south coast of England in the early part of the month. (ii) another rumour, not so widespread, is that an invasion by sea was started but was destroyed before reaching this country.

On Thursday, 26th September the front page of the *Daily Telegraph* announced in a bold headline that: - AXIS WEAKENS ON INVASION. It was claimed (from European sources) that the Germans had postponed their proposed invasion of Britain until the spring. Under a small sub heading entitled 'Rumour Denied' it was reported that the War Office sources said that: 'there was no foundation for the stories in circulation to the effect that an actual attempt at invading this country has been made by the Germans' and reference was made to stories of a 'circumstantial' kind: One report said that the enemy was supposed to have landed a force that was immediately overcome and the suggestion was inferred that large numbers of dead invaders had been picked up off the Goodwin Sands. These stories were discussed behind closed doors at the weekly meeting of the Home Defence Executive Committee. Apparently, the Ministry of Home Security had received no reports of any kind relating to these 'incidents' but the War Office did not always 'share' information with their Home Office colleagues.

Within weeks of the UPC meeting on 27 September, outright official denials of invasion disappeared and the stories appearing in the press would also curiously change in tone. However, in the three week intervening period before this happened there appeared two more significant invasion stories. On Monday, 7th October appearing in the *New York Sun*, was yet another report of a failed landing attempt. The second, appearing in the *War Weekly* magazine, referred specifically to the rumours and dismissed them as unfounded. The *Sun*'s story appeared beneath the bold headlines: 'British Fire Halted Invasion as Nazis Tried to Rush Coast'. Although reference was made to the *Sun*'s earlier report of 11 September, this time it was claimed that the attack took place on the southeast coast of England (not the west coast) 'in the latter part of August; probably the

25th.' Part of the report, said to have come from an 'unofficial British source', claimed that Royal Navy personnel involved in the action had been 'cautioned to tell no one about it for the time being.' It was also said that a British newspaper, the 'Daily Herald of London,' had published a three line notice about these events. This was not true, no details relating to such an event had appeared, or would ever appear, in the Herald. In fact, unlike the other reports that had appeared in American newspapers, this story did not find its way into the British press at all, at least not as printed in the *New York Sun*.

On 8 October the *Daily Sketch* briefly referred to the *Sun's* story beneath the heading - 'Invasion Tried and Smashed', but claimed that the RAF and Royal Navy had 'bombed and shelled barges somewhere near Dover and Folkestone.' Up to this point this was the nearest any British newspaper had come to printing a story that was in any way similar to the rumours still in circulation. Then, just days later, a short article in the 11th October issue of *The War Weekly* magazine, pointedly asked the question: 'Was an Invasion of England Attempted.' Written by staff writer A. G. MacDonnell, the article began by referring to the famous 'Russian Army in Scotland story of December 1914' and how a rumour spread but no one ever saw a Russian soldier. According to the author, 'now we have a similar story: thousands of drowned German bodies are being washed up on the east coast. Clear proof that an invasion has been attempted and has been a colossal failure.' He goes on to say that as with the 1914 story, the only person who seems to have seen the bodies is someone who told someone else who told someone else etc.

According to MacDonnell the *News Chronicle* had sent his friend and colleague Mr. John Pudney to investigate. John Sleigh Pudney was known for short stories, poetry, non-fiction and children's fiction. He was born at Langley Marish on 19 January 1909 and educated at Gresham's School, Holt in Norfolk, where he was a friend of W. H. Auden, leaving school at the age of sixteen in 1925. He later lived in Buckinghamshire. After leaving school, Pudney worked for an estate agent, for the BBC and for the *News Chronicle*. In the 1930s he moved on from journalism and poetry to publishing novels and collections of short stories. In 1940 Pudney was commissioned into the RAF as an intelligence officer and as a member of the Air Ministry's Creative Writers Unit. It was while he was serving as squadron intelligence officer at St. Eval in Cornwall that Pudney wrote one of the best-known poems of the war. *For Johnny* evoked popular fellow-feeling in the London of 1941. Written during an air raid, it was published first in the *Daily Chronicle* and featured significantly in the film *The Way to the Stars*. Wherever this roving reporter went he was told the same story, the bodies had been washed ashore alright - but always 'at a point farther north.' MacDonnell rounded of his sceptical report by stating: 'a variation on the story is that as soon as the bodies come ashore they are burnt by the authorities,' adding, tongue in cheek, 'so it's not surprising that people don't actually see them.'

Shortly after this story appeared official sources suddenly began to contradict their earlier denials and seemed to admit that an invasion attempt really had taken place after all. On Friday, the 18th and Saturday, 19th October, several newspapers quoted Air Ministry bulletins and reports suggesting that on Sunday the 15th or Monday, 16th September enemy invasion troops had been embarked for invasion, or had actually set out when the attempt was broken up by the RAF. Saturday's *Daily Herald* added that the news had been 'printed with great headlines in the American press yesterday'. RAF raids on the invasion ports were taking place at this time and English newspapers were full of accounts of smashing blows delivered at Hitler's barges assembled in the invasion bases; on that same Sunday night the RAF bombers left their mark on Hamburg and Wilhelmshaven, on Antwerp, Flushing and Ostend, on Dunkirk, Calais, Boulogne and Le Havre.[108]

Few newspapers mentioned casualties, except for Sunday's ever sensational *News of the World* which reported: 'Invasion Attempt Smashed by RAF - 50,000 Nazi Troops reported Drowned... September 16th, bodies washed up along coast of northern France.' Coincidently, on the same weekend that the initial Air Ministry reports appeared in the press, on Sunday, the 20th, the body of a German infantry corporal aged about thirty wearing the field grey uniform of a German infantry unit was washed ashore on the Kent coast near Littlestone-on-Sea. Six days' later the discovery was reported in the *Folkestone Hythe and District Herald* and immediately linked to the new story of a bombed invasion practice. The body, it was estimated, had been in the sea possibly as long as six weeks and as such fitted in with a report recently published that the RAF inflicted severe losses on the German invasion troops on the other side of the Channel about that time. The report ended by saying that death was probably caused by drowning and that the dead man would

---

108 On the night of the 15th/16th Bomber Command repeated their raids of the previous night and sent 155 bombers to attack all the Channel ports along the French, Belgian and Dutch coasts including a large attack on the docks at Antwerp where the hundreds of barges were docked in preparation for the planned invasion of England.

be buried at New Romney.[109] The *Felixstowe Times* also, reported that 'the bodies of three Germans believed to be airmen had been washed ashore on the 'southeast coast' and that: 'all three above average height and one still clutching a bundle' had been in the sea for 'some weeks.' It was also reported a few days later that the 'partially clothed' body of what was 'believed to be a German airman' had been washed ashore at Felixstowe.

Lars Moen, a former newsman and screenwriter who had been working for a Belgian film manufacturer had practically abandoned hope that the German military authorities would permit his departure before the end of the war. When he was suddenly offered the alternative, on 8 October, 'leave now or remain until the end of the war', he left. Fortunately, his passport gave no indication that he was a former newspaper man who was overtaken by the German offensive in May 1940 and remained in Antwerp until 22 October when he left to return to America on board the *Exeter*. In *Under The Iron Heel* (which he acknowledged was largely cobbled together from reports told by others en route from Lisbon) he wrote that: 'On or about 16th September (identified as 'Der Tag'), a considerable force of towed triple-barges set out from a point along the Belgian coast, constituting the first wave of the attack, which was to occupy a strip on the English coast at which liners could put in and disembark the invasion troops. At a point probably not far from the Belgian coast, they were spotted by the British. Destroyers of the Royal Navy then managed to cut them off and forced them well out into the North Sea. Here planes of the RAF dropped oil drums with great quantities of oil on and near the barges and then followed with incendiary bombs which turned the whole into a blazing inferno.

'During the first weeks of October, the bodies of hundreds of German soldiers were being washed ashore along the Belgian coast, especially in the vicinity of Ostend. Many of them were so badly burned as to be almost unrecognisable. Many of the invasion barges were missing, although the

---

[109] Today the grave of Heinrich Poncke of Anti-Tank Reserve Kompanie 19 can be visited at the Deutsche Soldatenfriedhof at Cannock Chase, Staffordshire. Poncke did not perish while attempting to invade Britain, nor was he one of thousands of similar casualties. He instead drowned either while training for Operation 'Sealion' or (as seems likely) during a successful Royal Navy 'cutting-out' operation against German flak trawlers moored in the Channel on 11 October. Three Felixstowe-based motor torpedo boats, using Dover as a forward base, sank two such trawlers north of Calais and captured a total of 34 crewmen, several others being drowned. Over the next few weeks Poncke's body was carried by the tide to Littlestone, with others arriving elsewhere and on both sides of the Channel. *The Bodies On The Beach; Sealion, Shingle Street and the Burning Sea Myth of 1940* by James Hayward, (CD41 Publishing, 1994: 2001).

naval craft and merchant liners were still in the harbour, their number having been increased by fresh arrivals. None of these facts, taken alone, could be taken as proof that an attempted invasion actually took place. Taken collectively, they all point in one direction. I believe these facts to be exact. I first learned of the burned patients from a Belgian nurse working in an Antwerp hospital; Americans living near Ostend confirmed reports of the bodies being washed ashore. Later, I heard these stories scores of times, which proves nothing - but it was extremely significant that reports from the most widely scattered sources were unanimous on one point: that a considerable number of German soldiers had been badly burned.'

On Monday, 21st October, hard on the heels of the Air Ministry bulletins, came a story in the pages of *The Times* that lent some support to the new claims and at the same time offered an explanation for the persistent rumours. It began with the headline: BOMBERS TOLL OF GERMAN TROOPS - WRECKED 'INVASION' BARGES - RAF raid coincided with dress rehearsal, bodies washed up along French Belgian and Dutch coasts for days afterwards'.

'Information which has reached the government through a variety of channels indicates that thousands of German troops have been killed and wounded in RAF raids on the 'invasion' ports. Most of these casualties occurred in one single raid, when the arrival of the British bombers synchronised with a full dress rehearsal being carried out by the Germans on a large scale at ports in northern France. For days afterwards the bodies of German soldiers were washed up all along French, Belgian and Dutch coasts. This gave rise to a rumour that an unsuccessful attempt to land in this country had been made, being repelled with heavy losses.' Many of the flat bottomed barges and ships, loaded with troops carrying their full invasion equipment, received direct hits and soon the water was dotted with soldiers, who in their heavy kit, stood little chance of regaining the shore. For days afterwards the bodies of German soldiers were washed up all along French, Belgian and Dutch coasts. This gave rise to a rumour that an unsuccessful attempt to land in this country had been made, being repelled with heavy losses. Official sources appeared to be claiming that the RAF had destroyed an invasion fleet, either after it had actually set out, or, according to *The Times*, while it was on pre-invasion manoeuvres. (And just for good measure the sinking of a German troopship by HMS *Sturgeon* had also been included in the picture). Here, or so it was claimed, were the real facts behind the unfounded rumours. There had been no invasion attempt, just a successful RAF raid that had left bodies washed up on foreign shores. *The Times* however, had avoided any mention of enemy corpses washed ashore on the English coast and in doing so it had been slightly economical with the truth. On Monday, 28th October the 2,000 ton tramp steamer, *Sheaf Field*, hit a mine and caught fire off the estuary of the River Deben. Later that week the bodies of three more German airmen would be washed ashore in the Hollesley Bay area.

But from the available evidence it is difficult to pin point a single catastrophic raid which led to the claimed results of substantial German losses. In late October official bulletins and press reports implied that the rumours, previously denied as being 'without foundation' were down to the RAF bombing an enemy invasion 'dress rehearsal' and the bodies of enemy soldiers subsequently floating across the Channel. Why did the government suddenly feel compelled to explain the 'facts' behind a rumour that they had previously dismissed as being without foundation? By the end of October 1940, stories relating to enemy invasion attempts and bodies on beaches had almost disappeared from the pages of the press. Two of the last notable references appeared in the *War Weekly* and *War Illustrated* on 1st November. Both magazines delved into the details of the Air Ministry claims made just two weeks earlier. The *War Weekly* referred to the 'Nazi Invasion Bid that Failed,' claiming: 'It has now become clear that the Germans did actually plan and try an invasion of Britain for 16th September and that it was smashed by the RAF before it began.' According to the report, initial enquiries by the magazine's reporters had received 'guarded' replies from Air Ministry sources. These were followed by an admission that: 'on 16 September the embarkation and disembarkation of German troops did actually take place.' Apparently, the RAF, in conjunction with a 'smooth working espionage system' had caught enemy forces off guard and 'smashed them down in a torrential bombing and machine gun attack'.

The *War Illustrated* article, which owed much to stories emanating from America, such as the report in the *New York Sun,* began by asking: 'What happened on September 16th?' 'Nothing less, it now seems probable, than an attempted invasion of England...' It then went on to state: 'It may have been a rehearsal or it may have been the real thing; whichever it was. Hitler's invasion fleet - if report speaks true - actually set out on 16 September only to be driven back in completest rout... The carnage was reported to have been terrific; neutral observers stated that the number of killed, drowned and wounded were to be counted in tens of thousands. All available hospital accommodation in and around the Channel ports had to be commandeered for the German wounded and one report quoted a French doctor who said he had seen several thousand severely burned German soldiers in hospitals in occupied France; they had been, said the doctor, on board transports and barges preparing for the invasion of England when they were caught by British oil bombs and the flaming oil on the surface of the water burned the troops as they leapt into the sea.' The explanation for these 'rumours', according to 'responsible sources in London', was that RAF bombers had caught the enemy invasion fleet during a 'rehearsal.'

Following the reports in both magazines, tales of failed invasion attempts seemed to disappear from the pages of the press entirely, at least for the time being. The rumours that had been circulating during the previous weeks also appear to have died down - but they were destined never to go away. A few days later some of the American papers were far more communicative. They did not hint at an invasion attempt; rather they stated in the most definite terms that the armada of invasion had actually sailed. Thus the *New York Sun* stated that the barges - 'very light, of wood and metal and obviously intended solely for a one-way trip' - each contained 200 Germans will full equipment. 'Evidently the Germans had counted on their airmen being able to silence the land batteries before these were able to annihilate the invaders, who were helpless because they did not carry artillery... They sank under a withering fire as soon as they appeared. Meanwhile, detachments of the British Fleet appeared to the rear cutting off the barges from France.' 'The carnage was reported to have been terrific; neutral observers stated that the number of killed, drowned and wounded were to be counted in tens of thousands.

Many stories were current, too, in the south of England concerning large numbers of dead Germans who, so it was said, has been washed ashore in several places. There were tales of closed lorries going to and from the beach at one point, of mysterious ambulances moving through the night; nor was there any doubt that some dead Germans had actually been washed up, but it was officially stated that these were Nazi airmen whose 'planes had been shot down into the sea. Perhaps more to the point were the many stories published in American papers of large numbers of German dead being washed ashore in the neighbourhood of the invasion ports, particularly on the beaches near Le Havre, Calais and Boulogne. At the time there were many stories in circulation concerning the supposed invasion attempt and the English newspapers were full of accounts of smashing blows delivered at Hitler's barges assembled in the invasion bases; on that same Sunday night the RAF bombers left their mark on Hamburg and Wilhelmshaven, on Antwerp, Flushing and Ostend, on Dunkirk, Calais, Boulogne and Le Havre.

By way of explanation of these American reports and English rumours, responsible quarters in London expressed the opinion that a considerable proportion of the German divisions detailed for the invasion of England had actually embarked, when the fleet of flat-bottomed barges was caught by the bombers of the RAF, whose bombardment was so effective that the enemy fleet was obliged to put to sea and lay a short distance from the French coast. Then rising winds compelled the vessels to return to their ports; and the French people who had seen their departure and witnessed their return, concluded that the invasion had been attempted and had been driven back. Yet another explanation was that the RAF bombers had caught the invasion fleet during a rehearsal... 'It was a fitting end to the day which Hitler had chosen to be Der Tag.'

In January 1941 there were large-scale Army manoeuvres in East Anglia, in response to as hypothetical landing by five German divisions on the Norfolk coast: the reports luridly describe the imaginary devastation of Lowestoft and Great Yarmouth. Winston Churchill was rather peeved by this Operation 'Victor', since he disliked the Army's assumption that the Navy and the RAF might not be able to stop an invasion happening in the first place.[110] Reginald O'Neill recalled[111] that at Dunwich during a night exercise with the Home Guard one night all off duty personnel had to assemble within the technical site to repel the Home Guard from gaining access. There was no moon to help either side. A searchlight had been mounted 30 feet up on the aerial tower, manned by a bod whose instructions were to expose the light in the direction of any disturbance. The defenders positioned themselves around the perimeter of the site within the wire. It was a little before midnight when sounds of the approaching 'enemy' were heard making their way towards the wire. The light was exposed, revealing well camouflaged Home Guards attempting to breach the wire. It seemed that all hell broke loose as yells and shouting, accompanied by the flashing and bangs of thunder-flashes broke the stillness of the night. It was some time into the ensuing battle that someone noticed that the siren was sounding. It had been arranged that should an enemy air raid alert take place during the exercise, then our operations would cease on hearing them

---

110 *The Battle of the East Coast (1939-45)* by J. P. Foynes.
111 *A Lighter Shade of Pale Blue* (Woodfield Publishing 2002).

but the fight continued; no one was giving way. What could the German aircrew flying overhead have thought as they looked down on what must have appeared to be a commando raid taking place. Perhaps they thought that it was those idiot English playing war games!

In May 1941 when the original rumours had all but been forgotten, the story of a failed invasion attempt in September 1940 made a brief re-appearance in print with the publication of *The Battle of Britain 1940*, an officially sanctioned account of the previous summer's events, authored by James M. Spaight, a former Principal Assistant Secretary at the Air Ministry. Spaight devotes most of page 95 to 'A Mid-September Mystery': the persistent rumour that a German invasion attempt had been foiled by British naval forces. According to Spaight the rumour that had spread the previous autumn was probably untrue, though he did state that a disaster of some kind had overtaken enemy invasion preparations: 'It is known that a large number of German soldiers were treated in hospital for burns, the result, it was reported, of a heavy raid by the RAF at that time.' He goes on to virtually repeat the story that had appeared in *The Times* the previous October, stating that enemy boats had been sunk 'and when they took to the water, the oil, set alight by the incendiary bombs, burned them severely before they could be rescued. For days after this incident bodies of dead soldiers were being washed up on the French, Belgian and Dutch coasts.' Spaight made no reference to bodies on English shores until the final chapter, where he repeated his previous statement and added: 'One particular series of [RAF] raids was especially damaging. It is believed to have caught the German soldiers and sailors just at the moment when a kind of 'dress rehearsal' was being staged and to have resulted in the killing and wounding of thousands of the troops embarked. There were certainly heavy demands on hospital accommodation in occupied France in mid-September. 'Bodies of uniformed Germans continued to be washed up on our shores for some days after that date'.

The rumour of burnt Germans would appear in *One of Our Pilots is Safe* by Flight Lieutenant William Simpson, who had been shot down in flames over Belgium in 1940 on 12 Squadron on the first day of the battle for France and suffered disfiguring burns to his face and crippling injuries to his hands. Hospitalised and confined to bed, he spent the autumn months of 1940 slowly recovering in the unoccupied zone of France and it was during his convalescence that he overheard many stories of German invasion preparations including the assembly of barges in Channel ports. He devotes about a page and a half to the rumours. 'French civilians and medical staff told how: 'On the sides of many of the barges the Germans painted 'Thos.

HITLER'S INVASION OF EAST ANGLIA, 1940

Cook & Sons' and the names of other British transport firms.' One day, or so he was led to believe, a large invasion fleet had set out and then been attacked by the RAF who had 'set light to the sea' and: 'Into the interior of France for days after went special hospital trains full of burned Germans. For months afterwards the burned bodies of many others were washed up on the shores of the Pas de Calais.' Simpson added an intriguing footnote to the story. Apparently undeterred by the disaster, the Germans created their own flame barrier on a lake and conducted experiments with asbestos clad barges and troops in protective clothing. What were literally 'live fire' exercises also ended in disaster resulting in yet more badly burned casualties appearing in French and Belgian hospitals. Simpson was repatriated to Britain in October 1941 and became one of the most famous of the 'Guinea Pigs' - a group of men treated by the skill of the great New Zealand plastic surgeon Sir Archibald McIndoe, in his pioneering burns unit at the Queen Victoria Hospital, East Grinstead. Nursing sister Mary Godson recalled 'He was not long married and had been a nice looking lad, but his wife did not want to see him. 'He was not a pretty sight. Only stumps remained on his right hand and his fingers had come away from his left hand when they changed the dressings on it badly while in France.' He later married one of his nurses. In 1942 while dictating the notes for his book, the Ministry of Information received a letter from a Chester schoolmaster, Captain Owen of Elton School, who referred to the rumour of 'two years ago', concerning the RAF bombing an invasion fleet and setting the sea alight, resulting in 'scorched bodies being washed ashore.' After enquiring if there was any truth in the rumours he suggested that a 'public and authoritative denial may effectively lay the matter to rest.' Owen received a fairly cursory reply from a civil servant identified only by his initials, stating: 'The story to which you refer is not one that has been widely circulated... to give it an authoritative denial would be likely to have the undesirable effect of increasing its prevalence.' It seemed that, at least for the time being, the authorities wished to 'let sleeping dogs lie' but three years later the Ministry of Information would reveal all and this time they were unconcerned about any 'undesirable effects'. But by the time Simpson's recollections were published the rumours of September 1940 had been almost forgotten.

On 7 April 1942 American journalist Charles M. Barbe, a former musician who had volunteered as an ambulance driver early in 1940 and saw service in France, gave a talk entitled 'None So Blind' to a small London audience at the Royal Institute of International Affairs at Chatham House in which he claimed that 33,000 men from three Waffen-SS divisions had perished in a sea of flame in September 1940. He added, 'Along with a few others who did not feel like the show was over I stayed on in Paris and during the last part of August this curiosity I speak of got the better of me again and along with another chap - a Frenchman, believe it or not, who felt an equal curiosity - we had been hearing stories of something which was going to happen around the 15th of September, during the first, second or third week in September. So we went up into the military zone, which was something I would not do again.

'From about the 10th to the 16th September we were in a small house about ten kilometres south of Dunkirk, a good healthy stone's throw from the Channel, during what is commonly termed the Battle of Britain. Maybe you remember it. Now I have broadcast several times for the BBC since I have been in London and I have written the story of what we saw happen there and what I was able to confirm later on in Paris and Berlin, but it has always been cut out of my scripts. I understand that I might be able to mention it here. Anyway I'll take a chance. The 161st and 197th Schleswig-Holstein SS divisions and the 67th Hessian Division, three of the prime, crack SS divisions, never bothered anyone after 15 September. The better part of 33,000 men started out from the shores of France and not one of them ever got back to the shores of France alive.

'I do not know what happened. About the 17th or 18th September on our way back to Paris we saw something strange... at a point on the coast quite near to Dieppe, we saw bodies on the shore like driftwood, something which could in some cases be identified as once having been human, while others looked like blackened tree stumps and I don't believe I shall ever get the stench out of my nose, not if I live to be 1,000 years old. They were just burned beyond recognition. I had previously spoken to a couple of German soldiers just north of Paris, who had told me that they had been badly burned during the latter part of August. One of the boys said he would be shot before he went back. He said he was out in a rowing boat, fishing, that is the official word, fishing, when, in his words, the sea exploded in flames. As I say, I do not know what happened. I only know what the results were.'

By the end of 1942 the only story of a German invasion attempt was confined to the cinema and the feature film *Went The Day Well?* Adapted from a story by Graham Greene and directed by Alberto Cavalcanti the film was produced by Michael Balcon of Ealing Studios and served as unofficial propaganda for the war effort. It tells of how an English village (Bramley End) is taken over by Nazi paratroopers disguised as British soldiers. At first they are welcomed by the villagers, until doubts begin to grow about their true purpose and identity. After they are revealed to be German soldiers intended to form the vanguard of an invasion of Britain, they round up the residents and hold them captive in the local church. The vicar is shot after sounding the church bell in alarm. In attempts to reach the outside world, many of the villagers take action. Mrs Collins, the postmistress, manages to kill a German with an axe for firewood and tries to telephone elsewhere.[112] The girls on the exchange see her light and decide that she can wait. Mrs. Collins waits until she is killed by another German who walks into the shop moments afterwards. The girl at the exchange then picks up the phone, getting no reply. The civilians attempt to escape to warn the local Home Guard, but are betrayed by the village squire, who is revealed to be collaborating with the Germans. Members of the local Home Guard are ambushed and shot by the Germans. They begin to bow in until a young boy, George, succeeds in escaping; despite being shot in the leg, he alerts the army. British soldiers arrive and - aided by some of the villagers, including a group of Women's Land Army girls, who have managed to escape, barricade themselves in and arm themselves - defeat the Germans after a short battle. The squire is shot dead by the vicar's daughter, who had discovered his treachery, as he attempts to let the Germans into the barricaded house. During the battle, many of the villagers who left to fight are wounded or killed; Mrs. Fraser is blown up by a grenade and Tom's father wrenches his ankle. The British troops then arrive at Bramley End and all ends well. The villager retelling the story to the camera shows the Germans' grave in the churchyard and explains proudly that 'this is the only bit of England they got'.

On 1 October 1944 the *News of the World* ran a story by John Parris, a British United Press correspondent who after speaking with Renee Meurisse, a Belgian Red Cross nurse in charge of a group of refugees at the time, reported: 'Thousands of German soldiers - 50,000 so it is said - were burned to death or maimed for life on that September day. 'A nightmare in hell' was how German soldiers described it after the RAF, catching the Nazi fleet in mid-Channel, dumped oil on the water and set fire to it with incendiary bullets. Belgians with whom I talked were surprised to learn that the British people had never been fully told of the attempt, which appeared to be common knowledge in Belgium.

---

112 In Crete when the Germans began the second wave of attacks which included more paratroopers and the amphibious assault, the civilian population joined in on the defence. There was one report of an older Cretan man who surprised a German paratrooper from the back with his walking cane and eventually beat him to death. While this story might be hearsay, there was little doubt that the civilian population of Crete greatly bolstered the defence.

WENT THE DAY WELL?

'During September 17th' said Meurisse 'we heard rumours that thousands of bodies of German soldiers were being washed ashore along the Belgian beaches. At seven o'clock that night a German Red Cross train of forty coaches pulled into Brussels Station. We had been expecting a refugee train, so we were surprised when we saw a train-load of Germans. The commandant; tired and in crumpled uniform, approached me and asked if we could help his wounded. He said that the train had been shunted on to the wrong line and his men were dying for lack of treatment. We agreed to help, sent a call for more nurses and ambulances and began taking the wounded from the train. The moans and screams were terrible. I personally helped to carry a young German soldier from the train. He was horribly burned about the head and shoulders. A doctor assisted me to put him in a corner and we determined to find out, if we could, exactly what had happened to him. We began by inquiring about his mother and sweetheart and after each answer I would ask, 'Where were you going and what happened?' Finally we managed to piece the story together. He said they had been told they were going to invade Britain; that nothing was going to stop them, that it was just a matter of getting into boats and crossing the Channel. He told me: 'It was horrible. The sea was ablaze, the British they bombed and machine-gunned us. Hell couldn't be worse.' Then he died, there on the stretcher. We looked after more than 500 soldiers as best we could, many of them died in Brussels railway station, others in our hospitals.'

Renee explained that other nurses told her more stories they had picked up from German soldiers. 'Thousands of us started out and we expected to be in England tonight,' they said. For days afterwards the bodies of German soldiers, their heads and shoulders burned, were washed ashore and it was impossible for the Nazis to preserve the secret any longer. 'The German Red Cross trains passed through Brussels for three days,' Renee went on. 'We asked for a supply of medical equipment for the Germans, but they didn't have much.'

W. A. Birkbeck, who took part in the liberation of Antwerp in September 1944 recalled: 'While we were enjoying the gaiety and celebrations a friend and I were invited to take tea with an old Londoner who had married a Belgian soldier after the First World War. Their daughter was a nurse in an Antwerp hospital. During our walk around the district watching collaborators tried, the nurse remarked, 'the best thing you ever did was set the sea on fire.' I asked when it was that we set the sea on fire, to which she replied 1940 and that, 'I know because I was on duty in the hospital. The British set the sea on fire and they were all so terribly burned.'

Meanwhile, by 1943 preparations were being made for the invasion of Europe and parts of east Suffolk became home to Allied soldiers rehearsing

HITLER'S INVASION OF EAST ANGLIA, 1940

for D-Day. Several villages were compulsorily, though temporarily evacuated by the War Office for use as Battle Training Areas. The area around Fritton Lake near Lowestoft was used by the 79th Armoured Division to test specially adapted tanks and armoured vehicles, 'Funnies' as they were known. After the war it would be alleged that some of these amphibious tanks had also been tested near Shingle Street in Hollesley Bay. Compared with what had happened in 1940 these evacuations turned out to be a relatively short term inconvenience and by 1945 the temporary Battle Training Areas had been returned to civilian ownership. Shingle Street, however, was another matter. Since first being evacuated in June 1940, the hamlet had remained a strictly prohibited area under military control. This state of affairs continued through the following years, although the hamlet was in fact never in a specifically designated Battle Training Area as such. Despite their best efforts the former inhabitants were denied permission to return to their homes and this would remain the case until long after the end of the war.

In 1943 Robert S. Arbib Junior USAAC - a part of the 'friendly invasion' in 1942 - discovered on a visit to the Suffolk coast that England's defences were once again equal to the attack (by coastal sorties and quick raids by the Luftwaffe). 'England was getting a tough little island to crack. East Anglia, that had been considered easy meat, was easy no longer.'

'Thank God we still had the navy' [in 1940] he was told. 'Yes [and] lads in battledress with the red ack-ack shoulder-flash and a handful of fliers, too. And surely something more than that. The hidden something... call it intestinal fortitude, call it guts, call it honesty and integrity or love of Country and of King. Call it sheer bravado, or a sense of the dramatic, or a sense of defiance - the kind of bravado and dramatics and defiance that has placed all the heroic lost causes first in the hearts of England - the Charge of the Light Brigade, the Battle of Bunker Hill, the breaking of the British Square, the Retreat from Dunkirk - that all through your history has honoured the charge into certain death - the fighting defeat - the doomed stand - the thin red line. Here it was again - Dunkirk and the famous 'Few' and now all England on the battle line. Call it courage, call it what you will. Say it is not an exclusive British quality - say that other nations and other soldiers and sailors and airmen equally have proved themselves courageous, foolhardy, brave, tough, stubborn, unyielding and magnificent. But never deny that England knows not gallantry...

'The invasion might have come. It might have succeeded and the German tanks and the artillery and the planes might have crunched across England and flattened it. But it would not have been a holiday or a parade. It would have been an historic, bitter, last-ditch fight and it would have been gallant and heroic to the end.'

Appendix A

Unternehmen Seelöwe (Operation 'Sealion') Order of Battle August 1940

Generalfeldmarschall Gerd von Rundstedt

16th Armee - Generaloberst Ernst Busch
First Wave XIII Armee-Korps - General Heinrich-Gottfried von Vietinghoff genannt Scheel.
17th Infanterie-Division
35th Infanterie-Division
Luftwaffe II./Flak-Regiment 14

VIIth Armee-Korps - Generaloberst Eugen Ritter von Schobert
1st Gebirgs-Division
7th Infanterie-Division
Luftwaffe I./Flak-Regiment 26

Second Wave Vth Armee-Korps - General Richard Ruoff
12th Infanterie-Division
30th Infanterie-Division

XXXIth Armee-Korps - General der Panzertruppen Georg-Hans Reinhardt
8th Panzer-Division
10th Panzer-Division
29th Infanterie-Division (motorised)
Infanterie-Regiment (motorised) Großdeutschland
Infanterie-Regiment Leibstandarte SS Adolf Hitler (motorised)

HITLER'S INVASION OF EAST ANGLIA, 1940

Third Wave
IVth Armee-Korps - General Viktor von Schwedler
24th Infanterie-Division
58th Infanterie-Division

XXXIIth Armee-Korps - General Walter Kuntze
45th Infanterie-Division
164th Infanterie-Division

9th Armee - Generaloberst Adolf Strauss
First Wave XXXVIIIth Armee-Korps - General Erich von Manstein
26th Infanterie-Division
34th Infanterie-Division

VIIIth Armee-Korps - General Walter Heitz
6th Gebirgs-Division
8th Infanterie-Division
28th Infanterie-Division

Second Wave
XVth Armee-Korps - Generaloberst Hermann Hoth
4th Panzer-Division
7th Panzer-Division
20th Infanterie-Division (motorised)

Third Wave
XXIVth Armee-Korps General Leo Freiherr Geyr von Schweppenburg
15th Infanterie-Division
78th Infanterie-Division

Heeresgruppe C
Generalfeldmarschall Wilhelm Ritter von Leeb
6th Armee - Generalfeldmarschall Walther von Reichenau
IInd Armee-Korps - General Walter Graf von Brockdorff-Ahlefeldt
6th Infanterie-Division
256th Infanterie-Division

Airborne Formations General Kurt Student
7th Flieger-Division

UNTERNEHMEN SEELÖWE

22nd Infanterie-Division (Luftlande)
Bau-Lehr-Regiment z.b.V. 800 Brandenburg

British Home Forces (General Alan Brooke)
Chief of Staff: Lieutenant General Bernard Paget
38th (Welsh) Infantry Division
21st Army Tank Brigade
IV Corps - Lieutenant General Francis Nosworthy
2nd Armoured Division
42nd (East Lancashire) Infantry Division
31st Independent Infantry Brigade Group

VII Corps - Lieutenant General Andrew McNaughton of Canada
1st Armoured Division
1st Canadian Infantry Division
1st Army Tank Brigade

Northern Command - Lieutenant General Ronald Forbes Adam
I Corps - Lieutenant General Harold Alexander
1st Infantry Division
2nd Infantry Division
45th Infantry Division

X Corps - Lieutenant General William Holmes
54th (East Anglian) Infantry Division
59th (Staffordshire) Infantry Division

London District - Lieutenant General Bertram Sergison-Brooke
20th Independent Infantry Brigade (Guards)
24th Guards Brigade Group
3rd London Infantry Brigade

Eastern Command - Lieutenant General Laurence Carr
II Corps - Lieutenant General Edmund Osborne
18th Infantry Division
52nd (Lowland) Infantry Division
37th Independent Infantry Brigade

HITLER'S INVASION OF EAST ANGLIA, 1940

XI Corps - Lieutenant General Hugh Massy
15th (Scottish) Infantry Division
55th (West Lancashire) Infantry Division

XII Corps - Lieutenant General Andrew Thorne
1st London Infantry Division
43rd (Wessex) Infantry Division
New Zealand Division
1st Motor Machine Gun Brigade
29th Independent Infantry Brigade

Southern Command - Lieutenant General Claude Auchinleck
V Corps - Lieutenant General Bernard Montgomery
3rd Infantry Division
4th Infantry Division
50th (Northumbrian) Infantry Division

VIII Corps - Lieutenant General Harold Franklyn
48th (South Midland) Infantry Division
70th Independent Infantry Brigade

Western Command - General Robert Gordon-Finlayson
2nd London Infantry Division
III Corps - Lieutenant General James Marshall Cornwall
5th Infantry Division
3rd Motor Machine Gun Brigade
36th Independent Infantry Brigade

Scottish Command - Lieutenant General Harold Carrington
46th Infantry Division
51st (Highland) Infantry Division

Appendix B

Commando Operations 1940-43

During the Norwegian Campaign, Narvik and its surrounding area saw significant fighting, initially from 9th April 1940 between German and Norwegian forces, subsequently between Allied and German forces, conducted by the Norwegian 6th Division of the Norwegian Army as well as by an Allied expeditionary corps until 9 June 1940. Unlike the campaign in southern Norway, the Allied troops in Narvik would eventually outnumber the Norwegian troops. Five nations participated in the fighting. From 5-10 May the fighting in the Narvik area was the only active theatre of land war in the Second World War. The Norwegian force eventually reached 8,000-10,000 men after a few weeks. The total number of Allied troops in the campaign in and around Narvik reached 24,500 men. The early phase of the invasion was marked by the German advantage of surprise.

The initial British detachment was reinforced on 28 April by a French expeditionary force, Three battalions of Alpine troops and two battalions of 13th Demi-Brigade of the Foreign Legion were deployed both north and south of the Ofotfjord, but later, the north would be the main French area of operation. Four Polish battalions arrived on 9 May. They were first deployed north of the Ofotfjord, but later redeployed to the area south of the fjord. In early June they were formed into the Polish Independent Highland Brigade under Zygmunt Bohusz-Szyszko.

At 2340 on 28 May, a naval bombardment commenced from the north. Two French and one Norwegian battalion would be transported across the Rombaksfjord and advance on Narvik from the north. In the south, the Polish battalions would advance toward Ankenes and inner Beisfjord. The maximum capacity of the landing barges was 290 men and these troops could not be reinforced for 45 minutes. These first troops were able to get a foothold on Ørnes by the time the rest of the French and the Norwegians were landed. The French moved west toward the city and east along the railway. The Norwegians moved toward Mount Taraldsvik, circled around and moved down toward the city. The German commander decided to evacuate before 0700 and retired along Beisfjord. This was the first major Allied victory on land.

It seemed now that it was only a matter of time before the Germans would have to surrender. They were pushed from the north by the Norwegians, from the west by the French and from the southwest by the Poles. It appeared that Bjørnfjell would be the Germans' last stand, but London had already secretly decided to evacuate on 24 May. The Norwegian government and commanders were first told in early June and the news was met with disbelief and bitterness. The Norwegians still hoped to defeat the Germans alone but on 8 June Narvik fell and on 10th June the last Norwegian forces in Norway surrendered.

In 1940 Winston Churchill had decreed that Britain must be able to strike back at the Germans so as to keep up morale, tie down German forces and to foster an offensive spirit into an army and people who were staring into the face of an invasion. 'Commando' was the name to be given to the new force of volunteers being formed. The term 'commando' itself came from the Boer War in South Africa from 1899-1902 where bands of irregular Boers called 'commandoes' would strike swiftly and suddenly at the British army. The first commando raid, conducted by the British forces in WWII was Operation 'Collar' on the night of 24/25 June 1940 when 115 men of No.11 Independent Company reconnoitred four locations on the coast of France. Each group was landed on one of the target beaches at Neufchâtel-Hardelot, Stella-Plage, Berck and Le Touquet. They were to spend no more than 80 minutes ashore before returning to their RAF boats but these were not equipped for a mission like this and lacked exact navigation equipment and the compasses were known to be unreliable. Crossing the Channel they also came to the notice of patrolling RAF aircraft who not being aware of the mission, came in close to investigate. At around 0200 hours on the 24 June, the boats reached France and put their men ashore. The group that landed at Le Touquet had the Merlimont Plage Hotel as an objective. Intelligence had suggested that the Germans were using the hotel as a barracks. When the group reached the hotel they discovered it was empty and the doors and windows boarded up. Unable to find another target, they returned to the beach, only to discover their boat had put back out to sea. During the wait, two German sentries stumbled on the group and were quietly killed by the troops' bayonets. Another German patrol then approached across the sand dunes and the group was forced to swim out to the boat, leaving its weapons behind. The group that landed at Hardelot penetrated several hundred yards inland and returned to its boat without meeting any Germans. The men that landed at Berck discovered a seaplane anchorage, but it was too heavily defended for them to risk any attack. The final group landed at Stella Plage. It encountered a German patrol and in the short exchange of fire that followed, one man was slightly wounded. The operation failed to gather any intelligence or damage any German equipment.

Operation 'Frankton', a commando raid on shipping in the German occupied French port of Bordeaux in the Bay of Biscay during 7-12 December 1942 was the most famous commando raid mounted from Britain in WWII. The raid was carried out by a small unit of Royal Marines known as the Royal Marines Boom Patrol Detachment (RMBPD), part of Combined Operations. Twelve men from No.1 section were selected for the raid; including the commanding officer, Herbert 'Blondie' Hasler and the reserve Marine Colley. A Royal Navy submarine, HMS *Tuna* (N94) sailed from Holy Loch in Scotland with the six canoes and raiders on board. The plan was for the canoes to be taken to the area of the Gironde Estuary by submarine. The raiders would then paddle by night to Bordeaux. On arrival they would attack the docked cargo ships with limpet mines and then escape overland to Spain. Two men survived the raid: Hasler and his No.2 in the canoe, Bill Sparks. Of the other eight, six were executed by the Germans while two died from hypothermia.

The Commando Order (Kommandobefehl) was issued by Adolf Hitler on 18 October 1942 stating that all Allied commandos encountered by German forces in Europe and Africa should be killed immediately without trial, even in proper uniforms or if they attempted to surrender. Any commando or small group of commandoes or a similar unit, agents and saboteurs not in proper uniforms who fell into the hands of the German military forces by some means other than direct combat (through the police in occupied territories, for instance) were to be handed over immediately to the Sicherheitsdienst (SD, Security Service). The order, which was issued in secret, made it clear that failure to carry out these orders by any commander or officer would be considered to be an act of negligence punishable under German military law. This was in the second 'Commando Order', the first being issued by Generalfeldmarschall Gerd von Rundstedt on 21 July 1942, stipulating that parachutists should be handed over to the Gestapo. At the Nuremberg Trials, the Commando Order was found to be a direct breach of the laws of war and German officers who carried out illegal executions under the Commando Order were found guilty of war crimes.

Winston Churchill believed that Operation 'Frankton' shortened the war by six months. The words of Lord Mountbatten, the commander of

HITLER'S INVASION OF EAST ANGLIA, 1940

Combined Operations, are carved into a Purbeck stone at Royal Marines Poole (current headquarters of the SBS): Of the many brave and dashing raids carried out by the men of Combined Operations Command none was more courageous or imaginative than Operation 'Frankton'.

During 1941-43 several Commando raids were conducted in Norway by the British and Norwegian commandoes. One of the very first commando operations was Operation 'Claymore' on 4 March when 800 men of 3 and 4 Commando and a party of Norwegians stormed ashore in the Lofoten Islands at Svolvær and Stamsund. The targets were a number of fish oil factories which produced glycerine for use in munitions. The mission was a complete success with very little fighting taking place and the targets destroyed. The force returned with 315 volunteers for the Norwegian forces, sixty 'Quisling' collaborators and 225 German prisoners. The only casualty was a British officer who accidently shot himself in the thigh. In addition some parts to an 'Enigma' code machine were captured which significantly helped the code-breakers at Bletchley Park. One humorous incident which took place was the sending of a telegram from Stamsund addressed to 'A. Hitler, Berlin'. It said: 'you said in your last speech German troops would meet the British wherever they landed. Where are your troops?

On 24 August in Operation 'Gauntlet' 1,500 Canadians and others who had been trained in amphibious warfare landed at Spitsbergen (Svalbard) and Bear Island (Bjørnøya) to destroy the coalmines on Svalbard to prevent them falling into German hands and to evacuate 2,000 Soviet miners to Archangel in Northern Russia and 800 Norwegians to Great Britain. The radio and weather installation on Bear Island was also destroyed and the people there evacuated.

From 26 to 28 December in Operation 'Anklet' 300 members of 12 Commando, 'Linge' company raided the Lofoten Islands at Reine, Sund and Sørvågen as a diversion for Operation 'Archery'. The 'Anklet' force which included men from the Norwegian 'Lingekompaniet' landed unopposed and captured the German garrison without a fight. They left two days later after having destroyed installations and taking with them 29 German prisoners as well as over 200 Norwegians.

Operation 'Archery', the first combined Army-Navy-Air Force operations raid of the war is one of the best known and certainly the most photographed as the raid was accompanied by official photographers and cameramen. The raid was to destroy the German iron-ore convoy assembly base at Vågsö on the Norwegian coast between Bergen and Trondheim and the force was to be supported by the RAF who provided air cover and attacked the airfield of Herdla just north of Bergen. Five hundred and twenty-five Army Commandos were landed on the island by Royal Navy assault craft and successfully overpowered the German garrison in a sharp engagement, suffering only light casualties. In support of this raid, 404 Squadron RCAF dispatched two Blenheim fighters from Sumburgh on the Shetland Islands to cover the landing, while Bomber Command contributed nineteen Blenheim and ten Hampden sorties. As a diversionary tactic, six Blenheim crews on 110 Squadron at Lossiemouth carried out a shipping sweep off the coast near Stavanger with the aim of drawing off German fighters from the Commando raid. Five of the Blenheims found a convoy off Egerö and four attacked but two Blenheims fell victim to flak and the other two were destroyed by Bf 109s of I/JG77 from an airstrip at Herdla. Seven Hampdens on 50 Squadron were sent to lay a smoke-screen at Vågsö but two were shot down, most likely by shore defences. The three other Hampdens bombed a German gun position covering the approaches to Vågsö. The naval part of the force consisted of one cruiser, four destroyers and two landing ships, the warships opened the proceedings with a bombardment of the island of Måløy. Some 800 commandoes (including 36 Norwegians) were split into five groups, 2, 3, 4 and 6 Commandoes and 'Linge' company. One group landed to the West of South Vågsö to secure the area then move up to the town. The second group landed to the North of the town to prevent German reinforcements getting in. The third group landed on Måløy to deal with the guns and garrison there. However the navy had done their job well and the guns were silent and it did not take long for the garrison to be subdued. The fourth group landed at the town itself and this proved to be the main centre of resistance. The last group was kept onboard ship to act as a floating reserve.

The Germans in the town were in greater numbers than expected and the group there called for reinforcements from the group to the West, from the floating reserve and from elements of the group on Måløy. Fierce House to house fighting developed but by 1345 the fighting was over and an hour later the force re-embarked. Behind them they left 15,000 tons of shipping destroyed, warehouses, dockyards, fish-oil processing plants and all German installations destroyed. Ninety-eight Germans were taken prisoner along with four 'Quislings' and 77 Norwegians also decided to come with them to Britain. The cost to the Germans had been around 150 killed; the British lost nineteen men and 57 wounded and the Norwegian force lost one man and two wounded. The Norwegian killed was an especially painful loss as it was their commander Kaptein Martin Linge who fell during the assault on Måløy. The Germans took reprisals against the Norwegian population which prompted protests from the Norwegian King Haakon VII and the government-in-exile. The Germans also began to reinforce and strengthen their defences, which was to the allies advantage as this tied down many troops which could otherwise be used elsewhere.

The SOE (Special Operations Executive) which had responsibility for conducting espionage, sabotage and liaison with local resistance groups were heavily involved in planning and coordinating the raids carried out after 'Archery'. 10 (Inter-Allied) Commando was formed in June 1942 and consisted of troops from the occupied countries. Each troop initially would consist of four officers and 83 other ranks. Countries represented included France, the Netherlands, Belgium, Poland, Yugoslavia and No.5 (Norwegian) Troop. A 'miscellaneous' troop was also created with members coming from the axis countries such as Germany and Austria.

On the night of 20/21 September 1942 in Operation 'Musketoon', a dozen men of 2 Commando were given the task of destroying the power station in Glomfjord which was providing power to an aluminium plant in the area. Captains Black and Houghton along with eight other ranks and two Norwegians set off from Scotland onboard a Free French submarine on 11 September. Arriving four days later they then had a three day approach march over the mountains to the target arriving on the 18th, they decided to attack the objective on during the night of the 20th/21st. Complete surprise was achieved but as the party withdrew and the charges were going off they encountered Germans which forced them to split up. In the confusion one of the British was killed, one of the Norwegians mortally wounded and the two officers wounded. They along with four others were captured however the other Norwegian and three of the British managed to make their way into Sweden and eventually on to Britain individually. The two officers were to become the first to suffer under Hitler's infamous 'Commando order' by being shot by firing squad.

Operation 'Cartoon', which went ahead on 23/24 January 1943 with the aim to destroy the pyrite mine on the island of Stord near Leirvik was a complete success. Sixty-three members of 12 Commando were accompanied by ten men from the Norwegian troop of 10 (IA) Commando under Captain Harald Risnes. Seven MTBs of the 30th (Royal Norwegian Navy) MTB flotilla were used as transport. Half the force was landed at Sagvåg quay and engaged the defending German positions there whilst the remainder were landed on the other side of the bay. The mine, which was two miles away, was reached in 25 minutes by the men who were each carrying 50lbs of explosives. The charges were set and the mine put out of action for a year. Meanwhile three of the MTBs went on to Leirvik in search of shipping but found none but on the way back a ship was attacked and left in a sinking condition and mines were also laid. The raid netted three German prisoners as well as a quantity of papers and equipment. This was achieved for the loss of one commando killed and two commandoes and eight sailors injured.

Operation 'Brandy' on 14/15 February 1943 was a Norwegian operation and involved seven members of 10 and 12 Commando led by Lieutenant Rommetveldt who boarded two Norwegian MTBs for an operation into Florø harbour. Two German ships were torpedoed and a third struck a mine laid by the MTBs. One of the MTBs ran aground and had to be abandoned. In Operation 'Checkmate' on 29 April 1943 six members of 14 Commando attempted an attack on shipping at Haugesund. Four attempts to pick up the party failed due to bad weather and no trace of them was found. One ship may have been attacked.

Numerous other operations were planned, trained for and begun before being called off for many different reasons ranging from weather to long daylight hours in the summer and from bad luck to bad planning.

Appendix C

Airborne Operations 1941-43

At first Hitler developed in detail his general views, politically and strategically, about how to continue the war against his principal enemy. Herein he also mentioned the issues in the Mediterranean. After that he turned to the question of invading England. Hitler said that during the previous year he could not afford to risk a possible failure; apart from that, he had not wished to provoke the British, as he hoped to arrange peace talks. But as they were unwilling to discuss things, they must face the alternative. Then a discussion followed about the use of the 11th Air Corps in an invasion of Great Britain. In this respect I expressed my doubts about using the Corps directly on the South coast to form a bridgehead for the Army - as the area immediately behind the coast was now covered with obstacles. These doubts were accepted by Hitler. I then proposed that, if it proved absolutely necessary to use the 11th Air Corps on the south coast, then airfields in the hinterland (25 to 35 miles distant from the coast) should be captured and infantry divisions landed on them.

Suddenly Hitler pointed to the Cornwall - Devon Peninsula and drew a big circle on his map round Taunton and the Blackdown Hills, saying: 'Your airborne troops could be used here as flank protection. This is a strong sector and, besides, this important defile must be opened.' He then pointed to Plymouth and dwelt on the importance of this great harbour for the Germans and for the English. Now I could no longer follow his thought and I asked at what points on the south coast the landing was to take place. But Hitler kept strictly to his order that operations were to be kept secret and said: 'I cannot tell you yet'.

General-Leutnant Kurt Student, an aggressive, innovative leader and a pioneer of the use of paratroops as part of the 'Blitzkrieg', who in January 1941 had a meeting with Adolf Hitler to discuss the invasion of Britain. Student had been badly injured during the invasion of Holland in May 1940 and did not return to action until 1941. After

AIRBORNE OPERATIONS 1941-43

the war Student wrote that if he had been on the scene he would have urged the use of parachute forces against England while the evacuation from Dunkirk was still in progress, to seize the ports where German troops were landing.

German transport units were instrumental in the rapid build-up of German forces for the invasion of Greece and Yugoslavia which took place on 6 April 1941. The assault opened with a dive-bomber attack on Belgrade and eleven days later Yugoslavia capitulated. By 24 April British and Greek forces were beginning to retreat from Thermopylae and the Germans planned a large-scale parachute drop to capture intact the road bridge over the Corinth Canal, but the paratroop assault on 26 April was unsuccessful. However, the Germans successfully captured the Peloponnese and only Crete stood in the way of Axis domination of the Balkans. On 20th April General-Leutnant Kurt Student, leader of the new XI Fliegerkorps which took in under its control all air transport units, had suggested to Göring that an attempt be made to invade Crete from the air. The plan was put to Hitler on 21 April and four days later he issued Führer Directive No. 28; Unternehmen 'Merkur' ('Mercury').

General Major Gerhard was made air commander of a force of transport aircraft which was to include 493 Ju 52/3ms and over eighty DFS 230 gliders. All told, 750 glider-borne troops, 10,000 paratroops, 5,000 airlifted mountain soldiers and 7,000 seaborne troops were allocated to the invasion. The Germans planned to use Fallschirmjäger to capture important points on the island, including airfields that could then be used to fly in supplies and reinforcements. The Luftwaffe commander, Colonel General Alexander Löhr and the Kriegsmarine commander, Admiral Karl-Georg Schuster, wanted more emphasis on Máleme, to achieve overwhelming superiority of force. Major-General Kurt von Student wanted to disperse the paratroops more, to maximise the effect of surprise. As the primary objective, Máleme offered several advantages: it was the largest airfield and big enough for heavy transport aircraft, it was close enough to the mainland for air cover from land-based Bf 109 fighters and it was near the north coast, so seaborne reinforcements could be brought up quickly. A compromise plan by Hermann Göring was agreed and in the final draft Máleme was to be captured first, while not ignoring the other objectives.

Fliegerkorps XI was to co-ordinate the attack by the 7th Flieger-Division, which would land by parachute and glider, followed by the 22nd Air Landing

Division, once the airfields were secure. The operation was scheduled for 16 May but was postponed to 20 May, with the 5th Mountain Division replacing the 22nd Air Landing Division. To support the German attack on Crete, eleven Italian submarines took post off Crete and the British bases of Sollum and Alexandria in Egypt.

Even before the huge aerial armada took-off, things had begun to go badly wrong. Enough fuel for the first attack wave arrived only a few hours before take-off and the pilots had no idea whether they would have sufficient petrol for the two succeeding waves. Only seven Ju 52/3ms were lost during the initial assault, but when they returned to their airfields many could not land because of the heavy dust. Those that did attempt a landing collided with others and the whole situation became chaotic. A second attack wave was planned to depart at 1300 hours to drop paratroops against Retimo and Heraklion, but the confusion led to the spreading of the unit's take off times and the last Ju 52/3m unit arrived three and a half hours after the first, KGrzbV 105. The German plan for the assault split the airborne forces in half: the first drop coming against the airfield at Máleme on the western end of the island; the second coming later in the day, against Heraklion on the eastern end of the island. The Germans significantly underestimated the number of Commonwealth troops available to Freyberg (the Greek forces consisted of approximately 9,000 troops; the British Commonwealth contingent consisted of the original 14,000-man British garrison and another 25,000 British and Commonwealth troops evacuated from the mainland) and they completely underestimated the determination of the Cretan population to defend their homes. The landing at Heraklion was an unmitigated disaster. The operation against Máleme airfield did not go much better. The attacking paratroopers took horrendous casualties and managed to establish only a few footholds against the New Zealand battalion defending the airfield. Moreover, throughout the first day the German airborne command in Athens largely failed to glean how badly things were going.

At 0800 on 20 May German paratroopers, jumping out of dozens of Ju 52 aircraft, landed near Máleme airfield and the town of Chania. The 21st, 22nd and 23rd New Zealand battalions held Máleme airfield and the vicinity. The Germans suffered many casualties in the first hours of the invasion, a kompanie of III Battalion, 1st Assault Regiment lost 112 killed out of 126 men and 400 of 600 men in III Battalion were killed on the first day. Most of the parachutists were engaged by New Zealanders defending the airfield and Greek forces near Chania. Many gliders following the paratroops were hit by mortar fire within seconds of landing and the glider troops who landed safely were almost annihilated by the New Zealand and Greek defenders. A second wave of German transports supported by Luftwaffe and Regia Aeronautica attack aircraft, arrived in the afternoon, dropping more paratroopers and gliders containing heavy assault troops. As night fell, none of the German objectives had been secured. Of 493 German transport aircraft used during the airdrop, seven were lost to anti-aircraft fire. The bold plan to attack in four places to maximize surprise, rather than concentrating on one, seemed to have failed, although the reasons were unknown to the Germans at the time.

Fortunately for the embattled Fallschirmjäger, Major General Bernard Freyberg VC, a New Zealand Army officer who was appointed commander of the Allied forces on Crete (Creforce) and the local commanders failed to reinforce the defenders at Máleme. That evening Freyberg, whose battalion had also suffered heavy casualties - but no heavier than the Germans - took his troops off the crucial hill that dominated the airfield. The next morning the German paratroopers found themselves in control of Máleme. Soon a steady stream of Ju 52s flew in reinforcements and the Germans managed to build up sufficient forces to overwhelm the Commonwealth defenders. This was the first time that the Germans encountered widespread resistance from a civilian population and they began massacring civilians, killing over 500 people from around twenty villages in mass exterminations.

Despite defiant resistance from the British Commonwealth and Greek troops, Crete finally fell to the Axis powers on 31 May 1941. Germany lost over 7,000 men killed or wounded, including one out of every four paratroopers dropped. The Luftwaffe's air transport units lost over 170 Ju 52/3ms destroyed or very seriously damaged.

The conquest of Crete occupies a special place in military history as the first successful invasion of an island carried out entirely from the air. Nevertheless, the German airborne victory proved to be enormously costly, which many historians have suggested discouraged Hitler from using airborne forces against Malta in early June 1942.

Hitler and the German commanders who fought on Crete were shocked by the very high casualties and Hitler cancelled airborne operations associated with Operation 'Barbarossa' and the Eastern Front. German paratroopers and airborne commandoes played a less significant role as airborne forces for the remainder of the war. For the most part German paratroopers fought as regular infantry But there were some successes: the seizure of the Tunisian bridgehead in response to Operation 'Torch', the Allied landing in North Africa in November 1942 and Benito Mussolini's rescue from his internment in the Campo Imperatore Hotel at the top of the Gran Sasso Mountain and only accessible by cable car from the valley below on 12 September 1943 by SS officer Otto Skorzeny, the commando expert. (There was a failed attempt to rescue Mussolini on 27 July 1943. The Ju 52 that the crew was aboard was shot down in the area of Pratica di Mare. Otto Skorzeny and all but one of his crew bailed out safely). Flying out in a Fieseler Storch, Skorzeny escorted Mussolini to Rome and later to Berlin. The exploit earned Skorzeny fame, promotion to Sturmbannführer and the Knight's Cross of the Iron Cross.

Paradoxically, the Allies may have gained the most from the German success on Crete. According to US Army Major General James 'Jumping Jim' Gavin, the British captured the German doctrinal manual for paratrooper operations and immediately passed a copy along to Americans. That manual, with relatively few exceptions, was the basis for the training and preparation of Allied airborne forces. Besides providing a 'how-to' guide, the German success on Crete also persuaded Allied military and political leaders that they would need airborne forces if they were going to successfully invade Europe. Thus began the laborious process of building up the airborne divisions that were to assault Hitler's *Festung Europa*, or fortress Europe, in 1943 and 1944.

The first division-sized employment of Allied airborne forces came during Operation 'Husky', the invasion of Sicily, which began on 10 July 1943. While the landings succeeded, the drops were anything but a success. Gale force winds completely upset the navigation for the transport aircraft. Of 144 gliders carrying British infantry, only 54 landed in Sicily and only twelve near their objectives. An American force of 3,400 paratroopers was dropped all over the south-eastern part of the island - 33 sticks in the British area, 53 near Gela and 127 in the neighbourhood of the 45th Infantry Division. Only the 2nd Battalion of the 505th Parachute Infantry Regiment (PIR) was together when it landed - but 25 miles from its objective. Regardless of the lack of concentration, the American paratroopers immediately caused a massive headache for the defending Germans and Italians. As the official history suggests: 'Bands of paratroopers were roaming through the rear areas of the coastal defence units, cutting enemy communications lines, ambushing small parties and creating confusion among enemy commanders as to exactly where the main airborne landing had taken place.' Perhaps most important, some of these small groups of paratroopers were able to delay the deployment of the Hermann Göring Panzer Division against the Allied landings at Gela.

To the east, despite its small size, a party of British paratroopers seized Ponte Grande, but proved too few to prevent the Italian defenders from regaining the bridge. By the morning of the second day, both the British and Americans had a firm foothold on the eastern and southern shores of the island. Only at Gela were the Germans putting significant pressure on American troops. As a result George S. Patton ordered that the 504th Regimental Combat Team be dropped in to reinforce the line. Despite careful efforts at coordination to ensure that the US Navy would not fire on the incoming aircraft, the troop carrier formations came under intense anti-aircraft fire from the Allied fleet off Gela. By the time it was over, the troop carriers had lost 23 out of 144 aircraft dispatched, with a further 37 aircraft badly damaged. Six of the aircraft shot down had their full load of paratroopers on board. Altogether, the 504th lost 81 dead, 132 wounded and sixteen missing.

Under intense anti-aircraft fire the transport crews once again dropped paratroopers all over south-eastern Sicily; by evening on the 12th the regiment still only numbered 37 officers and 518 men. The difficulties encountered in mass parachute drops in Sicily did not deter the continuation of the build-up of Allied airborne forces. Moreover, the successful reinforcement of the Salerno bridgehead by a regiment of the 82nd Airborne Division in short order also helped to strengthen the belief that paratrooper formations could be very useful in future military operations.

The great moment for the Allied airborne forces came with Operation 'Overlord' in June 1944 when their contribution more than justified the considerable airborne resources employed by the British and US armies. The initial plan for the invasion called for a three-division amphibious landing, supported by the drop of one airborne division but the Combined Chiefs of Staff found the logistical and amphibious resources to increase the invasion force to a six-division landing force - three American, two British and one Canadian - supported by a drop of three airborne divisions. Air Chief Marshal Sir Trafford Leigh-Mallory argued that the American paratroopers would suffer upward of 95 percent casualties. Eisenhower countered with his belief that the airborne assault at night would not suffer such a high casualty rate, but that it did not matter what the casualty rate was so long as the airborne troops accomplished their mission. As the supreme Allied commander, he got his way.

HITLER'S INVASION OF EAST ANGLIA, 1940

The British 6th Airborne troops were to seize the solid ground on the east side of the Orne River, while a specially trained glider borne force was to seize the bridges over the Caen Canal and Orne at Benouville to achieve a linkup with the amphibious landings (See Appendix F). The task of the American 82nd and 101st Airborne were to link up with the American forces on 'Utah' and 'Omaha' beaches and disrupt German communications throughout western Normandy. Due to weather, bad navigation and German anti-aircraft fire, the troop carrier pilots dropped them all over Normandy but the small groups of paratroopers spread havoc and confusion throughout the countryside.

The airborne operations on D-Day proved largely successful with Allied paratroopers taking their objectives with speed and daring, often with incisive coup de main tactics and holding their positions until reinforcement. Two months later, 17-25 September, when Operation 'Market-Garden' went ahead, the opposite was true. Events in Holland that month were to prove that despite overwhelming numbers of air and ground forces, a large scale assault did not always guarantee success against well-organised defenders. Generalfeldmarschall Otto Moritz Walter Model, 54 years old, who commanded the German forces in Holland was a senior officer of the old school, squat, broad-beamed and was harsh, forceful and energetic. He had been awarded the Iron Cross First Class and Knight's Cross with Swords in the First World War. Despite his humble origins - he was a Prussian of non-aristocratic background - he always tried to appear as a Prussian aristocrat, even down to his habitual monocle fixed in the Prussian manner to a scarred and sternly handsome face. Appointed to command a division on 13 November 1940, by January 1942, with the German front before Moscow on the point of disintegration, Model had risen to the rank of field-marshal by virtue of intellect, ambition and Hitler's patronage rather than through the influence of the old, traditionally military families. Hitler had called Model 'the saviour of the Eastern Front' where he had shown himself a master of defensive action in Russia and Poland and had earned his reputation as 'the Führer's fireman', able to take charge of a rout and turn it into a counter-attack. Model gave Hitler his political support and in return was allowed much more freedom of action than other German generals had the courage to demand.

Operation 'Market-Garden' was designed to encircle the Ruhr in a pincer movement and give easier access into Germany. Allied forces were to penetrate north from Belgium and advance sixty miles through Holland, across the Rhine and then consolidate north of Arnhem on the Dutch/German border ready to close the pincer. 'Market' involved the massed use of airborne forces (First Allied Airborne Army) and 'Garden' - the ground forces (British XXX Corps).

AIRBORNE OPERATIONS 1941-43

It was the largest airborne operation in history, with over 34,600 men of the 101st, 82nd and British 1st Airborne Divisions and the Polish Brigade being delivered and 14,589 troops landed by glider and 20,011 by parachute.[113]

Unfortunately, 'Market-Garden' was doomed to failure from the outset. Field Marshal Montgomery's plan was ambitious and bold as well as imaginative but it was complicated by decisions taken by Lieutenant General Sir Frederick Arthur Montague 'Boy' Browning commanding 1st British Airborne Corps and Lieutenant General Lewis H. Brereton USAAF, commander of the First Allied Airborne Army. First Allied Airborne Army's poor choice of parachute drop zones and glider landing zones were too far from the objectives. British paratroopers were asked to land seven miles from Arnhem Bridge. Brereton also ruled that there were to be no glider coup de main tactics like those that had been so successfully employed at night at the Orne bridges and amongst Rommel's glider posts during the Normandy air assault. The other major failure of 'Market' was the inability of the USAAF commanders to fly the airborne forces in two lifts on the first day. Brereton made the decision to carry out the lifts over two to three days, thus ensuring that any element of surprise was completely lost and the longer each division had to devote to defending the drop and landing zones, weakened their offensive power. He also limited the use of ground-attack aircraft over the battlefield while escort fighters were in the air protecting supply drops. After 17th September, air drops were piecemeal and often a victim of cloud and foggy conditions and the drop zones were quickly overrun by the German defenders. Because not all the units could arrive together the 1st Airborne Division failed to hold the crossings of the Lower Rhine. This meant that a substantial part of the force that landed on the first day was tied down holding the DZs so that subsequent lifts could land in safety. Moreover, the aircraft available were either Dakotas (C-47s) which were slow, unarmed and unarmoured transport aircraft not fitted with self-sealing tanks, or Stirlings, Halifaxes and Albemarles not designed to fly in daylight at a low height over hostile territory. The whole operation was to be carried out by the light of day.

Several bridges between Eindhoven and Nijmegen were captured at the beginning of the operation but XXX Corps ground force advance was delayed by the initial failure of the airborne units to secure bridges at Son and Nijmegen. German forces demolished the bridge over the Wilhelmina

---

113 Gliders also brought in 1,736 vehicles and 263 artillery pieces. 3,342 tons of ammunition and other supplies were brought by glider and parachute drop.

Canal at Son before being secured by the 101st Airborne Division. The 82nd Airborne Division's failure to capture the main road bridge over the river Waal at Nijmegen before 20th September also delayed the advance of XXX Corps.

At the furthest point of the airborne operation at Arnhem, the British 1st Airborne Division encountered initial strong resistance. Delays in capturing the bridges at Son and Nijmegen gave time for German forces, including armoured divisions, to be moved into Arnhem from Germany. In the ensuing battle, only a small force commanded by Lieutenant Colonel John Frost of Bruneval fame, whose 2nd Parachute Battalion was to take the three bridges over the Rhine at Arnhem, managed to capture the north end of the Arnhem road bridge and after the ground forces failed to relieve them, the paratroopers were overrun on 21st September. The remainder of the 1st Airborne Division were trapped in a small pocket west of the bridge, having to be evacuated on 25th September.

The two American airborne divisions lost 3,664 men together: 1,432 from 82nd Airborne, 2,110 from 101st Airborne and 122 glider pilots. The total losses for 1st Airborne Corps were 6,858 men. Second British Army's casualties for 'Market-Garden' are estimated to have been 5,354 including 1,480 for XXX Corps, giving a total of 16,805 Allied casualties. Generalfeldmarschall Model estimated Army Group B casualties' in 'Market-Garden' at 3,300, but other calculations place them as high as 2,000 dead and 6,000 wounded.

The OB West report on 'Market-Garden' produced in October 1944 gave the decision to spread the airborne landings over more than one day as the main reason for the Allied failure. A Luftwaffe analysis added that the airborne landings were spread too thinly and made too far from the Allied front line.

The failure of 'Market Garden' ended Allied expectations of finishing the war by Christmas 1944. Despite all the command failures and mishaps, the performance of the airborne troops was magnificent. The Rhine remained a barrier to the Allies advance into Germany until offensives at Remagen, Oppenheim, Rees and Wesel in March 1945.

Appendix D

Operation 'Biting' February 1942

Operation 'Biting' was the code name given to a British Combined Operations raid on a German radar installation at Bruneval near Le Havre in northern France on the night of 27/28 February 1942. A number of these installations were identified from RAF aerial reconnaissance photographs during 1941, but their exact purpose and the nature of the equipment that they possessed was not known. However, a number of British scientists believed that these stations were connected with the heavy losses being experienced by RAF bombers conducting bombing raids against targets in Occupied Europe. The scientists requested that one of these installations be raided and the technology it possessed be studied and, if possible, extracted and brought back to Britain for further examination. Due to the extensive coastal defences erected by the Germans to protect the installation from a seaborne raid, it was believed that a Commando raid from the sea would suffer heavy losses and give sufficient time for the garrison at the installation to destroy the Würzburg radar set. (Already capable in 1940 of controlling flak and searchlights, Würzburg had since been adapted to control night-fighters). It was therefore decided that an airborne assault using twelve Whitley transport aircraft followed by seaborne evacuation would be the most practical way to surprise the garrison of the installation, seize the technology intact and minimise casualties to the raiding force. 51 Squadron under Wing Commander Percy Charles Pickard was selected to provide the aircraft and aircrew needed for the operation and 120 men of 'C' Company in the 2nd Parachute Battalion commanded by Major John Frost were selected to carry out the raid. Nearly all the men were drawn from Scottish regiments. They were to be accompanied by a technical expert, an RAF radar operator, Flight Sergeant C.W.H. Cox. His job was to identify the components needed and to remove them from the Würzburg. Cox, a former cinema projectionist, was ill equipped for such an operation. He had never been in a ship, or on an aircraft, before!

HITLER'S INVASION OF EAST ANGLIA, 1940

The Würzburg antenna was erected between a villa and the cliff. It consisted of a parabolic antenna about 10 feet in diameter, which worked in conjunction with 'Freya' to locate British bombers and then direct Luftwaffe night fighters to attack them. The two systems complemented each other: 'Freya' was a long-range early-warning radar system, but lacked precision, whereas Würzburg had a much shorter range but was far more precise. Würzburg also had the advantage of being much smaller than the 'Freya' system and easier to manufacture in the quantities needed by the Luftwaffe to defend German territory.

The radar station was permanently manned by Luftwaffe radar technicians and was surrounded by a number of guard posts and approximately thirty guards; the buildings in the small enclosure housed approximately 100 German troops, including another detachment of technicians. A platoon of German infantry was stationed to the south in Bruneval itself and was responsible for manning the defences guarding the evacuation beach; these included a strongpoint near the beach as well as pillboxes and machine gun nests on the top of the cliff overlooking the beach. The beach was not mined and had only sporadic barbed-wire defences, but it was patrolled regularly; a mobile reserve of infantry was believed to be available at one hour's notice and stationed some distance inland.

All but two of the twelve Whitleys put down their loads at the right time and place. The main force assaulted the villa in which the radar equipment was kept, killing several members of the German garrison and capturing the installation after a brief firefight. Flight Sergeant Cox dismantled the Würzburg radar array and removed several key pieces, after which the force withdrew to the evacuation beach. However, the detachment assigned to clear the beach had initially failed to do so, but the German force guarding it was soon eliminated with the help of the main force. The raiding troops were picked up by six landing craft and then transferred to several Motor Gun Boats. The journey back to Britain was uneventful, with the force being escorted by four destroyers and a flight of Spitfires.

The raid was entirely successful. Two men were killed in the operation and six were missing, all of whom survived the war. Two German prisoners were brought back, one of them the Wurzburg's operator. The German report on the raid commented: 'The operation of the British Commandos was well planned and executed with great discipline... although attacked by German soldiers they concentrated on their primary task.' The pieces of the radar that were brought back allowed British scientists to understand enemy advances in radar and to create countermeasures to neutralise them.

OPERATION 'BITING' FEBRUARY 1942

Examination of the components of the radar array showed that it was of a modular design that aided maintenance and made fixing faults far simpler than on similar British radar models. Examination of the radar array also allowed British scientists to conclude that they would have to deploy a countermeasure code-named 'Window' that had recently been developed. One final consequence of the raid was that the Telecommunications Research Establishment, where much of the Bruneval equipment was analysed and British radar systems were designed and tested, was moved further inland from Swanage on the southern coast of England to Malvern to ensure that it was not the target of a reprisal raid by German airborne forces.

Appendix E

Operation 'Jubilee'; the raid on Dieppe, 19 August 1942

Operation 'Jubilee', the assault on Dieppe on the northern coast of France began at 0500 hours on 19 August 1942 and by 1050 hours the Allied commanders were forced to call a retreat. Over 6,000 infantrymen, predominantly Canadian, were supported by The Calgary Regiment of the 1st Canadian Tank Brigade and a strong force of Royal Navy and smaller RAF landing contingents. It involved 5,000 Canadians, 1,000 British troops and fifty United States Army Rangers. Objectives included seizing and holding a major port for a short period, both to prove that it was possible and to gather intelligence. Upon retreat, the Allies also wanted to destroy coastal defences, port structures and all strategic buildings. The raid had the added objectives of boosting morale and demonstrating the firm commitment of the United Kingdom to open a western front in Europe. Virtually none of these objectives were met. Allied fire support was grossly inadequate and the raiding force was largely trapped on the beach by obstacles and German fire. Less than ten hours after the first landings, the last Allied troops had all been either killed, evacuated, or left behind to be captured by the Germans. Instead of a demonstration of resolve, the bloody fiasco showed the world that the Allies could not hope to invade France for a long time. Some intelligence successes were achieved, including electronic intelligence.

A total of 3,367 of the 6,086 men (almost 60%) who made it ashore were killed, wounded, or captured. The RAF failed to lure the Luftwaffe into open battle and lost 106 aircraft (at least 32 to flak or accidents), compared to 48 lost by the Luftwaffe. The Royal Navy lost 33 landing craft and one destroyer.

From a topographical viewpoint there were few locations on France's coast that were less suited to an assault landing. The 100 feet and 200 feet cliffs lining the main landing beaches were ideally suited for enfilade fire on the assault troops. The German defenders themselves were well aware that

OPERATION 'JUBILEE'; THE RAID ON DIEPPE, 19 AUGUST 1942

the depth of the beach shale made it an unsatisfactory landing ground for tanks. The information on the German defences was hopelessly out of date while more up to date information was available through 'Enigma' decrypts but was unfortunately, never passed down to the assault commanders. The assault was viable only when certain conditions of time and tide prevailed. These conditions (high tide at or near dawn) were as well known to the German forces as they were to the British planners. It was not surprising that during these periods of potential threat German forces would be on heightened alert. Despite this the plan counted on tactical surprise. Bombing was not a precision tool at the time of Dieppe when pin point accuracy was needed to keep German defenders running for cover. It's conceivable therefore that a much heavier weight of offshore bombardment was needed than was provided. If heavier capital ships had been present they could have kept the defenders heads down until the troops were within a few metres of the beach.

Appendix F

Operation 'Deadstick', June 1944

This was the codename for an operation by airborne forces of the British Army that took place on 5th/6th June 1944 as part of the Normandy landings. The objective was to capture intact two road bridges in Normandy across the Orne River and the Caen Canal providing the only exit eastwards, for British forces from their landing on Sword Beach. The object of this action was to prevent German armour from crossing the bridges and attacking the eastern flank of the landings at Sword Beach and was vital to the success of the Operation 'Tonga', the British airborne landings. Failure to capture the bridges intact or to prevent their demolition by the Germans would leave the 6th Airborne Division cut off from the rest of the Allied armies with their backs to the two waterways. If the Germans retained control over the bridges, they could be used by their armoured divisions to attack the landing beaches of Normandy. The 3rd Infantry Division and the commandoes of the 1st Commando Brigade were scheduled to land at Sword Beach at 0600 on the day then advance to the bridges where they were expected to arrive at 1100. Intelligence reports said both bridges were heavily defended by the Germans and wired for demolition. The Ranville Bridge spanning the River Orne was guarded by fifty men of the 736th Grenadier Regiment, 716th Infanterie Division commanded by Major Hans Schmidt and based at Ranville, 1.2 miles east of the River. On the west bank of the Bénouville Bridge, which crosses the Caen Canal there were three machine-gun emplacements and on the east bank a machine-gun and an anti-tank gun. To their north were another three machine-guns and a concrete pillbox. An anti-aircraft tower equipped with machine-guns stood to the south. At the Orne River Bridge, the eastern bank south of the bridge had a pillbox with anti-tank and anti-aircraft guns. To the north of the bridge were two machine-guns. Both bridges had sandbagged trench systems along the banks. Once captured, the bridges had to be held against any counter-attack until the assault force was relieved by commandos and infantry advancing from the British landing zone.

OPERATION 'DEADSTICK', JUNE 1944

A force of 181 men, led by Major John Howard, took off from RAF Tarrant Rushton in Dorset, southern England in six Horsa gliders towed by Halifax bombers to capture the bridges. The force was composed of 'D' Company (reinforced with two platoons of 'B' Company), 2nd Battalion, Oxford and Bucks Light Infantry, part of the 6th Airborne Division; twenty sappers of the Royal Engineers of 249 Field Company (Airborne); and men of the Glider Pilot Regiment.

Staff Sergeant Jim Wallwork, the first glider pilot to land, recalled: 'In training the briefing was very succinct: 'You will be towed at one-minute intervals to 4,000 feet, which will take about one hour. You will then release three miles away at a point decided by your tug, from where you will be able to see triangles marked with broad white tape. Numbers 1 and 2 and 3 will land on one, making a right hand circuit and 4, 5 and 6 on t'other from a left hand circuit. A daylight tow was made at various times and height was eventually set at 6,000 feet and two separate course and times developed. Gliders 1-3 to fly a three-sided path and 4-6 a dog-leg pattern. We were towed in line astern at one-minute intervals. Broadly, 1-3 flew downwind leg of 180 degrees at 90 mph for 3 minutes 40 seconds; then a 90-degree Rate One turn right on to second course for 2 minutes 5 seconds and a last 90-degree turn right for the run in, by which time the target should be directly ahead. Gliders 4-6 cast off at the same spot; operated half then full flap and in a dog-leg course flew in straight to the target. The drill in flight was to cast off at 90 mph while turning onto the decided course, immediately I was 'On', the co-pilot operated the stopwatch and timing started, countdown by Ainsworth, 'Five, Four, Three, Two, One, Zero and I made a controlled Rate One right turn to course 2: and when I was 'On' again Johnnie restarted the watch, Another countdown and at zero, another 90-degree turn right and the target lay ahead. At last we were told where and why the two bridges over the River Orne and Caen Canal had to be taken intact and held. Gliders 1-3, flying the three course path, were to take the canal, while 4-6 would drop straight down and take the river. We took off at 2245 through low cloud and into the clear at 6,000 feet over the Channel. It was a smooth flight and Howard encouraged the men to sing - none were airsick. Thanks to our tug crew we were dead on time and dead on target. 'Cast Off'. The singing stopped and that was when six Horsas tiptoes quietly into two little fields in Normandy and released 180 fighting men in full battle order to give the German garrison the surprise of their lives.

'The tug pilot said, 'Weather's good, the clouds are at 600 feet, a couple of minutes before we cast off. And we all wish you the best of luck'.

Alter course, air speed right, John Ainsworth with the stopwatch, I'm checking the compass; he's checking the air speed. We cruise along and then 5…4…3…2…1…bingo, right turn to starboard onto course. Halfway down the crosswind leg I could see it all, the river and the canal like strips of silver in the moonlight. Visibility was good - the temptation to fly in was forgotten as training, training and more training took over. I duly completed the crosswind leg as Johnnie timed me, made the regulation rate-one turn and there as expected was the target straight ahead. The final approach was a little fast and I landed probably at about 95 mph instead of 85 and 10 mph in the dark looks rather quick. I hit the field and caught the first bit of wire and so I called 'Stream' and by golly, the parachute lifted the tail and forced the nose down. It drew us back and knocked the speed down tremendously. It was only on for two seconds and 'jettison' and Ainsworth pressed the tit and jettisoned the parachute. Then we were going along only about 60, which was ample to take me right into the corner. We got right into the corner of the field, the nose wheel doors had gone. The cockpit collapsed and Ainsworth and I went right through the cockpit. I went over head first and landed flat on my stomach. I was stunned, as was Ainsworth. I came around and he seemed to be in bad shape. I said 'Can you crawl?' and he said 'No,' and then I asked if I lifted, could he crawl out and he said, 'I'll try'. I lifted the thing and I felt that I lifted the whole bloody glider when probably all I lifted was a small spar, but I felt like thirty men when I picked this thing up and managed to crawl out.

'Although we made an awful noise on landing we seemed not to bother the German sentries. I was stunned and pinned under the collapsed cockpit, but the troops were getting on with it. Exactly one minute later No.2 arrived and joined in, followed by No.3. This all justified those training flights. Long afterwards we all confessed to feeling rather pleased with ourselves at having pulled it off; this when 6th June was twenty minutes old and our little battle was just starting. Air Chief Marshal Sir Trafford Leigh-Mallory called it the greatest flying feat of the Second World War.'

From sixteen minutes past midnight five of the Ox and Bucks's gliders (three landing near the Canal de Caen Bridge, subsequently renamed 'Pegasus Bridge') and two others near the undefended Orne River Bridge) as close as 47 yards from their objectives. The attackers poured out of their battered gliders, completely surprising the German defenders and took the bridges within ten minutes. Two men were killed. Lieutenant Den Brotheridge was shot through the neck crossing the Ranville Bridge in the first minutes of the assault and Lance Corporal Fred Greenhalgh drowned in a nearby pond when his glider landed. Brotheridge thus became the first member of the invading Allied armies to die as a result of enemy fire on D-Day.

A sixth glider, assigned to the capture of the river bridge, landed at the bridge over the River Dives, seven miles away. Most of the soldiers in this glider moved through German lines towards the village of Ranville where they eventually re-joined the British forces. The Ox and Bucks were reinforced half-an-hour after the landings by 7th Parachute Battalion and linked up with the beach landing forces with the arrival of Lord Lovat's Commandos.

Appendix G

'Secrecy over Wartime File Remains Baffling'

A great many profound secrets are somewhere in print, but are most easily detected when one knows what to seek?
Sir Lewis Bernstein Namier (1888-1960)

On Monday, 4th June 1945, just four weeks after VE Day and just a month away from Britain's first General Election since 1935, *The Times* and the *Daily Express* revealed what was claimed to be: 'The truth about the war rumour that swept the world.' Beneath bold headlines proclaiming, 'FLAMING SEA BURNED GERMAN ARMY - 1940 invasion secret out' the *Daily Express* told its readers that: 'The rumour that swept the world in September 1940 that a German invasion against England had been destroyed by 'setting the sea on fire' was fostered by British intelligence'. *The Times* said much the same, although in a slightly less sensational manner. On its back page the *Express* referred to other stories of invasion attempts being 'wiped out' and hundreds of bodies washed up on the south coast' and that 'The secret of what really happened was revealed last night by Mr. Geoffrey Lloyd, Minister of Information'. Lloyd, who in 1940 had been minister for petroleum[114] was quoted as saying that British intelligence agencies had fostered the burning sea rumour overseas and it was allowed to grow and was whispered through the ranks of the Wehrmacht with disastrous effects on morale.

'It always seemed to happen that when we were conducting full-scale experiments and making a tremendous blaze there was a German aeroplane about' recalled Lloyd. 'On many occasions it came and bombed

---

114   It was not until August 1944 that the existence of the PWD was revealed to the public for the first time when Geoffrey Lloyd held a press conference and released details of assorted petroleum weapons. Quoted in *Myths & Legends of the Second World War* by James Hayward (Sutton, 2003).

'SECRECY OVER WARTIME FILE REMAINS BAFFLING'

us. In this way the Germans must have known what we were doing and in fact they showed us they expected us to use flames as a defence, for they carried out experiments with asbestos suits. And the Germans killed thousands of their own troops in an effort to restore confidence where terror of the fire weapon spread fastest - through the ranks of the Wehrmacht. They arranged a great demonstration to show that specially equipped troops could pass unscathed even if the sea was on fire. Thousands of asbestos suits were made and each man of the troops to take part in the demonstration wore one (10,000 asbestos suits were ordered in Paris alone). Huge quantities of oil were spread off the French coast and set on fire. The trial armada set out - to disaster. A large number of the headpieces of the suits were defective and the men inside were roasted to death. For weeks afterwards the burnt bodies of German soldiers were being washed up on the south coast.'

With these new revelations the rumours of attempted invasion and German bodies on east coast beaches had finally been solved, or so it seemed. But in the House of Commons on 18th November 1946 Clement Attlee, now Prime Minister was asked by a backbencher, Sir Hugh Lucas-Tooth: 'if the prime minister will now make a statement about the German plans for invading this country in 1940; and also about the circumstances which led up to all military units in the United Kingdom receiving a warning that invasion was impending on the evening of a date in September 1940.' In his written reply Attlee stated: 'It has been widely believed in this country that a German invasion attempt was actually launched in 1940. This belief is based partly on the fact that a number of German bodies were washed up on the South coast of England between Great Yarmouth and Cornwall in August and September 1940 following RAF raids on enemy embarkation exercises along the French coast; and partly on the knowledge that the 'invasion imminent' signal was issued by General Headquarters, Home Forces on 7th September 1940.' The general public may have been unaware of Attlee's statement, but what he said was repeated by Winston Churchill in his book *Their Finest Hour*, published in 1949. 'During August the corpses of about forty German soldiers were washed up at scattered points along the coast between the Isle of Wight and Cornwall. The Germans had been practicing embarkation in the barges along the French coast. Some of these barges put out to sea to escape British bombing and were sunk, either by the bombing or bad weather. This was the source of a widespread rumour that Germans had attempted an invasion and had suffered either by drowning or by being burnt in patches of sea covered in flaming oil.' And he added a little spin of his own: 'We took no steps to contradict such tales, which spread freely through the occupied countries in a wildly exaggerated form and gave much encouragement to the oppressed populations. In Brussels, for instance, a shop exhibited men's bathing suits marked 'For Channel Swimming.'

The 'corpses of German soldiers' were none other than those from the armed trawlers sunk north of Calais on 11 October 1940 by the three Felixstowe-based motor torpedo boats, using Dover as a forward base, when they captured a total of 34 crewmen and 'several others' were drowned. The arrival of these bodies, according to Attlee, should have been recorded in the war diaries of coastal units stationed along the south eastern seaboard but they are not. Apart from the German infantry corporal washed ashore at Littlestone there appears to be no other recorded incidents of this nature in any war diary. Under established protocols both the British and German governments were obliged to record the details of enemy casualties and pass them on via the International Red Cross but no records of thirty (or more) corpses being washed ashore along the coastline from Yarmouth to Cornwall appear to exist.

Even before Attlee had made his statement Britain had begun the massive task of rebuilding itself after almost six long years of war and whatever may or may not have happened in September 1940 was of little interest to Britain's war-weary population. But in the fifties things changed. In 1950 CAB 101/347 'German Army Plans for Operation 'Sealion' July-October 1940'[115] was compiled by the 'historical branch' of the Cabinet Office. Basically a 'retrospective' overview of the German planning for 'Sealion', it was created using a number of sources, including captured enemy documents. Much of it has been repeated many times, including the assertion that the Germans seemed to view the whole operation as no more than a 'river crossing'. However, it is noted that the landing, as planned, 'would have taken place on a broad front in order to reduce the effectiveness of [British] counter attack divisions held in the rear.' The Germans were also aware that by mid-August 1940 the greatest strength of British forces had been 'focused on the southern coast,' anticipating that this is where the attack would fall. From this evidence it appears that if the German build up in France really was a feint, it was working. It is also revealed that the Germans, realising it would be impossible to conceal the invasion

---

115 This slim folder is now in the National Archives at Kew.

preparations, set out to 'camouflage actual invasion assembly areas by activity along the whole [European] coast.' By mid-August invasion preparations were in progress along the continental coastline from western France to the Baltic involving thousands of troops (more than would have been used in an actual invasion). With this level of activity over such an extended front it would have been difficult, if not impossible, for the British to determine from where exactly the invasion would come.

The file also reveals that the Germans were preparing several major diversionary operations, including a surprise assault in force between the Wash and Harwich, followed by an advance south west to secure a line from Peterborough to Maldon in Essex. At the same time, following a landing on the northeast coast, another force would advance south threatening the Midlands and Birmingham. Apparently, full preparations for the diversionary attacks went ahead with only a very few senior commanding officers aware that the operations were intended as a feint. In effect, during the summer of 1940 preparations were being made for not just one, but at least three separate landings. Therefore, conceivably, it would have been possible for the Germans to have launched several simultaneous assaults and exploited the one yielding the most immediate success, while the others split the defending forces. The file ends: 'The extent of the military preparations described here, when added to those of the [German] navy, should clearly prove the reality of the German threat to the UK during those three anxious months of 1940'.

In 1955 *The Big Lie*, a memoir by John Baker White was published. Born on 12th August 1902, Baker White graduated from Malvern College in 1920. In the early 1920s he was a member of the Anti-Socialist Union and was part of a tendency within that group that sought to co-operate with the British Fascists. He then worked for the Economic League, a privately funded anti-Communist pressure group and intelligence organization, serving as its Director from 1926 to 1939. Immediately before the war, he spent time in Germany as a spy; accepted there as an ardent anti-communist, he was invited to attend the Nuremberg Rally of 1937; he wrote about this experience in *Dover Nurenberg Return*. After publicly exposing Nazi propaganda and fifth column activity, he was obliged to slip out of Germany in April 1939. He joined Section D and was a leading figure in Britain's propaganda campaign, including attempts to convince German soldiers of a failed German landing attempt along the south coast of England. The job of Baker White and of his handful of co-workers was to fabricate stories to be fed to the enemy and give him a quite false impression of the state of Britain's defences.[116]

In 1940 Baker White was a major serving with the Directorate of Military Intelligence under the newly appointed DMI, Major-General F. J. 'Paddy' Beaumont-Nesbitt. Nesbitt was convinced that Germany would attempt an invasion of the British Isles, even going so far to inform the Joint Intelligence Committee in September that 'anyone who says the Germans will not invade is mad.' In August Baker White was assigned to a small DMI sub-section operating from offices in Berkeley Square, whose brief was the delivery of propaganda and disinformation to enemy troops. 'Our task was not to stop the Germans finding out about the real state of our defences. That was the job of the security agencies. What we had to do was to create in the minds of the German High Command and of Hitler himself a completely fictitious picture of what they would have to face if they launched an invasion attempt. A picture of a powerfully armed Britain and above all armed with new weapons of terrible destructive power. We had to put over the 'Big Lie'. We know today that the aim was achieved. A combination formed of the vigilance of the RAF and our security forces blindfolded the German Staff planners and compelled Hitler to seek information from rumours culled from the secret reports of hundreds of Gestapo and Abwehr agents in neutral countries. By methods that must remain forever secret, Britain supplied many of the rumours. I cannot say today, any more than I could have said at the time, how the thought and the wish became a rumour that was to go around the world. Certainly I do not claim complete authorship. I believe that, as in the case of so many successful rumours, it was not any one man's invention but was born from conversation between two or three people devoting their thoughts and discussion to the same question.

'Before the rumour was fed into the pipeline that ran to the bar of the Grand Hotel in Stockholm, the Avenida in Lisbon, the Ritz in Madrid and other places in Cairo, Istanbul, Ankara and elsewhere, not forgetting New York, it had to get over certain hurdles, including the committee that had to study all rumours before they were launched. This was a very necessary precaution, because it was quite possible for the rumour inventors to manufacture a story that would quite unwittingly disclose something of

---

116 He was elected Member of Parliament for Canterbury in the 1945 General Election and served until 1953. He was also chair of the Freedom Association in Kent and he published three other autobiographical books: *It's Gone for Good*, *Sabotage is Suspected* and *True Blue*.

'SECRECY OVER WARTIME FILE REMAINS BAFFLING'

operational importance… The burning sea story was our first large-scale attempt at a 'Big Lie' and it proved amazingly successful. It was 'produced by people who were still amateurs at the game and projected through a machine still far from complete. But it worked.

'When we engaged upon building up the Burning Sea deception we considered a hundred and one ways of adding substance to it. One ingenious plan involved the use of human bodies… Our scheme was to take the charred bodies of Luftwaffe men shot down in the Battle of Britain, dress them in the burnt uniforms of German infantry soldiers and float them ashore on the tide at various points along the invasion coast…[117] So far as I know, it was never put into operation but it had a much more important counterpart later in the war.'[118]

In 1957 *Invasion 1940* written by Peter Fleming was published. Fleming asked: 'Did the Germans launch an abortive attempt at invasion? How many corpses in field grey were washed up on the south coast? Did the British set the sea on fire?' Fleming was of the opinion that none of this could have happened and concludes that the rumour that swept the country in 1940 was: 'spontaneous, baseless and inexplicable.' On Friday, 22nd November 1957, through the new medium of television, the wartime generation was confronted with the mysterious rumours of 1940 once again. *The Finest Hour*, broadcast as part of the BBC's *First Hand* series, recalled 'the tense days when Britain prepared for a German onslaught' The *Radio Times* listing promised films and photographs from British and German sources, as well as 'eye-witness' contributions from Peter Fleming, Major General A. J. H. Dove and General Günther Blumentritt.[119]

---

117 If true, the scheme would never, have been cleared for publication under the D notice procedure and an embargo would last forever, either for reasons of national security, to protect confidential information supplied by the public, or where publication of records would distress or embarrass any living person.

118 *The Man Who Never Was*.

119 Blumentritt (10 February 1892-12 October 1967) was a German officer in WWI who became a Staff Officer under the Weimar Republic and went on to serve as a general for Nazi Germany during WWII. He served throughout the war, mostly on the Western Front and mostly as a Staff Officer, though he was eventually given his own Corps and made a General der Infanterie. Instrumental in planning the 1939 German invasion of Poland and the 1940 invasion of France, he participated in Operation 'Barbarossa' and afterward bore a large part of the responsibility for planning the defence of the Atlantic Wall and Normandy. Blumentritt gave an affidavit at the Nuremberg Trials, though he never testified in person and then later helped in the rearmament of Germany during the Cold War and the development of the modern German army.

HITLER'S INVASION OF EAST ANGLIA, 1940

A number of other participants included William Robinson, a former gunner in the Royal Artillery who over a period of several days and along with others, helped to collect the bodies of Germans from the beaches between St. Mary's Bay and Hythe. He said: 'The first day we found two soldiers. They had no badges. Later we found five more.' Robinson was definite that the bodies were soldiers, not aircrew. He also maintained that the corpses had been in the water for some time and appeared to have been 'slightly burned on the lower part of the body.' He was 'officially' told and he believed that the bodies had floated across the Channel after the RAF had 'caught them on a pre-invasion manoeuvre'. Robinson was searching the beach in the sector patrolled regularly by the 5th Battalion, Somerset Light Infantry, a patrol of which had found the body of the German infantry corporal several miles further down the coast on Sunday, 20th October. This is recorded in both the battalion's war diary and that of the 135th Infantry Brigade. If, according to Robinson, the corpses of at least eight other German soldiers had been found on the beach in this sector, why were special details being drafted from far off and organised to collect this relatively small number? It seems a lot of effort for a relatively minor task that could have been carried out by local troops stationed in the respective areas. And what happened to these bodies? According to Robinson the bodies were taken to 'some kind of improvised mortuary' at New Romney where all items of identification were collected by an NCO before burial. Were they disposed of without trace and remain hidden away in unmarked burial pits or were they buried in local cemeteries and then exhumed and re-interred at the Deutsche Soldatenfriedhof, the large German War Cemetery at Cannock Chase, Staffordshire, during the 1960s? The vast majority of the 3,700 graves are identified by name rank and number. There are however ninety headstones that bear no name. Robinson's story seems to suggest that some kind of orchestrated cover-up had taken place, but the British and German governments were obliged under the Geneva Convention to pass information concerning enemy casualties to the International Red Cross. If bodies had been collected in secret from a Kent beach the same could have been done on a Suffolk beach where the men of the Suffolk regiment had been dispatched from Bury St. Edmunds to beaches near Shingle Street in order to pick up German bodies.[120]

---

120 A 1992 investigation revealed that some cemeteries in the eastern region do have a few headstones bearing the inscription 'Ein Deutscher Soldat', literally translated as 'A German Soldier' (at time of writing there is one such headstone in the war graves section of Lowestoft cemetery). Almost as soon as the existence of the mystery graves was revealed there were counterclaims that the inscription is in fact a general term, simply meaning 'a German serviceman' and that the body in the grave was in all probability an unidentified airman.

'SECRECY OVER WARTIME FILE REMAINS BAFFLING'

As the post-war austerity of the 1950s gave way to the 'Swinging Sixties', wartime stories of an attempted invasion and a burning sea had faded into almost total obscurity. As for Shingle Street itself, by 1949, after what must have seemed to them to have been an eternity, the inhabitants had at last been allowed to return to completely rebuilt homes. The old ramshackle wooden bungalows had been replaced by modern dwellings and the isolated hamlet on the Suffolk coast could finally return to its quiet existence. Those who could tell anything of the strange events that had taken place there in 1940 became forgotten voices - at least for the time being. Post-war the stories surrounding Shingle Street had become no more than local tales, remembered only by a few and occasionally told in hushed tones to the curious and anyone else who cared to listen. But on Saturday, 3rd August 1974 on the inside pages of the *East Anglian Daily Times*, barely noticeable alongside the car sales and Public Notices, was a short article that undoubtedly grabbed the attention of many older readers. Beneath the heading: 'WAR FILE ON HAMLET CLOSED FOR FORTY YEARS', it was revealed that the contents of - HO 207/1175 - a wartime file on Shingle Street held at the Public Record Office, Kew, had been placed under a 75-year extended closure order, which puzzled some researchers. Extended closure is only possible with the approval of the Lord Chancellor and is granted for reasons that may include highly confidential information or related to national security. The same source also stated that: 'it was not known which category this file fell into but the maximum embargo is 100 years.' Norman Scarfe, a local historian and former resident of Shingle Street was quoted as saying, 'I cannot imagine what happened could still be regarded as highly confidential.' Obviously someone still regarded something as 'highly confidential' or 'sensitive' enough for this file to be kept closed until 2021 and not released, like thousands of other wartime files, under the more usual '30 year rule.' There was speculation that the secrecy might be associated with the top secret radar station at Bawdsey Manor.[121] Or perhaps it related to Orfordness and the secret military work that had taken place there in both world wars. Whatever the case, the obvious reluctance of the PRO to release

---

121 In the 1950s the Bawdsey CH station was upgraded as part of the ROTOR programme and gained an underground control centre with living quarters and air filtration to make it capable of operating during nuclear attack. The command centre was accessed by way of a small bungalow which can be seen on the left of the road which runs from Bawdsey village to Bawdsey Manor. The Manor continued as an RAF base throughout the Cold War and Bloodhound missiles were sited on the cliffs until the Bloodhound force ceased operations in 1990, when all the missiles were withdrawn to RAF West Raynham. RAF Bawdsey was closed in 1991.

HITLER'S INVASION OF EAST ANGLIA, 1940

a secret file relating directly to Shingle Street seemed to lend some credence to the wartime stories.

Best-selling author Jack Higgins would later recall that during research for his book, *The Eagle Has Landed*, which was first published in 1975 and made into a feature film in 1976, he had heard rumours in Suffolk pubs of 'Germans dressed as British soldiers turning up on the shoreline.' He is also on record as saying that the plot of the book, which involves a German commando unit disguised as allied paratroopers, is 50% historical fact. Higgins was not the only one to be intrigued by wartime stories of beaches littered with German corpses, but at the time that is all they seemed to be, just stories. The first indication that there might be something more to these curious tales appeared when a local newspaper revealed the existence of a secret wartime file. A file that for some unknown reason the authorities seemed eager to keep sealed - for as long as possible. Higgins made the astute observation that the original events may never have been recorded in the first place, therefore it was: 'hardly surprising that the reports cloaked the real facts.'

In *East Anglia at War* published in 1978 Derek Johnson devotes half a page to Shingle Street, including the evacuation of the hamlet and the extended ban on the mystery file at the PRO. He also speculated that the area and specifically Orfordness may have been used as a proving ground for secret weapons including early atomic experiments. The author stated that during the course of his research, locals, including former wartime police and coastguard, had revealed that they knew things but 'refused to divulge any information' and he also reveals that later in the war, long after the invasion period, the hamlet had been used for some kind of bomb trials. Johnson also makes an unconnected but nonetheless interesting reference to the wartime defences of nearby Felixstowe that included a 'novel flame gun'. Apparently a series of giant flame-throwers had been situated at several strategic points along the east coast ready to meet the German invasion armada with a 'sea of blazing oil.'

An unidentified skeleton was found in mud beside the River Ore near to Shingle Street, in June 1985 and was taken to Gorleston Hospital and examined by Home Office pathologist Dr. David Harrison. It was revealed that 'the skeleton was of a man believed to be 18 to 20 years old, 5 feet 7 inches tall' but no details were given as to how the man had died, or how long he had been lying in the mud. No positive identification has ever been forthcoming. As far as can be ascertained there appears to have been a strange reluctance on the part of the authorities to investigate these remains any

'SECRECY OVER WARTIME FILE REMAINS BAFFLING'

further. Enquiries have met with a curt rebuttal. All of this seems odd, given that ultra modem forensic techniques are now available and at a time when many police forces were actively pursuing cold cases that are even older.

In November 1987 many newspapers reported a ceremony commemorating a disaster that had taken place off Slapton Sands on the Devon coast early on the morning of 28 April 1944 when 749 American servicemen had been killed when a D-Day invasion exercise, codenamed Exercise 'Tiger', was attacked by German E-boats. Just as at Shingle Street, the residents of Slapton Sands had been evacuated, when in late 1943, the British Government set up a training ground to be used by Force 'U', the American forces tasked with landing on Utah Beach. Approximately 3,000 local residents in the area of Slapton were evacuated. Some had never left their villages before being evacuated. Within a week a writer to the letters page of the *East Anglian Daily Times* compared the long secrecy surrounding Slapton Sands[122] to that which still hung over Shingle Street: 'Someone in Whitehall knows and has taken stringent steps to suppress the truth'. The author, after acknowledging the 'reticence of Suffolk folk to talk', went on to pose the following questions: 'Would the facts explode the myth that the Germans did not land in England?' 'Was there a battle?' 'Did they really set the sea on fire or did the boffins at nearby Orford or Bawdsey come up with something that even now has potential or would cause condemnation from the rest of mankind?' This brief resurgence of interest was soon over and Shingle Street's wartime past slipped back into obscurity. Shingle Street hit the headlines again in

---

122 Several wartime disasters like this were 'covered-up' but only until the end of the war. (The casualty statistics for 'Tiger' were not released until August 1944, along with the casualties of the actual D-Day landings). On the night of 3 March 1943 172 people, 62 of them children, were crushed to death in an incident at the Bethnal Green Tube Shelter. The bodies were pulled out of the stairwell by civilian rescue workers then laid along on the pavement before being loaded onto lorries. By the next morning the pavements had been washed down, removing all evidence of the event. All those involved, even survivors pulled from the crush, were told not to say a word about what had happened. News of the event was also suppressed in the newspapers and the full details were not made public until after the war's end. All of this took place in a heavily populated area of London and yet the authorities still managed an effective cover-up. By comparison, removing dozens of German corpses from prohibited beaches in the defence areas, beaches that could easily be cordoned off, would have presented no problems. On 27 March 1943 the aircraft carrier HMS *Dasher* sank in the Firth of Clyde following a sudden and unexplained explosion. Immediately all details of the event were suppressed. Survivors were ordered not to talk about what had happened and the bodies of 379 men were buried in a mass unmarked grave. Again, details of the incident were not revealed until after the war.

1992 when the MoD stated: 'There is no evidence of any German invasion attempt or even German commando-style raids by sea or air. Indeed, there is no evidence in either the most highly classified contemporary British records, or apparently in contemporary German records, of an actual attempt by the Germans to land in Britain' [and] 'there was no evidence to suggest that 'British troops dressed in German uniforms landed at Shingle Street' [and] there are no records of large numbers of bodies being recovered from Suffolk beaches during August or September 1940. Any bodies washed ashore were those of German aircrew shot down by the RAF, or German soldiers killed while rehearsing for an invasion of the UK.'

On Friday, 6th March 1992 the tranquil slumber of Hollesley Bay was disturbed by an arresting article on page 15 of the *East Anglian Daily Times*, appeared beneath the headline: 'SECRECY OVER WARTIME FILE REMAINS BAFFLING'. There was speculation that the 'classified' file contained 'politically sensitive' information about a disaster or loss of life and suggested that the information might relate to pre D-Day manoeuvres of wartime exercises at Shingle Street involving the 79th Armoured Division, or the development of radar at Bawdsey Manor. The article ended by stating that the Ministry of Defence was unable to comment on the new information and briefly mentioned the wartime incident at Slapton Sands. The following day Shingle Street finally made it onto the front page with the bold headlines: 'DOZENS KILLED IN WARTIME BLUNDER' and the sub heading, 'British soldiers died as sea set on fire'. Henry Creagh revealed to readers that: 'Dozens of British soldiers were burnt to death by one of their own men in a wartime exercise on the Suffolk coast which went tragically wrong, it was claimed yesterday. New information has come to the *East Anglian Daily Times* about the secret of Shingle Street, an isolated coastal hamlet which was evacuated in 1940 for use by the armed forces. The incident allegedly occurred during a training exercise near the radar installation at Bawdsey, just south of Shingle Street. Part of the base's defences consisted of drums of petrol chained to concrete blocks under the sea and wired to detonators. In case of an enemy assault from the sea, the drums would be blown and the petrol would rise to the surface, where it could be set alight using tracer rounds. The Army had decided to carry out a mock assault on Bawdsey and contacted the base to say it would be doing so, but somehow the message was not passed on. Later that night, a sentry saw rubber dinghies approaching the base and, assuming it was the enemy, detonated the charges. The petrol was set alight by tracer bullets from a machine gun post. Many soldiers died in the inferno and their bodies

'SECRECY OVER WARTIME FILE REMAINS BAFFLING'

were carried out on the tide, only to be washed up at Shingle Street. The Ministry of Defence could not comment on the claims. The *East Anglian Daily Times'* source was said to be an anonymous telephone caller 'close to the Ministry of Defence' who had seen the classified papers by chance. Although the MoD mole allegedly telephoned on a second occasion, the *East Anglian Daily Times'* news desk were given no name or contact number and the source fell silent after the story broke nationally in wildly exaggerated form. Crucially, Creagh's report omitted one important detail: the tragedy was said to have occurred during training for the Normandy landings, presumably in 1944.[123]

On Tuesday, 10th March an intriguing story concerning Shingle Street appeared on page 4 of the *East Anglian Daily Times* and on Anglia Television News. John Rux-Burton, a Long Melford gallery owner, claimed that his grandfather John Edgar Burton, a former wartime intelligence officer with the Naval Intelligence Division had seen 'dozens' of charred bodies in British uniforms on the beach near Shingle Street after being sent there following reports that a German force had attempted to invade. Initially he was led to believe that they were Germans dressed as British soldiers but shortly afterwards he was told by an army officer that they were British soldiers who had been killed by accident when an exercise had gone wrong. However John Burton was suspicious because a rubber dinghy he saw at the scene had German markings. The dinghy was subsequently removed and all involved were told to 'keep quiet, it never happened.' (During October 1940 the Admiralty's chief officer in Harwich did express the concern that 'enemy troops disguised in British uniforms may enter Harwich by train.') Apparently the incident had a profound effect on Mr. Burton senior and eventually led to the end of his career in Naval Intelligence. His grandson stated that 'he always maintained the truth of his story.'

Within days of the Rux Burton story appearing a former soldier came forward with evidence that seemed to support it. In 1940 Tom Smith had been a signaller with the Royal Artillery at Kessingland. He recalled a 'terrific flap one night with lots of lights and anti-aircraft fire down the

---

[123] *Myths & Legends of the Second World War* by James Hayward. The story was declared secret until 2014, but was leaked in the *Daily Mail* in 1992. In the article it was stated that Mr. Ron Harris, a resident of Shingle Street since before the war and a former coastguard, was allowed to stay in Shingle Street after the other inhabitants had been compulsorily evacuated. He did recall receiving written orders to look out for charred bodies, but he could not remember the exact date of the orders or any incident when the sea was set on fire.

coast'. At first he had assumed it was an air raid, but the word going around the following day was that an advance party of Germans, in British uniform, had attempted a landing and had all been killed. He distinctly remembered being told that it was an invasion attempt and recalled that there were 'stories of German bodies in the sea, but it was all hushed up.'

A few days later another newspaper story involving a military style bag found five years earlier in 1987 by a member of the Suffolk Underwater Studies Group on the seabed off Bawdsey was also linked to the mystery. The bag was said to have contained WWII equipment including ammunition and documents. The report suggested that the bag 'could have belonged to an officer involved in the secret Shingle Street wartime operation'. The stories were beginning to suggest that a German invasion attempt was at the heart of the mystery, rather than the supposed 'friendly fire' incident. However, as the continuing story unfolded others came forward offering different solutions to the riddle: A local history teacher made the sensational claim that some civilians had refused to be evacuated and subsequent bombing by the RAF had caused casualties. A former wartime fireman from Woodbridge claimed that Barnes Wallis, of bouncing bomb fame had carried out secret tests with a special bomb at Shingle Street, but the tests had taken place in 1943.

On 5 April, beneath the headline: 'DID THE EAGLE REALLY LAND?' the *Sunday Telegraph* devoted a double page spread to the Shingle Street mystery. The report began with the claims that there had been a tragic accident and then went on to the more dramatic theory that German commandoes in British uniform had attempted a raid on the radar station at Bawdsey Manor. It was alleged that Churchill himself had ordered that the dead bodies of the enemy invaders be buried in secret - and all records of the event destroyed. Pictured in the article was a facsimile of a file headed GOC Eastern Command Top Secret Bawdsey Manor August 1940: 'Category A risk, liable to seaborne attack, probably a smash and grab raid by a hundred men launched from a submarine or ship offshore'. The Rux Burton story was also featured, as did the story involving Barnes Wallis and the secret bomb test. A former Royal Marine sergeant, who had been posted to the area later in the war, told of villager's stories of a 'beach covered with bodies' at Shingle Street and 'the whole sea being set ablaze'. A former army major, who in 1940 had been on anti-invasion duties, stated that the stories had been 'going around for a long time'. While speculating that the raid theory was plausible, the article did state that 'in 1940 British 'black' propagandists merrily spread rumours of burnt German bodies to

'SECRECY OVER WARTIME FILE REMAINS BAFFLING'

undermine the morale of the Wehrmacht'. Obviously someone had done their homework and found the June 1945 report in the *Daily Express*. The *Telegraph* did raise a couple of interesting questions by asking: 'why do stories of Shingle Street persist when other wartime rumours have been long discounted' and why are government files relating to Shingle Street 'still closed'?

Stories continued to appear in the local press and television news almost on a daily basis. A former Home Guard recalled that his section had been given orders to search for enemy soldiers who may have come ashore 'after the sea had been set alight'. Pensioner Agnes Mann, who in 1940 had been a schoolgirl in Belgium, told of seeing 'hospital trains loaded with burned German soldiers' and recalled being told that they had attempted to invade England. On Anglia TV an elderly woman said that in September 1940 she had seen a mysterious convoy of army trucks winding through the back roads of Norfolk. She was told that they were loaded with the bodies of German soldiers that had been washed ashore following a failed invasion. John Rux-Burton also appeared on camera with his story, stating that the bodies his grandfather saw were: 'burnt beyond recognition.'

In the *East Anglian Daily Times* in June 1992 a man told how his uncle, a civilian lorry driver with a transport firm in Great Barton, 'had spent two days with other civilians in the Felixstowe area helping to clear the bodies of German soldiers from the shoreline.' This, it was claimed, had happened following a bungled German invasion attempt 'when the sea had been set alight.' This story seems to tie in with what was witnessed by former Flight Sergeant Philip Taylor, who served on 110 'Hyderabad' Squadron at Wattisham in Suffolk who claimed to have seen the actual bodies of German soldiers lying on Suffolk beaches. Having borrowed a motorcycle Taylor attempted to ride to Felixstowe to visit relatives, but was stopped at a road block some distance from the town and ordered to go no further. Movement was restricted in all defence areas and identity checks at roadblocks were a fact of life in 1940, but his identity card should have been enough to get him past the Home Guard sentries. Using his knowledge of the back roads he eventually made his way round to Felixstowe, only to stumble upon a beach clear up operation in which 'heaps of bodies in German uniforms' were 'partly concealed beneath tarpaulins bearing the name of a local haulage company.'

Taylor was not the only motorcyclist experiencing difficulty on the back roads of east Suffolk that weekend. A dispatch rider (Don-R) carrying orders for a coastal battery was also halted on the outskirts leading to the coast. The carrying of an AB64 document, backed up with orders that under no circumstances were despatch riders to be detained, was normally enough to get past the tightest of security but not on this occasion. William Hall, a former gunner in the 72nd Medium Regiment RA based near Southwold was also convinced that the Germans had tried to invade Suffolk. He told how: 'Soldiers guarding the East coast in Suffolk were put on guard after an invasion by German forces dressed in British uniforms'. He also said that all the troops knew about it at the time, adding that he didn't know why it had all been 'hushed up'. Both the *East Anglian Daily Times* and its sister paper, the *Ipswich Evening Star*, published what was said to be a German report of a failed invasion attempt. The story, originally published in the German magazine *Der Landser* during the late 1950s told how German troops, including Waffen SS had mounted a small scale raid to test British defences and had been engulfed in a wall of fire.

There was by now a growing consensus of opinion that the answer to the enigma lay within the contents of the mystery file in the PRO but on 16 May 1992 PRO sources were quoted as saying that searches 'had failed to locate the file' and this simply aroused the suspicion that it had been destroyed because of the evidence it contained: allegations the PRO were quick to deny. Within days a PRO source was quoted as saying: 'the wartime dossier - believed to contain details of an operational blunder involving the loss of military and civilian lives - had probably been transferred to the PRO from a Government department thirty years after being classified. If found its contents could be released early if a request was made'. Hopes that the file might be released before its 2021 deadline had already been given encouragement by Prime Minister John Major's pledge of 'open government' in which government departments had been asked to carry out a review of any files they held under extended closure. The Foreign Office had released some of its previously classified files in 1992, including documents relating to Hitler's deputy, Rudolf Hess. With this in mind and with the support of local Ipswich MP Jamie Cann, the *East Anglian Daily Times* mounted a campaign to secure the early release of the Shingle Street file.

On 26 June in the House of Commons Cann asked the then Home Secretary, Kenneth Clarke: 'if he will now release his Department's files relating to the Shingle Street incident of 1940 into the public domain.' Mr. Clarke replied: 'I have been in correspondence and discussion with my right honourable Friend the member for Suffolk Coastal, Mr. Gummer, in whose constituency Shingle Street is, on the matter. As a result of these discussions, I am reviewing the files held in the Department dealing with the evacuation of the civil population from several villages on the east coast, including Shingle Street, during the Second World War with a view to opening them to the public.' Now, at last, it seemed the file that held the key to a mystery that had intrigued writers and researchers for years would be released - and the truth finally revealed.

On 7 July the early edition of the *East Anglian Daily Times* announced that HO 207/1175 would be opened at 0930 that morning and reporters would be at the PRO when it finally revealed its secrets. It was promised that all would be revealed in the following day's issue. The *Ipswich Evening Star*'s final edition carried the front page headline: 'SHINGLE ST. THIS IS IT? Underneath it was stated, 'So where is the mystery that had to be hidden for 75 years' but the report continued: 'despite widespread speculation that German invaders were repelled or that British troops died in an accident the file reveals only that the inhabitants were evacuated and later bombing trials took place.' The article also contained Home Office denials that any secret files had been suppressed.

The following day's edition of the *East Anglian Daily Times* devoted almost a double page spread to the disappointing contents of the file which only revealed was that the inhabitants had been evacuated, the hamlet had fallen into disrepair and in 1943 there had been some kind of test involving chemical bombs. Far from solving the speculation surrounding wartime events at Shingle Street the early release of the file had only deepened the mystery so why had a file that appeared to contain nothing sensitive been closed for so long? Normally, extended closure was granted if a file contained information damaging to national security or international relations or contained information that had been passed in confidence from one government department to another. Also, the file might contain information about people or events deemed to be highly personal or distressing. Also, the *Ipswich Evening Star*'s headline THE GREAT COVER-UP; Shingle Street Still Has Secret' capped an article that contained several interesting comments. Jamie Cann, the MP instrumental in engineering the file's early release, said: 'there are so many witnesses, I'm not accusing anyone of lying but I think there's still more information to come out.' The *Star*'s front page report ended with Shingle Street's surviving wartime inhabitant, Ron Harris, saying: 'the matter should now be closed'. But many, including Jamie Cann, believed that there may be other 'unopened' files lying in government vaults and he arranged to meet the junior defence minister, Lord Cranborne, to see if the MoD had anything else relating to Shingle Street hidden away on its 'dusty shelves.' But the story remained the same. On 15th July Cann told the national press: 'About forty bodies washed up on the beach in August [1940] were aircrew and soldiers killed when the RAF surprised a combined German force taking part in a pre-invasion exercise in the North Sea. They were burned by falling or jumping into burning oil in the sea. It took about a week for the charred corpses to reach the Suffolk coast...'

The MoD offered to release what were claimed to be 'other files' relating to wartime events at Shingle Street but added the proviso that if the 'new' information failed to solve the mystery 'the media will have two weeks to submit further questions to officials at the government department'. When the new information was released, over the weekend of 17th/18th July, much of it turned out to be from War Office files and Ministry of Supply documents relating to the Petroleum Warfare Department, all of which had been open to the public at the PRO for some time. One newspaper report claimed that the new information came from: 'once secret diaries kept by Army officers, which were in fact the War Diaries of army units dating from 1940; practically all of which had also been openly available at the PRO for almost twenty years. The 'new' MoD information refuted all stories of an attempted invasion or tragic accident and listed a number of specific factors as being the probable cause or origin of the stories surrounding Shingle Street. It was claimed that 'there are no records of large numbers of bodies being recovered from Suffolk beaches during August or September 1940. Any bodies washed ashore were those of German aircrew shot down by the RAF or German soldiers killed while rehearsing for an invasion of the UK'. If the MoD or anyone else in Whitehall expected that this new information would finally draw a line under the proceedings, they were mistaken. Following the release of the new information the *East Anglian Daily Times* reported Derek Johnson as saying: 'they are giving us the tip of the iceberg.' The editorial opinion published in the *Ipswich Evening Star* of 17 July posed the still puzzling question: 'if nothing much occurred at Shingle Street, why did someone slap a 75-year extended closure order on telling the world that nothing happened?'

Jamie Cann however, now seemed satisfied that the mystery had been solved. In the *Daily Telegraph* of 20 July he was quoted as saying: 'The truth has emerged - and the truth is not very much happened.' According to the *Telegraph* Cann had been shown a synopsis of all the files as well as some of the documents and was now convinced that 'the charred bodies did not belong to a secret German invasion force.' Instead the documents, apparently, revealed that: 'About forty bodies washed up on the beach in August [1940] were aircrew and soldiers killed when the RAF surprised a combined German force taking part in a pre-invasion exercise in the North Sea. They were burned by falling or jumping into burning oil in the sea. It took about a week for the charred corpses to reach the Suffolk coast. Other bodies were washed up on the shores of Europe in September.' This directly contradicts the MoD statement made just two days earlier, that: 'there are no records of large numbers of bodies being recovered from Suffolk beaches during August or September 1940.'

In the meantime yet more wartime stories surrounding Shingle Street emerged. 85-year old widow Rose Aldous revealed to the local press how her late husband, Claude, a former driver with Ipswich Co-op, had been sent to Shingle Street in 1940 to help pick up German bodies and 'put them in boxes.' She remembered being told that the bodies were slimy and had German uniforms on: 'it was awful... they picked up the bodies and put them in boxes.' When this article appeared, sources in the *East Anglian Daily Times* (and the *Ipswich Evening Star*), stated that they had received other reports of Co-op vehicles and drivers being involved in this gruesome task. In one published account of this story, a spokesman for Ipswich Co-operative Society was quoted as saying that 'nothing could be found in the records,' but also added: 'whether we did do something and were told not to make a record, at this stage we can't tell.' The *East Anglian Daily Times* stated that it had received other reports of Ipswich Co-op drivers retrieving dead bodies from Shingle Street in 1940. Derek Johnson, author of *East Anglia at War*, also claimed to have discovered an Ipswich Co-op connection while carrying out some earlier research for his book. According to his version, lorries sent with coffins were offloaded at roadblocks near to the hamlet then sent back.

Another new claim in 1992 was made by Gerald Wallis who in 1940 was a 14-year old living in the family home at Buckanay Farm, roughly half a mile inland from Shingle Street. He remembered seeing a battle out at sea: 'the sky was all red and looked like it was alight'. Later his uncle, a Regimental Sergeant Major at Felixstowe, had visited the family and told them that the Germans had attempted a landing but: 'the sea had been set alight and burned a lot of them in their boats.' Wallis also recalled the rumours of dead Germans in British uniform being washed up on the beach, but said that he personally did not see any bodies. A former Military Policeman, Donald Garnham, dismissed talk of large numbers of bodies and said it was all down to the accidental deaths of a few 'top brass' during a military exercise. In October 2004 as contributors to BBC Radio 4's

'The Battle of Shingle Street', Donald Garnham would tell a very different story, maintaining that there had been no deaths at all and while Wallis still recalled the faint glow in the night sky out to sea that 'grew brighter and brighter' on that occasion he made no mention of his sergeant major uncle or the stories of Germans being washed up on the beach and simply stated that there was 'no invasion whatsoever' and that he 'saw no bodies.' Garnham was even more dismissive than he had been in his original account, stating that as a member of the military police at Woodbridge, he would have been 'the first to know if anything had happened' but had heard nothing. He also expressed the opinion that the area was so heavily defended that the Germans would have been 'fools to try' [an invasion].[124]

At the end of July 1992 one of the final newspaper articles concerning Shingle Street resurrected the 'Mid-September mystery' and bodies floating across the Channel as proof that: 'the riddle of Shingle Street' had been solved over forty five years earlier in 1946. Placing the stories of attempted invasion alongside UFOs and corn circles, it was suggested that the only reason the stories had lasted for so long was because 'people wanted to believe them.' But even this debunking attempt ended by posing the still highly pertinent question: 'why were the top secret papers [that had apparently held no secrets] classified for so long?' The five month saga of Shingle Street's secret file eventually came to a close on the pages of *The Times* on 15 August beneath the headline: 'WHITEHALL SLOWLY UNVEILS ITS SECRETS.' The article referred to the unimpressive revelations of the file, along with those of the Rudolf Hess files, as being 'damp squibs'. It also outlined the problems facing researchers, including the fact that many wartime files, particularly those of the Joint Intelligence Committee, were closed [and still are]. One of the most notable authors on intelligence matters, Professor Hinsley, was quoted as saying that he'd been allowed to see many of the Joint Intelligence Chief files and that: 'they ought

---

124 Another contributor pointed out that during the Napoleonic wars, when Britain faced a similar threat of invasion, there had also been 'wild and unfounded rumours', including a story that Napoleon Bonaparte himself had landed on the south coast of England (this may be so, but on 22nd February 1797, 1,400 French troops did set foot on British soil). The programme's producers came to the general conclusion that the story of Shingle Street was one of: 'a few slim facts carried further by a liberal coating of mystery.' One of the 'slim facts' discussed was the red glow that filled the night sky. This, it was said, was the result of an RAF blitz on the Belgian port of Ostend, far across the North Sea. The final analysis was that the black propaganda exercise coupled with other factors, including the invasion alert of 7 September 1940 was the most likely explanation for the invasion stories.

'SECRECY OVER WARTIME FILE REMAINS BAFFLING'

to release the whole lot and not worry about it.' The article did make it clear that the Security Services were exempt from the Public Records Act and under no obligation to submit their files to the PRO.[125]

Even as *The Times* article appeared, media interest surrounding Shingle Street had already begun to evaporate. It seemed that the media had lost interest in a mystery that appeared to be unsolvable. Although the stories surrounding Shingle Street would never excite such a level of interest again, they have never entirely gone away. Among the many stories that have emerged there is one that should, on the face of it, be verifiable. This relates to the decomposed and burnt body of a man in German army uniform, said to have been washed up at Felixstowe ferry, just across the Deben estuary from Bawdsey Manor in 1940 which was supposedly recorded in the wartime diary of a Felixstowe police Inspector, Claude Rush, the existence of which resulted from a question posted in the Answers to correspondents feature of the *Daily Mail*, in July 1999. The body is said to have been buried in the war graves section of the town's cemetery; 'the headstone bearing the simple inscription, 'a German soldier', carved in German.'

The writer claimed to have seen the actual diary, said to reside in Ipswich museum, in 1970. However, subsequent requests made by researchers, have been met by difficulties, or have simply been ignored. Could it be that the diary contains something that must be kept from the public gaze? In 2012 there were six German WWII graves in Felixstowe New Cemetery, all with relatively new headstones, at least more recent than the 1970s. All but one bear a name along with a date of birth and date of death and all but one are German aircrew. Only two - Herman Camp, a Luftwaffe Warrant Officer and Unteroffizier Karl Fritz - date from late 1940. The body of Herman Camp was washed ashore on Sunday, 27th October. His funeral was reported in the *Felixstowe Times* on Saturday, 2nd November. The body of Karl Fritz on the crew of a Dornier Do 17Z shot down by Hurricanes while attacking Martlesham Heath was washed up on the foreshore at Landguard Point seven weeks later and he was buried on 15 December. One headstone that bears no date is simply inscribed with a name: Jentschin. Could this be the grave of the man in German army uniform referred to in the Rush diary and has the newer headstone replaced one that bore the simple inscription 'Ein Deutscher Soldat'? Records simply state that this is the grave of an

---

[125] They are also exempt from the new Freedom of Information Act 2000 (sections 23 and 24). Therefore, if the Security Services do hold any material relating to Shingle Street it is unlikely that it will ever see the light of day.

'unidentified airman'. Even so, it would be expected that, in keeping with the other headstones, it would at least have the date of burial.

Ordinarily the next step would be to examine Inspector Rush's diary itself but its exact whereabouts are unknown, though it is rumoured to be in the possession of Suffolk Police at an undisclosed location. It is also said that certain relevant pages are missing. There is in existence a 'Felixstowe Police Station War Diary' held in the Suffolk Public Records Office at Ipswich. This neatly typed journal was certainly compiled by Inspector Rush and may or not be the diary referred to by the writer in the *Daily Mail* of 3 July 1999, but it was clearly written up post war using information from a number of sources, which must include Rush's own notes but as a serving police officer, was he allowed, or even willing, to openly record all that he witnessed or heard during WWII? As expected, the police war diary does record a number of bodies being washed ashore at Felixstowe or along the nearby coast during wartime. The majority of them, whether enemy or allied, airmen or sailors, are identified, including four of the German aircrew buried in Felixstowe cemetery and the body of an American airman, still identifiable after having been in the sea for twelve weeks but there is no mention of a Jentschin and nowhere in the diary is there a record of a 'decomposed and burned body of a man in German army uniform' being washed up at Felixstowe Ferry.

The only report of an unidentified body being washed ashore during the autumn of 1940 was recorded on Thursday, 24th October. The body, described as 'apparently [a] German Air force Officer' is almost certainly Herman Camp. The only other report of a body washed ashore, recorded on Wednesday, 8th May was the identified corpse of a British sailor. There are no bodies, identified or unidentified recorded as being washed ashore during the intervening five months and this includes the crucial period of September 1940. So if military personnel and civilians did spend days removing the bodies of German soldiers from Felixstowe beaches it was not recorded, at least not officially.

The *Felixstowe Times* of Saturday, 26th October 1940 reported that, 'a body, believed to be that of a German airman was washed ashore at Felixstowe on Thursday [24th], it was partially clothed and had been in the water for some time'. This is obviously the 'German Air force Officer' referred to in the police war diary. However it was also reported that three other bodies, 'believed to be Nazi airmen' had also been washed ashore. The bodies, 'all above average height, one still clutching a bundle,' had apparently been in the water for some weeks. There is no reference to these bodies in the Felixstowe police diary, or in the war diary of the local army unit. On the 29th; the same day that Herman Camp was buried, the body of another German airman was washed ashore at Shingle Street. The following day two more enemy airmen were washed up; one in Hollesley Bay and another nearer to Bawdsey. The bodies washed ashore near Shingle Street and Bawdsey are recorded in the war diaries of the Liverpool Scots and the 165th Infantry Brigade, but they do not appear in the Felixstowe police diary.

In September 2002 during an edition of BBC Look East's 'Inside Out' series one contributor suggested that several hundred gallons of petrol might have actually been ignited off the east coast and even a few bodies dropped in the sea, all with the purpose of adding a touch of realism to the propaganda campaign. It was also suggested that the rumours may have been connected to the sinking of Royal Navy destroyers in the North Sea on the night of 31st August 1940. It was claimed that the arrival of casualties at east coast ports in the wake of the disaster and the secrecy surrounding the event may have given rise to some of the stories associated with Shingle Street. One man did go on camera to relate how his father, who had been stationed at Felixstowe with the army during 1940, had been called out one night to pick up the bodies of German soldiers from nearby beaches. Mick Paintin stated that during 1940 his father had been stationed at Landguard Fort: 'sometime after Dunkirk he was alerted during the night and together with other serving soldiers detailed to remove from the sea at Felixstowe a number of bodies in full Wehrmacht uniform and 'very badly burned'.' Paintin's father was adamant that this could not have been a small raiding party, owing to the large number of bodies that had been recovered. Apparently, after the bodies had been loaded onto army vehicles and driven away, all those involved were given 'very strict orders that this matter was never to be discussed.'

In 2004 Peter Haining's book *Where the Eagle Landed* uncovered the facts behind a real German landing on the Suffolk coast by a solitary E-boat crew. The author makes an interesting reference to comments made by his late friend and fellow writer, Dennis Wheatley, who had worked for the Intelligence Services during WWII and had apparently heard stories circulating among colleagues of an attempted German landing on the east coast near Sizewell. In 2005 Shingle Street and the stories of a failed invasion were featured in Sky 1's 'Conspiracies' series. The programme generally provided a reasonable balance of opinion from many contributors, including the German perspective from historian Dr. Peter Schenk. Having looked at the available evidence, it

HITLER'S INVASION OF EAST ANGLIA, 1940

was suggested that the most probable explanation for the invasion rumour was a secret anti-invasion black propaganda 'whispering campaign' aimed at demoralising enemy troops. One contributor referred to the rumours as being 'a very successful 'Sib'.

On 1 December 2005 on the high profile BBC 'peoples war' website there appeared the story of Desmond Sibley, a member of the Home Guard, who was sent to Shingle Street where he witnessed a shoreline littered with bodies, all in German army uniform. Along with his comrades he was ordered to guard the area until relieved by the regular army and told 'never to tell anyone what he'd seen.' This story had been told to his son Chris when his father was 60 years old and after he was prompted by a television programme where someone from Shingle Street was talking about these events.

'Dad was medically excused from military service and he worked on the land in Coggeshall, Essex but he was able to join the Home Guard in the later years of the war. On one occasion they were called to Colchester Barracks where they were transferred to an unknown destination, being told not to look out of the back of the truck. It seemed to dad as if they were travelling forever and towards the end of the journey he did peep out of the vehicle and it appeared to him that the sun was setting in the east because of a large orange glow on the horizon. When they eventually reached their destination, which he later found out was Shingle Street, he said that the sea looked as if it was alight and he assumed that a tanker had gone down and the fuel was blazing. When they got to the edge of the shore it was awash with burnt bodies which dad said were wearing full German uniforms. They had to stay at Shingle Street, guarding these bodies, until relieved by the regular army. Before they got into the trucks to return home, dad said they were told never to tell anyone what they had done or seen.

'I visited Parham airfield where there is a museum for the Secret Army [Britain's Auxiliary Units] and during a conversation with the curator about dad's story, which the curator was familiar with, he said that the Dutch Resistance had corroborated this story by saying that their hospitals had filled up with burnt German military personnel at the time of the Shingle Street episode. Apparently the story has been denied by MoD and dad always thought that it was an invasion attempt or a practice by the German Military, but we'll probably never know exactly what did happen at Shingle Street.'

Did a wartime exercise go badly wrong resulting in a tragic friendly fire incident? Did German commandoes mount a raid on 'top secret' Bawdsey

'SECRECY OVER WARTIME FILE REMAINS BAFFLING'

Manor radar station? Was there a diversionary attack against the east coast or even a full blown invasion attempt? Was the sea set on fire and were the burnt bodies of German soldiers wearing British uniforms washed up on nearby beaches? Or was it none of these and are the stories no more than a rumour that was fostered by British Intelligence to provide badly needed good news and boost morale in desperate times?

What has become the most readily accepted explanation, the 'black propaganda' spread in order to bolster the morale of a nation facing defeat, does seem believable. A tragic friendly fire incident is equally plausible and would certainly explain stories of burnt bodies and the cloak of secrecy surrounding the event. A commando raid on the radar station at Bawdsey Manor is dismissed simply on the basis that there is, apparently, no 'official' record that one ever took place. It is also claimed that by the summer of 1940 the area was heavily defended, so heavily defended that a German landing attempt of any kind would have been futile. It is true that flame defences, including burning oil/petrol mixtures on the sea would have been used in 1940. There still exists impressive film footage showing a 'flame barrage' turning the calm waters of a south coast bay into a raging inferno within minutes. But the Petroleum Warfare Department, the body that oversaw the development of such weapons, did not come into existence until July 1940. It was many months later before the first practical working flame barrage was installed and this was on the south coast, not the east.

And last but by no means least there are the intriguing tales of Germans wearing British uniforms. While there are stories of German troops using such unorthodox tactics, especially during the invasions of Holland and Belgium, many of those stories, it is claimed, are hearsay. It is also argued that while such tactics may have been used they were not used all that often. Therefore, many of the tales of Germans impersonating French or Belgian army officers, or even Dutch policemen, have simply grown with the telling and owe more to the mythology rather than reality. All of the above may be true, but none provides absolute proof that anything extraordinary, at least for those times, happened at Shingle Street.

Index

Aalborg airfield xviii
Adlerangriff ('Eagle Attack') 62, 67
Adler Tag ('Eagle Day' 62, 67
Afridi HMS 159
Air Exercises, 1937 52
Alde, River 137
Aldeburgh 58, 87, 89, 100, 111, 136-137, 139-141, 195
Aldous, Rose 261
Amsterdam 1, 11, 115
'Anklet', Operation 222
Arbib, Robert S. Jnr. USAAC 214
'Archery', Operation 222-224
Arethusa, HMS 91
Arnhem 16
Ashfield, Flying Officer Glyn 'Jumbo' 45
Ashford, Ronald 136-137, 147
Attlee, Clement 245-246
'Auk', Operation 187
Auxiliary Units 74-85, 178-179, 181, 189, 194-195, 266

Bader, Wing Commander Douglas 166-167
Baldry, Henry 138
Baldwin, Stanley 45
Banks, Major General Thomas MacDonald 'Donald' KCB DSO MCTD 148-149
'Banquet/Banquet Light', Operations 99
Barbe, Charles M. 210-211
Barbie, Klaus 104

Barnes, Pat 144
Basildon 141
Battle of Britain xxi
Bawdsey 44-45, 47, 49-51, 53-58, 68, 86-87, 91-92, 97, 112, 138, 142, 159-160, 177, 183-184, 186, 251, 253-254, 256, 263, 266-267
Beachy Head radar station 136
Beaumont-Nesbitt, Major General F. J. 'Paddy' 248
Bentley Priory, RAF 47, 58, 62-63, 162
Biggin Hill, RAF 111, 136
Birkbeck, W. A. 213-214
'Biting', Operation (Bruneval) 235-237
'Black Book' 115
Blackett, Baron Patrick Maynard Stuart OM CH PRS 46
Blenkinsop, Colonel Harry 182
Bletchley Park 61-62, 222
Blumentritt, General Günther 249
Bock, Colonel-General Fedor von 10
Bognor Regis 45
Bonaparte, Marie 156
Bowen, Dr. Edward George 'Taffy' 48
'Brandenburg Concerto', Operation 176-196
Brandenburgers 13-19, 41, 103-106, 122, 125, 177-178, 186-189, 191, 194-195
'Brandy', Operation 225
Brauchitsch, General Walther von xiv, 31, 114, 119, 124, 185
Breuning, Dr. Ernst 55-56

INDEX

Brighton 33, 120-121, 123-124, 127, 132-133, 141
Bromley radar station 59
Brown, Richard 170
Bruneval raid 235-237
Burchall, Squadron Leader P. R. 46
Burg, Konrad 103-104, 106-107
Burnell, Flying Officer 2
Busch, Generaloberst Ernst 120
Buwalda, Major Jan 19-20

Calvert, Captain Mike 76-77
Camp, Herman 264
Campbell HMS 112
Canaris, Wilhelm 117
Canewdon radar station 51, 59
Cann, James MP 259-261
'Cartoon', Operation 224
Chamberlain, Arthur Neville ix, x, xvi, xix
'Checkmate', Operation 225
Churchill, Squadron Leader Walter Myers DSO DFC 173
Churchill, Winston S. vii-viii, x; xix-xx, xxi, 24-25, 29-30, 38, 40, 56, 62, 67, 71, 73-75, 91, 95, 100, 125,126,134, 141, 150-151, 154, 158, 162, 169, 173-174, 208, 220-221, 245, 256
Clacton 91, 201
Clarkson, W. J. 49-50
'Claymore', Operation 222
Colbeck, Colonel 151-153
Colchester 59, 91, 266
Coleshill House 80-81
'Collar', Operation 220
Coltishall, RAF 138, 161, 165-166
Colville, Sir John 'Jack' 141
Cooling, Rupert 'Tiny' 21, 24
Copenhagen xviii
Corton 141
Cransford 179
Crete 10, 212, 227-230
Croft, Captain Andrew 78-80
Croydon 52, 55, 110, 173

Darré, Richard Walther 88
Darsham radar station 57-58, 68, 178-179, 189
Dasher HMS 253
de Broke, John Willoughby 52
de Witte, Vera 117-119
'Deadstick', Operation 240-243
Debden RAF 59, 111, 138
Deenekamp 1
Delmer, Sefton 155-156
Detling 109
Dick, LAC 2-3
Dieppe 211, 238-239
Dönitz, Grand Admiral Karl xiii, 33
Donovan, Colonel William 'Wild Bill' 149-150, 200
Dordrecht 12, 20, 28, 106, 178
Douglas, Sergeant 'Duggie' 21, 24
Dover radar station 10, 51, 53, 65
Dover 31-32, 35, 37, 105-106, 111, 129-130, 132-133, 162, 174, 183, 202, 204, 246
Dowding, Air Vice Marshal Sir Hugh Caswell Tremenheere 43-44, 46-47, 54-55, 62-64, 162, 164
Dreyer, Admiral Sir Frederic Charles GBE KCB 68
Drugge, Karl Theodore 117-119
Dundee 51
Dungeness 115
Dunkirk evacuation xvi, 29, 72, 89, 140, 171, 214, 227
Dunkirk radar station (Kent) 65
Dunkirk xvi, xx, 29, 36-38, 59, 65, 77, 87, 101-102, 120, 129, 144, 149, 152, 172, 200, 203, 208, 211, 214, 265
Dunwich Common 186
Dunwich, RAF xiv, xv, 49, 57-59, 68, 87, 95, 139-140, 178, 189, 193, 195, 208
Duxford, RAF 111, 166-167
Dymchurch 115
'Dynamo', Operation 72, 171

'Eagle Day' 67
Eastchurch 109

Ében-Émael, Fort 6-8, 10, 86, 137, 186, 193
E-boats 100, 103, 128-130, 145, 171, 178, 187, 253, 265
Eddis, Sir Basil 137
Eden, Anthony 71, 73-74, 125
'Enigma' 61-62, 124, 144, 188
Esk HMS 142-145
Express HMS 142-145

Fairburn, W. E. 'Dan' 81
Falkenstein, Major Sigmund von 124
'Fall Gelb' ('Case Yellow') 141
'Fall Grün' ('Case Green') 177
'Fall Weiss 2' ('Case White') 177-178, 183, 185
Farnborough 44, 109
Farnie, Flight Lieutenant Scott 60
'Felix', Operation 125
Felixstowe 50, 68, 87, 91, 96, 111, 138, 143, 155, 159, 168, 171, 177, 183-185, 204, 246, 252, 257, 261, 263-265
Felmy, General Helmuth xi, xii
Fiebig, Kommodore Martin 19
Fifeness radar station 60
Fleming, Captain Peter 76-78, 80, 104, 249
Fleming, Ian 76
Folkestone 33, 105, 119, 120, 121, 124, 127-130, 132-133, 202-203
Foreness radar station 136
Forster, Major General 104
Framlingham 139, 179, 182
Franco, General Francisco 125
'Frankton', Operation 221-222
Fritton Lake 214
Fritz, Unteroffizier Karl 263
Führer Directive No.16 32-33

Gablenz, Oberstleutnant Carl-August Baron von xviii
Ganges HMS 91, 97
Garnham, Donald 262
'Gauntlet', Operation 222
Geneva Protocols 98

Gennep 17
Gerhard, Generalmajor 227
Gerken, Richard 1-2
Giddings, Flight Lieutenant Herbert Selwyn 138
Goetzel, Colonel Hermann 189-190
Gordon-Finlayson, Sir Robert 71, 218
Göring, Reichsmarschall Hermann xv, 5, 28, 33, 39, 44, 53-54, 62, 66, 68, 109, 122, 124, 129, 136, 150, 163, 172-175, 185, 227
Gossage, AVM Ernest Leslie 52-53
Grabert, Leutnant 18
Graf Zeppelin 55-57
Great Driffield 67
Great Glemham Out Station 178, 182-183
Great Yarmouth xiv, 100, 102, 140, 144, 245
Greene, Graham 211
Gubbins, Brigadier Colin McVean 75-78, 80

Hague, The 22, 26
Haining, Peter 76, 90, 107, 265
Halder, General der Artillerie Franz 31-32, 185
Hankey, Lord 149, 152
Hannington Hall 81
Harwich 97
Hawkinge 60, 67, 111
Hayward, James 145, 156, 204, 244, 255
Heinz, Lieutenant Colonel Friedrich Wilhelm 13-14
Henry, Mike 37, 39-40
Herdla 222-223
Heyde, Oberst Friedrich August Freiherr von der 187
Heyford, Handley Page 52
Higgins, Jack 252
Himmler, Heinrich 104
Hindenburg 55
Hippel, Theodore von 13, 105
Hitler, Adolf ix-xiii, xvi, xx, 7, 31-32, 36, 53, 103, 107, 125, 172, 175, 232

270

INDEX

Hoare, Samuel 71
Holland, Major General John 'Jo' 74-75
Hollesley Bay xiv, xv, 68, 91-93, 102, 137, 152, 160, 183-184, 206, 214, 254, 265
Hollmann Unit 104
Home Guard 41, 70-73, 77, 79, 82, 96, 99, 105-106, 131, 136-137, 165, 168-169, 177, 180, 184, 189, 194-195, 208, 212, 257, 266
Hornchurch, RAF 52, 111, 136
'Husky', Operation 230-231

Icarus HMS 142-143
Intrepid HMS 142
Ipswich xiv, xv, 50, 58, 91-92, 145, 170, 182, 258-261, 263-264
Ironside, General William Edmund GCB CMG DSO 96, 126
Ivanhoe HMS 142-145

Jenkins, Barbara 182
Jeschonnek, General Hans 124, 172
Jodl, General der Artillerie Alfred xii, 30-31, 119, 130, 185
Johnson, Derek 252, 261
Johnson, Pilot Officer 'Johnnie' 161-162
Joyce, William ('Lord Haw-Haw') 135
'Jubilee', Operation 238-239
'Julius Caesar' defence plan 70
Jupiter HMS 112, 141-143
Jutland xviii

Kapp Putsch 13
Keitel, Field Marshal Wilhelm 119, 130
Kelvin HMS 112, 136, 141-143
Kemsley, Lord 69
Kenley RAF 110
Kennedy, Joseph P. 149-150
Kesselring, Generalfeldmarschall 5, 163
Keyes, Admiral of the Fleet, Sir Roger xix

Kieboom, Charles van der 116
Kirke, General Sir Walter Mervyn St. George GCB CMG DSO 70-71
Kleffens, Mr. Van der 27
Knox, 'Dilly' 61
Koch, Hauptmann Walter 7, 10
Kristiansand xviii

Lawrence, T. E. 13
LDV (Home Guard) 71-73, 77
Lee, Raymond 173
Lettow-Vorbeck, General Paul Emil von 13
Leyland, Sergeant Reginald H. 45
'Lion', Unternehmen (Operation) 119
Littlestone-on-Sea 203
Lloyd, Geoffrey 148-149, 153, 244-245
'Lord Haw-Haw' 135
Los Angeles, USS 55
Lowestoft xiv, xv, 58, 87, 91, 102, 108, 140, 171, 208, 214, 250
Lozère, Madame Pauline 200
Lucas-Tooth, Sir Hugh 245
Lundby 41, 177, 183, 185, 191
Lydd 116
Lympne RAF 111, 120

Maastricht 6, 16
MacDonnell, A. G. 202
MacLean, Fitzroy 80
Malden Bridge 17-18
Manston RAF 45, 67, 111, 195
Marham, RAF 2
'Market-Garden', Operation 232-234
Martini, General Wolfgang 55-56, 64, 66
Martlesham Heath, RAF 44-45, 109, 263
Meier, Karl 115-116
'Merkur' ('Mercury') Unterhekmen 227
Meurisse, Renee 212-213
Milch, Field Marshal Erhard 5, 52-54, 172-173, 186-187
Mildenhall, RAF 52
Mill House 179

271

Model, Generalfeldmarschall Otto Moritz Walter 5, 232, 234
Moen, Lars 204-205
'Molotov Cocktail' 99
Moore, Jim 'Dinty' viii-ix, xix-xxi, 35-38
Morris, Pilot Officer G. E. 45
Mountbatten, Captain Louis 141, 143, 221
Murrow, Ed 198
'Musketoon', Operation 224
Mussolini, Benito 72, 119, 230
Mustard gas 98

Newall, Chief of Air Staff 55
Nikolayevsky, Boris 148, 176
North Coates, RAF 143
North Weald, RAF 45, 59, 111, 166-167
'Northwest' plan xiv, xv
Norwich 33, 58, 124, 144-145, 161, 165

'Oboe' 44
Observer Corps 46-47, 55, 62, 110, 162
Ockenburg 10, 21-23
Odiham 52, 109
Ore, River 68, 91, 152, 183, 252
Orford Ness 48, 91, 102
Oslo xviii, 11, 14, 41, 135
Oslo-Fornebu 14
'Overlord', Operation 231-232

Paintin, Mick 265
Parham airfield Secret Army Museum 266
Park, AVM Keith 62, 164
Parris, John 212
Pegasus Bridge 242
Perry, Colin 161
Petter, Robert 117-119
Pevensey radar station 65, 136
Pickard, Wing Commander Percy Charles 235
Poling CH Radar station 45
Pons, Sjoerd 116

Portsmouth docks 64
Powell, 'Sandy' 37
Pretty, Flight Lieutenant Walter 56
Prickman, Wing Commander Thomas 110
Pudney, John Sleigh 202
PWD (Petroleum Warfare Department) 149-150, 153-155, 159, 244, 267
PWE (Political Warfare Executive) 155-156

Raeder, Grand Admiral Erich Johann Albert xii-xiii, xiv, xvi, 31, 33, 36, 119, 122, 129-130, 185
'Razzle' incendiary device 158
RDF (Radio Direction Finding) 40, 44
Reeves, Alec 44
Reitsch, Hanna 5-7
Rendlesham Forest 138
Richmond, Sergeant 'Rich' 37
Robinson, Flight Lieutenant Denis 164
Robinson, William 250
Roosevelt, Franklin D. 125
Rose, Nigel 63
Rotterdam 10, 12, 19, 21-22, 25-26, 28-29, 35, 120, 123, 136, 143, 146, 189
Rowe, Albert Percival 42, 44, 56
Rubensdörffer, Hauptmann Walter 64-65
Rundstedt, Generalfeldmarschall Gerd von 120, 221
Rush, Claude 263-264
Rux-Burton, John 255-256
Rye 65, 69, 93, 121, 130

Sammt, Albert 55-56
Sandhurst, Royal Military Academy 126
Saxmundham 57, 178
Scapa Flow 110, 141
Schalburg, Vera (Vera de Witte) 117-119
Schenk, Dr. Peter 153, 265-266
Schiff, Dr. Paul 200

INDEX

Schiphol 11, 19, 21
Schmid, Joseph 'Beppo' xii
Scott-Moncrieff, Captain George 179
'Sealion', Operation xiii, 29, 33, 36, 38-39, 62, 79, 102-105, 108-109, 115, 119-127, 130, 132, 183, 186-187, 189-190, 196, 204, 215-218, 246-247
Shaw, Vera 162
Shepherd, Bob 158
Sheringham 140-141, 143
Shingle Street 42, 90-93, 97, 137-139, 147, 152, 159, 168-169, 178, 204, 214, 250-263, 265-267
Shirer, William Lawrence 197-199
Sibley, Desmond 266
Simpson, Flight Lieutenant William 209-210
Six, Dr, Franz 115
Sizewell 87, 96, 102, 110, 140, 195, 265
Skipjack HMS 171
Slapton Sands 253
Slessor, Air Marshal 90
Smith, Flight Lieutenant Christopher Dermot Salmond DFC 45
Smith, Tom 255-256
Solberg, Robert 199-200
Sparks, Bill 221
Spens, Sir Will 90-92
Sperrle, Generalfeldmarschall Hugo 163
Stanmore, RAF 62
Stavanger xviii
Stavanger-Sola 117
Stephens, L. J. 167
Stirling, David 80
Stösser, Operation 187
Stratton Strawless Hall 165-166
Stringer, Captain Hubert 89
Student, Major-General Kurt 10, 121, 226-227
'Study Red' xiii, xiv
Stumpf, General Hans-Jürgen xi
Sturgeon HMS 145
Sykes, Eric 'Bill' 80-81, 83

Tangham Forest 138-139
Tangmere, RAF x, 63, 109
'Tannenbaum', Operation 177
Taylor, Flight Sergeant Phillip 257
Thorne, General Andrew 'Bulgy' 77
'Tiger', Exercise 253
Tizard, Sir Henry 40, 43, 46
Townsend, Peter x, 4-5, 53-54, 56-57, 65
Tuna HMS 221
Turner, LWO 179

Udet, Ernst 12
'Ultra' Secret 61
Underground Propaganda Committee 156
Uxbridge, RAF 53, 62, 162

Vågsö 222-223
Valkenburg 10, 21-23, 25, 188
Ventnor radar station 60, 64-66
'Victor', Operation 208
Vindictive HMS 151
Vortigern HMS 112, 141-142

Waalhaven 10, 12, 19-23, 25, 189, 192
Wakeful HMS 171
Waldberg, Jose 115-116
Wallis, Gerald 261-262
Wallwork, Staff Sergeant Jim 241-242
Walmsley, Corporal Bunty 165-166
Walther, Oberleutnant Wilhelm 14
War Game, 'Sealion' 126-134
Warmwell, RAF 164
Watchful HMS 97
Waterhouse, Captain Charles 170
Watson-Watt, Robert Alexander 43-44, 48-50, 54
Wattisham RAF 110
Wavendon Towers 156
Wedgwood, Josiah MP 69
Went The Day Well? (feature film) 211-212
Weserübung, Operation xiii, xvii-xviii, 14
West Malling 111

273

HITLER'S INVASION OF EAST ANGLIA, 1940

Weybourne 141
Wheatley, Dennis 88-90
White, John Baker 247-249
Wilhelmina, Queen 122
Wilhelminabrug 16
Wilkins, Arnold 43-44, 48
Wimperis, Harry Egerton 42-43
Winkelman, General Henri Gerard 28
Wintringham, Captain Tom 70-71
Wood, Peter 163-164
Woodbridge 76, 78-79, 188, 256, 262

Woodhall, Wing Commander Alfred
   Basil 'Woody' 166
Worth Matravers 51
Wright, Flying Officer Robert 65

Youell, Peggy 58
Ypenburg 10, 19-23
Y-Service 60

Zech-Burkersroda, Count Julius
   von 3-4